LAU

POLICING UNDER FIRE

COLLE

SUNY Series in New Directions in Crime and Justice Studies
Austin T. Turk, Editor

POLICING UNDER FIRE

Ethnic Conflict and Police-Community Relations in Northern Ireland

RONALD WEITZER

State University
of New York
Press

Published by
State University of New York Press, Albany

© 1995   State University of New York

Production by Susan Geraghty
Marketing by Nancy Farrell

Printed in the United States of America

For information, address State University of New York Press,
State University Plaza, Albany, N.Y., 12246

Cover photo: Joint police-military foot patrol, courtesy of the
Royal Ulster Constabulary

Library of Congress Cataloging-in-Publication Data

Weitzer, Ronald, 1952–
    Policing under fire : ethnic conflict and police-community
relations in Northern Ireland / Ronald Weitzer.
        p.   cm. — (SUNY series in new directions in crime and justice
studies)
    Includes bibliographical references and index.
    ISBN 0–7914–2247–X (hard : alk. paper). — ISBN 0–7914–2248–8
(pbk. : alk. paper)
    1. Public relations—Police—Northern Ireland.   2. Royal Ulster
Constabulary—Public relations.   3. Police—Northern Ireland.
I. Title.   II. Series: SUNY series in new directions in crime and
justice studies.
HV8197.5.A3W45   1995
363.2'09416—dc20   94–816
                                                                          CIP

10 9 8 7 6 5 4 3 2 1

CONTENTS

TABLES

ABBREVIATIONS

CR: Community Relations, a branch of the RUC

DMSU: Divisional Mobile Support Unit, units of the RUC

DPP: Director of Public Prosecutions

DUP: Democratic Unionist Party

ICPC: Independent Commission for Police Complaints

IRA: Irish Republican Army, an illegal Republican insurgent organization, also called Provisional IRA or the Provos

NIO: Northern Ireland Office, executive arm of the British state in Northern Ireland

PCB: Police Complaints Board, replaced in 1988 by the ICPC

RIC: Royal Irish Constabulary

RUC: Royal Ulster Constabulary

SDLP: Social Democratic and Labour Party

UDA: Ulster Defense Association, a Loyalist insurgent organization, banned in 1992

UDR: Ulster Defense Regiment, a British army regiment

UFF: Ulster Freedom Fighters, an illegal Loyalist insurgent organization connected to the UDA

USC: Ulster Special Constabulary, abolished in 1970 and replaced with the UDR

UUP: Ulster Unionist Party

UVF: Ulster Volunteer Force, an illegal Loyalist insurgent organization

Northern Ireland

From Ronald Weitzer, *Transforming Settler States: Communal Conflict and Internal Security in Northern Ireland and Zimbabwe,* Berkeley: University of California Press, 1990, p. iii.

ACKNOWLEDGMENTS

This book is based on field research in Northern Ireland, made possible by a grant from the Law and Social Sciences Program of the National Science Foundation (grant no. SES–8911898). The research could not have been done without NSF's support, which is greatly appreciated. Needless to say, NSF is not responsible for any of the book's contents or conclusions.

As my research assistant for the duration of the project, Cheryl Beattie made a tremendous contribution to the study. She assisted me in gathering documents and other published materials, collected and analyzed the historical data in Chatper 2, and read several drafts of chapters. Her participation in the project was invaluable and is deeply appreciated.

During the field research in Northern Ireland, I was affiliated with the Institute of Irish Studies at Queen's University in Belfast. I am grateful to the institute's director, Ronnie Buchanan, for making the institute's facilities available to me. While working in Northern Ireland, I benefited greatly from conversations about policing with a small circle of friends who have done their own research on the Royal Ulster Constabulary: John Brewer, Adrian Guelke, and Graham Ellison. They know how difficult it is to conduct research on policing in this society, and their support, hospitality, and intellectual stimulation were essential to my peace of mind and the progress of the study. John Brewer deserves special thanks; we spent hours discussing everything from methodological issues to analytical frameworks, and his input and enthusiasm for the project are greatly appreciated. He also shared with me some of his field notes on policing in West Belfast, which I use in the book a few times, with his permission.

For a decade, ever since I first began to study the Royal Ulster Constabulary in 1983, David Page has been a constant source of support and intellectual stimulation. From him I have learned a great deal about policing in Britain and its troubled province, Northern Ireland.

I conducted approximately 70 intensive interviews with government officials, members of agencies responsible for overseeing the police, members of local police-community liaison commitees, security spokesmen of the various political parties, some police officers, and a number of community leaders (clergy, local politicians, and community workers) in Catholic and Protestant neighborhoods. As interested parties, many of my respondents will probably disagree with some of the arguments and conclusions in this book. But I am deeply indebted to them for taking the time, sometimes several hours, to speak to me, and for the hospitality they bestowed. In addition to their specific information and observations, they brought the subject matter to life as no other source can. Because of the conditions in Northern Ireland, these interviewees must remain anonymous, except for a few persons of national standing who are frequently quoted by the mass media and who granted me permission to name them. One key informant in Belfast, whom I cannot name, deserves special thanks for going out of his way to line up interviews with several community workers and for facilitating my research in other ways.

Data from the Northern Ireland Social Attitudes Survey were used with permission of Social and Community Planning Research in London, which conducted the survey, which contains the largest number of questions on policing issues ever asked in Northern Ireland.

Part of Chapter 7 appeared, in a slightly different form, as "Northern Ireland's Police Liaison Committees," in *Policing and Society*, 2 (1992): 233–243. I am grateful to Harwood Academic Publishers for permission to reprint parts of the article.

CHAPTER 1

Policing Ethnically Divided Societies

The quality of relations between the police and the public is an important part of successful policing in any society. Good relations can facilitate police work in every area where police come into contact with citizens. Poor relations may strain interactions between police and members of the public, make citizens reluctant to report crimes and come forward as witnesses, heighten the danger of police work, lower police morale, and hamper recruitment of new officers.

Primarily Anglo-American and focused on liberal democracies, the literature on policing has largely neglected "deeply divided" societies where the police are highly politicized, prone to violence, unaccountable, and heavily biased in favor of one ethnic, racial, or religious group. With some exceptions, many of the classics in the policing literature deal with issues that are of secondary importance in these societies.[1] The result is that some fascinating questions have been ignored, such as the conditions under which a highly repressive, sectarian police force can be overhauled and the conditions under which its relations with a subordinate ethnic population can be improved. Regarding the first question, most studies of police reform examine cases where large-scale change was fairly gradual or where modest organizational innovations have taken place.[2] There is little research on societies where sweeping and relatively rapid transformation has been attempted. Regarding the second question, we know little about societies where police-community relations are at their very worst, where policing is the source of deep grievances and intense conflicts. In deeply divided societies, the police face more serious legitimacy problems, at least with respect to one communal group, than in more integrated societies. Moreover, the police are evaluated not only on their own merits but also in terms of what they symbolize as defenders of a particular system of sociopolitical domination. This points to the importance of the relationship

1

between the police and the state, also neglected in the literature.[3] Even when a police force undergoes reform, its continuing association with a discredited political system and social structure typically retards improvements in police-community relations. In these societies, police reform becomes meaningful, at least for the subordinate group, only in the context of larger political and social changes. Yet, these very changes are likely to infuriate and fuel resistance on the part of the dominant group.

Northern Ireland (or Ulster) is an excellent case for examining police-community relations in a divided society. Along with the protracted conflict over Northern Ireland's territorial and constitutional status and its political system, policing (and the larger system of law and order) is one of the most hotly contested issues in this society.[4] Police actions are frequently and vigorously condemned and praised by prominent clergy, politicians, and other notables whose statements are often reported by the media. These national-level disputes not only politicize policing to an infinitely greater degree than elsewhere in the United Kingdom, but they also infuse popular discourse at the neighborhood level and affect people's attitudes and interactions with police.

Conflict over policing in Northern Ireland occurs largely along ethnic lines—between an Irish Catholic minority (38 percent of the population) and an Ulster Protestant majority (62 percent)—and police relations with Catholics differ from their relations with Protestants.[5] Relations between the police and Catholics are not as universally bankrupt as is commonly thought, but they are palpably worse than for any other minority group in the United Kingdom. Indeed, some of Northern Ireland's Catholic neighborhoods show just how bad (and seemingly irreparable) police-community relations can become. In areas where armed insurgents thrive and where the state lacks moral authority, we find the ultimate in popular estrangement and enmity toward the police, manifested in violent attacks on the police and the demand that they withdraw completely from the neighborhood. On the other side, relations between the police and Protestants are not as cordial as one might predict from the fact that the police force is almost totally Protestant in composition and historically was tied to a Protestant-dominated state. One of the findings of the present study, absent in most of the literature on Northern Ireland, is the remarkable degree of discontent over policing in some militant Protestant neighborhoods, largely due to reforms in policing over the past two decades. The police are now under fire from sections of both Protestant and Catholic populations.

This study examines the structural factors that shape police relations with Protestant and Catholic communities and that give rise to conflict, as well as the substantive nature of those relations and struggles. Both the larger social, political, and policing arrangements and the micro-level relations (interactions and attitudes) between police and citizens are examined. I argue that police-community relations in Northern Ireland are largely determined by what I call *counterinsurgency policing* and by Protestants' and Catholics' differential *orientations to the state*, neither of which is a major factor in police-community relations in societies that are not ethnically polarized or politically violent.

This chapter presents a model of policing in divided societies, posits a set of determinants of police-community relations in these societies, and concludes with a discussion of the research methods and sources used in the study.

A MODEL OF POLICING

Compared to the extensive theoretical work on crime in the field of criminology, the policing literature is fairly atheoretical. Some of the literature, however, contains arguments that lean toward either functionalist or conflict theory. Functionalist theory holds that the police protect the citizenry as a whole from crime and disorder and contribute to the stability of the social system.[6] Police thus act in the general interest, or the interests of the law-abiding majority, even if they sometimes depart from strictly universalistic law enforcement. Conflict theory maintains that the police protect powerful interests and suppress resistance on the part of oppressed groups such as the working-class and ethnic minorities.[7] Functionalist theories examine the police in isolation from the state, because each contributes to social cohesion in its separate way. Conflict theory portrays the police as a repressive arm of the state, with the rider that the state cannot be neutral but is allied with hegemonic forces in civil society.

Presented as general theories of policing, both approaches are untenable. The police must be theorized in specific societal contexts, not in terms of some a priori, universal "functions" or "interests." As Marenin argues,

> Policing is too complex to fit simple schemes which . . . glorify
> the police as last-ditch defenders of order against the onslaught
> of anarchy and subversion, or calumnify them uncritically as
> always and only instruments of class rule, repression, and
> exploitation. Both the orthodox [functionalist] and Marxist
> images of the police are clearly wrong. The police are not neu-
> tral and disinterested servants of the state, law, or order who
> provide a service which helps all equally and makes orderly and
> civilized life possible; nor are the police merely the blue shock-
> troops of repression who impose upon the dominated a system
> of values, order, and selective coercion which maintains and
> benefits an exploitative and unequal system. The police some-
> times fit either view and sometimes neither.[8]

This does not mean that policing is purely situational. Policing
reflects its societal context, which means that we should expect to
find patterns in policing associated with different types of
sociopolitical orders. I would argue that the more democratic the
political order and the more egalitarian the social order, the more
benign policing should be. In liberal democracies, therefore, conflict theory has less explanatory power in accounting for police
structures and practices than what is claimed by conflict theorists.
Although the police in those societies have intervened to suppress
social movements and working-class struggles and to control
minority populations, the police cannot be *reduced* to agents of
class or ethnic oppression or state domination.[9] They also provide
a host of services and perform ordinary law enforcement and
order maintenance on behalf of the entire population. Policing in
liberal democracies is a mixture of what we would expect from
conflict and functional theories, but leans toward the latter.

Conflict theory is better suited, in my view, to explaining
policing where state repression and/or social inequality is
extreme, as in communally divided or highly authoritarian societies.[10] Our interest is in societies that are sharply polarized along
racial, ethnic, or religious lines. One group enjoys institutionalized privilege and dominance, while others suffer severe eco-
nomic, political, and social deprivation. Communal cleavages are
the defining features of these societies, not secondary to other
social structures.[11]

Relatively little research has been done on policing in divided
societies. There are several case studies but little comparative or
theoretical work.[12] Is policing in these societies qualitatively distin-

guishable from policing in more integrated societies? I will argue that the social and political structures characteristic of divided societies do indeed lend themselves to a distinctive type of policing that is entirely consistent with conflict theory. A *divided society model of policing* with the following dimensions is posited:[13]

1. Systematic bias in law enforcement, with members of the subordinate communal group policed more aggressively and punitively than members of the dominant group.
2. Politicized policing: strong police identification with the regime, a politicized organizational mission, and vigorous police actions against the regime's political opponents.
3. Dominant-group monopoly of the top positions in the police force and disproportionate representation in the rank and file.
4. Dual responsibility of the police for internal security and ordinary law enforcement.
5. Legal or extralegal powers giving police great latitude in their control of the subordinate population, including the use of force.
6. An absence of effective mechanisms of accountability with respect to police abuses of power. The police show differential sensitivity to the concerns of one side of the divided society, but this particularistic slant should not be mistaken for genuine, universalistic accountability transcending sectional interests.
7. Polarized communal relations with the police, with the dominant group as a champion of the police and the subordinate group largely estranged from the police.

Policing in divided societies is organized first and foremost, then, for the defense of a sectarian regime and the maintenance of a social order based on institutionalized inequality between dominant and subordinate communal groups.[14] Consequently, conflict over policing is endemic in these societies. Features 1 through 6 of the model may each contribute to chronic or acute struggles between citizens and the police and disputes between dominant and subordinate groups. The seventh element is a consequence of the other six.

It is the *combination* of the model's elements and their *magnitude* that distinguishes the policing of divided societies from that

of more integrated societies.[15] Some dimensions of the model
(biased law enforcement, political influences on policing,[16] inadequate controls on police misconduct) are by no means unique to
divided societies, but they are much greater in scope and/or intensity in divided societies and, in combination with the other elements, constitute a communally repressive system of policing.
There are also some important qualitative differences between relatively integrated and divided societies. In the former, the police
are judged according to perceptions of their impartiality, their
restrained use of force to achieve lawful purposes, and their
record in crime fighting. In communally divided societies, the first
condition is typically inverted: sectarian law enforcement is
expected and demanded by groups who want preferential treatment from the police. The second condition is equally particularistic: the ideal of minimum force is reserved for one's own population, whereas maximum force may be viewed as necessary to
control the opposite group. The third condition, policing of ordinary crime, is important in divided societies, but its salience may
be diluted in communities where the police are held in ill repute
and where their crime-control efforts are seen as a ruse for sinister
aims.

As with all ideal types, there is variation in the degree to
which empirical cases approximate this model. The fit is quite
close for some societies (e.g., white-ruled Rhodesia, Namibia, and
South Africa), but less so in others. There is also likely to be variation *within* societies in the manifestation of elements of the
model. The balance between security policing and conventional
policing, for instance, may vary considerably depending on the
ethnic profile of a community. In South Africa, white areas traditionally enjoyed conventional policing while black townships
were policed in a militarized and highly authoritarian fashion.
Qualification is also necessary for feature 7 in the model—the
idea that "the dominant community looks on the police as the
guarantor of its position, while the subordinate community tends
to see the police as the agents of their oppression by the dominant
community."[17] Communal populations are internally differenti-
ated by class, age, political orientation, and other factors, each of
which may affect perceptions of policing. Within a subordinate
ethnic group, for example, persons who are elderly, middle class,
and politically conservative are likely to be less critical of the
police than their young, working-class, radical counterparts.

Moreover, the police may actively strive to co-opt the former, driving a wedge between them and other sections of their ethnic group.

At the same time, the dominant ethnic group's approval of the police is not automatic. Although they are generally predisposed to support and defend the police, this acceptance is not unconditional. Much depends on whether police remain steadfast in upholding the right kind of "order," which spells tight control over the subordinate population. Problems arise when the police actively distance themselves from sections of the dominant community, as may happen when the latter's demands clash with police interests or capacities. This can produce serious tensions which may explode in violent incidents, as illustrated recently in South Africa in altercations between police and militant white supremacists.

The model suggests a rather close affinity between the police and ruling elites, but this does not mean that the police are always readily available instruments of state power, whose interests are wholly compatible with the government's.[18] Empirically, the degree of congruence in their interests varies over time and place. The police have a measure of autonomy from the regime, which allows them to pursue their own *organizational interests*—interests that may sometimes clash with regime policies or enforcement of certain laws, and lead to subtle forms of noncompliance or active resistance to regime demands. Interest in improving the image of the force or in minimizing danger to police officers, for example, may make police wary of implementing especially controversial policies. (It should not be assumed that these police forces are necessarily oblivious to the value of generating at least some consent in the subordinate community, if only to make their work easier.) The *political orientation* of police officers also may create friction with the regime—for example, if a hard-line regime refuses to endorse minor concessions to a subordinate population that might reduce unrest and thereby ease pressures on police or, conversely, if a modernizing regime begins to promote reforms that police strongly oppose. An example of the latter is police opposition in South Africa to the reforms (in apartheid structures and in policing) introduced by President F. W. de Klerk since 1990.[19] In short, the police in divided societies may act in ways that are not always consistent with the priorities of political elites or the wishes of the dominant communal group, but as a general rule their ties to regime and partisan interests are substantially stronger than in more integrated, democratic societies.

The divided society model best characterizes unreconstructed and relatively stable societies (though some of its features are potentially destabilizing). Some of the qualifications above become especially salient during periods of progressive change in the social and political order, which may lead to the withering of some traditional patterns of policing. Northern Ireland allows us to examine policing in both a traditionally divided society (under Protestant, Unionist rule, 1921–1972) and a modernizing one (under British rule, 1972–present). Under Protestant rule, Catholics were politically powerless and socioeconomically disadvantaged. As a minority whom Protestants deemed disloyal to the state, they were denied civil rights and discriminated against in housing and jobs. Under British rule, Protestants no longer wield executive and parliamentary power, and the British regime has attempted, with some success, to dismantle the institutional supports for ethnic inequality. (Since Protestants continue to control much of the economy and disproportionately staff the institutions of law and order, I will refer to them as the "dominant" ethnic group, but it is a dominance that has been diluted under British rule.)

The two regimes can also be compared for their respective impact on policing. Policing under Protestant rule closely resembled our model, as Chapter 2 shows, whereas under British rule policing has in some respects moved away from the model. Northern Ireland is one of the few divided societies where a sustained attempt has been made to revamp policing, and it may have gone the furthest in police reform of any contemporary divided society.[20] Since British intervention in the early 1970s, the aims have been to universalize law enforcement, depoliticize the force, increase accountability, and build popular confidence in the police. Changes have occurred in some of these areas, as Chapter 3 shows.

Since each of the dimensions of the divided society model may cause serious discontent and conflict, we might predict that reforms running counter to the model should help reduce discontent in the subordinate group. But in Northern Ireland progressive changes (in the direction of greater accountability, more even-handed law enforcement, depoliticization) have not helped to defuse conflicts over policing or generate popular confidence in the police force, the Royal Ulster Constabulary (RUC). Policing remains fiercely contested and police relations with certain communities abysmal. For Catholics, this is partly because the objective changes are not perceived as meaningful in a context where Protestants are still heavily overrepresented in the force, the RUC retains its dual role in conventional law enforcement and internal security, and formal norms have not satisfactorily constrained police use of force and other questionable conduct. Foremost in importance is the counterinsurgency role of the police (discussed below). For Protestants the reforms have already gone too far, demonstrably undermining law and order and constraining the RUC in its fight against Catholic insurgents. The reforms are thus devalued by both groups, seen by many Catholics as insubstantial or cosmetic, by Protestants as unwarranted concessions to Catholics.

EXPLAINING POLICE-COMMUNITY RELATIONS

Our dependent variable, community orientations toward police, has both attitudinal and behavioral dimensions: it includes neighborbood residents' views, preferences, and complaints about policing, and their behavior toward police officers. (I follow conventional usage in treating these community orientations as synonymous with "police-community relations," bearing in mind that it is citizens' attitudes and behavior that will be explained, not so much police attitudes and behavior.) I will show that community orientations to police in Northern Ireland, and arguably in other divided societies, are shaped by four main variables:

1. Police effectiveness in performing their ordinary duties, such as crime fighting, at the neighborhood level, and their treatment of civilians (e.g., fairness, civility, restrained use of force) in the course of this ordinary work.
2. The intensity of counterinsurgency policing in a neighborhood.
3. The legitimacy of the state in the neighborhood political culture.
4. National-level controversies over policing that receive attention in the mass media and that spill over into local communities, becoming part of neighborhood discourse and evaluations of policing.

In socially integrated, liberal democracies, variable 1 is the primary determinant of police-community relations and the others are of secondary importance or absent altogether.[21] Relations are primarily a function of ordinary law enforcement practices at the neighborhood level, though publicized incidents occurring elsewhere may also have some effect.[22] Counterinsurgency policing is not unknown in liberal democracies (apparent in riot policing and police surveillance of suspected subversives), but it is typically limited, not the hallmark of police organization and practice.[23] The state is a background factor. Considered basically legitimate by most of the population (whatever their specific criticisms of its performance), the state has a positive, if largely unseen, effect on evaluations of the police. Even for those persons who are alienated from the state, this appears not to adversely affect their views of the police.[24] As for major policing controversies, they are much less frequent in relatively integrated, liberal democracies than in divided societies.[25] When they occur only occasionally, the police may be able to weather the storm without long-term damage to their image.

In deeply divided societies like Northern Ireland, all four variables are important. Together, they determine whether a particular neighborhood evaluates the police favorably or unfavorably and how residents interact with police. But it is counterinsurgency policing that, I argue, is the master variable shaping police-community relations in Northern Ireland. Central during the period of Unionist rule, counterinsurgency policing has increased dramatically under British rule, largely as a result of the civil unrest that began in the late 1960s.

Counterinsurgency policing (or security policing) refers to efforts to maintain public order, combat sectarian, intercommunal violence, and protect the state from subversive and violent opponents. We find it in crowd control during demonstrations and riots; surveillance of suspect individuals and groups; undercover operations against special targets; militarized patrolling in troubled areas; and the use of exceptional legal powers on the street, during house searches, and to detain and interrogate suspects. Compared with conventional policing, counterinsurgency policing has generated little scholarly attention, largely because it is not prominent in the liberal-democratic societies studied by most researchers.

Counterinsurgency policing is not necessarily "evil"; it may be motivated by legitimate state interests, implemented judiciously, and beneficial for the population at large. But, if not properly controlled, it is conducive to gross abuses of power, serious deviation from what is considered normal policing, and popular estrangment from the police and the state in communities experiencing it as oppressive. Northern Ireland is familiar with each of these outcomes.

Counterinsurgency policing is of paramount importance in Northern Ireland because of its independent effects on citizens' attitudes, observations, and interactions (largely negative in neighborhoods that experience most of it, in contrast to those that see little of it), *and* because of its effects on the other three variables outlined above: (1) it fuels most of the national-level conflicts over policing, (2) it is the primary means of defending the state, and (3) it affects how well the police handle conventional crime. In other words, counterinsurgency policing has both direct effects on community orientations to police and indirect effects as mediated by larger conflicts over policing, its connection to the state, and its impact on ordinary policing. In areas where counterinsurgency operations are a prominent part of neighborhood life, the direct effect on residents is paramount. Where counterinsurgency policing is relatively rare, its direct effect on residents is low, but it may still affect evaluations if perceived as detracting from ordinary policing or when it becomes a contested issue on the national stage.

Citizens' attitudes are shaped not only by police behavior but also by what police symbolize. In some societies they are perceived as the linchpin of public order and protectors of the citizenry, rather than defenders of a system of power and privilege. In divided societies, the association of the police with a particular power structure is a critically important determinant of police-community relations. However much autonomy the police have from a regime, they remain the most visible agents of state power. A community's perception of the state thus has major effects on its relations with the police, much more consequential than in less polarized societies. Policing in Northern Ireland is inextricably tied to the legitimacy of political institutions; perceptions of the state condition perceptions of the police. The legitimacy of the Unionist state for Protestants predictably inflated their views of the RUC, whereas Catholics' distaste for that state lowered their opinion of the police. Under British rule since 1972, the moral authority of the state is low for both Catholics and Protestants, which adversely affects both groups' evaluations of the RUC.

In Northern Ireland attitudinal polarization on the police and other institutions of law and order is pronounced and few people take a centrist position. But, under British rule, relations between the police and the Protestant and Catholic populations have become more complicated than a simple dichotomy of orientations. There are increasingly significant differences *within* the Catholic and Protestant populations, differences important enough to justify an analysis based not only on the two larger populations but also on their major subgroups. Following the standard distinctions made in the literature on Northern Ireland, I examine four groups: staunch Republicans, moderate Catholics, staunch Loyalists, and moderate Protestants. (One of the groups was predominant in each of the specific neighborhoods I studied.) Staunch Republicans and Loyalists hold more extreme views than their moderate Catholic and Protestant counterparts regarding the British state and the national question, and they are more prepared to condone or participate in protest actions and political violence. The book shows that each group's distinctive relationship with the police is shaped by the four variables outlined above.

Since the study deals with police-community relations, the concept of "community" deserves clarification. I follow the common definition of community as a small territorial area that is fairly well integrated and homogeneous, the members of which have, or perceive themselves to have, shared interests, values, and identity. Some locales clearly do not have these characteristics, but others do. In highly segregated societies, we are likely to find communities with high degrees of territoriality, resistance to external encroachment, and shared experiences and perceptions of state authorities. They may be "defended neighborhoods," to use Gerald Suttles' term, exclusive and aggressively protected against outsiders.[26]

Many of Northern Ireland's communities are defended neighborhoods par excellence. Residential segregation of working-class Protestants and Catholics traditionally has been high, but it increased markedly in the early 1970s as a result of a series of attacks on persons living in the "wrong" neighborhoods. From 1969 to 1972 approximately 15,000 people were driven out of their former neighborhoods by firebombings of homes, threats of forcible eviction, or fear of attacks. (Relocation for these reasons continued for several years after 1972 but on a much smaller scale.) During this four-year period the proportion of Belfast's Catholics living on streets where Catholic households constituted more than 90 percent rose from 56 percent to 70 percent; the proportion of Belfast's Protestants living on streets over 90 percent Protestant rose from 69 percent to 78 percent.[27] Today, residential segregation remains high in Belfast and in some other areas, and in 1993 half of Northern Ireland's population lived in areas whose inhabitants were over 90 percent of one religion or the other.[28]

Segregated housing is one reason why people in Northern Ireland "have quite definite ideas about what their neighborhood is" and a strong sense of its boundaries.[29] Residential segregation traditionally has been associated with loyalty to a locale whose identity is shaped in part by its differences with neighborhoods of the opposite ethnic group, which are often nearby. Segregation has a narrowing effect on a person's circle of contacts and fosters prejudice toward the other side, but it also has a positive effect insofar as it contributes to the formation of fairly cohesive communities organized to protect members from violent attacks by outsiders. In turn, as Georg Simmel pointed out, such attacks (which continue to occur in Northern Ireland) increase communal solidarity and foster a distinctive neighborhood identity.[30] Especially in Northern Ireland's troubled communities (but also in other areas), residents are highly suspicious of outsiders, who might pose a threat—a sensitivity conducive to the development of strong overarching allegiances, despite internal differences. Indeed, the largest cities of Belfast and Londonderry are often referred to as clusters of "urban villages"—relatively insulated, self-sufficient, integrated localities. (At the same time, people have a keen sense of their larger ethnic identity—as Protestants or Catholics—that transcends the local neighborhood and fosters identification with their ethnic counterparts in other locales. Catholics and Protestants have their separate schools, newspapers, churches, political parties, voluntary associations, clubs, and pubs, and there is very little intermarriage.)

All of this is to suggest that the concept of "community" is appropriate in studying local-level relationships with the police in Northern Ireland. We shall see that Northern Ireland's communities, particularly those in the most segregated areas, are the locus of strong collective views and experiences of the police.

The final theme addressed in the book is the question of the *possibilities and limits of improving police-community relations in an ethnically polarized and strife-torn society.* Under what conditions can the police gain the confidence of each of our four types of communities, and under what conditions will they lose support or see their relations deteriorate further? Since the model of police-community relations in divided societies is more complex—that is, there are more determinants and they are interrelated—than what obtains in less divided, liberal democracies, we should expect that improvements in relations would be more difficult in divided societies. In Chapter 7 and the Conclusion, I address questions of improvement and deterioration in relations with the help of the four factors outlined above. I also assess the state's efforts to improve relations via community policing. *Community policing* refers to a style of policing that seeks to build ties between police and residents to reduce crime, deal with other local problems, and make police more responsive to neighborhood needs. It may take the form of regular meetings with community groups, foot patrols, youth programs, and so forth. We shall see that residents of Northern Ireland's troubled neighborhoods are skeptical or suspicious of virtually all police actions, however benign, and that community policing cannot compensate for the more common police practices that aggravate people, nor for the state's basic lack of legitimacy. Not only will such experiments fail in these neighborhoods, but they may also backfire. Indeed, in Northern Ireland's most troubled neighborhoods, community policing has had an *adverse effect* on police-community relations, making an already bad situation even worse. Chapter 7 shows how this dynamic works.

None of this is to say that police-community relations are frozen solid in Northern Ireland. Police and citizens are not destined to harbor as much ill will or to interact as belligerantly as they do in some areas. I will argue that relations can be improved, to some extent, where they are presently poorest not by community policing but instead by *progressive changes in counterinsurgency policing.* Liberalizing security policing is not a contradiction in terms. Public order and internal security can be maintained in ways that are much less aggravating and alienating than in contemporary Northern Ireland.

SOURCES AND METHODS

Three types of data sources were used in the study: documentary, survey, and interview. Written materials included annual reports of the police and the civilian complaints board, reports of commissions of inquiry, parliamentary debates, publications of Northern Ireland's political parties, and newspaper reports. Particularly useful newspapers were the *Belfast Telegraph*, the *Irish Times*, the *Irish News*, and the *Independent*.

Several surveys have tapped public attitudes on policing. The most comprehensive are the 1987 Policy Studies Institute's poll and the 1990 Northern Ireland Social Attitudes Survey, conducted by Social and Community Planning Research. I use these data to help profile each of our four types of community's attitudes toward the police. However, the survey data are not sufficient for understanding these orientations. Since they typically sample large populations, the generalized results mask geographically specific neighborhood patterns; they yield fairly superficial data and are not designed to elicit respondents' interpretations and understandings and the contingencies on which specific attitudes hinge; and the often dichotomized response options may conceal respondents' ambivalence on particular questions. For example, the question "Are you satisfied with the police?" tells us very little. An affirmative response may conceal underlying reservations or dissatisfaction with a specific aspect of policing, and it tells us nothing about the reasons why subjects report satisfaction. Neither are surveys designed to unravel apparent contradictions in responses to different questions. It is not uncommon to find people reporting "satisfaction" or "confidence," but then critically evaluating specific aspects of policing.

Surveys in Northern Ireland present additional problems. The sensitivity of some questions may yield responses that exaggerate approval of the police and underreport extreme views. Support for various aspects of policing may be more shallow than affirmative responses suggest, even if there is a high degree of consistency across different polls. Another vexing problem is the sometimes significant number of respondents who select the "don't know" option. The survey findings presented in this book should therefore be treated cautiously. Fortunately, these data have been triangulated with other data sources.

Insofar as sensitive issues are covered, in-depth interviews have advantages over surveys, since they permit greater rapport between researcher and subject. They also allow us to explore respondents' ambivalence about specific matters and the qualifications untapped in answers to fixed-choice questions. Intensive interviews are not only sensitive to the complexities of individuals' attitudes, preferences, and complaints, but they can also help explain why people subscribe to those views. Researchers have rarely used in-depth interviews to explore public attitudes on policing, and never in Northern Ireland.[31] A few participant-observation studies in Northern Ireland have reported, inter alia, on a community's experiences with the security forces, but they have not presented members' own accounts in any depth, nor have they explored the range of issues covered in my research.[32]

I sought interviews with a broad range of individuals who were well situated to discuss police-community relations. This resulted in four sets of respondents, over 70 individuals. One sample is drawn from the elected city and district councillors who sit on Police-Community Liaison Committees. Most of Northern Ireland's local councils have established such committees, and I interviewed representatives from 17 committees, traveling to each city and town where they are located. A major purpose of the committees is to help improve police-community relations, and I examined their efforts and impact in this area (see Chapter 7).

Northern Ireland's political parties have been passionately involved in policing issues, particularly since the outbreak of political violence in the late 1960s. Most of the major parties represent Protestants or Catholics almost exclusively and tend to articulate ethnically specific perspectives on policing. Frequently voicing criticisms and demands that are antithetical, the Protestant and Catholic parties play a major role in contesting policing at the national level. Their general positions can be derived from media reports, but interviews were necessary to probe their perspectives more deeply and to raise questions neglected in the mass media. I interviewed the security spokesman or another top leader of the Ulster Unionist Party, Democratic Unionist Party, Social Democratic and Labour Party, Sinn Fein, and Alliance Party.

A third group of subjects work in government departments and official bodies involved in some way in policing. The Police Authority, the police complaints commission, and the Northern Ireland Office play a role in formulating policing policies, handling complaints, or attempting to improve relations between the police and public. Information was sought on agency practices and goals, perceptions of community concerns and attempts to address them, and the nature of each agency's relations with the RUC. I also interviewed two chairmen of the Police Federation, the union representing 95 percent of the RUC.

Repeated attempts were made to gain permission from the RUC to interview officers attached to its Community Relations Branch. I hoped that the chief constable might see this as potentially in the RUC's interest, a way of highlighting a type of gentler policing as a counterbalance to the security policing that draws so much attention. But my requests for access were denied. Van Mannen notes that "antipathy and distrust of the academic researcher are endemic to most police departments,"[33] but the RUC arguably has better grounds than many others to worry about the consequences of research for the morale and safety of officers. While I awaited decisions on my requests to conduct interviews, some police officers and soldiers were killed or injured in attacks by the Irish Republican Army (IRA).[34] The tremendous physical danger facing RUC officers reinforces a siege mentality and galvanizes organizational norms of secrecy and suspiciousness of outsiders—present in other police forces but extreme in the RUC. This understandable protective insularity converges with a compelling interest, on the part of RUC chiefs, to minimize adverse publicity, whether it results from academic research, journalistic exposés, or government investigations. This may explain why research on even a seemingly innocuous side of policing like community relations was rejected by the RUC's gatekeepers.[35]

As it turned out, I did manage to interview some officers unofficially and to attend some community policing functions, thanks to introductions from third parties. I have kept their identities and police stations strictly confidential, since they acted without official permission. Data on community constables' attitudes and experiences are reported in Chapter 7, with the proviso that they are drawn from a small number of individuals and are intended simply to illustrate how some community cops view the RUC's relations with the public and what they are doing to improve matters. The study is not primarily about community policing or police perspectives, but about community orientations to the police.

This brings us to the fourth group, a sample of 40 community-based informants close to the grass roots of their respective neighborhoods: community workers, local politicians, and clergy located in 20 neighborhoods, most in Belfast. (A list of these interviewees appears in the Appendix.) A few of the community workers have worked in both Catholic and Protestant areas, and their comments on both areas are used, but most of the informants worked exclusively in one type of community. Interviews were conducted in Catholic, Protestant, and mixed lower-class and middle-class areas. Some of the neighborhoods were well insulated from those of the opposing ethnic group, whereas others were in borderline or interface areas. The initial respondents were drawn from two short lists of voluntary civic groups (I approached all these groups) and from the 21 community centers administered by Belfast City Council (I interviewed workers at 10 centers).[36] Snowball sampling was used to identify other informants. Subjects were asked for names of persons knowledgeable about the community, which generated a second sample. Where possible, I tried to cross-check the responses by interviewing other persons in the neighborhood.

The purpose of these interviews was to *examine in depth predominant community evaluations and experiences of policing.* My informants' positions in the community and their activities on behalf of constituents means that they often hear comments and complaints from ordinary people, some of whom request help in dealing with the police; that they are in a position to observe interactions between police and residents; and that these informants are well versed in the neighborhood culture. They are therefore uniquely situated to articulate the perspectives and describe the experiences of ordinary people in their areas.

The interview schedule contained some standard questions asked of all respondents and others tailored to the specific respondent's position in the community or the type of community in which he or she lived and worked. Questions addressed, inter alia, community complaints, approval, demands, and experiences of policing; changes in attitudes over time; perceptions of policing on the other side of the ethnic divide; views of various community policing mechanisms; awareness of and attitudes toward the civilian complaints board; views on the composition, impartiality, and legitimacy of the RUC; assessments of how the police handle their ordinary duties; and what, if anything, the police could do to elicit more local support. Responses to the standardized questions were analyzed across interviewees on a question-by-question basis, with special attention to similarities and differences in responses of persons located in the same neighborhood as well as in different neighborhoods.

I have no reason to believe that my interviewees deliberately camouflaged attitudes or distorted them in a socially acceptable direction. I judged the interview data to have a high degree of validity, in terms of being reasonably accurate descriptions of community orientations toward the police. But two sources of bias may have crept into the data. First, there is a danger that at least some respondents will discuss only the negative aspects of policing and that, by virtue of the probability that they hear mostly complaints, their characterizations of local opinion may exaggerate the criticisms held by average members of the community. People with praise for the police may make favorable remarks in passing but they are less likely than the aggrieved to make a special effort to contact community leaders to express their views. Some of my interview data appear to reflect this tendency; that is, I got an earful of criticisms and complaints in the militant Catholic and Protestant neighborhoods (though I also heard positive comments in the Protestant areas). I am confident, however, that the data reflect the *dominant* neighborhood culture in each type of community, which prevails over individuals holding minority views. I found substantial consistency in informants' descriptions of prevailing community orientations toward police in staunch Republican areas and in staunch Loyalist areas, both among informants located in the same neighborhood and across different neighborhoods of the same type, although naturally there were differences related to the specificities of each locale. The degree of consistency in the findings suggests that these data can be taken as a barometer of the most serious issues pertaining to policing in the neighborhoods studied. The data on moderate Protestant and Catholic communities also clustered around a dominant set of themes, largely positive for the moderate Protestants and more mixed for the moderate Catholics, depending on the dimension of policing in question.

A second possible source of bias relates to snowball sampling, which may yield a sample of informants who share one anothers' views to such an extent that the data are skewed and variations within the population are not tapped. I tried to minimize this in two ways. First, I had several snowballs rolling, each based on a different list of community organizations, as noted above. Second, some interviewees provided names of persons they knew well and others they did not know but considered useful contacts. A few even referred me to people on the opposite side of the ethnic divide. I believe these procedures helped broaden the sample sufficiently.

Access to community informants was remarkably easy and, in most cases, rapport was quickly established. Most respondents did not hesitate to grant interviews, and they gave freely of their time and hospitality. Only one person declined to be interviewed—a priest concerned about the sensitivity of the subject matter. It is surprising that this concern was not voiced more often. Other researchers in Northern Ireland have been accused of being spies for the security forces, British intelligence, or the CIA; no one made any such comment to me. After I described my research objectives and why I was requesting the interview, rarely was I questioned about my motives or sympathies. And I was only once asked to show my university credentials (to officers in Sinn Fein, the political arm of the IRA).

Ease of access was perhaps partly due to the fact that respondents were anxious to express their views to an American researcher. Had I hailed from Northern Ireland, elsewhere in the United Kingdom, or the Republic of Ireland, I almost certainly would have found it more difficult to gain access to and the confidence of both sides of the society; questions about my impartiality and motives would have been more salient. To preempt suspicions of bias, I stressed in my letters of introduction or initial phone conversations that I had already begun to interview both Protestants and Catholics in different parts of Belfast, and that I wanted the views of all groups. A second reason for the high response rate may be the profound salience of policing and security issues in Northern Ireland, issues that figure prominently almost daily on the nightly news and in the press. Policing is a matter of long-standing public controversy, and my respondents were clearly eager to discuss their perspectives and experiences with me. Indeed, most of them spoke without hesitation about controversial and sensitive issues, apparently seizing the opportunity to discuss community orientations or to "set the record straight" about local relations with the police.

Interview responses were recorded by hand as largely verbatim statements.[37] Because of the sensitive nature of many of the questions and concern for the safety of my interviewees, tape-recording was judged unwise. Tape-recording would have been refused by many informants and, if used, might have interfered with rapport and distorted responses to questions about delicate matters. The handwritten recording method, coupled with the rapport that usually developed in preinterview conversations, seemed to facilitate frank responses to the sometimes sensitive questions. On only a few occasions did a respondent decline to answer a specific question. Respondents were assured of anonymity in my written work, with the exception of a few informants of national standing who are frequently quoted in the press and who granted permission to be identified.

The sensitive nature of the research suggested that it would be wise to take a low profile during the fieldwork. Not only did I keep the identities of my informants confidential, but I also concealed my research activities from strangers. When asked what I was doing in Northern Ireland, I usually responded that I was visiting friends or traveling throughout Ireland. Declining to reveal that I was studying policing may have meant some missed opportunities, but I considered it the safest choice.

Other field researchers in Northern Ireland have reported fears of having their data confiscated by the authorities or being detained and interrogated about their research activities and contacts. I knew that the police were aware of my research, since I had formally requested permission to interview officers. Was the data I gathered of interest to the authorities? Perhaps. Although I did not ask informants, and was not informed by them, about specific illegal activities in their communities, many comments, if traced to the individual, might be grounds for harassment by the security forces. I was surprised to learn that the phones of community workers were tapped—something I could not verify but which nevertheless heightened my concern about risks to my subjects and to myself. The usefulness of the data to the authorities, as another source of intelligence on the residents, is doubtful since the data do not reveal the specific kinds of information sought by the security forces. Moreover, these are communities on which the security forces already have a wealth of intelligence. I would hope that the authorities would derive other lessons from the book—in terms of corrective measures that might help to reduce some of the sources of tension between the police and the public, a point taken up in the Conclusion.

There was a risk of unwanted attention not only from the security forces but also from militant Catholic and Protestant organizations that became aware of my research. Some academics have been threatened, wounded, or killed in Northern Ireland. I had originally planned to minimize personal risk by steadfastly avoiding any contact with the Irish Republican Army, the Ulster Defense Association, and their kindred spirits. But my respondents in Sinn Fein were probably connected in some manner to the IRA, and I was told that one of my Protestant informants was close to the UDA. This was perhaps unavoidable in some of the neighborhoods studied. I did not, however, intentionally make contact with individuals active in insurgent (or "paramilitary") organizations, even when offers were made by third parties.

Another delicate aspect of the research involved my study of both Protestant and Catholic communities. I alternated between Protestant and Catholic neighborhoods in the hope that issues raised in one would be useful in studying the other. Almost every other community researcher has studied one side exclusively, taking pains to avoid contact with their antagonists. Researching both groups raised a number of problems, particularly since I informed respondents of this fact. Occasionally I was asked with whom I had spoken "on the other side"; I replied that all names were confidential, including the questioner's. But I was surprised to learn that some informants already knew the identities of some of my informants on the other side. I discovered that at least some Catholic and Protestant clergy and community workers have contact with their counterparts in the other ethnic group or some kind of intelligence grapevine, whereas ordinary members of their communities tend to be insulated from the other side. Though somewhat disconcerting to me, this backstage communication between members of opposing groups seems to have enhanced my credibility and facilitated rapport with a number of respondents. Indeed, the success of my movement between conflicting groups appears to be due to the following: they perceived me as truly an outsider with no strong biases in favor of either side; I was honest about studying both sides; I kept my contacts and findings confidential; and I did not play one side off against the other. Similar precautions by other researchers who have studied conflicting parties seems to have facilitated their research as well.[38]

Another problem with the decision to study both sides involved scheduling: on some days an interview in a staunch Republican neighborhood would be followed by one in a staunch Loyalist neighborhood, and I knew that taxis (my mode of transportation) traveling between communities had not infrequently been attacked in the past (taxi companies are sometimes identified with a Protestant or Catholic area). One driver was visibly shocked that I was traveling between community centers in neighborhoods he described as being "at each others' throats." In retrospect, it probably was not advisable to travel so cavalierly between opposing communities. But the back-to-back interviews in these neighborhoods did facilitate my comparative research goals, throwing into immediate and stark relief community differences and sensitizing me to their similarities.

Qualitative researchers have often been criticized for failing to link their findings to larger structural and cultural conditions. In my data analysis, I have attempted to draw connections between police-community relations at the micro level and the macro-level factors that affect them: institutional factors (especially with regard to policing structures), broad ethnic relations and inequalities, and the ongoing political conflict in Northern Ireland.[39] In other words, part of the analysis examines how local-level patterns of police-community relations are conditioned by larger structures. We can also move from the micro to the macro: our analysis of police-community relations on the ground, although by no means a microcosm of the larger society, can be instructive in illuminating certain features of Northern Ireland society as a whole.

The book is organized as follows. Part 1 examines the transition from Northern Ireland's traditional system of policing under Protestant rule to more liberal policing under British intervention. We shall see that the reforms are a welcome departure from the traditional order, but they are limited by various factors. Part 2 examines the three most important substantive problems bearing on police-community relations: police legitimacy and professionalism, counterinsurgency and conventional policing, and police accountability. For their part, the authorities have responded to community relations problems with "community policing" initiatives. Part 3 evaluates these efforts and then draws some conclusions about the prospects for improving police-community relations in Northern Ireland and more generally.

PART 1

From Protestant to British Rule

CHAPTER 2

Protestant Policing: 1922–1968

To fully comprehend policing in Northern Ireland we need a historical perspective. Historical investigation allows us to assess how closely policing in the past resembled the divided society model presented in Chapter 1; enables a longitudinal analysis of continuities and changes between the past and the present; and provides a reference for understanding contemporary actors' efforts to invoke, either critically or enthusiastically, Ulster's policing traditions. This chapter begins with a brief examination of nineteenth century patterns, and then turns to the period of Unionist rule, focusing on the Royal Ulster Constabulary's composition, relations with Catholics and Protestants, political leanings, and conduct. Data are drawn from secondary sources, parliamentary debates, and the reports of several commissions of inquiry.

NINETEENTH CENTURY POLICING

Ulster's policing traditions predate the creation of the Unionist state in 1921, originating during the nineteenth century when the entire island of Ireland was ruled by Britain. In 1836 a national Irish Constabulary replaced the disparate local police forces in Ireland. Controlled by an inspector-general, the new force was responsible for policing everywhere except in Dublin, Belfast, and Londonderry, which retained their own forces. From the very beginning Ireland was policed more heavily than the rest of the United Kingdom. The number of police officers per capita in Ireland in 1836 was more than three times that of England and Wales and four times that of Scotland. By 1897 Ireland still had over twice as many constables per capita than the rest of the United Kingdom.[1] Large, centralized, militarized, and armed (with guns, batons, bayonets), the constabulary faced chronic legitimacy problems: it was discredited by radical Catholics (who saw it as an army of imperial occupation and a champion of Protestant supremacy) as well as by Northern Protestants (who claimed that Catholic officers were sympathetic to the Republican struggle to end British colonialism in Ireland).

Over time, however, the constabulary grew more impartial, professional, and representative of the two ethnic groups. It became less amenable to local sectarian influences; intervened to prevent clashes between Ulster Protestants and Catholics; prohibited police membership in the Orange Order (a bitterly anti-Catholic organization) and the Catholic Association; and recruited an increasing number of Catholics.[2] Catholics constituted only 16 percent of the force in 1816 but 76 percent in 1880, although the officer corps remained largely Protestant.[3] Police were forbidden under the 1836 Constabulary Act (s. 17, 18) from belonging to any political organization, save the Freemasons, and from voting in elections. The act (s. 24) also provided for police inquiries into allegations that officers had neglected or violated their duties.

Nineteenth century Ireland was governed by a British colonial regime based in Dublin, but northern areas with sizeable concentrations of Protestants were given some autonomy in local affairs. Belfast, for example, was policed by a local Protestant force numbering 160. (A small constabulary unit was also stationed there to provide support as needed.) The local police came under the authority of a Police Committee appointed by the Town Council. The committee handled all matters connected with the local force including the hiring of constables. Members of both the council and the committee were almost all Protestant, as was the chief of police, and only between five and seven members of the local police force were Catholic in the mid-nineteenth century. (The chairman of the Police Committee told a commission of inquiry, examining policing in Belfast in 1864, that he had no objection to Catholics joining the force but then revealed that, if the force somehow attracted a large majority of Catholics, he would not hesitate to restore Protestant hegemony, out of sympathy with the Protestant population). This was not simply a Protestant force but a fiercely anti-Catholic one; many of the Protestant constables were members of the supremacist Orange Order. The 1864 commission concluded that the ethnic composition of the force was "decidedly calculated to create, and does create, suspicion on the part of the Roman Catholic population," and the fact that the police force was controlled by the Town Council itself deprived the force of the confidence of "a considerable portion" of the population.[4] No wonder so few Catholics considered joining this force.

The Belfast police force also had a reputation for differential law enforcement.[5] An 1857 commission of inquiry found that the police acted with less belligerence in managing disturbances in Protestant than in Catholic neighborhoods, but it claimed that this was not due to partiality on the part of the police. Instead, most of the variation could be explained by the different circumstances in the two areas. Unlike Protestants, Catholic crowds reportedly refused to disperse when so ordered and often attacked the police. The police were thus provoked to act more harshly against Catholics than Protestants. Unfortunate though it was, the 1857 commission did not see the Protestant composition of the force as the central problem; hence, it recommended simply increasing the size of the force (which did not occur).[6]

For the 1864 commission, by contrast, the composition of the force and Catholic alienation from it were at the very heart of the problem. It highlighted the "grave inexpediency" of a purely Protestant force and noted that an ethnic balance would enable officers of different backgrounds to check one another.[7] Foremost among its recommendations was the abolition of the local police force and replacement with a greatly expanded constabulary of 400 to 450 men drawn from all over Ireland. The goal was to improve police-community relations:

> Considering the peculiar circumstances of Belfast, the violent religious and party animosities that have so long prevailed there, and no less the spirit of suspicion necessarily generated by such an unfortunate state of things, any force of a strictly local character would inevitably give dissatisfaction. . . . It would in all probability never win the general confidence of the people. None of these objections apply to the constabulary. Recruited . . . from every part of Ireland, . . . the local and personal predilections or antipathies of its members are insensibly softened down. . . . If any of its members should fall under the supicion of becoming impregnated injuriously with local feelings, they could at any moment be removed. . . . [8]

Also troubling was the Town Council's political control over the police; the commission recommended that the management and control of the force be transferred from the council's Police Committee to a commissioner of police. The 1865 Constabulary (Ireland) Amendment Act incorporated these recommendations, replacing the Belfast police force with the Royal Irish Constabulary (RIC) under the control of an inspector. By the 1880s the RIC's officer corps in Belfast was mainly Protestant, but the force as a whole was fairly evenly divided among Protestants (330) and Catholics (268), in a city with a 2:1 ratio of Protestants to Catholics.[9]

Whether the agency policing Belfast was the local Protestant force or the Irish Constabulary, its neutrality was disputed by one ethnic group or the other. The local police identified with and favored the Protestants, which fostered Catholic discontent. Once the control, composition, and conduct of the police began to change—as a result of the 1864 commission—a shift in police-community relations became noticeable. Protestants now began to argue that police were biased against them. The constabulary was accused of being insensitive to the Protestant population and an instrument of the British government, and it periodically came under physical attack. Over a two-week period of violence in 1872, for example, one-sixth of the force was injured and one officer killed.[10] New disturbances broke out in 1886 at a time when Protestant discontent with the Crown was at a high point. Westminster was debating a Home Rule Bill for Ireland, which Protestants feared would lead to religious discrimination in an independent Catholic state. Sectarian feelings were running high and they boiled over into rioting.

The commission investigating the riots concluded that many Protestants believed the government was "packing" Belfast with Catholic police from the south who were "charged with the duty of shooting down the Protestants," and being used "for the purpose of coercing the Protestant population of Belfast into an acceptance of the Home Rule scheme."[11] The commissioners considered this an "insane idea," but it fired Protestant attacks on Catholics and the police. With unprecedented ferocity and duration (a period of four months), police were stoned, beaten, shot at, and branded "Fenian whores" for intervening to protect Catholic businesses against Protestant attacks. A large number of Protestant rioters acted with "wild and unreasoning hostility" toward the police.[12] So intense was the hostility that the police were withdrawn from Belfast's Protestant Shankill area and replaced with the military. In the end, 31 people had been killed.

The 1886 commission found that police officers had performed admirably in the face of prolonged attacks and that they had acted impartially. It rejected proposals for a return to a locally recruited force and for the creation of a special reserve constabulary, because they would lack broad-based support and would only fuel more conflict. Also rejected was a proposal by the Town Council that the chief of police take instructions from and report to a local committee. The commissioners dismissed the idea on the grounds that "the unhappy dissensions of Belfast would render it most difficult to form any committee which would command the confidence of the general body of the inhabitants."[13] They noted that the council already had a Law and Police Committee that occasionally communicated with the police chief.

The commission recommended that, since the command of the force was tenuously divided between the police chief and the divisional magistrate, full authority should be vested in the former, who should be entirely independent of any outside authority (except for the inspector-general of the RIC in Dublin). Concerned with the state of police relations with both Catholics and Protestants, the commission suggested that a code of conduct be introduced to nurture a civic ethos in the police culture, to teach cops "the art of dealing discreetly and with tact with an urban population."[14] Another problem was the paramilitary character of the RIC, which did not befit a civil force. Accordingly, it recommended that constables be armed only with batons, not guns— advice the government rejected. In the years to follow, the RIC became even less of a civil force and more involved in counterinsurgency, largely as a result of violent Republican opposition to British rule in the latter part of the century and the first two decades of the twentieth century.[15] Armed struggle escalated into a full-scale civil war in 1919, which ultimately led to the birth of the Northern Ireland state.

PROTESTANT POLICING: 1922–1968

In 1921 the British government partitioned Ireland, granting home rule or dominion status to the south and a semiautonomous state to the north. The boundaries were drawn in a way that guaranteed that neither part would become a secular state. The north would have a confortable Protestant majority and the south would be almost entirely Catholic. Northern Ireland remained part of the United Kingdom, and the new Protestant regime sought simultaneously to cement this link to prevent a future grab by the southern state (which laid claim to the north) and to achieve maximum autonomy from the Crown to preempt interference in internal affairs. Central to the process of consolidating state power was the regime's need for full control over the institutions of law and order. A police force was created with dual responsiblities for ordinary crime and internal security. The new Royal Ulster Constabulary (RUC) was insulated from British traditions of minimum force, "policing by consent" of the public, and political independence. Reminiscent of the past, the RUC was from the beginning armed and militarized, and Northern Ireland continued to be policed more heavily per capita than the rest of the United Kingdom. The force was closely tied to the Ministry of Home Affairs, whose top officials were strident defenders of Protestant interests and whose policies with regard to law and order were sometimes purely political and biased against Catholics. Supporting the RUC was another paramilitary force, the Ulster Special Constabulary (USC), which was formed at the end of 1920 largely from the ranks of the outlawed Ulster Volunteer Force, a Protestant vigilante group dedicated to keeping Northern Ireland within the United Kingdom. The USC provided assistance to the RUC during public disturbances; it staffed checkpoints on various roads; and it was involved in border patrols and other, more mundane tasks.

Information about policing during the period of Unionist rule is limited.[16] The remainder of the chapter is based largely on an examination of material in the Northern Ireland House of Commons (or Stormont) debates from 1921 to 1968.[17] These data were analyzed in terms of the ways in which policing conformed to the divided society model outlined in Chapter 1 and the major areas of conflict over policing. Parliamentary debates are lacking in certain information that would pertain to the divided society model, but they do contain information (from government ministers and opposition MPs) on some core features of policing, and, coupled with other sources, the data suggest that traditional policing in Northern Ireland was largely consistent with the divided society model. This source is also an imperfect guide to conflicts over policing in the wider society, but, combined with the few secondary accounts, the data suggest which issues generated the most conflict. Some of the parliamentary comments undoubtedly reflect the exaggerated posturing of politicians, but for the most part the views expressed appear to be rooted in real concerns and abiding party interests regarding policing. There is an overall consistency in the content of nationalist and Unionist discourse, although the intensity of the debate changed over time.

Party Perspectives

Our analysis focuses on the leading political forces in Northern Ireland, the ruling Unionist Party and the nationalist parties, who represented most Protestants and Catholics. However, other parties (labour, independent Unionists) contributed to debates on policing, and when the nationalists boycotted parliament these minor parties were alone in challenging the policies of the Unionist Party. The labour parties usually echoed nationalists' criticisms of the police, and the independent Unionists sometimes criticized policing from the right of the government, demanding more police protection of Protestants and less intervention against Orange marches.

Nationalists.   Moderate Catholic leaders were ambivalent about political participation in the Northern Ireland state. All elected nationalists abstained in 1921 from taking their seats in the new Stormont parliament, because participation might have been seen as a vote of confidence in a state they considered illegitimate and hoped would be short-lived. But after the 1925 election two nationalists entered Stormont in the hope of winning some concessions. In the following decades there were periods when they again refused to take their seats. The more radical Catholics, or Republicans, boycotted Stormont for its entire life.

Organized into a number of parties, nationalists articulated the concerns of the Catholic minority and were committed to the elimination of the Northern state and reunification of Ireland. They did not advocate the violent overthrow of the government but doubted that a Unionist regime could be persuaded by peaceful means to accept changes that might dilute Protestant dominance. Their opposition to the Northern state did not translate into sweeping condemnation of the RUC; instead they were at times conciliatory and at other times quite critical of the police.

Criticisms grew during the regime's periodic mobilization of the RUC to stifle Catholic political activity or quell unrest and when the police failed to intervene to protect Catholics from Protestant attacks. Over time, the seriousness and scope of their complaints increased. In 1925 the nationalist leader, Joseph Devlin, described the RUC as "a very efficient, very kindly, courteous, and tactful body of public servants."[18] But by the early 1930s frustration with the rigidities of Unionist rule and concern about unchecked Protestant violence against Catholics sharpened nationalist criticism of the RUC. Nationalist MPs questioned the impartiality of the force and its allegiance to the rule of law.[19] During a later period one MP characterized Catholic opinion as "complete detestation" with the "political police force known as the RUC."[20] This was something of an exaggeration, judging by other MPs' more tempered depictions of Catholic attitudes, but the trend was unmistakable: nationalist discontent mounted over time, peaking during major disturbances when the police came into direct physical conflict with Catholics.

If the intensity of criticism increased over the years, the litany of substantive grievances changed little. Nationalists routinely argued that the force was too large and costly and should be reduced—to no avail. (Northern Ireland was much more heavily policed than the rest of the United Kingdom. In 1924 the ratio of police to population was 1:160 in Northern Ireland, 1:669 in England and Wales, and 1:751 in Scotland.)[21] Nationalists also frequently called for the RUC to be disarmed (because an armed force deviated from other United Kingdom forces or for other reasons) and for the USC to be disbanded. And they routinely complained about the low number of Catholics in the RUC; police raids on homes to conduct searches and interrogate residents; politically biased handling of marches and demonstrations; crackdowns on the flying of the banned Irish flag; and the nefarious influence on the police of the Orange Order and the Unionist Party.

The fact that nationalists were at all willing to sit in the Stormont parliament suggests that their criticisms and demands might be more tempered than those of Republicans, who refused to participate in the state. Indeed, nationalists refrained from blanket damnations of the RUC as an institution and sometimes praised the force, they drew distinctions between the USC and RUC, and they tended to blame policing problems on senior officers or the

Home Affairs minister rather than ordinary constables. Although many of their criticisms resonated with those of Republicans, the latter considered the specific problems secondary to the fundamental illegitimacy of the RUC and the state, and they did not endorse nationalists' positive remarks about the police. Republicans sought the abolition of both the USC and the RUC, their arch-enemies, along with the dismantling of the entire Northern state. They supported the Irish Republican Army's (IRA) armed attacks on police, which occurred sporadically in the 1940s and during an abortive campaign to eliminate partition in 1956–1962.[22]

An analysis based largely on parliamentary data, which do not include radical, Republican perspectives, may give the impression that policing was less contested in Northern Ireland than it may have been. It is useful to keep in mind that the conflicts over policing examined in this chapter do not include Republicans' sweeping and unequivocal rejection of the RUC.

Unionists.   Partition guaranteed Northern Ireland a Protestant majority, and the Unionist Party virtually monopolized the political representation of that majority for fifty years. Unionists regarded the state as a Protestant preserve, but since Ulster was a majoritarian democracy, they could not exclude Catholics from the national electoral system.[23] Nevertheless, Unionists essentially controlled Stormont; there were never more than 19 opposition MPs (some of whom were not nationalists) sitting in the 52-member House.[24] The opposition's motions rarely mustered more than a handful of votes, and they were powerless to influence policing matters.

The Unionist Party was not hospitable to moderates who sought some kind of accommodation with the Catholic minority. Though it included both hard-liners and pragmatists, the party as a whole was fully committed to the maintenance of Protestant supremacy and to resolute defense of the Northern state against "papist" threats.[25] Almost all Unionist MPs (138 out of 149 serving between 1921 and 1969) were members of the Protestant supremacist Orange Order.[26] Unionists' prejudices and an obsession with the security of the state drove policy making and legislation in a direction that discriminated against the Catholic minority.

It was an article of faith among Unionists that the RUC compared favorably with police forces in more integrated societies.

Frequently proclaiming the RUC to be one of the best police forces in the world, they insisted that the force was absolutely impartial, disciplined, and professional. Occasionally it was conceded that "rotten apples" might exist, but they were few in number and did not reflect on the force as a whole. However, during periods of heightened ethnic tension or when the Irish Republican Army was active, there was less trumpeting of the normality and fairness of the police. Instead a premium was placed on mobilizing the force to maintain a particularistic brand of "law and order," one that rested on the pacification of the Catholic population. The IRA's rare armed ventures were not widely supported by the minority community, but Unionists seized on them to justify maintaining a militarized police force and to discredit all nationalist criticisms. As a Home Affairs minister declared, "Derogatory remarks have been made in the past about the semimilitary training of our police forces, regular and Special, but how clearly the necessity for such training has been demonstrated by recent events will now be obvious to all."[27]

The following sections examine in greater detail the major areas of conflict between Unionists and nationalists and several dimensions of the divided society model: police relations with Catholics and Protestants, composition of the force, political policing, and accountability.

Community Relations

In 1948, the minister of Home Affairs told parliament: "I am just as much concerned as any hon. Member in this House to see that the relationship between the Royal Ulster Constabulary and the public remains as perfect as possible. . . . I think we succeed."[28] Ministers flatly insisted that the RUC enjoyed the support of all sectors of the populace: "I should think 99.9 percent of the people of Northern Ireland, agrees that in point of fact the RUC is a respectable force, and that it is sheer nonsense to criticize it."[29] And Unionist MPs ritually praised the force for having won widespread legitimacy. Typical was the claim that the RUC "enjoyed the full confidence of the community . . . with the exception of those people who are the declared enemies of Northern Ireland."[30]

Relations between the RUC and the Protestant population were indeed generally good, in accordance with the divided society model. Unionists occasionally complained about some fairly minor things (such as police rudeness toward civilians) and isolated instances of police interference with Protestant rallies and marches. But in general, police relations with Protestants did not appear problematic.

Relations between the police and the Catholic community were problematic indeed, strained especially by the RUC's responsibilities for maintaining internal security and its reluctance to curb Protestant vigilantism. The lack of police accountability and the predominantly Protestant composition of the force also caused discontent. Relations soured during incidents of Protestant attacks on Catholics, when nationalists staged protests, and when the police meted out vicarious punishment to Catholics for the actions of the IRA. Since some Catholics were sympathetic to "those people who are out to murder the members of our police force and other loyal elements in our country,"[31] aggressive and intrusive policing was deemed necessary. That this could alienate innocent Catholics was apparently of little concern.

The Ministry of Home Affairs was never sufficiently concerned with the level of Catholic confidence in the RUC to initiate any meaningful program to improve relations, nor did nationalists call for such programs. Instead they called for changes in the composition of the force, elimination of its political duties, and creation of mechanisms of accountability, each of which might improve relations between the police and the public, even if that was not the primary aim.

Composition of the RUC

The composition of a police force can be an important variable affecting public attitudes toward the police in a divided society. If the force is drawn exclusively or primarily from the dominant ethnic, racial, or religious group, this may result in biased practices and polarize relations with the police. Constables in such forces are likely to develop strong prejudices and engage in discrimination toward members of the subordinate group. But, as I will argue in later chapters, it does not necessarily follow that a more representative police force will help to reduce police bias and discrimination or elicit greater popular support.

Tensions over the RUC's composition dates from the moment of its inception, with nationalists and Unionists expressing antithetical concerns. One question had to do with the political loyalty of former members of the RIC (which was dismantled in 1922). Unionists had never been satisfied with the RIC—which they considered too Catholic and of dubious loyalty to the new Northern state—and they balked at suggestions that a number of its former members might be absorbed into the new RUC. Concern was also expressed about the (few) English constables who entered the new force.[32]

A committee on the reorganization of the police was formed in early 1922. Assuming that the new force would have the same structure as the RIC and would be centralized, armed, and militarized, the committee gave most of its attention to matters of composition and recruitment. It recommended that, consistent with their proportions in the population, one-third of the new force should be drawn from Catholic members of the RIC and from the population at large and two-thirds from Protestants in the RIC and USC.[33] Stormont did not reject these recommendations, but neither did it incorporate them into the 1922 Constabulary Act. Instead, it left it to the RUC and Home Affairs Ministry to implement the committee's recommendations.[34] One year later, the force consisted of 1,400 former RIC members, 1,215 former USC members, and 62 new members; 20 percent of the force was Catholic.[35]

The fact that the government did not contest the recommended ethnic balance may seem surprising in light of Unionists' unfavorable view of the RIC and suspicion of Catholic police. Farrell cites practical reasons, such as the need for trained and experienced officers and the belief that only Catholic police could get information in Catholic areas, as the RUC inspector-general argued at the time: "It is quite useless to expect to obtain any information from the RC [Roman Catholic] areas unless there are RC police and detectives. The efficiency of the force suffers at present from a lack of RC police."[36] Years later a minister also saw some value in Catholic officers: "It is often desirable, where it is a mixed district, that there be at least one [officer] of that faith to whom people in the area, probably, if they have a personal complaint may turn."[37] But the one-third quota can also be interpreted as a means of *restricting* Catholic representation in the force. Given that the RIC had been well over half Catholic in Belfast (and 80 percent throughout Ireland), the one-third limit may have been less of a conciliatory gesture than a barrier to

Catholic policemen, as three members of the advisory committee argued in dissent.[38]

At first, even the one-third quota was too much for some Unionist politicians and Loyalist organizations. The former demanded in parliament that only "loyal Ulstermen"—a euphemism for Protestants—be recruited, and the latter expressed alarm to the prime minister over alleged Catholic overrepresentation in some towns. Later, during disturbances in Belfast in 1935, independent Unionists implied that Catholic policemen may have been responsible for attacking Protestant homes. But over the years, Unionists' concerns about the loyalty of Catholic recruits diminished. As it turned out, the Catholic proportion always fell far short of the one-third ceiling. At its peak in early 1923, Catholics constituted 21 percent of the RUC, which declined to 17 percent by 1927 and 10 percent by 1966.[39] Instead of trying to recruit Catholics, the RUC filled vacancies with former members of the all-Protestant USC.[40] All applicants were required to disclose their religion to the RUC.[41]

Nationalist MPs also expressed concern about the RUC's composition. In the late 1920s they proposed that Catholic applicants be given preference in joining the RUC in order to rectify the ethnic imbalance, to no avail. They also complained that Catholic constables were being overlooked for promotion. (In 1927, 31 percent of inspectors, head constables, and sergeants were Catholic, compared to 14 percent in the lower ranks.[42] By 1944 the proportion in the middle ranks had fallen to 20 percent, mostly because of retirements rather than promotions into the senior ranks.)[43] Nationalists argued that barriers to promotion would only further reduce the number of Catholic officers, increase the sectarian character of the RUC, and undermine Catholic confidence in the force: "Quite a number of non-Unionists have had to leave because there was no hope of promotion. When this happens . . . the police force . . . will not be looked up to."[44] The ministry's policy of inviting applicants from the despised USC (who constituted about half of the force in 1923 and a third in 1951) added insult to injury for the nationalists.

The increasingly Protestant complexion of the force was important not only because it represented institutional exclusion of Catholics and affected Catholic evaluations of the RUC but also because it increased the likelihood of anti-Catholic practices. It was claimed that because the RUC was "rapidly becoming a narrow sectarian one in composition" this was "widening the door to discriminatory acts against certain sections of the population."[45] Differential treatment of Catholics and Protestants is discussed below.

Unionist leaders faulted the Catholic community itself for its underrepresentation in the RUC. There was, it is true, some Catholic reluctance to apply—conditioned by the IRA's intimidation of recruits, fear of being ostracized in the Catholic community, and underlying alienation from the police and the state. But the attitude of the Home Affairs Ministry and developments inside the RUC also served to discourage Catholics from applying to the force. The first minister of Home Affairs, Richard Dawson Bates, was infamous for his hard-line political convictions and bigotry against Catholics.[46] Bates argued that there was a "rule (which has been in operation for a very considerable time) to have Protestants in the ranks of commissioner and assistant commissioner," and he sometimes asked the inspector-general, Charles Wickham, to transfer Catholic officers, on one occasion forcing a high-ranking Catholic officer out of Belfast.[47] Wickham complained about these efforts "to bring unfair influence to bear on [sic] the detriment of RC members of the force," but he protested in vain.[48]

Furthermore, since the one-third quota was an administrative rather than a statutory matter, it could be implemented as the Ministry of Home Affairs saw fit, and the ministry eschewed until the early 1970s any kind of recruitment campaign directed at Catholics. Ministers construed the one-third quota differently at different times. In 1927 it was held that the quota applied only to the initial creation of the RUC, not to future recruitment.[49] Some twenty years later, when the proportion of Catholics was even lower, it was claimed that the one-third pledge "is still existent, and is being observed at the present time." The minister added, however, that any shortfall in actual Catholic representation should be blamed on Catholics who discouraged their own from applying, including nationalist MPs whose criticisms of the RUC were intended to prevent Catholics from joining the RUC, "so they can then use the cry of bigotry as to the composition of the force."[50]

If the RUC's composition generated complaints, it was the all-Protestant, Ulster Special Constabulary (USC) that exemplified a sectarian police force in Northern Ireland. The USC was initially divided into A, B, and C Specials with distinctive duties. The Bs were the main target of nationalist criticism. They were a large, armed voluntary force responsible for manning roadblocks, patrolling along the border, assisting in riot control, and guarding buildings at night.[51] Catholics despised and shunned contacts with the B Specials, whom they labeled a reincarnation of the hated vigilante Ulster Volunteer Force.[52] Unionists insisted that the Specials were essential for internal security, and they expressed reverence for the force, Prime Minister Craig once declaring, "I love the Bs."[53] The A and C Specials were phased out by 1926, but the Bs survived until 1970.

Initially, it seemed that the force might not evolve in a sectarian direction. In 1922 the governments of Northern Ireland and the Irish Free State signed an agreement (the Craig-Collins pact) which contained some remarkable plans for the USC:

1. Units posted in Belfast's mixed districts would be half Protestant and half Catholic.
2. An advisory committee, composed of Catholics, would assist in the selection of Catholic recruits for the USC.
3. Arms searches would be carried out by units that would be half Catholic and half Protestant.[54]

The agreement met with stiff resistance from Unionists inside and outside the state and was never implemented.

The USC thus became an exclusively Protestant force, and there is ample evidence of its fierce anti-Catholic sentiments. It staged numerous reprisals against Catholics, who were punished for their apparent disloyalty to the state and for the IRA's real and perceived acts of treachery. Two ranking members of the B Specials resigned in protest at the bigotry and indiscipline of the unit, and gave remarkable testimony to a 1922 inquiry into the collapse of the Craig-Collins pact. One of them described the Specials as a partisan force involved in "unofficial patrolling" and "much offensive oppression" of Catholics, and he claimed that "criminal acts by the 'B' Specials have been and are 'cloaked' and evidence is unobtainable." The other officer elaborated:

> There can never be any . . . confidence or stability so long as the
> "B" force . . . [is] authorized to get "on top" . . . of his Roman
> Catholic neighbor. The latter resents it all the time and even the

most respectable and constitutional nationalist gets more bitter
as the record of raids and abuses by the uncontrollable elements
[in the USC] piles up and harmless and innocent people suffer. . . . Protestants . . . have always been taught to hate Roman
Catholics and it is against all reason to expect that, untrained,
undisciplined, and almost wholly without supervision, they can
be . . . entrusted with police duties.[55]

Many years later, in an interview with the author, a former chief
constable candidly summarized the USC's serious problems:
"They were not trained in normal policing, were not subject to
discipline, and tended to be a law unto themselves."[56]

Opposition MPs repeatedly criticized the Specials' indiscipline, partiality, and criminal acts and demanded that they be
replaced with a neutral and disciplined force.[57] Yet the Specials'
repressive adventures remained unchecked for fifty years; they
were disbanded in 1970 under British pressure.

Political Policing

After the turbulent formative years of the new state, the Catholic
population was never given much reason to identify with the
regime and the institutions of law and order. The Home Affairs
Ministry was responsible for policies and practices that discriminated against Catholics, whom top officials viewed with contempt.[58] Catholic protests were branded as subversive, and security measures were vigorously enforced against political suspects.
Protestant sectarianism, by contrast, was construed as an expression of ultra-loyalty to the state and usually treated leniently.[59]
Loyalist marches were much more likely to be approved than
nationalist marches. Similarly, the Special Branch—the RUC's
intelligence unit responsible for gathering information on security
threats—monitored suspected Republicans and IRA members but
paid little attention to Loyalist extremists. By the 1960s, the RUC
was mistakenly claiming that the Ulster Volunteer Force did not
exist and the Special Branch disclosed that it had "no records on
loyalists."[60]

The first inspector-general, Charles Wickham (an Englishman
disliked by many Unionists), remained chief of the RUC for
twenty-three years, but he failed to curb the institutional procliv-
ity for differential treatment of Catholic and Protestant protests
and marches or individuals suspected of political offenses. His

authority was partly compromised by his political masters at Home Affairs, who intervened in public order and security matters. Apart from Wickham, the top echelon of the RUC was closely tied to the Unionist establishment.

A 1936 inquiry conducted by London's National Council for Civil Liberties (NCCL) criticized the RUC's political role and departures from British policing traditions. Noting that the police were equipped with armored cars and machine guns, the NCCL complained that they were intimately tied to the Home Affairs Ministry, tolerant of the Orange Order's attacks on Catholics, and wielded exceptionally broad powers under the 1922 Special Powers Act. The act allowed for punishments of whipping or death for the possession or use of weapons or explosives, and it gave the Home Affairs minister power to introduce any regulation that he considered "necessary for preserving the peace and maintaining order." Among the regulations issued were those providing for curfews, arrests and searches without a warrant, the banning of clubs and organizations, censorship of publications, and the seizure of property. The act was used to proscribe Republican publications, ban nationalist meetings and marches, suppress labor protests in the 1930s, and harass individual Catholics.[61] During World War II and the IRA campaign of 1956-1962, the act was used for internment without trial of suspected subversives.

Enforcement of the Special Powers Act also brought police and Catholics into conflict during relatively tranquil periods. Police searches of homes without a warrant was apparently not uncommon, an activity which nationalists frequently objected to: "Raiding the house of a person at midnight is not a legitimate part of police duties."[62] Dramatizing the invasiveness of these raids, nationalists claimed that "searches can be made an engine of torture of innocent political opponents"[63] and that police frequently entered homes in the middle of the night because it was "calculated to inspire alarm and terror" in residents.[64] Examples were cited of police abusiveness during raids, such as strip-searches of elderly women. Many raids yielded nothing illegal, such as weapons or seditious materials, but the authorities consistently denied charges of police impropriety in specific incidents and disregarded the general allegation that the raids constituted a form of harassment. Even if raids failed to turn up anything sinister, one minister thought they might have a deterrent effect insofar as they "discourage [residents'] activities when they might not be so innocent."[65] The act was rarely used against Protestants,[66] though not without some prompting from opposition MPs, one of whom observed that "there must be . . . public enemies and unauthorized arms lurking amongst the supporters of the Ministry, but searches in that quarter are like angels' visits, few and far between."[67]

The Ulster Special Constabulary was even more palpably political. The NCCL doubted that the Specials were needed to maintain order and criticized the Orange flavor of the force and its alleged role in "partisan electoral" projects on behalf of the Unionist government.[68] Nationalists saw the Specials as undisciplined, costly, untrained agents of the government used to "overawe and intimidate" the minority population: "there is an underlying fear by the minority in the North—this is based on actual experience—that the B Specials are at times a threat both of intimidation and of actual murder to members of that minority."[69] Unionists, on the other hand, fiercely defended the USC. They credited it with having saved Ulster during the troubles in the early 1920s, and in later years they applauded whenever the Bs were mobilized to deal with real or perceived problems.

Nationalists portrayed the RUC in a more favorable light than the USC. At times, the RUC was even congratulated for acting professionally—praise intended to show that nationalists were not anti-police, even when they criticized specific aspects of policing, and to contrast the RUC with the dreadful Specials. Nationalist MPs sometimes pinned blame for police misconduct on the Unionist regime rather than on rank-and-file constables: "The majority of them are decent people, and if they were left alone by the [government] . . . I believe they would do their duty . . . with reasonable impartiality."[70] They criticized the regime for fostering loyalist sympathies among RUC officers, for interfering with the policing of disturbances, and for routinely deploying the force in security operations, which impaired its capacity to perform its civil duties.

Loyalist Sympathies.   With regard to the policing of Protestant and Catholic activities, the NCCL found that "the police do not act impartially" but display "favoritism" toward the Orange section, frequently tolerating attacks on Catholics.[71] Mirroring nationalist criticisms, the NCCL laid most of the blame for police partisanship on the Unionist regime rather than on rank-and-file members of the RUC:

> To some extent this apparent partiality may be due to a feeling of impotence rather than to a desire (particularly on the part of the ordinary rank and file of the RUC) to show favoritism, for there is no doubt that Orange hooliganism often reaches such a pitch as to require the most drastic use of force to suppress it. But even if this feeling does play some part in producing the effects of partiality, . . . the attitude of the government renders the police chary of interference with the activities of the Orange Order and its sympathizers.[72]

One minister of Home Affairs condoned the differential policing of Orange and nationalist processions on the grounds of the former's "loyalty" to the state and willingness to "take the advice of the police," versus the imputed disloyalty of the nationalists.[73]

Some police officers may, as the NCCL suggested, have been reluctant to intervene against Orange activities because of fears of being overpowered or because the regime discouraged it, but others were hesitant to intervene out of personal sympathy with the Orange Order. Whereas the RIC had prohibited its members from joining sectarian organizations, the Unionist government lifted the ban on membership in the Orange Order just three months after the RUC's creation. Early in 1923 a special Orange lodge for constables was formed, and the Home Affairs minister attended the first meeting.[74]

The government's position was that Orange cops would not be politically compromised. But membership in the Orange Order clashed with the RUC's own regulations. A 1924 circular from inspector-general Wickham (posted in police stations) prohibited officers from making political speeches or "entering into discussions where political or sectarian opinions are expressed."[75] And the RIC Code, which applied to the RUC, stipulated that "the expression or manifestation of political or sectarian opinions on the part of any member of the Force is strictly forbidden."[76] The contradiction—between authorized membership in a politically charged, ethnocentric body like the Orange Order and the prohibition on political or bigoted statements—manifested itself in one incident where a district inspector's speech at an Orange meeting appeared in the press, for which he was discharged from the RUC.[77] In the ensuing controversy in parliament, several Unionists accused ministers of creating the problem by allowing police to join an Orange lodge while forbidding political speeches. Both the Home Affairs minister and his parliamentary secretary responded by claiming that it was political speeches, not membership in the Orange Order or attendance at its meetings, that undermined one's impartiality. The incident was exceptional, however; the activities of most Orange meetings were kept secret, so there was little danger that a police officer would be held liable for his statements.

To nationalists the Orange Order was not simply a nasty, ethnocentric organization, but one that engaged in unlawful conduct against the minority population. Membership in the Order could not help but prejudice officers and contribute to biased law enforcement:

> A large proportion of the Royal Ulster Constabulary belong to the Orange Order. What effect is that going to have upon the impartial administration of law and order in a community like this? Imagine a young constable having sat in [an Orange] Lodge with a [civilian] brother who was probably guilty of some offense the morning after.[78]

Some nationalists even charged that police officers were directly influenced by the organization, that they were "under instructions from the local branch of the Orange Order."[79] But the influence of the Unionist Party was a more frequently mentioned concern. Nationalists alleged that police officers had to please Unionist politicians at the local and ministerial level or face transfer or denial of promotion. Individual constables were therefore motivated to "make mischief in the belief that if they attack the government's political opponents, the Nationalists or Republicans, they are establishing a record which will stand them in good stead later on with the people at [RUC] headquarters."[80] Pressures on constables either from the Unionist regime or the Orange Order clearly increased the probability of differential police treatment of Protestants and Catholics.

Public Order. Differential conduct became a heated issue in parliament when major public disturbances occurred. The police were accused of two kinds of discrimination: failing to protect Catholics from Protestant mobs and engaging in "police riots," that is, causing disturbances by interfering with or attacking

Catholic marchers.[81] An example of the first kind of bias was the tolerance shown toward Protestant rioters during the marching season in 1935. The traditional Orange marches in the summer always increased the potential for ethnic tension and violence. In response to attacks on Catholics in June of 1935, the Home Affairs minister had banned all parades, but he lifted the ban on June 27 when the Orange Order threatened to defy it on the biggest marching day, July 12. In the intervening two-week period, shootings and other attacks on Catholics occurred almost nightly; on July 12 Protestant mobs beat and shot at Catholics and burned 56 Catholic homes, while Catholics returned fire. The police refused to intervene.[82]

Subsequently, the minister of Home Affairs was accused of being "badgered" into issuing a warning that constables would be punished if they acted too zealously against Protestants. This warning apparently emboldened the Protestant mob, provoking further attacks on Catholics.[83] Labour MPs joined nationalists in criticizing the minister's capitulation to sectarian demands: "there is a fear creeping in on the police that they are in peril of further disciplinary measures if they offend a mob of a certain [Orange] hue."[84] Conversely, when the minister banned all processions and assemblies to try to bring the continuing violence under control, hard-line Unionists accused the government of capitulating to the nationalists.[85] The government seized on the clamor from both sides as evidence of its impartiality:

> You have, on the one hand, the . . . Member for Central complaining that the people who belong to his political party [Nationalist] and his political faith are murdered in the streets of Belfast; while, on the other hand, the Member for Duncairn complains that the dice has [sic] been loaded against the party [Unionist] to which he belongs. I can assure this House that so far as the administration of justice is concerned, the government does its best to see that justice is meted out with an even hand to both parties, and will continue to do so.[86]

The police were faced with "an unenviable job," but the government was certain that they "behaved with exemplary care and caution in all the steps they took, which, whether they were right or wrong, were taken with the one object of ensuring that the peace of the city is preserved."[87] These claims fell on many deaf ears.

One of the RUC's fundamental roles was to preempt or crush nationalist resistance to the Protestant state, but it was not until 1950 that a special riot squad was formed. The Reserve Force, specially trained for riot control and other emergency duties, was first deployed against Catholic marchers in the early 1950s, greatly fortified and mobilized against the IRA in the latter half of the decade, and mobilized for riot duties in the late 1960s. Nationalists saw the Reserve Force as the dark side of RUC.[88]

Police riots occurred in the 1950s during a number of Catholic protest marches. Since the end of World War II, nationalists had been organizing, in the Anti-Partition League, to convince the British government to reconsider the partition of Ireland. Their rallies and processions were often accompanied by a display of the flag of the Irish Republic, the tricolor. Outraged Loyalists called upon the authorities to suppress all gatherings where the tricolor was flown.[89] This led to a series of clashes between tricolor-waving nationalists and the police.

Nationalist determination to display the tricolor in the 1950s and the resulting disturbances prompted Stormont to expand police powers. In 1951, it passed the Public Order Act, which made it illegal to carry any flag that might disturb the peace and required that 48 hours notice be given to the RUC for all meetings and processions, save traditional marches. It empowered the police to reroute or ban any parade they believed would be likely to disturb the peace. However, the act did not specify which flags were offensive—technically, even the Union flag could be banned since it might provoke trouble when carried through Catholic areas—nor did it prohibit the flying of flags on poles or buildings. To close the loopholes, the government introduced a new law, the 1954 Flags and Emblems Act, which prohibited any interference with the display of the Union Jack and empowered the police to curtail the display of other flags deemed likely to disturb the peace. Needless to say, the act did not end disputes over the right to fly the tricolor.

Nationalists argued that the Union Jack should be treated on the same basis as the tricolor, that is, as a potentially provocative partisan symbol. They condemned the legislation and differential enforcement of it: "The police protect . . . the Union Jack, but they pull down the national flag [the tricolor] and often trample it in the dust."[90] Nationalists also charged that police intervention in such circumstances catalyzed disturbances rather than prevented them. The minister of Home Affairs countered that the flying of the tricolor itself caused public disturbances,[91] and he alleged that the organizers of Catholic marches were cynically manipulating the situation, ready to accuse the authorities of violating civil rights if the march or rally was banned and equally ready to blame them if a disturbance resulted.[92] Display of the tricolor led local Loyalists to threaten that if the RUC did not take action, they would take matters into their own hands. The Unionist MP for Enniskillen warned: "Had the minister of Home Affairs refused to forbid the tricolor being carried. . . . We, the Protestants of Enniskillen, would take steps to see that the flag was not carried up the streets of Enniskillen."[93] Police responsiveness to these threats outraged nationalists: "If Nationalists did the same kind of thing in connection with Orange processions, what would happen? They would be batoned and thrown into jail."[94]

Although Orange marches were much more frequently approved than nationalist marches,[95] some Protestant parades were banned. In 1953 a planned Orange march along the Longstone Road (a traditional nationalist route) was banned by the minister of Home Affairs and then dispersed by the RUC in the face of pressure from local nationalists. That the authorities were sometimes sensitive to the appearance of partisanship is illustrated by the incumbent minister: "I am quite satisfied that, were I to ban a Republican or any other opposition meeting in one part of the country and, not only to permit an Orange procession in a Nationalist district, but to provide police protection for that procession, I would be holding our entire administration up to ridicule and contempt."[96] But this enlightened position was short-lived. The ban on the march created such a storm of protest from Loyalists that the minister lifted the ban a year later, even providing a police escort to protect Orange marchers from nationalists intent on blocking their way. Orange processions over the Longstone Road, and the resentment they engendered, persisted well into the 1960s. Elsewhere, nationalist marches, particularly those in which the outlawed tricolor appeared, were typically broken up by the police. Reflecting on the marches, a nationalist MP concluded: "there are two laws in this country. There is one law for the people who support the minister and another for the [Catholic] people. . . . "[97]

Political Versus Conventional Policing. Whereas nationalists never conceded that the USC possessed any redeeming qualities, they had few complaints about the RUC when it performed its ordinary civil duties. It was the RUC's political role that caused problems: "They may do an undesirable kind of work some of the time, but I think they would do very good work if . . . the politicians let them do police work."[98] Even during periods of heightened unrest, when nationalists strongly denounced the political role of the RUC, they hesitated to condemn the force itself:

> The difficulty always is to determine whether we are dealing with an . . . ordinary, normal police force or whether . . . it is a militarized force which is used as an auxiliary to the occupying power in this country.[99]

> I am prepared to say that in matters of a non-political nature the Royal Ulster Constabulary is probably one of the best forces in the world, but in . . . the political field they take the view . . . that they are under an obligation to disregard the rights of the minority.[100]

The political responsibilities of the RUC produced lingering resentment toward the force, but this did not necessarily carry over into Catholics' mundane interactions with police officers. One writer asserts that "at street level, there grew between the police and the Catholic community a practical pragmatism [sic] within which both sides ignored the high-level contradictions between them and settled for low-level mutual respect and cooperation."[101] Although little information exists to evaluate this claim, it is roughly consistent with nationalist comments that they were fairly satisfied with ordinary law enforcement.

Ordinary policing could easily be suspended or overshadowed by counterinsurgency policing, however. Buckland writes that "at the first hint of trouble normal police behavior was suppressed as the RUC became a paramilitary force."[102] In addition, nationalists often charged that the political sympathies and duties of the RUC *interfered* with ordinary police work. In 1936 an MP, concerned about some unsolved murders in Belfast, argued that police membership in the Orange Order detracted from the performance of normal duties.[103] In 1946 a wave of purse snatchings in Belfast prompted another MP to ask if the minister of Home Affairs would ensure "that the existing police force would expend the same energy in tracking down thieves and robbers as they have been expending in terrorizing people of nationalist sentiments in some parts of Northern Ireland."[104] In 1952, one nationalist sarcastically called upon the government to reorganize the police "so that the political arm would be concerned with politics and with its duty of suppressing and batoning the Nationalist people, the nonpolitical arm being left free to go on with the normal, ordinary work of crime detection."[105] The police would "give a better return to the taxpayer if they devoted more of their time to the duties which the community expects," claimed another MP, "rather than in carrying out actions which are provocative and disturbing to the public peace."[106] Incidents of blatantly political policing in the 1950s and 1960s apparently made ordinary police work difficult in some Catholic communities. In Londonderry "the knowledge that [the RUC] are a political force so reacts upon our people that they withhold from them their co-operation in regard to matters which are non-political. It is bad form in Derry city to be associated with police officers."[107]

The degree to which the RUC's political duties impaired its efficiency in ordinary law enforcement is difficult to judge from the available evidence. Northern Ireland traditionally enjoyed the lowest crime rate of any part of the United Kingdom. Moreover, the average clearance rate for criminal cases was significantly higher than in the rest of the United Kingdom.[108] Still, the Home Affairs minister noted, "Our security problem in itself has meant a wide dispersal of police resources in areas where there is little ordinary crime." This stretching of resources meant that Belfast, which accounted for more than 50 percent of the country's ordinary crime, was underpoliced.[109] The commitment of resources to security-related functions therefore appears to have detracted, at least to some extent, from the quality of conventional policing, a problem that has become especially serious since the outbreak of civil unrest in the late 1960s.

Accountability

The inspector-general of the RUC was responsible to the minister of Home Affairs, who was always a Unionist politician, for general law-and-order policies. The inspector-general was completely autonomous, however, when it came to operational decisions and everyday enforcement of the law. Unlike other UK police forces, the RUC was exempt from the annual inspections of Her Majesty's Inspectorate of Constabulary. Mechanisms of accountability were therefore few and were confined to handling matters of individual misconduct: namely, the criminal courts and internal disciplinary procedures within the RUC. Completely absent was an agency—external to the RUC and Home Affairs and representative of both ethnic groups—with the power to review contentious policing matters or to handle citizens' complaints.

The RUC was not required by law to investigate complaints against officers from members of the public or even from inside the force. The Constabulary Code gave the inspector-general power to form (but did not mandate) an internal "court of inquiry" to adjudicate alleged breaches of regulations and to prefer charges of indiscipline against officers. The court's findings were presented to the inspector-general, who, if unsatisfied with the results, had the power to ask the court to reconsider its findings. In the case of departmentally generated charges of indiscipline, a court of inquiry was not open to the public, but when the complaint came from a civilian the hearing was open unless the inspector-general considered it unwise for security reasons.[110] The procedures for handling complaints from members of the public were rudimentary. There was no provision to ensure that complaints were properly investigated or even recorded; they could be summarily suppressed by the superiors of the accused officer.[111]

Figures on disciplinary action taken against accused police officers are scarce for the period under review. In the RUC's first two years, over 100 officers were dismissed for disobeying orders.[112] From January 1927 to April 1930, 288 officers were charged with disciplinary offenses, 194 of whom were found guilty. In 1931, 18 officers were charged and 16 found guilty.[113] (Thereafter, no comparable figures are provided.) It is difficult to draw conclusions from these sparse data, except to note that a relatively high proportion of accused officers were found guilty of disciplinary offenses in the RUC's early years. Unfortunately, there is no indication of the seriousness of the infractions, whether the charges originated internally or from a civilian complaint, or the kinds of punishment meted out to the guilty.

Officers could also be charged with a criminal offense as a result of a civilian's complaint. Allegations that appeared to have substance were examined by an investigating officer appointed by the inspector-general, whose report was then submitted to the attorney general. If the attorney general concurred that there was *prima facie* evidence of a criminal offense, the case was prosecuted. But in deciding whether to prosecute a case, the attorney general was completely dependent on the reports of police investigators. Although police investigators are not necessarily or consistently prejudiced in favor of their accused colleagues, the possibility of a conflict of interest always raises the question of bias, particularly where there is no external check on their decisions.[114] Neither could the attorney general be considered an entirely neutral party. As a member of the cabinet and a Unionist, some of his decisions may have been affected by political considerations.

Figures on criminal prosecutions and convictions of RUC officers are hard to come by, but it appears that few officers appeared in court and few were convicted. Between March 1957 and March 1963, for example, six RUC officers were convicted of criminal acts.[115] Even during the unrest and police excesses of the late 1960s, few prosecutions occurred: in 1968 three cops were charged, and from January to September 1969 two were charged.[116] No one was charged with serious criminal misconduct during 1969 and 1970.[117]

Contested Accountability.   Nationalists perceived the courts as biased in favor of police defendants: "every time a constable is brought before a court . . . the magistrate is always willing to bend over backwards to believe the defending constable."[118] They were also unhappy about the authorities' unwillingness to take complaints seriously. Nationalist MPs sometimes requested the cooperation of the minister of Home Affairs and the inspector-general in investigating complaints of their constituents. Ministers usually responded with investigations less rigorous than a formal court of inquiry; they typically reported back to parliament that the officers in question denied any wrongdoing, denials which usually satisfied ministers. The Home Affairs minister also had the prerogative to appoint an external investigator to conduct a public inquiry. Though MPs called for many such investigations, they were consistently refused.[119]

Opposition MPs frequently complained about the RUC being entrusted with investigating complaints against its own members, on the grounds that "a police inquiry into police conduct . . . is neither adequate nor will it satisfy the public."[120] They pressed, to no avail, for reforms. Following the 1935 riots in Belfast, a Labour MP recommended that an external review board be established to ensure that citizens would be protected from the "violence of certain outrageous individuals."[121] In 1965, the Ministry of Home

Affairs was asked to establish a police council with some lay members to investigate all matters concerning police relations with the public.[122] Three years later, a nationalist MP complained about the lack of checks on police who handled detainees and suspects under interrogation (over the years nationalists had alleged that suspects were subjected to prolonged periods of questioning, intimidation, and assault ranging from mild roughness to severe brutality):

> Over a number of years persons have come to me and told me that when under arrest they have been assaulted by members of the RUC. I immediately told them that they would find it very hard to prove. If a constable assaults a prisoner while under arrest the prisoner may complain, but to whom does he complain? He complains to the RUC station. Naturally the [senior officer] will not want to believe that one of the constables under his command could be guilty of such conduct. . . . How then does a prisoner prove that he was assaulted, because a constable's word will be accepted by the station sergeant, head constable, district inspector and finally by the Ministry of Home Affairs?[123]

He wanted a proposed office of parliamentary commissioner, which would oversee local government departments, to also review complaints against police officers:

> If we had a Parliamentary Commissioner, someone who would enjoy the confidence of the whole community . . . and if the members of the RUC . . . who committed an offence against human dignity or social justice in this state were to be accountable to such a person they would not be so likely to commit the acts in the first place.[124]

When the office of parliamentary commissioner was later established, the RUC and the USC were specifically excluded from its jurisdiction.

Even some Unionists pressed the government to make the RUC more publicly accountable, albeit for reasons quite different from those of the nationalists. These Unionists called for public investigations of police actions not because they believed accused officers were guilty but because they hoped that visible exoneration of them would improve the reputation of the RUC. In 1924, for example, an independent Unionist advocated such investigations because of allegations against the police; he wanted the police "protected" by investigations he assumed would absolve them.[125] Decades later, a right-wing Unionist argued that civilian complaints should be visibly investigated by an independent person because the public wanted assurance that the allegations were found to be groundless.[126] Unionists' calls for independent oversight mechanisms were thus motivated by an interest in inflating the RUC's image, whereas nationalists sought greater accountability to punish offenders and prevent future misconduct.

In response to criticisms and allegations against the force, successive ministers of Home Affairs habitually denied police wrongdoing. When they conducted inquiries into charges of misconduct, they typically accepted police accounts and regularly found that officers' actions were justified or within appropriate bounds. Similarly, Unionist MPs believed that the police would never "act against any individual in this country unless that individual was guilty."[127] Requests for formal public inquiries were repeatedly rebuffed, for reasons that included ministers' claims that the allegations were simply without substance.[128] The authorities also sought to defuse allegations of police misconduct with the help of various "techniques of neutralization"—Sykes and Matza's term for methods of excusing or justifying wrongdoing or challenging accusers' claims.[129] One technique was to blame the victim: a civilian complainant involved even on the "fringes" of dissent "has only himself to blame" for police harassment.[130] Anyone even remotely connected to the IRA or another radical organization would find their character easily assassinated; it was an article of faith that they were incapable of making a genuine complaint. Police abuse of innocent Catholics could also be rationalized in terms of threats to the state, the technique of appealing to a "higher purpose." For example, in response to opposition protests against police harassment of civilians in a Catholic area of Belfast, the minister of Home Affairs defended police actions because "at the present time [1940] there is a widespread conspiracy in Belfast and outside it on the part of people who are, beyond all question, organized against the state."[131]

The authorities also attempted to counteract charges and criticisms by contrasting the virtue of the RUC with the disrepute of its critics, including opposition MPs. Examples of this technique of "condemning the condemners" include the following:

> It would almost seem as if those [opposition MPs] who have
> spoken were minded to sow suspicion and distrust in the minds

of the public. . . . I believe it to be the duty of every Member of this House to promote . . . the confidence of the public in our Police Force. I would go further and say that if one were to take a census of opinion one would find that the force has in very full degree the confidence of the public.[132]

It is a sinister and significant fact . . . that these attacks are made from time to time by Members of the Opposition upon our police force, which the entire law-abiding population of our country knows is doing a splendid job.[133]

I must condemn most forcibly those people who are attempting to undermine the Royal Ulster Constabulary . . . [who] have behaved themselves in the most commendable manner and if it had not been for them we would have had a much more serious situation.[134]

Through such neutralization techniques officials sought to discredit nationalist grievances and to assure the police that criticisms were not being taken seriously by the regime.

The government also refused to accept more general demands for greater accountability. Ministers frequently declined to answer MPs' questions on the grounds that dissemination of the information would be contrary to the public interest. Similarly, instructions to the force and even the RUC Code were confidential, sensitive documents.[135] Such secrecy was deemed necessary because the RUC operated in a context that was radically different from what faced police forces elsewhere in the United Kingdom; its security duties and paramilitary style precluded the sort of democratic controls and public accountability sought by nationalists. The official position was succinctly articulated by the parliamentary secretary for Home Affairs in 1936 in response to a proposal that a board of control be formed:

Our police force is something different from the police force of a county in England. Our police force is now, and has always been, a semi-military force. . . . I do not see how a board of control could fit in with the character of the Royal Ulster Constabulary, and I cannot see how it would fit in under the circumstances in which we unfortunately find ourselves, where quick decisions have got to be taken in connection with duty that has got to be done.[136]

The RUC's exceptionalism thus exempted it from reforms that might enhance its accountability.

Another reason why new mechanisms of accountability were unnecessary, Unionist officials claimed, was the high level of public satisfaction with the RUC.[137] Since police relations with the public were good, there was "no point in . . . setting up any further investigating body" into police conduct.[138] Nationalists' claims that the lack of checks on the police undermined public confidence in the RUC fell on deaf ears.

The data presented in this chapter suggest that traditional policing in Northern Ireland closely resembled the divided society model outlined in Chapter 1. There is evidence of biased law enforcement in favor of Protestants; political partiality; ethnically unrepresentative police forces and official resistance to creating greater balance in the forces; an absence of effective, independent mechanisms of accountability; a substantial police role in internal security as well as conventional law enforcement; and broad and vague legal powers giving police enormous discretion conducive to abuses. Each of these factors had an effect on police relations with Protestant and Catholic communities, as suggested in the demands, criticisms, and praise expressed by MPs representing these populations. At the same time, we have seen that nationalist politicians articulated views that were more moderate than conventional portrayals of the Catholic population, which assume that virtually all Catholics are bitterly anti-police. There were important divisions within the Catholic population which survive today. Divisions among Protestants, at least on questions of policing and the state, were much less marked during the period of Unionist rule. But this remarkable solidarity began to shatter as the pillars of Protestant supremacy came under attack in the late 1960s.

In certain respects, contemporary policing in Northern Ireland resembles the traditional patterns described in this chapter. But there are also some important differences between the periods of Unionist rule and British rule, both in the structure and practice of policing and in police-community relations. Continuities and discontinuities between the two periods are identified in the following chapters.

CHAPTER 3

Reforming the RUC

After the turbulent early 1920s, Northern Ireland entered a long period of relative stability, despite Catholics' lingering discontent with a state and social order under which they suffered discrimination and deprivation. Public disturbances were not common, serious ethnic violence was sporadic, and the IRA remained dormant for most of the period. From the mid-1920s through 1968, only 18 deaths occurred because of political or interethnic conflict.[1] The turning point was the rise of the civil rights movement in 1968, which prompted a violent backlash on the part of Protestants, bloody actions by the security forces, and the rebirth of the IRA in defense of Catholics under siege. As a result of these disorders, 212 people died in just three years (1969–1971). The events of this period have been adequately described in other sources.[2] Here I show how the disturbances set the stage for reforms in policing during the final years of Unionist rule and I then examine the nature of the reforms and the factors constraining them under both Unionist and British rule.

DISORDER AND REFORM: 1968–1972

The RUC played a pivotal role during this period of rising public protest, disorder, and sectarian violence, generally acting insensitively or oppressively against the largely Catholic civil rights demonstrators and residents of Catholic neighborhoods. On occasion, officers intervened to keep civil rights protestors and Loyalist counterdemonstrators apart. Only rarely, however, did the police act to disperse the opposing Loyalist crowd, as it did during a march through the town of Bellaghy in January 1969. The RUC was generally unresponsive to requests from civil rights marchers that they be provided with adequate police protection, and police actions often fueled, rather than dampened, violent clashes between Protestants and Catholics. Indeed, the police themselves sometimes intervened violently in what had been peaceful protests.

The first bloody encounter occurred in Londonderry on October 5, 1968 when civil rights marchers clashed with police, many of whom were in the Reserve Force, the RUC's riot squad. Among the injured were 77 demonstrators and 4 constables. The government claimed that the police did nothing to provoke the violence but instead maintained a "tolerant" stance and "endured physical attack before employing force."[3] An official commission found otherwise, criticizing the police for indiscriminate use of batons and unnecessary use of water cannon.[4] No officers were charged with criminal or disciplinary offenses[5] (the Unionist Government in 1969 declared an amnesty for anyone, including cops, accused of criminal conduct during prior disturbances). The second major incident occurred on January 4, 1969 at Burntollet Bridge, when civil rights marchers were ambushed by a group of Loyalists, including off-duty members of the USC. Third, and most infamous, were a series of incidents following the stoning by Catholics of a Protestant march in Londonderry in August 1969. The RUC's Reserve Force retaliated by storming the Catholic Bogside district and going on a rampage—which included serious assaults and malicious damage to property—prompting the inhabitants to erect barricades to keep the police out, which they defended with petrol bombs. The police responded by attempting to drive landrovers through the barricades, thus provoking skirmishes throughout the night. This "siege of the Bogside," as it is now known, sparked riots and bloodshed throughout Northern Ireland, and the barricading of other communities. Angry Loyalist mobs were aided by police indifference or active support as they attacked civil rights demonstrators (in Armagh, Dungannon, Londonderry) or invaded Catholic enclaves (in Belfast) and engaged in arson and shooting. For many Catholics the apparent collusion between police and Loyalist mobs lent credence to the notion that the RUC was the "armed wing of Unionism."

The Cameron Commission's investigation of the disturbances of 1969 placed blame less on the decisions and actions of police on the ground than on the lack of sufficient manpower to control the rioting. The lack of manpower forced the RUC to rely on methods—baton charges and beatings, water cannon, tear gas, gunfire—that inevitably caused casualties. Investigating some of the same incidents, the Scarman Tribunal concurred with Cameron and added a second causal factor: the RUC's (mistaken) assessment that it was confronting an uprising planned by the IRA.[6] Both factors caused the police to overreact and to treat protestors as if they were the enemy. The two inquiries praised the attempt of the majority of police to carry out their duties impartially under extremely trying circumstances, but also found that the RUC was seriously at fault during several major incidents. The Cameron Commission was particularly critical of the RUC's failure to disperse Loyalist crowds hostile to the civil rights movement, which convinced the protestors that the police were cavalier about their safety and biased in favor of the Loyalists.

The methods, the casualties, and the appearance of bias in the various disturbances had the cumulative effect of ruining the RUC's reputation among Catholics throughout Northern Ireland. The Scarman Tribunal pointed to a "fateful split between the Catholic community and the police,"[7] and the Cameron Commission agreed that alienation from the RUC had deepened. Nationalist politicians, some of whom had been beaten during street protests, spoke in terms of a crisis in police-Catholic relations. After the incident in Londonderry in October 1968, one nationalist MP claimed that "the damage that has been done to community relations has put this entire area back a quarter of a century"[8] and a colleague declared that "the people of that city have an utter contempt for the RUC."[9] Another nationalist politician noted that "in view of the indiscriminate batoning of men, women and children in the aftermaths of some civil rights marches one could not reasonably be expected to believe in the impartiality of the police."[10] Subsequent events in Londonderry, Belfast, and other towns only seemed to confirm these indictments of the RUC. Indeed, the period marks a watershed in the deterioration of police relations with Catholics; police behavior during these years remains vividly inscribed in people's memories and continues to influence perceptions of the police today.

Over time, the tone of nationalist discourse on policing became increasingly bitter and indignant. Nationalist MPs called for major reforms, while more radical Catholics outside Stormont branded the RUC as unreformable and demanded the complete dismantling of the force. Most nationalist MPs refrained from castigating the entire force, directing their criticisms at the senior management or the "bad eggs" and "black sheep" who constituted either a small or a sizeable minority of the RUC. Similarly, they continued to draw distinctions between ordinary policing and counterinsurgency policing, comparing the latter unfavorably with the former. Two comments are illustrative:

> The question of normal police duties in dealing with crime . . . does not arise [and] no one has criticized the efficiency of the police force in this field. Let me also say that its efficiency is weakened by the recent disturbances and by its part in them, because when a loss of respect in the forces of law and order takes place their efficiency in doing normal police work is reduced as there are always vandals and people willing to take advantage.[11]

> With regard to the way the RUC carry out their duties, in the main, in the ordinary day-to-day duties where the RUC are concerned no one has any complaint to make. But we have very serious complaints to make with regard to the management of public affairs and the control of crowds and public order . . . [and] regarding the decisions they make to ban [or] . . . permit processions.[12]

Unionist MPs, by contrast, predictably defended and lavished praise on the RUC and denounced all of its critics.

The disturbances and their mishandling by the authorities generated unprecedented intervention from London. British cabinet ministers, concerned over the deteriorating situation, pressured the Ulster government to deal with the disorders more sensitively and effectively and to make concessions to the demands of the civil rights movement. As the situation worsened, London in August 1969 sent British troops to the province to keep the peace. This reduced the RUC's responsibility for public order and its presence in troubled Catholic neighborhoods, thus greatly reducing altercations with the public. With British troops on the scene, it was almost certain that London would turn its attention to larger problems of law and order. Indeed, the RUC came under outside scrutiny for the first time.

A 1969 inquiry by two senior British police officers, Robert Mark and Douglas Osmond, criticized the poor quality of leadership in the RUC, excessive autonomy of the inspector-general, outdated intelligence, fortress appearance of RUC stations, lack of a complaints system and a public relations branch, and the Special Branch's obsession with the IRA to the exclusion of Protestant extremists.[13] Later in 1969 another investigation, by the Hunt Committee, produced a seminal report critical of policing.[14] It found most objectionable the militarized style and security role of the RUC and USC. The report was unequivocal: "the protection of . . . the state against armed attacks is not a role which should have to be undertaken by the police, whether they be regular or special." A counterinsurgency police force could not help but strain police-community relations: "any police force, military in appearance and equipment, is less acceptable to minority and moderate opinion than if it is clearly civilian in character."[15] The committee recommended that the RUC abandon its "war-like" armored cars, be relieved of all security duties (except for intelligence gathering and enforcement of relevant laws), and be disarmed since firearms were "inappropriate" for a civil police force (clearly a British notion). The B Specials should be disbanded (not because of their sectarian reputation but because no police force should perform paramilitary duties) and replaced with a military force under the command of the British army chief stationed in Ulster.

The Hunt Committee recommended other sweeping changes to bring the police into line with the liberal model obtaining elsewhere in the United Kingdom:

- A major increase in RUC personnel.
- A vigorous program to recruit Catholics and removal of the requirement that applicants reveal their religion.
- Greater use of community relations programs.
- Repeal of much of the Special Powers Act.
- More training in crowd control for all uniformed officers and the annual replacement of one-third of the Reserve Force to reduce its insulation from the rest of the force.
- Creation of a system of independent public prosecution to replace police prosecution.
- Creation of a Police Authority to administer the force and to which the inspector-general would be accountable. An independent body representative of the society would provide a corrective to the politically sensitive link between the RUC and Home Affairs and a neutral mechanism through which the "wishes and fears of the community can be expressed."

- Regular evaluations of the RUC by Her Majesty's Inspectorate of Constabulary.[16]
- Changes in the handling of civilian complaints so that all complaints would be properly recorded and investigated by an officer from another county or district. Regarding civil suits by members of the public, the police chief should be liable for his subordinates' actions.

The committee also questioned the propriety of allowing police officers to join partisan organizations like the Orange Order and the Ancient Order of Hibernians (a Catholic society), but no recommendation was made to prohibit such membership, and the Unionist authorities ignored the query.

Sensitive to Protestant concerns and the need to bolster police morale, the Hunt Committee's progressive recommendations were balanced by proposals to inject more resources and manpower into the RUC and to create new security forces to replace the paramilitary USC. These proposals were duly implemented. With the addition of a new RUC Reserve force (an auxiliary force, not to be confused with the previous riot squad of the same name), manpower doubled in a few years (from 3,044 regular cops in 1969 to 4,256 regular and 2,134 Reserve officers in 1972); the police budget grew sharply; and the USC's duties were assumed by the RUC Reserve and the new Ulster Defense Regiment, a locally recruited branch of the British army.

Most of the Hunt Committee's progressive proposals were officially accepted by the Unionist government, but this hardly meant that problems would be swiftly addressed. Some reforms were rather easily implemented. A Community Relations Branch was formed in an effort to improve police relations with the public; screening mechanisms were created to exclude from the force individuals holding strong political or ethnocentric views; and police trainers gave more attention to inculcating in recruits the values of impartial law enforcement and sensitivity toward the public. Other proposals were delayed, diluted upon implementation, or later reversed. Catholics continued to form a small fraction of police recruits, the Special Powers Act remained on the books until 1973, the force was not demilitarized, and an independent system of public prosecution was delayed until 1972.

Plans to enhance police accountability and control met with mixed results. Under the 1970 Police Act the head of the RUC (now called "chief constable") was required to ensure that all citizen complaints were investigated and criminal cases forwarded to the attorney general, but the act provided no external mechanism to monitor how well the police complied. The act did create a Police Authority to administer the force, strengthen its accountability, and reduce the influence of the Home Affairs Ministry. Yet the Authority devoted most of its time to recruitment, budgetary matters, and the provision of police supplies, equipment, and buildings. Altogether secondary were the larger policy issues and the control of police misconduct.[17] The Police Act stipulated that the Authority should be representative of the community as a whole, yet most of its senior staff came directly from the Ministry of Home Affairs and hardly reflected minority interests.

Nor was the chief constable's autonomy reined in in practice. Indeed, he retained full legal control over operational matters— such as deployment and the handling of specific disturbances— although this was not always respected by politicians. As Graham Shillington, the chief constable, told me, "My biggest difficulty was to try to convince politicians at Stormont and from Britain that they had no authority to interfere with police operations. It was often very difficult to convince the Unionist politicians of this."[18]

Since it challenged the traditional style of policing, the Hunt Committee's key recommendations were received bitterly by Protestants, who believed that reforms were an attempt to appease Catholics while jeopardizing Protestants' security. Unionist politicians fought, as they continue to fight today, all changes that would "weaken" the RUC by reducing its legal powers or coercive capacity or by increasing its control by outside agencies. These political leaders, as well as ordinary Protestants, complained about the erosion of police morale, the transfer of counterinsurgency duties from the police to the British army, plans to create a Police Authority and to disarm the police, and the appointment of a British officer, Arthur Young, as the new RUC chief. Unionist MPs were adamant during parliamentary debates that the Special Branch should remain intact (it did) and that Her Majesty's Inspectorate of Constabulary, after conducting its annual assessment of the RUC, would not report to the Home Office in London but only to Ulster's Minister of Home Affairs and the Police Authority (this became the procedure). Particularly galling to the Protestant population was Hunt's plan for dismantling the USC; this provoked two days of rioting by Protestant mobs during which sixteen soldiers were shot and one police officer killed, the first constable killed during the troubles. The Unionist cabinet only agreed to abolish the USC when British Prime Minister James Callaghan threatened to have Westminster legislate unilaterally on the matter.[19]

Inside the RUC the Hunt Report initially lowered morale, although there was sentiment in favor of some of the proposals. The plan to disarm and demilitarize the RUC, for example, had a remarkable degree of support inside the force. Indeed, the Central Representative Body of the RUC had previously sent a memorandum to the Hunt Committee expressing a "desire to abandon all military aspects of our present duties. . . . "[20] RUC officers were less united on the specific question of whether the police should continue to carry arms: a 1970 poll found that 1,196 opposed and 1,085 favored retaining arms.[21] The new chief constable felt that the army should be the sole armed force and that disarming the police might pay off. In fact, the force was disarmed for a brief period in 1970–1971, which the chief constable assessed positively: "Relieving the police of their former paramilitary duties has to some extent reduced the tension and hostility which existed in some areas. . . . "[22] But the police were rearmed in 1971 as a result of increasing political violence, including IRA attacks on officers.

Despite embryonic changes in the structure, official ethos, and control of the RUC during this period, traditional policing remained firmly institutionalized. The RUC continued to act in a visibly partisan manner; it enforced the same controversial security laws; it remained overwhelmingly Protestant; the police culture was impervious to the new ethos articulated by RUC chiefs; and changes to increase accountability were wholly inadequate to control police misconduct. What did change—with the advent of British military intervention—was the degree to which the police were required to deal with political violence, public disturbances, and hostile neighborhoods. Such police duties decreased considerably as they were largely transferred to the army.

Elsewhere I have explained the resilience of traditional policing arrangements during this period largely in terms of Northern Ireland's political environment, especially the intractability of a Unionist regime that had little taste for reforming the institutions of law and order.[23] A necessary, but not sufficient, condition for transforming policing was the installation of a new, modernizing regime. This occurred in March 1972 with the transfer of power to the British state.

REFORM UNDER BRITISH RULE

There are three competing perspectives on policing in Northern Ireland under British rule. One highlights the negative: the ways in which policing today is reminiscent of the era of Unionist rule or reflective of new innovations in state repression.[24] The essence of policing is inferred from the RUC's militarized style and appearance and from incidents of police brutality during marches and riots, mistreatment of detainees, shootings of suspects, and insensitive and provocative conduct on the street, at roadblocks, and during house searches.

A diametrically opposed argument—proffered by some scholars as well as the RUC and British officials—is that the RUC is now thoroughly reformed, indeed one of the most professional police forces in the world.[25] Proponents acknowledge that a few "bad apples" are sometimes involved in misconduct, but insist that most officers do a stellar job in light of the exceptional, exacting conditions under which they work. Additional reforms are not required, since the problems lie elsewhere: in the unjustified hostility toward police of a minority of Protestants and Catholics and in the political violence that makes extraordinary police methods necessary. A variant of this perspective denies that the RUC *ever* conformed to the image proffered in the first model. It has been an outstanding force all along and reforms have simply refined its traditional professionalism. The evidence presented in Chapter 2 refutes this claim.

A third approach, which I have advanced,[26] provides a corrective to these two extreme formulations. It recognizes that significant reforms have taken place since the advent of British intervention in the province, but also identifies a set of constraints on police liberalization. A modernizing regime will find it difficult to institutionalize reforms if strong countervailing factors are present—such as police resistance to reform, opposition from influential conservative groups in civil society, continuing political instability and ethnic strife, and a high level of political violence, particularly if insurgents target state institutions and if the police are the principal security force. Each of these factors is present to some extent in contemporary Northern Ireland. After describing the progressive changes under British rule, I examine the most important factor interfering with further liberalization, the growth of counterinsurgency policing.

Sharing responsibility for law and order with Ulster's state elites during 1969–1972 and having to persuade them to accept reforms, London's assumption in 1972 of the reins of state power enhanced, to some extent, its capacity to impose changes on the RUC. Accordingly, the British administration pressed senior police officers to cultivate an organizational ethos based on professionalism and greater fidelity to the British ideal of "policing by consent," to negatively sanction traditional attitudes and practices, to increase Catholic numbers in the force, and to improve screening and training of new recruits.[27]

A sense of mission is a core feature of the occupational culture of a police force; policing is not simply a job, but also a cause.[28] Under British rule the RUC's mission changed from that of defending a social order based on Protestant supremacy to enforcing the law impartially in a society undergoing a transition away from Protestant domination. This is hardly a cosmetic change. The new mission is frequently articulated by senior officers in public and to the lower ranks and is incorporated in the RUC's code of conduct, *Professional Policing Ethics*. One goal is to depoliticize the force; although officers are not specifically forbidden from joining political parties or partisan organizations like the Orange Order, the code of conduct warns that "a police officer shall not take any active part in politics or allow any personal political view to influence his actions."

Has the official mission changed the views of ordinary constables or contributed to more impartial law enforcement? It has taken many years for the norm of impartiality to gain acceptance among the rank and file, but the RUC today clearly pays greater attention than in the past to Catholic sensitivities and shows less favoritism toward Protestants. The official discourse of professionalism and universalism serves as something of a brake on discriminatory conduct, although this should not be exaggerated. Both Catholic and Protestant insurgents are vigorously pursued. In fact, unlike their comparative freedom under the Unionist state, Protestants today are *more likely* to be apprehended for political or "terrorist" offenses than their Catholic counterparts (see Chapter 5). And since the mid-1980s, the RUC has aggressively confronted Protestant rioters—another departure from its benign approach under Unionist rule.

Many of the rank and file now insist that they make no distinction between Protestants and Catholics,[29] but it would be surprising if the new ethos of neutrality and professionalism was enthusiastically embraced throughout the entire force. Research on other countries shows that the values championed by senior officers are often subverted by lower-ranking officers whose allegiance is to a different set of values and beliefs.[30] In Northern Ireland some long-serving officers[31] and some of their younger counterparts continue to harbor strong Unionist sympathies. It may be the case that only a minority of these officers allow their attitudes to affect their treatment of Catholics, but we lack observational data bearing on this question. Police stationed in areas with the most belligerent populations and the highest incidence of political violence are particularly likely to develop stereotypes about the residents—however well they have learned to conceal them—and to disregard formal norms of minimum force and impartiality. The survey and interview data presented in the following chapters show that there is a widespread perception among sections of the Catholic and Protestant populations that the police act in a biased fashion in their handling of marches, at roadblocks, during house searches, in dealing with sectarian attacks, and generally in their behavior toward members of the public. And it is these perceptions, however consistent or inconsistent with reality, that affect police-community relations.

The composition of the force has changed in some respects, but not in others. Most of the officers who served during the period of Unionist rule have retired; 81 percent of the current force was hired between the beginning of 1972 and the end of 1992.[32] That few officers are holdovers from the previous regime may be expected to have some positive effect on the force, though it certainly does not ensure more enlightened behavior.

The RUC remains overwhelmingly Protestant. The overall status of the force is high enough that the police have no difficulty recruiting Protestants; many see police work not only as a secure job but also as a way of contributing to "law and order" and suppressing challenges to the state. Catholics still constitute only a small percentage of the force (7 percent in 1992) and under a tenth of new recruits.[33] This record can be explained largely by

Catholic alienation from the RUC and by the IRA's threats and attacks on officers. In addition, it may be the case that the rejection rate for Protestant applicants is lower than for Catholics. *Police Review* reported in 1989 that the RUC rejects 5 percent of Protestant applicants and 20 percent of Catholic applicants.[34] These figures are challenged by the RUC, which provided me with the following figures: from January 1, 1990 to August 31, 1991, 41 percent of Catholics and 38 percent of Protestants examined by interview boards were rejected.[35] Interviews, however, are conducted only after an applicant has advanced through two prior stages: the initial review of his or her qualifications and the background check on the individual's criminal record and security status. The aggregate rejection figures for all three stages may indeed approximate those reported by *Police Review*.

The authorities have repeatedly called on Catholics to apply for jobs in the RUC, which they hope would pay dividends for the image of the force. On occasion, however, the RUC's ethnic imbalance has been downplayed. One government minister stated: "It is more important that we have good policemen in the higher ranks of the RUC than a balance between the communities," and he noted that Catholics were well represented in the higher ranks.[36] But government figures show that Catholics are only slightly better represented in some of the higher ranks: 9 percent of inspectors, 13 percent of superintendents, and 14 percent of chief superintendents—nowhere near their number in the population.[37]

Under British rule the RUC has simultaneously accepted the need for improved relations with Catholics and Protestants and fought to preserve as much autonomy as possible from civil society. On the one hand, it is appreciated that greater accountability and consultation with the public are necessary elements of modern policing and have public relations potential. On the other hand, there is a strong institutional inclination to insulate the RUC from outside pressures, driven by an interest in shedding the stigma of its traditional favoritism toward Protestants and in removing the police from the political battlefield. (The RUC places a certain construction on "apolitical" policing, which means leaving virtually all decisions up to the "professionals" and rejecting all but the tamest kinds of civilian input.) Claiming that the force is now "above politics" and fully reformed, senior officers and the Police Federation (the union representing 95 percent of RUC officers) have distanced themselves from political parties, pressure groups, and state elites. (One important exception deserves mention here. Whereas the Police Federation previously was represented at Westminster by a British Conservative MP, its parliamentary advisor is now a leading Unionist: the Ulster Unionist Party's Ken Maginnis. Regarded by many as a moderate Unionist, his advisory role nevertheless raises questions about the federation's declared neutrality. In fact, he originally declined the position in order to avoid the appearance of bias.[38] Since the arrangement is not common knowledge, it has not generated public controversy.)

"Interference" from British government ministers is rejected almost as stridently as "meddling" from Unionist and nationalist politicians. As the head of the Police Federation warned, "Neither are we seeking to be the instrument of political enforcement of any government."[39] At times, this has manifested itself in struggles between the chief constable and officials at the Northern Ireland Office (NIO)—the executive branch in Ulster under British rule. As one senior NIO official confided, "There is more suspicion of the government by police officials here than anywhere in England. There is no disposition by the RUC to let the NIO know much about recruitment, training, and so on."[40] He cited a general "lack of collaboration" between the police and civil servants. Similarly, the Police Authority has had problems convincing the chief constable to comply with some of its requests (see Chapter 6).

This remarkable stress on professional independence and apolitical policing naturally does not appeal to all constables. Some find it hard to disregard the pressures coming from civil society and others still identify strongly with the interests of the Protestant population or maintain close ties to militant Loyalist groups. But over the past two decades, the police force as a whole has grown increasingly isolated from the civilian population. Police have been threatened and attacked in both Catholic and Protestant neighborhoods, making them wary of developing social contacts with civilians to a much greater degree than is normal for cops in other societies. Traditionally living in the communities they served, most constables now reside outside those communities, in peaceful middle-class areas.[41] Belfast is one example. Partly because of attacks on the homes of constables living in the city, including a wave of attacks in some Protestant areas in the mid-1980s, officers have relocated to outlying suburbs and nearby towns.

Institutional autonomy of a police force can be a double-edged sword. In Northern Ireland it is a sign of progress, given the RUC's historically close link to the Ministry of Home Affairs and identification with the abiding interests of the Protestant population. At the same time, excessive insularity breeds a subculture of hostility to outsiders and disregard of perfectly legitimate demands from outside the force, hinders (at least to some extent) officers' accountability, and makes difficult the building of positive relations with the public—all of which give the RUC the appearance of being superimposed on society rather than rooted in it. Autonomy may thus help to reduce political and communal interference in policing, but when pushed to the extreme creates police insensitivity to citizens' criticisms and concerns and loss of their base of support in civil society. The evolution of American policing in the twentieth century followed a similar pattern to Ulster's. Police departments became progressively detached from the grip of urban political machines, but also rather indifferent to popular input.[42]

The changes discussed above indicate that, in some respects, police work in Northern Ireland is increasingly guided by liberal standards. In comparison to the era of Unionist rule, the RUC today is better trained, more sensitive to the effects of its actions on both ethnic groups, more likely to enforce the law impartially, subject to greater accountability, and less politically driven in its mission. Formal norms and values have been reconstituted, and over the past two decades have been internalized to some extent by individual officers. But the reforms have been limited by several factors: a traditional police culture that has not totally withered away and that clashes with the liberal ideals articulated by police managers; insufficient institutional commitment to reducing repressive practices and sanctioning serious misconduct; and the larger context in which reforms have been implemented, marked by political stagnation, interethnic strife, and antistate violence. The larger conflict contributes to another trend in policing, which coexists tenuously with liberalization: the increasing fortification and militarization of the RUC in response to its growing counterinsurgency duties.

FORTIFICATION AND MILITARIZATION

The RUC is today one of the most formidable, militarized police forces in the world. Heavily armed units patrol on foot and in "thick-skinned" vehicles like armored landrovers. Police stations are imposing fortresses, galvanized to minimize damage if attacked by the IRA, which occurs fairly often. The force commands the most advanced computer system in the United Kingdom, and is heavily involved in surveillance of political activists, "known terrorists," and ordinary citizens.[43] The police budget has climbed steadily since 1972, tripling during the 1980s, and per capita expenditure in Northern Ireland is three times higher than in England and Wales (Table 3.1). A great proportion of this is security related, costs that would not be incurred were it not for the troubles; Northern Ireland has a low rate of ordinary crime by United Kingdom standards.

From 1970 to 1976 the British army replaced the RUC as the premier security force responsible for street patrols, house searches, intelligence gathering, riot control, and undercover operations. Boyle, Hadden, and Hillyard distinguish two systems of law and order during this period.[44] Organized around the goal

TABLE 3.1
Expenditure on Police[a]

	Northern Ireland		England and Wales	
	Total Expenditure (£ millions)	*Expenditure per Capita (£)*	*Total Expenditure (£ millions)*	*Expenditure per Capita (£)*
1979/80	125	83	1443	29
1980/81	159	105	1712	35
1981/82	202	132	2078	42
1982/83	218	142	2303	46
1983/84	236	154	2498	50
1984/85	258	166	2870	58
1985/86	278	178	2827	57
1986/87	319	204	3040	61
1987/88	365	232	3352	67
1988/89	384	243	3731	74
1989/90	420	265	4261	84
1990/91	468	294	NA	NA

[a]Net expenditure (gross expenditure minus receipts appropriated in aid).
NA = not available.
SOURCES: Police Authority and Northern Ireland Office.

of incapacitating suspects, the "military security" approach included summary internment without trial of suspected insurgents and fairly indiscriminate use of security powers in the interrogation of civilians and blanket house searches in Catholic neighborhoods. (Twelve army battalions were stationed in militant Catholic areas, three or four in Protestant areas.) Considerations of due process did not figure prominently in these operations. The police (except for the Special Branch which assisted the army) were largely relegated to duties of ordinary crime control in less disturbed, Protestant and mixed areas. There, they followed the "police prosecution" approach, investigating specific crimes with a view toward prosecuting offenders in court. Differential deployment of the army and the police in Catholic and Protestant areas thus guaranteed differential treatment of suspects in the two kinds of areas.

The policy of military primacy championed by Britain's Conservative government in 1970–1974 came under review in 1975 by a new Labour government, which appointed a committee of inquiry (the Gardiner Committee) to assess the security situation.[45] It concluded that the military approach had failed and that a shift of responsibility to the now "rehabilitated" RUC would result in more selective and sensitive operations, which would lessen the disturbance to Catholic communities. But the logic went deeper: it was considered necessary to take steps to radically redefine the nature of the conflict and the image of the antagonists. Challenges to the state should no longer be met by military force, which gave the impression that a war was being fought, and insurgents should no longer be detained without trial by the army or given special privileges in prison because of their political motives. Insurgents would be criminalized and the conflict recast as strictly a law-and-order problem to be handled by the police and the courts.

Consequently, beginning in 1976 the police resumed their senior position in the security field. Primary responsibility for public order and internal security was transferred back to the RUC. Both the number of soldiers and their visibility declined: the strength of the army fell by 50 percent from 1972 to 1990, from 22,000 to 10,500 troops, though it has increased since 1990. Today, only in those areas that are most dangerous—such as West Belfast and the southern border areas—does the army play a major role. Elsewhere, it provides support to the police when called upon. The shift in the balance of responsibility from the military to the police became known as the "primacy of the police" which was part of the larger "Ulsterization" of the security enterprise, that is, the use of indigenous forces (RUC and UDR) and reduction of British military involvement. Essentially, the RUC now performs both counterinsurgency and ordinary policing roles—as it did prior to 1970—although one style normally predominates in any given locale depending on its security profile.

As the role of the British military decreased, in a context where political violence remained serious, it was inevitable that the RUC would be galvanized. The fortification and militarization of the RUC is thus a direct effect of its growing counterinsurgency role. The police are now frequently involved in managing public order situations (traditional marches, political funerals, demonstrations, riots, clashes between groups of Protestants and Catholics) and in security duties such as running undercover surveillance operations, manning vehicle checkpoints, stopping and searching pedestrians, and conducting house searches—all of which occur much more frequently than during the era of Unionist rule. These counterinsurgency duties tend to invite police aggression and abrasive encounters with citizens, continually reinforcing resentment in the communities most affected, as the military learned in the early 1970s.[46] Less frequent but even more controversial are incidents resulting in fatalities, including deaths caused by plastic bullets during public disturbances and killings of suspected insurgents by regular constables or undercover squads.

It is useful to examine the effects of counterinsurgency policing not only on the civilian population (the theme of Chapter 5) but also on the police themselves. First and foremost, it places officers in extreme danger and increases their chances of suffering casualties. According to Interpol, RUC officers perform the most dangerous policing job in the world.[47] Table 3.2 chronicles the annual number of officers killed and wounded, in attacks that are typically premeditated and politically motivated—neither "senseless" nor incidental to other crime, as is normally the case in other Western societies. Neither armored landrovers nor fortified police stations are safe havens; both are frequently assailed with rockets and mortars, and a substantial proportion of the 2,544 attacks on police stations from 1969 through 1991 caused significant dam-

TABLE 3.2
RUC Casualties, 1969–1991

	Officers Killed	Officers Injured	Attacks on Police Stations
1969	1	711	28
1970	2	191	31
1971	11	315	261
1972	17	485	271
1973	13	291	204
1974	15	235	158
1975	11	263	85
1976	23	303	138
1977	14	183	77
1978	10	302	66
1979	14	165	39
1980	9	194	37
1981	21	332	134
1982	12	99	43
1983	18	142	48
1984	9	267	68
1985	21	415	52
1986	12	622	84
1987	16	246	151
1988	6	218	143
1989	9	163	109
1990	12	214	112
1991	6	139	205
TOTAL	284	6,874	2,544

SOURCE: Figures provided by RUC Headquarters.

age. Serving officers have seen many of their colleagues wounded or killed or have themselves been the target of violence. The fact that the RUC is under such fire helps explain why officers act overzealously or vengefully toward civilians living in certain neighborhoods.

Second, the dangers inherent in counterinsurgency policing can adversely affect morale if police feel they have inadequate resources or are laboring under under excessive restrictions. This is the case in Northern Ireland. The Police Federation has for years fought against liberal reforms and for more resources and broader legal powers. The rationale is that, as long as police primacy in the security enterprise remains, officers should be properly empowered to combat insurgency. Judging by the federation's frequent complaints, which are directed at government ministers, two decades of growing expenditures and overall fortification of the RUC have been wholly unsatisfactory. According to the federation, the RUC is forced to operate with insufficient manpower, with cuts in overtime pay, with inadequate equipment, and without the necessary powers to deal with insurgents. The federation has campaigned for the following changes: abolition of the right to silence for persons accused of security offenses; intensified surveillance and more frequent counterinsurgency operations; stiffer punishment for persons convicted of insurgent offenses (including mandatory sentences and the death penalty); relaxed restrictions on the discharge of weapons; prosecution of complainants for wrongful accusations against officers; more sophisticated equipment; and summary internment of "known terrorists." Fearing that excessive accountability would hamstring police on the street, the federation has opposed the creation of oversight agencies and has complained about the criminal prosecution of wayward cops, who are defended with federation funds.

The British government has responded favorably to some of these demands while rejecting others. It accepted the principle of prosecuting persons who lodge false complaints against officers; lengthened the time in prison served by political offenders, by cutting the previous 50 percent remission of sentence to 33 percent; abolished the right to silence in trials of insurgents; and banned radio and television broadcasts of statements by members of the IRA's political branch, Sinn Fein. The federation interprets the government's refusal to budge in other areas as symptomatic of a general lack of will to defeat the IRA and official satisfaction with simply "containing" political violence. The current chairman told me, "We need the same determination as Britain showed in the Falklands, more resources and more commitment. . . . There is still the idea of an acceptable level of violence."[48] Frustrated with this state of affairs as RUC casualties mount, the federation passed at its 1990 conference a vote of no confidence in the Northern Ireland Office because of its lack of "willingness and determination to defeat terrorism."[49] This illustrates the relative autonomy of the police from the British regime, discussed in Chapter 1.

Although police forces throughout the world commonly press for increased powers and some of the federation's demands seem reasonable in light of the security situation, many of the changes would only further entrench the exceptional features that the police claim to dislike. Indeed, because of continuing police casualties, the federation has grown increasingly strident in its public articulation of constables' frustrations with their security duties. In 1974 the chairman of the federation insisted that "there is no way whereby a successful system of civilian policing can be intermingled with military duty,"[50] and in 1981 paramilitary operations were branded "distinctly unnatural" for police.[51] Five years later the chairman called for an enhanced army role and insisted that "the government is being totally unrealistic in its policy of putting the emphasis of security onto the police."[52] In recent years, the organization has even demanded that the RUC be *relieved* of these duties, so that it can return to "normal policing." Witness the chairman's remarkable speech to the federation's annual convention in 1989:

> The gradual erosion of the normal policing role reveals a fundamental failure by Government to understand the need of the RUC to perform as a normal civilian police service. . . . We are being pushed quite visibly more and more into a purely combative purpose. We reject this singular destiny. . . . We need to perform the more general police duties[;] otherwise we are in danger of being brutalized by continuous exposure to terrorists and their crimes. It is neither a good thing for the police nor the public that their Force should be dealing only with the sharp end of terrorism.[53]

Likewise, the current chairman worries about the serious consequences of decades of counterinsurgency policing: "They are trained as policemen, but when they go to the station they're doing a soldier's job with police overtones. . . . The policing that some of our people do is not policing."[54] Noting that "our capacity to deliver this normal civilian police service is . . . gradually and irrevocably being eroded," he laments the "brutalization" of officers caused by years of abnormal policing: "The loss of routine public contact may not even distress some of our younger members; this in itself would show the growth of a hardened . . . attitude among officers. Police officers should not be confined permanently to the sharp end of policing."[55] Chapter 5 shows that these concerns are shared by sections of both the Catholic and Protestant populations.

In a nutshell, policing in Northern Ireland under British rule reflects both traditional commitments (survivals of Unionist rule) and the demands of liberalization and militarization. The latter two trends are a function of the contradictory imperatives of coping with ongoing ethnic conflict and armed insurgency while trying to abide by the ideals of professional, liberal policing. Each demand has a limiting effect on the other, but the counterinsurgency dimension predominates. There appears to be no politically acceptable alternative to this state of affairs (e.g., a reversion to military primacy), but later chapters suggest how counterinsurgency policing itself can be partially liberalized, promising some important benefits in reducing the "brutalization" of cops and perhaps improving police-community relations.

PART 2

Core Problems in
Police-Community Relations

CHAPTER 4

Police Legitimacy and Professionalism

The progressive reforms described in Chapter 3 are under fire from sections of the Protestant and Catholic populations, who see them, respectively, as unwarranted and dangerous in the context of armed insurgency or as cosmetic and meaningless in the context of aggressive counterinsurgency policing. At the same time, attitudinal data presented in this and later chapters show that there is considerable *general* approval of the RUC among both Protestants and Catholics, in addition to substantial dissatisfaction with certain aspects of policing. This chapter focuses on questions of the RUC's legitimacy and professionalism. Legitimacy is defined as acceptance of the moral authority of a police force and its right to enforce laws and issue commands. Professionalism is defined broadly to include organizational autonomy from external forces and fidelity to rational-legal norms such as impartiality and political neutrality.

CATHOLIC AND PROTESTANT ATTITUDES

The chief constable claims that the "so-called alienation of the police and the public is often a political manipulation of the facts."[1] The official line is that most people in Northern Ireland, Protestants and Catholics alike, support the police. The chairman of the Police Authority reflects:

> There is a perception that Catholics are alienated but we find limited evidence of that. It's a perception, not a fact so far as the great majority of Catholics are concerned. The police say there is little alienation from, say, 85 percent of the Catholic population. Members of the RUC are deemed [by Catholics] to be far more impartial than ever before. The Catholic [Church] hierarchy says the quality of policing has improved dramatically over the years. But there is still a considerable number who are anti-RUC.[2]

Survey data confirm that there is substantial Catholic approval of the police, but also a sizeable number who express disapproval, which is consistently higher among Catholics than among Protestants. Levels of general approval are indicated in Table 4.1 by the number expressing "satisfaction" with the RUC and saying the police do a "good job" or do their job "well." Another item that may be related to satisfaction is approval of an increase in the size of the RUC, which far fewer Catholics than Protestants endorse. Large majorities of Catholics and Protestants say they have never personally experienced police behavior that was annoying, though Catholics are more likely to report annoyance and less likely to say they have been pleased by police behavior toward them. Almost half the Catholics and two-thirds of Protestants think the police understand local problems. But large proportions of both groups think the police could improve on the service they provide, although some of the most important improvements for Catholics are not mentioned by Protestants, such as showing greater courtesy and impartiality.[3]

One dimension of police professionalism is impartial treatment of different social groups. Ulster's Protestants and Catholics differ in their views of how the RUC fares on this score. Table 4.2 shows that Protestants are in remarkable agreement that the police are fair, and three-quarters endorse the idea that the police treat Catholics and Protestants "equally"; relatively few think Protestants are treated better. Catholics are pretty evenly split on whether the police are fair or unfair, and they are less inclined to believe that the police treat both groups equally; a majority believe Protestants are treated better. Hardly anyone thinks Catholics are treated better.

Attitudes on police impartiality may also be inferred from perceptions of the degree of police vigor in dealing with interethnic attacks. Most Protestants think the police try hard to stop Protestants' attacks against Catholics, but only a minority of Catholics agree. Protestants and Catholics are in closer agreement regarding police action against Catholics who attack Protestants.

Another measure of perceptions of police impartiality is the question of whether Catholic or Protestant demonstrators are disproportionately restricted by the police. Table 4.2 shows that Catholics are seven times more likely than Protestants to say that police impose controls too often on Catholic demonstrations, whereas Protestants are four times more likely than Catholics to say

TABLE 4.1
General Attitudes on Policing
(% responding affirmatively)

	Protestants	Catholics
Satisfied with police (1990)	85	50
Dissatisfied with police (1990)	6	27
RUC does its job well (1978)	94	73
Police do a good job (1987)	80	64
Police do a good job (1989)	65	61
RUC is helpful when contacted (1990)	86	85
RUC is unhelpful when contacted (1990)	12	13
Ever annoyed by police behavior toward you (1990)	14	27
Ever pleased by police behavior toward you (1990)	32	23
RUC's size should be increased (1985)	90	38
Police understand problems people have in this area (1987)	68	45
Police could improve their service (1987)	70	63
Better for Northern Ireland if more Catholics in RUC (1990)	54	63

SOURCES: 1978 poll: Northern Ireland Attitude Survey, Edward Moxon-Browne, "The Water and the Fish: Public Opinion and the Provisional IRA in Northern Ireland," *Terrorism 5*, 1–2 (1981): 41–72. (N = 1,277)

1985 poll: Ulster Marketing Survey, *BBC Spotlight Report*, British Broadcasting Corporation, May 1985. (N = 1,008)

1987 poll: Continuous Household Survey, Northern Ireland Office, *A Commentary on Northern Ireland Crime Statistics*, 1989. (N = 6,000)

1989 poll: Jan van Dijk, Pat Mayhew, and Martin Killias, *Experiences of Crime Across the World: Key Findings of the 1989 International Victimization Survey*, Daventer: Kluwer, 1990. (N = 689 Catholics, 1,219 Protestants)

1990 poll: *Northern Ireland Social Attitudes Survey*. (N = 324 Catholics, 436 Protestants)

TABLE 4.2
Attitudes on Police Impartiality
(% in agreement)

	Protestants	Catholics
Police are fair (1985)	96	47
Police are unfair (1985)	4	53
Police treat Protestants and Catholics equally (1986)	75	42
Police treat Protestants and Catholics equally (1990)	75	38
Police treat Protestants better (1990)	12	55
Police treat Catholics better (1990)	4	0
Police try hard to stop Protestant attacks (1986)	86	46
Police try hard to stop Catholic attacks (1986)	74	82
Controls on Catholic demonstrations are used too much (1990)	6	42
Controls on Catholic demonstrations are used too little (1990)	24	6
Controls on Protestant demonstrations are used too much (1990)	13	7
Controls on Protestant demonstrations are used too little (1990)	13	34

SOURCES: 1985 poll: Northern Ireland Consumer Panel poll, *Belfast Telegraph* February 6, 1985. (N = 955)
1986 poll: David Smith, *Equality and Inequality in Northern Ireland*, London: Policy Studies Institute, 1987. (N = 594 Catholics, 1,059 Protestants)
1990 poll: *Northern Ireland Social Attitudes Survey.* (N = 324 Catholics, 436 Protestants)

they are used too little. The two groups also disagree on the control of Protestant demonstrations, although the gap is not as wide.

Finally, the ethnic composition of a police force may tell us something about its acceptance to the major ethnic groups in a society. Catholics now constitute only 7 percent of the RUC and

between 7 and 10 percent of new recruits over the past few years.[4] It appears that more Catholics would be willing to join the force were it not for the IRA's standing threat to kill Catholic officers and discouragement from fellow Catholics. On the question of whether it would be better for Northern Ireland if the RUC employed more Catholics, 63 percent of Catholics and 54 percent of Protestants agreed. But substantial numbers thought it would make no difference: 26 percent of Catholics and 30 percent of Protestants.[5] Catholics say that the two most important reasons (out of four choices) why Catholics do not join the RUC are that their fellow Catholics pressure them not to join and that prospective recruits believe they will be treated badly by the RUC. Most Protestants single out the former reason, dissuasion by Catholics, as the most important explanation for the low number of Catholics in the force.[6]

Intraethnic Variations

Some of the above findings run counter to a divided society model that would paint communal divisions in black and white. There appears to be substantial approval for the RUC among both Protestants and Catholics, which differs from conventional images of Catholics, although Protestants are clearly more supportive than Catholics. There are also some important intraethnic differences, particularly among Catholics, by residential neighborhood type, social class, age, and political affiliation.

Some of these variables also appear to affect attitudes of minority group members in other societies. Nonwhite Americans living in areas with high percentages of nonwhite residents are less impressed with the police than nonwhites living in mixed areas.[7] Similarly, Northern Ireland's Catholics who live in neighborhoods that are overwhelmingly and majority Catholic are more likely to believe that the police treat Protestants better than Catholics living in fairly evenly balanced neighborhoods and in mostly Protestant areas.[8] Regarding social class, the evidence from other societies is not conclusive. Some studies find significant differences between lower-class and middle-class people, whereas others do not. In Northern Ireland, middle-class Catholics have more favorable views of the police than working-class or poor Catholics.[9] Most of the studies that examine the age variable find that it is associated with attitudes toward police—

with youth, and particularly minority youth, holding more negative views than older age groups.[10] This is also the case in Ulster, for both Catholic and Protestant youths.[11] The political orientation variable has not been examined in studies of police-community relations, but it is likely to play a role in highly politicized societies. In Northern Ireland, supporters of Sinn Fein (the political wing of the IRA) take a decidedly more critical view of the RUC than supporters of the Social Democratic and Labour Party (SDLP) (see Table 4.3). Thus it is among the following Catholics that we find the most negative orientations to the police: residents of mostly Catholic neighborhoods, poor and working-class people, youth, and Sinn Fein supporters.

Ulster's Protestants, like whites in Britain and America, are less divided on policing issues, and large majorities report favorable attitudes. However, in some working-class and politically militant communities a significant proportion are critical of the police. Supporters of the moderate Ulster Unionist Party (UUP) are the most satisfied with policing of any political party, as Table 4.3 shows. Protestants who are less satisfied are apt to support the right-wing Democratic Unionist Party (DUP) or Loyalist paramilitary, insurgent organizations and to live in working-class or poor Protestant neighborhoods. DUP supporters are more likely than their UUP counterparts to be dissatisfied with the RUC generally, to see the police as partial, and to express concern that the police interfere with Catholic protests too infrequently and Protestant protests too frequently.

The variables of political party affiliation, social class, and religious or ethnic composition of a community can be used to construct a four-cell typology of neighborhood orientations to the

TABLE 4.3
Attitudes on Policing by Political Party Affiliation
(% responding affirmatively)

	SDLP	Sinn Fein	UUP	DUP
Satisfied with police (1990)	54	4	91	80
Dissatisfied with police (1990)	26	86	3	12
Ever annoyed by police behavior towards you (1990)	28	77	12	14

TABLE 4.3 (continued)

	SDLP	Sinn Fein	UUP	DUP
Police treat Catholics better (1986)	0	0	11	23
Police treat Catholics better (1990)	1	0	2	14
Police treat Protestants better (1986)	61	90	8	11
Police treat Protestants better (1990)	50	90	9	8
Police treat Catholics and Protestants equally (1986)	37	10	80	64
Police treat Catholics and Protestants equally (1990)	44	6	82	72
Police try hard to stop Protestant attacks (1986)	42	19	88	89
Police try hard to stop Catholic attacks (1986)	80	81	79	60
Controls on Catholic demonstrations are used too much (1990)	41	82	5	12
Controls on Catholic demonstrations are used too little (1990)	3	2	23	41
Controls on Protestant demonstrations are used too much (1990)	6	18	10	24
Controls on Protestant demonstrations are used too little (1990)	36	27	12	22
Better for Northern Ireland if more Catholics in RUC (1990)	67	23	56	33

Note: 1990 figures for Sinn Fein should be treated with caution, given the low N, but they are fairly consistent with the 1986 figures, based on a higher N.

SOURCES: 1986 poll: David Smith, *Equality and Inequality in Northern Ireland*, London: Policy Studies Institute, 1987. (N = 247 SDLP, 63 Sinn Fein, 550 UUP, 239 DUP)

1990 poll: *Northern Ireland Social Attitudes Survey*. (N = 143 SDLP, 25 Sinn Fein, 271 UUP, 83 DUP)

police that offers a more refined picture of police-community relations in Northern Ireland than a simple dichotomy; the typology allows for comparisons of the dominant and subordinate groups but is also sensitive to divisions within each group. The four types are consistent with distinctions commonly made in the academic literature and by ordinary people in Ulster: moderate Catholic, staunch Republican, moderate Protestant, and staunch Loyalist.[12] The groups are moderate or staunch in relation to the RUC and in political outlook, and they correspond fairly well to political party identification as reflected in Table 4.3: moderate Catholics as SDLP supporters, staunch Republicans as Sinn Fein supporters, moderate Protestants as UUP supporters, and staunch Loyalists as DUP supporters. It is not suggested that the four types are exhaustive, but they do account for most of the population. Very few people in Northern Ireland are neutral with regard to policing.[13]

The analysis is organized around both *types of individuals* and, because the book is concerned with police-community relations, *types of neighborhoods*. There is a correspondence between these two units of analysis because neighborhood types are defined by a preponderance of a certain type of person (staunch or moderate). The type of neighborhood, hosting a critical mass of residents who hold a particular view of the police, is an important contextual variable, in that it serves to amplify existing relations between residents and police. Staunch and moderate communities are also perceived differently by RUC officers; areas are categorized as "green" or "orange" and "hard" or "soft." Residents are thus subject to ecological contamination, a pattern also found in other heterogeneous societies.[14] Police typifications of neighborhoods incline constables to treat all residents in the "appropriate" manner, which, in turn, shapes residents' collective experiences and perceptions of the police.

There is a parallel correspondence between the two types of data: the surveys provide data on types of persons (e.g., staunch Republican, Sinn Fein supporters), and the in-depth interviews asked key informants to discuss at length the views of the majority of people in a particular locality (e.g., one that votes heavily for Sinn Fein). Generally I found that the interview data corroborate and enrich our understanding of the survey findings, although some of the latter, such as levels of overall "satisfaction" with the RUC, need to be understood in the context of other survey items and the qualitative interview data.

The congruence between the individual level and the neighborhood level is not perfect, because the four kinds of neighborhoods are ideal types. Some of the 20 empirical neighborhoods I studied conformed to type better than others; but despite this variation within type, the similarities were much stronger than the differences. And where there are significant numbers of atypical persons, they are under pressure to conform to the dominant neighborhood norms in visible interactions with the police, although their private relations may contradict their outward behavior. Thus, where staunch individuals predominate and exercise power, a moderate minority is constrained in its relations with police; fearing sanctions, moderates tend to act in ways that confirm the importance of the dominant neighborhood culture.

At the societal level, however, staunch Republicans and Loyalists are minorities within their respective Catholic and Protestant populations. Some analysts of survey data focus exclusively on majority views or, because they weight all respondents equally, underplay the importance of minority views. This is always a danger when researchers divorce attitudes from circumstances. The significance of minority views in a society like Northern Ireland is much greater than the sheer proportion holding them, and it can be argued that, in some respects, they deserve more attention than majority views—because of their sociological significance as extreme or intractable orientations to the police and their practical importance for the RUC, much of whose time and resources are devoted to monitoring and controlling neighborhoods where persons holding staunch views thrive, many of whom are prepared to go to great lengths to challenge or attack officers. Staunch Republicans and Loyalists are largely responsible for fueling the conflict in Northern Ireland, which makes their perspectives disproportionately important for a proper understanding of police-community relations.

In the remainder of the chapter each community type is analyzed in terms of its distinctive orientation to the police, both in terms of its level of "diffuse support" for the RUC as a legitimate institution and general satisfaction with its performance and in terms of its level of "specific support" for particular aspects of policing, such as the RUC's composition, political neutrality, and impartiality in law enforcement.[15] Although diffuse support is somewhat independent of specific support—that is, a person may hold the police in general high regard but criticize specific policies

or arrangements—an increase over time in the number and intensity of specific criticisms may influence the degree of diffuse support.

MODERATE CATHOLICS

Moderate Catholics support British withdrawal from Ulster and a
reunification of Ireland or a power-sharing government in Northern Ireland, composed of Catholics and Protestants. But they disapprove of the use of political violence to achieve these ends.
Rejecting the IRA and Sinn Fein, they vote for the SDLP or the
small, centrist Alliance Party. Many of them live in Ulster's middle-class, mixed areas, where policing is relatively benign. Consequently, the RUC's overall status among moderate Catholics is
significantly higher than for Republicans, but lower than for most
Protestants.

The SDLP is the political representative of moderate Catholics
and a frequent participant in national-level controversies over
policing, which influence, at least to some extent, the opinions of
constituents. The problem is that the SDLP has a somewhat less
coherent platform on policing than the other major parties. Blanket condemnations of the RUC are infrequent today, but the party
also refrains from endorsing the force. When asked in 1984
whether the party supports the RUC, its security spokesman, Seamus Mallon, responded: "No. We say there must be order and we
recognize that the community needs an impartial enforcement of
law. We do not give support to a system and its elements which
have been seen to be very partial [in favor of Protestants] and
almost incapable of sustaining the highest standards of justice."[16]
In recent years Mallon has begun to temper his criticisms. In 1989
he called for the disbandment of the UDR and expansion of the
RUC on the grounds that "whatever hope there is of getting
impartial treatment rests with the police."[17] The official party
position today is that it gives conditional support to the RUC,
contingent on constables fulfilling their duties within the law. The
SDLP admits that the RUC has made progress over the past two
decades, but some leaders are more prepared than others to praise
the force. A survey of nine SDLP members of the (now defunct)
Northern Ireland Assembly found that all but one disagreed with
the statements that the RUC does its job well and that it treats

Protestants and Catholics fairly.[18] Other leaders believe that the RUC is indeed carrying out "impartial policing" and concede that officers have "shown themselves to be worthy of support from everyone."[19] They are unhappy with what they consider the party's ambivalent positions on policing and would like it to play an active role on bodies dealing with the police, like the Police Authority and liaison committees. (Party policy prevents members from accepting positions on such bodies, just as the party does not urge Catholics to join the RUC.) One district councillor remarked: "I think SDLP policy ought to be changed. We ought to be in there pitching. This boycotting of things hasn't helped."[20] But this is a minority view.

The SDLP has been in the forefront of the campaign to reform the RUC and tame its repressive proclivities. It has repeatedly pressed for commissions of inquiry to investigate controversial incidents; an end to indiscriminate stops and searches on the street, careless and destructive house searches, and use of excessive force; empowerment of the complaints board and the Police Authority; the repeal of exceptional legal powers which invite police abuses; tighter control of the RUC's Special Branch; improved training of officers; and creation of local police-community advisory committees. However, these reforms are considered secondary in importance to resolution of the central problem, that is, the larger political conflict.

The SDLP has consistently argued that full support for the police is contingent on a satisfactory political settlement to the conflict. Such a settlement seemed possible during a brief power-sharing experiment in 1974, in which the SDLP held important posts. At that time the party expressed support for the RUC, but when the experiment crumbled, it immediately withdrew its endorsement of the police. A 1975 position paper emphasized the "political causes of non-acceptability" and insisted that fundamental political changes, including the incorporation of both ethnic groups in government, were "a prerequisite for acceptable policing." Reforms will be of "little avail" until this precondition is realized.[21] The document implies that once a political settlement has been reached, Catholic support for the police would be readily forthcoming, perhaps an overly optimistic prognosis in light of prevailing opinion of the RUC.

The party's stance on this central issue—the political preconditions of police legitimation—has been constant since 1975.

John Hume, the SDLP's leader, recently insisted that "we will only have total unequivocal identification with the institutions of law and order when there is agreement among the people as a whole as to how we are governed. . . . "[22] The police continue to "protect the constitutional position of Northern Ireland" as part of the United Kingdom.[23] This is also cited as an obstacle to the recruitment of Catholics into the force: "The only way to get Catholics into the RUC is when they have something to defend. The police represent a *form of government* with which they cannot identify. It's not a question of religion; its a question of the form of government. . . . Catholics have to feel they can identify with the state before they can identify with the police" (U). Therefore, one reason why the reforms in policing have not had the positive impact on attitudes that might have been expected—and that the police feel they deserve—lies *outside* the domain of policing, in the political system.

It is not clear whether the RUC would have to be dismantled and replaced under a new political order, as Sinn Fein insists. The SDLP believes that the kind of police force appropriate to a new Northern Ireland would be negotiable among the principals involved in constitutional deliberations.

Some of the SDLP's positions are strongly endorsed by ordinary party supporters while others command less support. Is the RUC fundamentally illegitimate or basically acceptable? The available data suggest that moderate Catholics subscribe to neither position. They do not reject outright the RUC's claim to authority, but their opposition to British rule—which the police are seen to uphold—has a contaminating effect on the legitimacy of the force, rendering it at least somewhat precarious. Moderates doubt that the police are sufficiently autonomous of the executive branch: "They'd think there was a political coloring, and they would remember all of the ways in which the police have been used by the government in the past" (KK). The nature of the state thus has some bearing on moderates' perceptions and confidence in the RUC, although my interview data suggest that this is less salient for ordinary people than for SDLP politicians and staunch Republicans.

The level of general satisfaction with the RUC is also somewhat higher for the SDLP's constituents than for its political leaders. A majority of SDLP supporters (Table 4.3) say they are satisfied with the police, and interviews uncovered some fairly positive attitudes consistent with the survey findings. One Catholic priest flatly stated: "Catholics here support the police. . . . People experience the police as a service" (NN). Another priest said, "Middle-class people would feel more comfortable around the police and will treat them with authority. Middle-class Catholics would be looking for law and order. They have an instinctive desire to think well of the police" (O). There is also "a great deal of sympathy for the police" when the IRA attacks them,[24] whereas Republicans tend to greet such attacks with applause. One informant paints this picture of his moderate Catholic neighborhood:

> Police get on quite well with people here. . . . This doesn't mean they are 100 percent happy with the police. . . . People would find the police extremely helpful in times of trouble. People would not feel inhibited calling the police to their homes; more and more they are doing that. And the police would get a good reception generally in the homes. But there are still some people who won't call the police because they view the RUC as an alien force; they are a minority. (V)

Twenty-six percent of SDLP supporters say they are unsatisfied with the RUC (Table 4.3), and others are rather ambivalent: "Catholics think the police are needed. They don't bend over backwards, but they don't say 'get them out of the area.' . . . They don't love them but they do see them as necessary, and not as a necessary evil."[25]

A significant proportion of moderate Catholics judge the RUC as impartial. They are considerably more likely than Republicans to believe that the RUC treats Protestants and Catholics equally, much less likely to say that the police treat Protestants better than Catholics, and twice as likely to say the police try hard to stop Protestant attacks on Catholics (Table 4.3). Still, a significant number of moderates say the police are not impartial, and they remain concerned about instances of blatant police bias. One way of gaining greater acceptance in moderate areas is "if police could be seen as being totally and utterly impartial" (KK).

Two-thirds of moderate Catholics think that more Catholic police officers would be good for Northern Ireland (Table 4.3). They endorse the principle of Catholics joining the RUC, evidently because they expect that Catholic officers would behave more sensitively toward Catholic civilians and/or because a more balanced police force might yield symbolic dividends—demonstrating that the RUC is no longer a Protestant preserve, perhaps giving it more credibility. One priest surmised that "if Catholics were in charge of checkpoints, then the ballgame would be different" because Catholic officers would be less prone to engage in harassment (D). (This differs radically from staunch Republicans' opinions of Catholic police officers, as shown below.) But moderates also appreciate that the composition of the RUC is unlikely to change under conditions where the disincentives for prospective Catholic recruits are overwhelming. Sixty-one percent of SDLP supporters say that the most important reason why Catholics do not join the RUC is intimidation or dissuasion by other Catholics, and about a fifth believe the most important reason is that Catholics fear bad treatment if they join.[26] Catholic cops also face ostracism from their relatives and neighbors and attacks by the IRA.

In general, then, despite the problematic legitimacy of the RUC, moderate Catholics have a more positive impression of the force than what is suggested by conventional accounts that paint all Catholics as alienated from the institutions of law and order. Still, the security role of the police causes great concern, as the next chapter shows. Moderates who do not experience counterinsurgency policing to any significant extent are still aware—in greater or lesser degree—of the problems it causes in other communities. Their perceptions of the RUC are affected not only by personal experiences and observations in their own neighborhoods, but also by national-level conflicts over incidents of security policing. The frequency with which unsettling incidents occur, and the complaints of Catholic leaders that are continually aired in public, have a profound, cumulative effect on their attitudes. Such incidents are frequent enough to suggest that the problem is not confined to a few "bad apples," although moderate Catholics are less likely than staunch Republicans to jump to the conclusion that the RUC is a thoroughly "rotten barrel."

STAUNCH REPUBLICANS

Staunch Republicans support the goal of a united Ireland, to be won by armed struggle and political mobilization. They vote for Sinn Fein, are supporters of the IRA or the smaller Irish National Liberation Army, and are heavily represented in poor and working-class Catholic communities. Sluka's study of one Republican community (Divis Flats in Belfast) distinguishes "hard" and "soft" supporters of the IRA. Hard supporters define themselves as IRA loyalists, agree with the IRA's goals and methods, and are prepared to participate in at least some of its activities, legal or illegal (on the legal side, attending Republican demonstrations and political funerals; on the illegal side, hiding weapons, providing safe houses, acting as couriers and drivers, gathering intelligence). Soft supporters strongly endorse the IRA's goals but are more ambivalent about the means—approving of its campaign for a united Ireland and its efforts to defend Catholics, but uneasy about its offensive attacks on Loyalists, the security forces, and commercial property.[27] It is the hard supporters who play the dominant role in shaping the neighborhood culture of staunch Republican areas.

Judgments of the police are not solely an individual matter, particularly where a vibrant neighborhood culture exists. In Ulster's Republican areas collective sentiment is quite antagonistic to the British state and institutions of law and order, views that are continually fed from many sources: personal experiences with police; observations of others' encounters with police; ongoing socialization, including what people learn from older generations who keep alive tales of incidents (some long past) of gross police repression; impressions of how the police treat Protestants; and national-level conflicts over policing and the state conveyed by the mass media. The combined and cumulative effect of these factors is such that even persons who have had positive experiences or observations of the police tend to rate them negatively.

The role of neighborhood culture is examined in some American research. A study of black ghettos in Milwaukee, Wisconsin, found that neighborhood culture can be decisive in shaping perceptions: "The general reputation of the police in the black neighborhood has become so bad that good experiences do not bring about correspondingly good evaluations." At the same time, bad experiences are not limited to the affected individuals, but have broader neighborhood effects: "The proportion of the black ghetto with bad experiences is much greater than in other neighborhoods, so that the indirect effect of their experiences is considerably multiplied."[28] Similarly, observations of others' treatment by police can contribute in a major way to the neighborhood culture. Another study of black ghettos in the United States found that observations of persons being abused by the police were very strongly related to general subcultural beliefs about the prevalence of police misconduct in the neighborhood.[29] These findings are borne out in Northern Ireland, but what distinguishes Northern Ireland's communities is the importance of exogenous factors—the state, frequent national-level conflicts over policing, perceptions of how the opposing ethnic group is policed—in shaping neighborhood orientations.

The sparse literature on Ulster's Republican communities suggests that most residents are estranged from the RUC, in large part because of the counterinsurgency enterprise, which is omnipresent in these neighborhoods. One study of West Belfast found that police were perceived as sectarian, prone to harassing civilians, trading favors with common criminals in return for their intelligence on the community, and deliberately ignoring calls from citizens as a form of community punishment.[30] Another study, of the Divis Flats neighborhood, found that residents avoided contact with the police; saw them as heavily biased in favor of Protestants; were resentful over street harassment, disruptive house searches, brutality during demonstrations and riots, and arrests of innocent people; and believed the police operate with impunity, so that reporting a complaint is a waste of time.[31]

My data generally support these findings, but since my research centered on policing, and covered several neighborhoods, it allows for a more extensive analysis and explanation of patterns in police-community relations.

James Baldwin once compared the status of police in America's black ghettos to that of "an occupying soldier in a bitterly hostile country."[32] A somewhat exaggerated characterization of American ghettos in the 1960s, it fits perfectly Ulster's Republican neighborhoods, where police are seen as alien oppressors, branded as agents of the British state and as defenders of Protestant supremacy. In Sinn Fein's view, the institutions of law and order are thoroughly contaminated by British and Unionist interests: the RUC is both a British occupation force and, in the words of Sinn Fein's president, the "armed wing of Unionism."[33] Sinn Fein is the only political party that condemns all aspects of policing and insists that the RUC is beyond redemption as long as British involvement in Ulster continues. It shares the SDLP's criticisms of all the specific objectionable aspects of policing in Northern Ireland (Sinn Fein supporters are more critical than SDLP supporters of repressive police measures), but considers them merely symptomatic of more fundamental policing problems. While the SDLP presses for reforms, Sinn Fein holds that the RUC is patently unreformable and must be dismantled and replaced with a new police force after Britain withdraws from the country.

Sinn Fein's unqualified rejection of the RUC is very strongly shared by the residents of Republican areas, as the survey and interview data show. Only 4 percent of Sinn Fein supporters say they are "satisfied" with the RUC, and very few think the force is impartial (Table 4.3). On other issues there is some variation, ranging from the extreme view that the "only good policeman is a dead one" (S) to sublethal antipathy, but Republicans are united in their feeling that the RUC is *totally illegitimate*. The problem lies not with a few "bad apples" in the force; the entire barrel is rotten beyond repair. I was told repeatedly in each of the different Republican neighborhoods I studied that an anti-police attitude is widespread and that the RUC has no credibility whatsoever:

> People grow up feeling the RUC is an alien force and that they will get no justice from them. (A)

> Generally, the police here aren't acceptable. The RUC have such a bad record. (B)

> People have undisguised fear and hostility toward the police. (Z)

> Most people here have never known the police as anything other than an oppressive force. The view here is that the RUC isn't a police force at all but an armed, sectarian paramilitary force. . . . Most are totally opposed to the RUC. (UU)

> Here . . . the police are nonacceptable in any form. They're seen as a Protestant police force, even if there are Catholic cops, enforcing the government's rules. People here would accept the army quicker than the RUC! (MM)

Indicative of the RUC's illegitimacy is the consensus among my informants that people in their respective communities want the police to *withdraw completely from the area*. There is a sense that nothing would be lost if the police left since they perform no positive role now, and that residents would gain by the lifting of this yoke of oppression. This contrasts sharply with black Americans, who—although critical of certain aspects of policing—are adamant that police should not leave their communities and should instead expand their crime control efforts therein.[34] A poll in Los Angeles, for example, revealed that only 1 percent of blacks felt there were too many police in their neighborhoods; 74 percent said there were not enough.[35] Blacks in London are somewhat more likely to reject the police, but it is still a small minority. Fourteen percent of London's blacks believe there are too many police in their neighborhoods; 20 percent, too few; and 63 percent, the right amount.[36]

People do not accept that the RUC has made any progress in the past twenty years. The police have "all the vestiges of the old order" (N). Reforms described earlier in the book are dismissed as window dressing. A community worker stated: "People don't believe the police have reformed. They are the same police force. Nothing is different. They've always been armed and militarized and they are doing nothing different than before" (W). In fact, the RUC is characterized as "unreformable": under British rule no less than Unionist rule it is an inherently ethnocentric force designed to repress Catholics. What is required is a "complete overhaul" or "dismantling" of the institution (LL). One informant insisted that people "wouldn't accept restructuring of the RUC, but only the complete disbandment and creating an entirely new force. Even then it would have to prove its neutrality and that would be difficult because you're always going to have one side or the other demanding the police act a certain way" (MM).

The illegitimacy of the RUC and the demand for its transformation or replacement is largely due to the moral bankruptcy of the state. It is not accepted that the police are now autonomous of the regime, nor does the British regime have greater standing than the Unionist regime that preceded it. Sinn Fein's legal affairs officer is adamant:

> The RUC have never really progressed from defenders of the orange state. The whole ethos was to sit on that population who didn't accept the state. Sinn Fein contends that, to the present day, the majority of RUC officers would still see the defense of the orange Unionist state as their first priority. Policing is secondary.

> *But the orange Unionist state no longer exists; it was abolished in 1972.*

> The trappings of the orange state were abolished in 1972, but that state was under British sovereignty before 1972 and Britain

gave its blessing to what the orange state did. Very little of the state has changed for the nationalist community since Unionist rule was suspended. We believe the RUC can't be reformed; they are beyond reform because of their ethos. The only thing that's changed is the color of their uniform.[37]

Indeed, to acknowledge that progressive changes have occurred would contradict Sinn Fein's fundamental position that Northern Ireland's institutions can only be transformed in a united Ireland free of British involvement. "There will never be proper, civilian policing here until Britain withdraws," says a Sinn Fein officer, "When that happens policing here would not be unlike the type they have in Britain."[38]

Many Republicans appear to accept this position, convinced that a police force would be acceptable in their communities only after Ireland is united, but this seems a less prominent element of the neighborhood culture than the more immediate desire to see the police leave the area. For some people the RUC's political hue may not be the foremost concern, and the issue of whether people condition their support for the police on a political settlement to the conflict may be "almost a philosophical question" that is somewhat divorced from daily experiences (S). Some informants thought that politically active people are more likely than ordinary people to link acceptance of the police to a political settlement (TT), whereas others claimed that most people would endorse this view (LL). The director of one community organization observes that Catholics attending meetings at the organization frequently "express very strong views that the police operate in a way that propagates British rule" (G). Another community worker stated that people wanted the police to have "no political masters who use the police to keep the people down. The police are seen as an arm of Unionist parties. People believe the police are still being used as a political weapon" (W). And another study found that working-class Catholics living in a small border town believed the RUC helped to maintain Protestant supremacy.[39]

Contributing to the illegitimacy of the RUC is its prominent security role, which is defined not as a genuine, necessary response to political violence but as a means of propping up an illegitimate state. In other words, counterinsurgency policing demonstrates that the RUC is thoroughly politicized. The RUC's security role is examined in depth in the next chapter.

Republicans are more likely than other groups to report having had bad encounters with police officers. In 1990 (Table 4.3) 77 percent of Sinn Fein supporters said that they had been "annoyed" by police behavior toward them at some time, much higher than what is reported by SDLP supporters (28 percent) or the two Protestant groups (12 and 14 percent). The large number of Sinn Fein people reporting negative experiences may be expected to produce neighborhood effects in Republican communities in the direction of *generalized* tension and discontent, not just isolated, individual resentment. This generalized tension infuses police-citizen encounters, with both parties expecting problems when they come into contact. "Normal friction" is also found in police-citizen interactions in some minority neighborhoods in other countries, such as America's black ghettos, because police work causes an irreducible level of tension in areas with high crime rates or because a segment of the population is frequently uncooperative with police.[40] But the normal friction in American ghettos pales in comparison to what we find in Ulster's Republican areas, where animosity toward police is much more palpable and serious and has political as well as interactional sources.

The degree to which the police are shunned by ordinary people is remarkable: "People will not go to functions if a policeman is there. If there is *any* RUC involvement at any level, they will not have anything to do with it" (B). And "anyone using the police or being on friendly terms with the police is regarded with suspicion. . . . When the police go to a house, it draws attention and neighbors will wonder if they are informers" (A). Avoidance of the police is indeed widespread in these communities, as the RUC readily admits. Even those who are not anti-police "don't identify with them," and "you wouldn't see anyone stopping and talking to a policeman" (U). In Republican neighborhoods with a minority of moderate Catholics who support the RUC, their outward behavior is constrained by community norms against most kinds of contacts with the police.

Not all Republican neighborhoods are equally hostile to the police, however. In some areas relations are slightly less contentious than in other areas. A comparison of two neighborhoods suggests that the local level of political violence may affect relations with police:

On the Falls Road attitudes to police are more politicized and people are more belligerent. [Here] there is joyriding, dope, thieving—police are looking for these people, rather than the terrorists. Yet terrorists still operate here; there's been a lot of shootings. . . . On the Falls Road, kids will ignore police if they say hello. There you will find random stoning of police and paramilitary attacks on landrovers. That has never happened here—only one or two bombings of landrovers, by dropping [petrol] bombs from balconies. People up the Falls say the police are letting people [here] do what they want, because they are using them for information. On the Falls, people phone police as a last resort. Here they phone the police immediately. This is surprising given the reputation of the place! It's strange in what is supposed to be a Republican area. For broken windows and other kinds of crime, people here are inclined to phone the police. Up the Falls, they sort it out themselves.

This does *not* mean that residents of this neighborhood see the RUC in a positive light:

> Here attitudes are more ambivalent. People will say hello to them. . . . Police call people by first names and chat with kids. But the police are looking for information; it's an intelligence-gathering approach. . . . People are very suspicious of the police. (W)

A former community worker in this neighborhood confirmed that it was slightly more tolerant of the police than where she now works, which is "totally anti-police" (MM). She suggested that this is partly because Orange parades are allowed to pass through the latter, but not the former, community every year, which leads to clashes between residents and the police or Orange marchers, and "very strongly reinforces bitterness" toward the RUC.

Despite the fact that some Republican areas are less overtly anti-police than others, distrust is endemic and palpable in all Republican communities. Facing a cool or hostile reception in these neighborhoods, police officers are prone to develop sweeping stereotypes about the residents. The official RUC line is that most people in these areas are decent, law-abiding people, sick of the IRA's bloody campaign and its stranglehold over the community, but fearful of and intimidated by the "terrorists." But the prevailing stereotypes held by constables working in these neighborhoods are rather different. A Neighborhood Branch inspector noted that in Republican parts of West Belfast there were "some decent peo-

ple, but basically they're very mistrustful." He surmised that
Catholics in the area think the police are "all ultra-Unionist. . . .
That's probably because they're all ultra-bigots."[41] One of my
sources, a Community Relations sergeant, said of the same population, "It's very hard to get the locals to trust us, and we don't trust
them."[42] Even among officers whose discourse differentiates
between "decent" Catholics and troublemakers, these distinctions
may not be invoked in encounters with residents of staunch
Republican areas. Like many American cops' interactions with
inner-city blacks,[43] RUC officers behave as if they paint all residents of Republican areas with the same brush, as the enemy. The
master typification of the neighborhood as "anti-police" obscures
for all practical purposes differences among individual residents.

Police impartiality toward different ethnic groups is one measure of their professionalism. Chapter 3 noted that the RUC's official discourse now emphasizes impartial treatment of Catholics
and Protestants. Such formal norms can coexist, however, with
high levels of police prejudice and discriminatory conduct.
Indeed, we should expect to find significant levels of police prejudice in troubled areas with high concentrations of staunch Republicans or Loyalists, areas where police encounter the most problems with local people.[44] One study suggested that the principle of
impartiality is indeed regarded more skeptically by RUC officers
stationed in Republican neighborhoods than in undisturbed
areas. It cited some constables who insisted that they act toward
civilians without regard to their ethnic background, but others
who admitted that they harbor prejudice toward one side. "Since
I've come into this job it's made me really biased against
[Catholics]," one officer stated, "I'd probably feel biased against
the Prods [Protestants] if I was in one of the hard Prod areas."
And a colleague remarked, "I think the Catholics are the worst;
you can't help being biased up here."[45]

Unfortunately, we have no information on the number of constables who subscribe to these views or the extent to which they
translate into discriminatory behavior, and the observational evidence from other societies regarding police treatment of minorities is mixed.[46] What we do know is that the "normal friction"
between police and civilians in Republican areas, where residents
are highly sensitive to signs of police bias and enter into encounters with negative expectations, allows these encounters to be
readily *invested* with sectarian meaning and politicized. An

authoritarian or brusque interpersonal demeanor on the part of police officers, which arises out of their need to command compliance from civilians,[47] can be construed as an expression of police prejudice or domination over Catholics. The fact that most police officers are Protestants, are seen as agents of the British state, are members of a discredited organization, and enforce laws that indirectly maintain the partition of Ireland (which serves Protestant interests) makes it rather easy for their routine authoritarian conduct to be defined as bigoted. This *sectarian overdetermination* of perceptions of encounters with the police is almost automatic in Republican areas, where it is firmly embedded in the neighborhood culture.[48]

Clearly, the RUC's growing impartiality over the years has not registered among staunch Republicans. Constables are perceived as strongly inclined to act with bias for the reasons outlined above. In a survey of members of the (now defunct) Northern Ireland Assembly, all four Sinn Fein members disagreed with the notion that the RUC acts fairly toward Protestants and Catholics.[49] Likewise, few Sinn Fein supporters think the police treat Protestants and Catholics equally, and they are almost unanimous in believing the police treat Protestants better. Four-fifths believe the RUC tries hard to stop sectarian attacks by Catholics but not by Protestants. They also think the police hinder Catholic protests far too often, unlike their occasional intervention in Protestant demonstrations (Table 4.3).

My interview data from several Republican communities in Belfast help to enrich our understanding of the reasons why people reject the idea that the RUC is impartial. Perceptions are rooted not only in people's experiences and observations in their own neighborhoods but also in subcultural assumptions about what policing is like in Protestant areas. Even when people are aware of specific police actions against Protestants, it has little effect on the conviction that anti-Catholic bias is endemic in the RUC. They may "understand that the police are *capable* of hassling Protestants" and they may not "believe Protestants will automatically be protected by the police" (Z), as one informant pointed out, but this does not translate into impartiality. Consider the following claims:

> The police instinctively have a bias in favor of the Unionist people. Patrolling and harassment in Protestant areas is nothing

like the patrolling of Catholic areas; that's the perception in Catholic minds. (O)

If you told anyone here that the police were impartial, they would laugh at you. They just wouldn't believe it. Where are officers going to live? They can't be impartial if they live in Protestant areas. . . . You can't live among your own and be impartial. (W)

People think Protestants are treated softly. . . . They don't think people have any problems with the police in Protestant areas and that you can't make even the slightest comparison between the two areas. (MM)

[There is] a belief that Protestant areas are policed more leniently. You often hear people say, "That wouldn't happen in the Shankill," when they see abuses by the peelers. . . . The general perception is that police would be favorably treated in Protestant areas and also that they treat people in those areas better than in Catholic areas. (LL)

People here know very well that the police will behave better toward people in Protestant areas and mixed middle-class areas. . . . They also know the police belong to Orange lodges and live in Loyalist communities. People know the reasons why police act differently toward Catholics and Protestants. (Z)

In interface areas between Protestant and Catholic neighborhoods, as opposed to the insulated heartlands, differential policing can be most clearly observed and experienced:

People believe they are treated more harshly here than Protestants are. And there is evidence in their own experiences. The police station is located at a flashpoint, an interface between our community and the Protestant [housing] estate. People from the Protestant community can throw stones here and get away with it, but if Catholics do it in [the Protestant area] they get arrested. This is what local residents have experienced. A friend of mine was attacked by Protestant teens close to the police station and he couldn't understand why the police didn't respond. . . . Some of our teenagers used to go to a disco near the Protestant estate and they were sometimes attacked by Protestants who were never pursued by the police. (RR)

We shall see in Chapter 5 that grievances about partisan policing are most pronounced with regard to matters of public order and security.

It is commonly assumed that the composition of a police force in an ethnically heterogeneous society is an important variable shaping attitudes toward the police, and that the more representative a police force becomes, the greater its legitimacy. Two major American commissions of the 1960s recommended recruitment of minority police officers on the grounds that they would enhance the status of the police in minority neighborhoods and reduce the potential for tension and violence.[50] And the U.S. Civil Rights Commission believes it is "axiomatic" that a police force representative of the population will have good relations with the public.[51] In Northern Ireland the fact that Catholics constitute only 7 percent of the RUC appears to be one of its deficiencies from the perspective of moderate Catholics, two-thirds of whom favor increasing the number of Catholics in the force. Republicans are not troubled by the low numbers: only 23 percent believe more Catholic police would be good for the country (Table 4.3). As the interview data below show, many Republicans feel there are already *too many Catholics* in the RUC. They are half as likely as SDLP supporters to say the most important reason why Catholics do not apply is because they are pressured by fellow Catholics not to join (33 percent), and more likely to say it is because they expect bad treatment in the police force (43 percent).[52]

My interviews uncovered some other important subcultural evaluations of Catholic police. There is a historical dimension: "People just hate Catholics who go into the police force. In the 1940s we remember Catholic police torturing people on the Falls Road and coming into homes and ripping things up" (W). And there are other concerns: "I don't advise Catholics to join the RUC. . . . I will tell them all the consequences: isolation from their families, the [RUC's] denial or insult to their own symbols of nationalism or religion, and danger to their own lives" (Q). Not only is there pressure from family members and other Catholics, but also a concern that joining the RUC would be a betrayal of the Catholic population:

> Most people here would look upon someone joining the RUC as betraying his or her own people and probably doing it only for the money. (Z)

> A Catholic policeman is seen as a traitor, a turncoat. So that's why people will not worry if he's shot, because he shouldn't have been there. (W)

They would see Catholics as traitors, betraying their nationalism and their own people. (MM)

It would also mean relocating out of a Republican area because of the danger they would face there:

He can't join and stay in the community because he'll be shot. (U)

A Catholic patrolling in West Belfast would have only difficulties with people and a Catholic cop living and working in West Belfast wouldn't survive. Catholics here would be stupid to join the RUC—they'd be committing suicide. (LL)

How would people feel if more Catholics joined the force?

I don't think it would make any difference. People don't talk about the lack of Catholics in the force. It's a bigoted police force. (TT)

If the RUC was to get more Catholics, it wouldn't make any difference. It doesn't really matter what the religion of the person is. I want people in the RUC who will enforce the law impartially. In Northern Ireland that is virtually impossible to do because the force is anti-nationalist. (U)

Nor would the presence of Catholic constables improve face-to-face interactions in Republican neighborhoods:

A Catholic in the force today has to act more aggressively than a Protestant to prove himself. (W)

The comment which is always made is "your own are always the worst."

What does that mean?

If a Catholic joins the police he has to prove that he is a policeman first and foremost and to do that he may be more oppressive than a Protestant cop, especially toward Catholics. This is frequently stated here, that a Catholic officer might be worse than a Protestant officer. (RR)

Catholic officers would be *more disliked*, perceived as traitors. "Your own's the worst," people say. (LL)

If people knew the cops [dealing with them] were Catholic it would make no difference. They would give Catholic cops a harder time, although the different age groups would act differently. Teenagers would torture the hell out of them, call them Fenian bastards; older people, those over 50, would be more willing to accept Catholic cops, because they accept authority figures in general.

Why would people give Catholic police trouble?

Because they have sold out to the establishment. Catholic and Protestant cops would be assumed to be the same. And the Catholic cops I know tell me they have to be harder on people in their own areas. There is considerable pressure from other cops to act more aggressively. They always have to prove they are as good as their Protestant colleagues.

Catholic officers have said that to you?

Aye, some Catholic cops have actually told me this. (MM)

Catholic cops aren't going to treat us any differently than Protestant officers. In fact they treat us worse to show that they're tough, like the black policemen in Los Angeles! (TT)

The little research that has been done on the attitudes of RUC officers lends some support to Republicans' perceptions of Catholic constables. One study found that some Catholic officers made blatantly anti-Catholic remarks, presumably as a way of conveying their trustworthiness to Protestant colleagues.[53] And a survey of part-time RUC officers—whose work includes guard duties and patrolling—found that Catholic officers took a much harder line on law-and-order issues (death penalty, stiff sentences for lawbreakers, belief that even "wrong" laws should be obeyed) than the Catholic population, and that they even took a harder line (on the second and third items) than their Protestant colleagues in the RUC![54]

The evidence from other societies suggests that the behavior of police officers from a minority ethnic group usually differs little from that of their majority-group counterparts, although their presence may be symbolically meaningful to the minority population. As minority representation on a police force rises, it may have a subtle effect on the police culture and perhaps some overall constraining effect on police behavior.[55] But there are strong institutional pressures on minority-group officers to act like their colleagues. First, the fact that police are authority figures responsible for the control of citizens inevitably brings them into conflict with some members of their own ethnic group, and, second, minority-group officers have an interest in winning acceptance from majority-group colleagues, which may depend on their demonstrated willingness to act firmly toward civilians of whatever ethnicity.[56] This helps to explain why the growing number of black police officers in the United States and Britain has not markedly improved black ghetto residents' views of the police, nor is there a strong preference for black officers.[57] A minority are highly suspicious and critical of black cops and believe they are harder on black people than white cops, but few go so far as to label them traitors to their communal group or to oppose them joining the police force, as do Republicans in Northern Ireland and many blacks in South Africa.[58]

The data presented above suggest that a more representative RUC—holding all else constant—clearly would not improve staunch Republican's perceptions or positively affect their interactions with officers. On the one hand, it is difficult for people to "see" the religion or ethnicity of an officer (unlike racial identity). Catholic constables are not readily recognizable as Catholics, and most people probably assume that the officers on the street are Protestants, a fair assumption since 93 percent of the RUC is Protestant. One informant referred to the "perception that officers are Protestants here to lord it over us" (B). On the other hand, even if officers' ethnicity could be discerned, it arguably would make little or no difference in encounters with residents of Republican areas. The master-status of constable or "peeler" is so negative in these communities that it renders the officer's ethnicity largely irrelevant. A Catholic officer would therefore command no more deference than a Protestant officer and perhaps even less respect among those who brand Catholic officers traitors to their people. It follows that the solution is not to recruit more Catholics or deploy more Catholic constables in Republican neighborhoods. The RUC requires fundamental overhaul before Republicans will accept it, which is dependent, for many people, on a political settlement:

> People around here would like the RUC disbanded; only then would they accept Catholics in the force. (MM)

> A completely new force is needed before any Catholic with any sense would join it. . . . You'd have to solve the problem of Northern Ireland as a whole before Catholics would join the police. The Irish question. (LL)

MODERATE PROTESTANTS

If there is one thing that brings moderate and radical Protestants together, it is their stiff opposition to a reunited Ireland. Most Protestants today favor a political solution that maintains the link with Britain while devolving substantial power to the local state in Northern Ireland. What separates moderates from their militant counterparts is their unwillingness to countenance violent methods. Generally law-abiding, moderate Protestants do not support Loyalist political violence, although they might endorse armed resistance if a united Ireland loomed on the horizon. Heavily concentrated in middle-class communities, moderates constitute the majority of the Protestant population.

Survey data indicate that most Protestants tend to view the RUC favorably and are much less divided than Catholics over policing issues. Moderates are particularly likely to hold pro-police views; they are significantly more positive in their assessments of policing than staunch Loyalists and much more so than both types of Catholics. Of UUP supporters, 91 percent say they are satisfied with the RUC, and a high proportion think the police are fair and impartial in their conduct toward Catholics and Protestants (Table 4.3). Fifty-six percent support the idea of recruiting more Catholics into the RUC and they overwhelmingly (82 percent) believe that the most important reason why Catholics do not join is because they are intimidated or discouraged by other Catholics.[59] Moderate Protestants might accept that the RUC contains a "few bad apples," but they would reject the argument that the force is structurally conducive to large-scale police deviance.

What does concern moderate Protestants is the British government's involvement in policing. In a 1985 poll 92 percent of Protestants agreed with the statement that the security forces were "politically restricted" by the government.[60] Similarly, among moderate Protestants living in a small mixed town near the border, one study found a widespread feeling that the government was tying the hands of the security forces.[61] Concern about government meddling in policing does not, however, translate into criticism of the RUC itself. Moderates are reluctant to criticize the police, and they dismiss the frequent criticisms made by Catholics and staunch Loyalists. In a middle-class Protestant area, most people are not willing to say anything critical of the police because the police are being criticized in the media by nationalists and people don't want to be identified with those critics. . . . A lot of people feel police are doing a good enough job; those who have grievances wouldn't want to criticize the police. People would be loathe to criticize the police. (QQ)

Moderate Protestants' generally high opinion of the police is partly due to the lack of security policing in their neighborhoods, which only occasionally see vehicle checkpoints or landrovers on patrol. Living in untroubled areas, they "don't know what abnormal policing is" (SS), and the complaints reported in the media from Catholics are more likely to cause them to defend the RUC than to question policing.

When individuals in moderate areas have bad experiences with the police, the generally positive neighborhood reputation of the RUC tends to preempt any serious deterioration in police-community relations. This pattern is similar to research findings for white neighborhoods in the United States, in contrast to black communities.[62] Neighborhood effects are, of course, not static. The standing of the police may deteriorate if growing numbers of individuals have negative experiences or if serious incidents outside the neighborhood or trends on the national level tarnish the police.

I studied several Protestant communities (middle class and working class) which are predominantly moderate but contain small minorities of staunch Loyalists and, in some areas, Loyalist insurgents or "paramilitaries." Informants consistently drew distinctions between the two subgroups. The paramilitaries and their supporters are critical of the police or even "anti-police" because the police interfere with their illegal activities (R, QQ). But the moderates "are very supportive of the police, even if the police are in the wrong" (R), and people feel that "if we are good to the police, they'll be good to us" (SS). Police harassment of ordinary people is rare (J). Resentment toward the police is low, and people have no reluctance in calling them to report crimes or ask for assistance. (In some areas, however, there is frustration over the RUC's slow response to calls from residents, discussed in Chapter 5.) A clergyman describes the dominant neighborhood view: "People support the police, . . . are pro law and order, and supportive of authority in any shape or form" (P).

Communities that are insulated from unrest and security policing and free of insurgents naturally register the most favorable attitudes and cordial relations with the police. Attitudes tend to be somewhat less positive in interface areas (where Protestant and Catholic neighborhoods adjoin) and in enclaves surrounded by communities of the opposite ethnic group. In one area, where Protestants and Catholics live on different sides of the street and conflict flares up occasionally, Protestants lean toward supporting the the police, but "the nature of the community means there is a much greater degree of tension and a greater degree of suspicion about the police" (P). In one Protestant neighborhood there is anger that the police do not treat the area with the proper specificity that it deserves, but instead lump it into the category of "troubled West Belfast":

> Police in this area have a consistent response throughout the area. They respond in the same way in Protestant and Catholic areas. . . . They treat this Protestant locality as being just as dangerous to them as Catholic areas. . . . There was a period prior to three years ago when the police valued this community and thought it important to maintain good relations with the community. Now they treat it as being part of the troubled area of West Belfast. In 1986 and 1987 three police families were attacked here [because of the Anglo-Irish accord described below]. This led the police to change their attitude toward the area. (R)

Even in moderate Protestant communities with historically cordial relations between residents and police, a rift may develop over a particular incident and bitter feelings may linger over time. The most notorious case in point is the uproar that accompanied the 1985 signing of the Anglo-Irish Agreement between the British and Irish governments, giving Dublin an unprecedented consultative role (but no real power) in Ulster's affairs by providing for regular meetings to discuss policy issues, including policing. The agreement sparked violent clashes between Protestant protesters and police with dramatic effects on police relations with staunch Loyalists, but the events also shook moderate Protestants' faith in the RUC and heightened concern about political interference in policing, now from both the British and Irish governments. The UUP's security spokesman articulated the views of some moderate Protestants when he expressed surprise that the "police were able to justify to themselves implementing a political decision against the will of the majority."[63] Surveys taken a few years later (Table 4.3) suggest that moderates' confidence in the RUC has largely been restored, although it appears that lingering doubts persist about government manipulation of the police.

With regard to the question of police impartiality, the survey findings show that four-fifths of moderate Protestants believe the RUC treats Protestants and Catholics equally. Most moderates would also agree that officers *should* act impartially. Some, however, believe Catholics are getting off easy: "They do feel the police 'deal with us harder than they deal with Catholics,'"[64] and "there's a perception among Protestants that because of the RUC's lack of access in Catholic areas, they don't act strongly enough there" (K). Others are concerned that the police treat Catholic and Protestant areas *too similarly*, as evidenced above. But complaints about excessively impartial policing or favoritism toward Catholics are more likely to be heard in staunch Loyalist areas.

STAUNCH LOYALISTS

Staunch Loyalists are fierce opponents of a united Ireland, suspicious of the British government's actions with regard to Ulster, and at least somewhat sympathetic to the activities of Loyalist insurgent organizations. Heavily concentrated in poor and working-class Protestant neighborhoods, staunch Loyalists tend to support the right-wing Democratic Unionist Party,[65] though some see even this party as too mainstream; they may vote for it but also support insurgent groups such as the Ulster Defense Association or the Ulster Volunteer Force.[66]

Staunch Loyalists are more likely to criticize the RUC than moderate Protestants (Table 4.3) and, although 80 percent express overall satisfaction with the RUC, many harbor grievances over specific aspects of policing. In most respects their grievances are qualitatively different from or antithetical to those of Catholics, but there are also some points of convergence in the criticisms from each quarter. Naturally there is a degree of attitudinal variation among Loyalists, ranging from conditional support to outright hatred of the police, and they are divided between those who believe that police misconduct is confined to a few individuals and those who think it is more widespread or even institutionally reinforced. Some of this variation is evident in the data presented below, but we shall also see that there is considerable agreement among Loyalists on a number of important issues.

Longitudinal changes in police relations with staunch Loyalists—in the direction of gradual deterioration—have been much more substantial than anything experienced by moderates. The most serious rupture in relations to date followed the signing of the Anglo-Irish Agreement in November 1985. Loyalists promptly condemned the agreement as a monumental betrayal and an infringement on Ulster's sovereignty by a foreign state, the Irish Republic. Mass street protests brought protesters into direct confrontation with the police, during which the RUC was ridiculed for "enforcing" the unpopular accord and for "selling out" the Protestant community. That the RUC was simply maintaining order was not accepted; instead it was accused of implementing the "dictatorial" policies of the Thatcher government or, even worse, facilitating the subversive, irredentist designs of the Irish government.

Disaffection with the police reached an all-time high during 1986–1988. In a series of violent clashes between demonstrators and police, stones and petrol bombs were hurled at police, who were called "pigs," "scum," and "traitors." Resentment over the RUC's vigorous control of these protests also resulted in anonymous death threats and a total of 550 attacks on police officers and their homes (stonings, shootings, petrol bombings); attacks on officers' homes forced 140 families to relocate to more hospitable neighborhoods.[67] Although Loyalists' sense of outrage over police behavior in "upholding" the accord has waned since 1988, the rift between them remains and relations are unlikely to return to their pre-accord level.

The data presented below are drawn from staunch Loyalist areas in Belfast. But the general findings are corroborated in a couple of other sources. A qualitative study of one of Londonderry's largest Protestant working-class public-housing estates drew the following conclusions: "There was no confidence, most marked among activists, that the police were there to ensure peace and stability in the estate. There was a feeling that they provoked trouble, and harassed and victimized young people unnecessarily; the stories of the language used and the general attitude of the police would suggest that they were careless of gaining the goodwill of the community."[68] And a report of a conference of Protestant community workers is unequivocal: "Protestants also experience the police as oppressive, and there is little respect for the police in many working-class areas. . . . The police should consider ways of regaining confidence in Protestant areas."[69] This assessment pertains to areas where staunch Loyalists, not moderates, are predominant.

For Republicans and Loyalists alike, the legitimacy of the RUC is heavily dependent on the *nature of the state*. Republicans consider British rule wholly beyond the pale. Loyalists find it distasteful (albeit preferable to a reunited Ireland) since it creates political insecurity over the future of the province. Yet it is not only the state as such that concerns Loyalists, but also the *nature of state intervention in policing*, also a concern of moderate Protestants. British rule is associated with unwarranted executive interference and judicial restraint on the police, which hamper effective policing of Catholic communities and the incapacitation of Republican insurgents. At the same time, the government is accused of putting excessive pressure on the RUC to crack down on Loyalist insurgents.

The DUP's security spokesman summarized the problem when he complained that the police are "hindered in their fight against terrorism because of political considerations. We see a lot of interference from the NIO."[70] Some people blame the government more than the police for the feeble response to Republican insurgency and for oppressive actions against Protestants:

> Protestants still feel today it is a Protestant police force which should protect Protestant rights and be as tough as they want to be against Republicanism. I hear lots of comments that the British government gets in the way of this. Lots of times. (VV)

> Anti-police attitudes are due very much to the political situation; people feel the government is leaving them in an uncertain situation regarding their political identity. They don't understand why the police—who once were connected to the Protestant population—are now turning attention to Loyalist paramilitaries. (QQ)

> People no longer see it as their police force. Since the Anglo-Irish accord, people have become more and more suspicious of the RUC, believing they've been sold down the river. (II)

The police are now seen as an oppressive force being used to implement the ongoing talks [between political parties in 1992]. Before that they were involved in implementing the Anglo-Irish Agreement and before that they were gathering information to arrest people for the supergrass[71] trials. (OO)

For the most militant Loyalists the RUC faces a legitimacy crisis nearly as severe as what we have seen in Republican areas. Other Loyalists, however, describe the RUC as "a Protestant force" or "our boys," while yet others seem ambivalent. Informants pointed to these differences of opinion in their communities:

A major section of the community would view police with immense mistrust. They would not perceive them as the enemy, per se, but with mistrust. Only if you're involved in paramilitary activity would you see them as the enemy. Some people feel oppressed—the connected ones [i.e., connected to an insurgent group]—and they get hassled. People who aren't in trouble don't have problems with police, but there is a certain amount of "them and us" that is felt by the majority. Some feel that they are "our police" and that the police are getting enough trouble from Republicans, so we shouldn't be giving them more trouble. (JJ)

[Residents see the police] as "our boys," but also as a nuisance when the police stop them on the street. (A)

There is a dichotomy of views. On the one hand, there is an anti-authoritarian streak: "Don't tell the authorities anything." On the other hand, the police are seen as our police, Protestants. These two attitudes are running side by side. (Y)

People won't accept what the police tell them; there's no respect for them; they're wary of them. But beat police are accepted in that they won't be interfered with in doing their job. . . . People are quite content to have police walking about. . . . Community police walk down the road every day and people talk to them. (F)

The [neighborhood] is one-third elderly, who would be total supporters of the RUC. The remainder, especially the unemployed, wield more influence than they should and have a lot of venom toward the police. (T)

Now there is a generation growing up with little respect for authority in any shape or form. . . . Among the unemployed and working-class Protestant people, some do not have very high intelligence levels and they are more susceptible to pressures of the peer group to take issue with authority. . . . They would be willing to take on the police, and have running battles with authority. But in the main, in Protestant working-class areas there is respect for law and order. . . . Relations between Protestants and the police in those areas is one of uneasy peace, more peace than uneasy. (P)

Police are tolerated because they are doing a job, but people are not totally supportive of them. Young people especially are not supportive. . . . People don't go out of their way to help them. . . . A lot has happened since the beginning of the troubles to make the police and the whole system of law and order suspect. A lot of people think Protestants are quite supportive of the police, but that isn't the case here. (X)

Notwithstanding the different attitudes captured in these statements, it is clear from them that there has been an overall decline in confidence in the RUC, compared to the period of Unionist rule.

If many residents of Loyalist communities have mixed feelings about the police, a sizeable number are truly alienated. For example, in one neighborhood "a substantial minority would be anti-police; I'd say about 40 percent" (JJ). I was told that there are areas of another neighborhood "where police would fear to go at night as much as in Republican areas" and that a very large section of the community "is as anti-police or anti-authority as the nationalist areas" (T). The views of those who are most hostile to the police are reflected in nasty graffiti, such as "SS-RUC" and "peelers are pigs," although this is less common than in Republican areas. (Much of the graffiti dates from the Anglo-Irish disturbances of 1986–1988.) Many Catholics and moderate Protestants would be surprised to learn that this virulent anti-police sentiment is not confined to a small minority in Loyalist areas. An incident illustrates the lack of goodwill toward police on the part of a section of one community:

Even if one [officer] was lying on the road, people wouldn't help him. A policewoman got hit by a car up the street, not seriously but she was knocked to the ground, and people standing on the street actually cheered! They thought it was quite funny and talked about it the next day, asking their friends if they had heard about it. (WW)

Verbal abuse is also directed at officers: "People call them black bastards all the time. I hear women standing on the road saying to themselves, 'Look at those black bastards.' But they usually don't talk loud enough for the peelers to hear" (WW). (A "black bastard" in Northern Ireland originally referred to a person biased against Catholics, but the term has been bastardized and is now used to insult police officers. The term is not infrequently directed at the police in Loyalist areas.) In communities where anti-police elements are dominant, the neighborhood culture discourages public articulation of opposing views. I asked what would happen if a person who expressed hatred for the police was challenged by another person:

> They would call you a cop-lover and suspect you of informing on people. You can think what you want but you can't say it—definitely! A pro-police person wouldn't stand up for the police. You don't challenge people here who are anti-police because you'd get a brick through your window or get shot! (WW)

Loyalists' attitudes to the police are not only rooted in everyday experiences and observations of police conduct and neighborhood assessments of the RUC, but are also shaped by notions about what policing is like in Republican neighborhoods. This raises the question of the RUC's perceived impartiality. DUP adherents are somewhat less likely than their UUP counterparts to say that the RUC treats Protestants and Catholics equally (Table 4.3) and much more likely to take the extreme position that the police treat Catholics better than Protestants. At the height of the Anglo-Irish disturbances in 1986, 23 percent of DUP supporters subscribed to this view, declining to 14 percent in 1990 (Table 4.3). A DUP leader, Rev. William McCrea, claims that the police treat Protestant and Catholic suspects similarly, but then cites examples where the police seem to have favored Catholics:

> I can assure you there is no difference whatsoever. The Protestant community feel that some policing leans against them. The police live in mixed or Protestant areas and therefore are more apt to police Protestant areas for minor things. Protestants feel that because the police don't stay in Catholic areas and don't police some Republican functions that the Protestant community is being sat upon, for minor things. Very often Protestants will say to officers, "Why don't you go in and police the Republican area?"

But do the police act impartially?

It depends on how you look at it. Some Republicans may be stopped in their car longer and detained longer, or harassed. But Protestants feel they are sat upon because the RUC are *always in their community*. But there is no evidence of the security forces victimizing any community. They are usually more careful in policing nationalist areas because they feel the NIO would be on their backs [if they aren't careful] and Protestants resent that. The police should police all areas similarly. There should be no place the police don't go.[72]

People do appear to believe that Republican and Loyalist

areas are policed differently, and it is not the case that people [in this Loyalist area] are treated leniently. People will tell you the very opposite. Because police have easy access to [this Loyalist area] and can come in at any time, they believe the police use their full access to prosecute people for things like traffic offenses. We estimate that 75 percent of traffic arrests are made in Protestant areas because police spend so much time there. We see ourselves as being under more police supervision than we should be.

And people resent this?

People resent this and you'll hear people say, "You're doing this to us but not on the Falls." This creates a great deal of animosity. (PP)

The notion that Loyalists are getting the punitive policing that Catholics deserve is a refrain in all of the Loyalist areas I studied:

When the police get tough on Protestant thugs, Protestant women tell police, "Why don't you go do that on the Falls?" . . . Other Protestants ask, "Why are they wasting time in our area when they could be fighting terrorists?" (A)

Because I've lived in a Catholic area—I'm married to a Catholic—I know that police are biased toward Catholics, but most people here [a Loyalist area] wouldn't agree with that. People would think I'm talking shit. They think Catholics are getting off, that the security forces aren't dealing with them heavily enough. They would like police to go into Catholic areas and root out the terrorists. (II)

People in this area say police are afraid to go into Catholic areas and instead spend too much time harassing us. When the police are arresting a drunk, or dealing with a fight in a bar, or giving traffic tickets, people say, "Why don't you go into the Falls area and do that?" They shout at them, "Yous must be too scared to do that in a Catholic area." People give police a lot of hassle like that, they definitely do, all the time. (WW)

In a conversation after the interview, a community resident (not one of my interviewees) confirmed that the admonition "Why don't you go up to the Falls and do that?" is a "usual comment" made in the neighborhood. Asked how the police respond to this, my informant replied, "Normally police wouldn't respond, but once I heard one say, 'I get sick of listening to that all the time'" (WW).

Some people appear to have little concern for the law-abiding people living in Republican areas:

Working-class people still believe that the most fearsome thing is the IRA and that damaging ordinary, innocent Catholics will be a way of getting at the IRA. The damage the police might do to Catholic houses [during searches] in West Belfast, they don't care about this, as long as it helps police destroy the IRA. . . . And they tend to forget about the outrages in the opponents' area, like the Falls Road. It wouldn't be a major tragedy if a bomb killed innocent Catholics; but in a Protestant district, it would be a major tragedy. (VV)

Also telling is an incident involving Protestants who had just committed a robbery:

The police shot and killed one of the robbers. There was a feeling in the community that this was a killing of a good Protestant who should have been arrested and that the police should have been doing this [shooting suspects] in Catholic areas. If that had been a Catholic boy, the police would have been seen as heroes! . . . It's tribalism: it's OK for the police to attack the other tribe but not one of their own. (QQ)

Staunch Loyalists think the police also show an ethnic bias in the way they deal with suspected political offenders, as the next chapter shows.

A number of Loyalists also see bias in the handling of Protestant and Catholic marches, seeing the former as too often restricted and the latter as insufficiently controlled (Table 4.3). Traditional parades of the Orange Order have occasionally (since 1985) been banned or rerouted away from Catholic areas, to prevent the sectarian violence which sometimes accompanies these events. But a banning or rerouting has sometimes resulted in bloody clashes between Orange marchers and the police. Loyalists consider these restrictions a violation of their "traditional rights" meant to appease Catholics, and they see a world of difference between Protestant and Catholic parades, as a DUP leader explained: "What is the Loyalist demonstrating? He is demonstrating his loyalty to law and order and to British rule in this country. What are Republican parades demonstrating? They are demonstrating their support for murder, terrorism, and the overthrow of the state."[73]

What lies behind many of the complaints just described is frustration with liberal reforms in policing, which are antithetical to the traditional style of policing that Loyalists revered. Like dominant ethnic groups in other divided societies, a large section of the Protestant population, especially the Loyalists, believe police reform threatens their traditional supremacy and personal safety. Changes in the direction of more restrained, impartial, and accountable policing have been branded as appeasement of Catholics, criticized for impeding the RUC's capacity to deal with Republican subversion and violence, and castigated for directly or indirectly harming Protestants. Most Loyalist leaders have been careful not to disparage the *principle* of reform and instead focus their sights on the negative consequences of specific procedural and organizational changes. On occasion, however, they have condemned the very principles of liberal policing. For example, in the period after the Anglo-Irish accord, when police clashed with Loyalist demonstrators, a DUP leader complained, "There must come a time when the conscience of each police officer must overrule the brainwashing . . . that professionalism must overrule conscience on every occasion." He lamented the "attitude within the RUC that officers . . . must carry out their task in a professional manner."[74] If police were true to their consciences, they would refrain from acting in defense of unconscionable things, like the Anglo-Irish accord.

What about the question of the composition of the RUC? In the Northern Ireland Social Attitudes Survey, three-quarters of Loyalists say that the most important reason Catholics do not join the force is that they are intimidated by fellow Catholics. It is not only the IRA but also Catholic politicians and priests who are to blame. A DUP leader complained, "They never tell Catholics to join the police, but then they criticize the police for being Protestant. But *they* are the ones preventing people from joining the police!"[75] But do Loyalists actually want to see more Catholics in the RUC? In fact, only one-third of Loyalists think that more Catholic constables would be a good idea (Table 4.3), which puts them closer to the views of their Republican arch-enemies than their moderate Protestant counterparts (the chi-square difference between the DUP and UUP on this question is 22.9, significant at p < .001). Interviews uncovered approval, disapproval, and ambivalence on this issue. Some people "think more Catholic cops would improve relations between Catholics and the police" (II). One informant described some other reasons for this approval as well as a certain uneasiness about contacts with Catholic police:

> A high proportion of the people would like to see more Catholics in the RUC. This is even true for some militants. A fair percentage of staunch Loyalists hold contradictory views; they'd like more Catholics in the police, seeing it as the only way forward, either because they believe this is how it should be or because they are pragmatic. The idea is that "We have to give these things, we can't always be saying no." But for many people, if they knew a cop was Catholic [in a confrontation], it would become an issue; it would be used as a way of getting back at them—the Catholic card. They would say, "You're only picking on us because you're Catholic and we're Protestants." (JJ)

Others are more lukewarm about the idea of more Catholics in the RUC: "Most people wouldn't really care. They might like to see it happen, but they know it won't. The police are still seen as the enemy anyway; so it wouldn't matter if a cop was Catholic, Protestant, or Hindu" (X). And others flatly oppose the idea:

> They wouldn't want more Catholics in the force. There's too much distrust of Catholic officers. They don't trust Catholics, full stop. Because they are Catholics, they are seen as a threat, as a Trojan Horse. . . . It is difficult to tell whether an individual officer is Catholic, but they would be suspicious of a Catholic police officer, absolutely, because they'd see him as spying on their community. (Y)

> [Some Loyalists] see the police as becoming *Catholicized* and being out to get them.

But the RUC is under 10 percent Catholic!

They perceive that it is higher than 10 percent Catholic. A small percentage of Loyalists will believe that the police force has been taken over by nationalists. They feel these police treat them tit for tat [i.e., punitively, because of other Protestants' sectarian crimes]. (T)

At the same time, since the signing of the Anglo-Irish accord in 1985, staunch Loyalist areas have become inhospitable to Protestant constables who live or spend time there. In one community, for example,

people here suspect cops. I wouldn't tell my neighbors that my brother was a policeman and I wouldn't tell them he was visiting. I don't feel safe and he doesn't feel safe when he is here. So many families have had to leave the area when a member became an officer. I know what would happen if I declared I had links to the security forces and trouble later broke out in the area. Stones might be thrown at the house. One person's house was spray-painted "police lover" during the supergrass trials. (OO)

Unlike some other policing issues on which there is considerable agreement among Loyalists, the neighborhood culture of Loyalist areas contains no single, dominant perspective on the RUC's composition. There is room for the view (held by one-third of Loyalists) approving of more Catholic officers, the opposite view despising Catholic constables, and the idea that neither Catholic nor Protestant officers are to be trusted. But the issue of the composition of the force did not figure high among my Loyalist informants' core concerns, perhaps because the RUC is almost entirely Protestant. More important were the concerns that the RUC has become politically compromised, acts with bias against Protestants, and is losing its moral authority.

CONCLUSION

Catholic alienation from the RUC is not as widespread as is commonly thought. The attitudinal data presented above indicate that orientations range from charitable evaluations to unequivocal rejection of the RUC. Confidence in the police among moderate Catholics does not appear, however, to be very deep and is easily shaken by events. Moderates are reluctant to give enthusiastic support to the RUC or to praise it for its accomplishments on the path toward reform. Republicans refuse to accept that any progress has been made by what they consider a repressive, illegitimate political force. They find laughable the notion that the RUC has grown more impartial, politically neutral, or worthy of popular support.

Protestants clearly view the RUC more favorably, although there are important differences between moderates and militants. Moderates' historical identification with and continuing diffuse support for the RUC creates a "halo effect" which, during normal times, blinds them to most allegations of improper police conduct (particularly when made by Catholics) and gives police officers the benefit of the doubt. But this does not mean that they unconditionally support the RUC, since it is vulnerable to "political restrictions" imposed by the British government and now the Irish government as well. Staunch Loyalists' approval of the police has eroded over the past two decades. Many still believe it is wrong to criticize the RUC, which would put them in the company of Catholics, and they express qualified support for the force. But for many others, the RUC's legitimacy is now problematic, its impartiality questionable, its professionalism suspect, and its political orientation has been turned on its head. Their confidence in the RUC is now tempered or absent altogether, and what was once a revered institution defending a Protestant state and population now appears prostituted to the British government in ways that violate Protestant interests. This chapter clearly shows that Protestant approval of the RUC is not as widespread as the conventional wisdom holds.

The views of many Protestants and Catholics reveal a degree of ambivalence about policing, which can be traced to the tension between liberal reforms and surviving aspects of traditional policing. Many moderate Protestants are skeptical about the value of the reforms, and staunch Loyalists believe the reforms either hurt their communities or cripple the RUC's ability to control Catholic unrest and political violence. Moderate Catholics' ambivalence follows an obverse logic. They welcome reforms, but believe they are too often honored in the breach. The police frequently seem to act without regard for the norms of due process, minimum force, and impartiality, and too often commit abuses with impunity. Staunch Republicans agree, but they are convinced that the RUC is incapable of acting as a neutral, professional force in the context of the existing political order.

CHAPTER 5

Dual Policing:
Fighting Crime and Insurgency

Chapter 3 described the uneven development of policing in contemporary Northern Ireland, one of liberalization and militarization. The RUC has made significant progress since the demise of the Protestant state. Officers are better trained, less politicized, more impartial and accountable, and more sensitized to their delicate position in the divided society. But further reform is limited by a number of factors, foremost of which is the RUC's militarization and conspicuous counterinsurgency role. Counterinsurgency policing also interferes with the RUC's other duty, ordinary crime control.

One analyst writes that "police cannot do a satisfactory job at both security and police work," and another declares that there is a "fatal incompatibility" in the two roles.[1] These conclusions may be somewhat exaggerated, given cases where police perform conventional duties and limited security duties well. Rather than simply declaring the two roles "incompatible," we need to examine the consequences where a police force is expected to fight both crime and insurgency. What is clear is that, in Northern Ireland, each role has a distorting effect on the other. Counterinsurgency operations are constrained to some extent by norms of due process, minimum force, and accountability. But the main dynamic is the effect of security demands on ordinary law enforcement.

First, in a context of civil unrest and armed insurgency, precautions taken to enhance officers' safety may detract from conventional police work. The dangerousness of police work in Northern Ireland contributes to an offensive and forbidding patrolling style, a slow or nonexistent response to calls from residents living in troubled communities, and difficulties in proper investigation of crimes in unfriendly neighborhoods. Second, the resources devoted to security policing are highly disproportionate to those earmarked for ordinary policing. According to the chief constable, 80 percent of police time is spent on matters related to insurgency and unrest.[2] As a result, much ordinary crime is neglected. In his annual report for 1982, for instance, the chief constable stated, "As a consequence of the resources of the police being deployed principally to combat [politically motivated] murder and terrorist acts generally, there was an increase in ordinary crime and a fall in the detection rate."[3] Third, media coverage of counterinsurgency operations that go awry or seem excessive helps to tarnish the image of the entire police force and undermine public cooperation with police in the communities most disturbed by the incidents. Disputed killings, brutality during demonstrations and marches, allegations of mistreatment of detainees, and other troubling incidents are publicized frequently enough to fuel serial controversies in the public arena. This adversely affects police efforts to perform their normal duties.

Since security problems are not evenly distributed across Northern Ireland, there is geographical variation in the degree to which counterinsurgency or conventional policing predominates. Many parts of the province are largely unaffected by the political violence, subversive activity, and interethnic discord which are facts of life elsewhere. A semblance of ordinary policing—fighting common crime and dealing with social problems—prevails in the untroubled areas. Brewer and Magee's study of one peaceful Protestant neighborhood in East Belfast highlights similarities to ordinary policing in other societies. Police there typically engage in foot patrols without military backup, and are primarily involved in investigating crimes and providing services to the public. Encounters with members of the public are fairly relaxed; officers are not verbally abused by citizens on the street and do not have to contend with physical attacks from angry residents; and they are much less preoccupied with the threat of deadly strikes by insurgents than their counterparts in violent neighborhoods. However, police working in these relatively untroubled areas still take precautions to limit their vulnerability, and the threat, and occasional reality, of violence remains an important consideration in their daily work. Even here, policing is conditioned by larger security imperatives:

> The fact that police in "soft" areas routinely carry arms, have stations with the look of gulags, and drive reinforced Land

Rovers, has been incorporated into what passes for normal policing in the locale. So too has the sight of police manning vehicle check-points and doing other low-level security work in "soft" areas: this is normal policing Northern Ireland-style.[4]

By conventional standards this is far from "normal" policing, but policing in "soft" areas still contrasts sharply with policing in troubled areas.

In troubled areas, conventional policing is the exception to the rule, if not wholly absent.[5] Policing is largely reduced to order maintenance and internal security, and officers' personal safety is a major concern. Constables routinely are greeted with verbal abuse and pelted with stones; less frequently they are the target of petrol bombs and sniper attacks. The extreme danger and the high-profile security duties place narrow limits on the kinds of interactions police can have with residents. Patrols are typically conducted by a caravan of armored police and military vehicles, which appear menacing and unapproachable to residents. And the dangerousness of police work in these communities also hampers their responses to calls from the public, which are routinely delayed and sometimes nonexistent. Officers are wary of being lured into traps and ambushed, something that has happened often enough to justify their fears.

When police and residents do interact, their encounters are often fraught with tension or mutual hostility. It is an exaggeration to say that police and soldiers engage in "constant and systematic harassment of thousands of people within clearly defined areas," but vexatious police conduct is frequent enough to be a fact of life in some communities.[6] Such conduct is a result of police frustration and anger over the taxing and dangerous conditions under which they work, which includes routinely dealing with belligerent civilians and the constant threat of becoming casualties like so many of their dead and wounded colleagues. Abusive behavior is also very much a function of the unenviable tasks RUC officers are forced to perform. These include the stressful public order duties, such as controlling marches, political funerals, and riots, which sometimes result in confrontations and casualties. Much more frequently, they are involved in stopping, searching, and questioning people on the street and at roadblocks all over the country, encounters that sometimes turn uncivil or physically nasty. (The power to stop, search, and interrogate individuals does not require suspicion or probable cause.) People who travel in both troubled and more peaceful areas report worse treatment in the former, and it is also reported that those who appear to be Catholic (from names and addresses) are more likely recipients of harassment than putative Protestants. Those who previously have been arrested are particularly liable to be stopped and questioned, and perhaps rearrested. The vast majority are Catholic.

Under the Prevention of Terrorism Act a person may be detained after arrest for up to 48 hours, and for an additional five days if authorized by the Secretary of State for Northern Ireland.[7] (The European Court of Human Rights ruled in 1988 that detention for such a long period violated the European Convention on Human Rights, but the British government decided to derogate from the convention rather than alter the law.) Many of the persons arrested and detained are pressured to provide intelligence on their community or to become informers; in fact, many arrests are motivated by this aim, rather than in reaction to specific offenses with a view toward prosecution. From 1978 to 1986 only 13.7 percent of the persons arrested under the Emergency Provisions Act (EPA) were charged with an offense. Under the Prevention of Terrorism Act, 30 percent of those arrested from 1974 to 1989 were charged with an offense.[8] The others were interrogated and released. (In Britain 80 to 90 percent of those arrested under the ordinary criminal law are charged.) A 1980 study found that only 28 percent of those arrested were questioned about a specific offense.[9] Instead, interrogators grilled detainees about their associates, family members, and political sympathies. Since 1973, over 60,000 people have been arrested, interrogated, and released without charge. The cumulative effect of such dubious arrests is the blackening of the RUC's neighborhood reputation in the communities where most of the arrested persons live, that is, Republican communities.

Another major component of the RUC's security role involves house searches for arms, ammunition, and explosives. Warrants are not required, but the EPA requires a senior police officer's determination that reasonable grounds exist to suspect that contraband is present. In Republican areas, early morning raids are frequently conducted on either a specific house or a few houses (previously they did less selective, blanket house-to-house searches). Some of these operations yield illegal material; others produce nothing except property damage.[10] Many searches include partial removal of walls, floorboards, and ceilings. Figures are scarce on the proportion of raids that are successful, but the NIO reports that in 1990 only 5 percent of the army's house searches were "positive."[11] This low success rate suggests that many of the searches are not based on reasonable suspicion, as the law requires. The significance of these operations for the affected communities becomes apparent when we consider their sheer magnitude. The police and army carried out 308,000 house searches between 1971 and 1979 and 22,000 between 1980 and 1988.[12] Though declining, the raids still have a profound alienating effect on the inhabitants, who feel victimized by what they consider vicarious punishment for the deeds of the insurgents in their midst.

Such visible security policing has its covert counterpart, which has grown under British rule. An undercover RUC department, E4, supervised by the Special Branch, is involved in photographic surveillance, planting electronic listening and tracking devices, and phone tapping. Undercover cops are also stationed in observation posts (in unoccupied premises, cars, or attics of houses), where they track movements of "known terrorists" and suspicious persons and feed the information into a central computer, which may then be conveyed to uniformed officers in the area; occasionally their observations are such (e.g., of men carrying guns on the street) that they demand immediate action.[13] Intelligence is also gathered through the infiltration of Republican and Loyalist organizations and constant efforts to turn arrested insurgents, and common criminals, into informers. Occasionally, covert operations go badly awry (e.g., when civilians are killed) or come to light in some other way that raises public concern or provokes a public outcry. But the collective awareness that other, undiscovered undercover activities are ongoing also causes discontent in both Republican and Loyalist communities, as discussed later in the chapter.

Northern Ireland's policing problems are not primarily due to "rotten apples" within the RUC. There are, of course, constables who violate formal norms and act excessively toward civilians, but the problem is much larger. It lies in an institutionalized mode of policing—counterinsurgency policing—that is highly conducive, if left unchecked, to uncivil and abrasive police behavior, use of force against civilians, intrusions on the liberty of persons on the street and at home, and civilian and police casualties. It is so entrenched that a former chief constable was prompted to declare, "We'd have a stupendous job of reorienting the whole force to a community service role. . . . [Each officer] would have to become almost an entirely different sort of policeman."[14]

None of this is to suggest that counterinsurgency policing is intrinsically evil or unjustified. It may be a legitimate response to serious problems of armed insurgency against the state or sectarian violence between ethnic groups, and it may lead to the demise of subversive movements like the neo-Nazis or help to reduce ethnic strife. Yet it also tends to agitate communities on the receiving end, which means that special efforts must be taken to check or limit its harsh effects. Such controls have not been satisfactory in Northern Ireland.

One "positive" dimension of counterinsurgency policing in Northern Ireland deserves mention before we begin to examine its effect on police-community relations. Although the majority of security operations are concentrated in Republican areas, Loyalists are not exempt from such attention. This marks a change from the RUC's traditional bias in favor of Protestants. In the early 1970s Loyalist paramilitary organizations like the Ulster Defense Association (UDA) and Ulster Volunteer Force (UVF) killed a sizeable number of Catholics. The police brought remarkably few of the killers to court. Today, political offenders in the Protestant population are no longer treated leniently by the police. One inquiry concluded that the RUC "has been increasingly even-handed in its efforts to eradicate terrorism" by Republicans and Loyalists alike.[15]

A willingness to pursue Loyalists is suggested in figures on persons charged with murder, attempted murder, and explosives offenses. Although Republicans have been much more heavily involved in insurgent-related offenses than Loyalists,[16] a much higher proportion of Loyalists than Republicans have been charged with these offenses. Table 5.1 reports data for murder, attempted murder, and explosives offenses for 1981 through 1988. The ratios of persons charged per incident for these years show that charges were preferred four times more often against Loyalists than Republicans for murder (1.55:1 and .35:1, respectively), almost five times more often for attempted murder (.82:1 and .17:1, respectively), and almost eight times more often for explosives offenses (1.32:1 and .17:1, respectively). It is possible that more Loyalists than Republicans were actually involved per incident—which would explain some of the difference—but the differential incident-charge ratios remain striking. Other reasons for the incident-charge disparity include the following: the Protestant population is more prepared to give information to the police regarding Loyalist insurgents; the UDA and UVF have been infiltrated by the RUC to a greater degree than the IRA; Loyalists are less likely to hold up under interrogation; Loyalists do not have the option of escape into the Irish Republic; and Loyalists have a reputation for being less proficient than their Republican counterparts in executing their attacks and in concealing material evidence.[17] For these reasons the police have found it easier to pursue Loyalist offenders, and their willingness to do so is a departure from their more tolerant approach during the era of Unionist rule. It is also noteworthy that the "supergrass" tactic— the method used in the early 1980s to prosecute large numbers of persons allegedly involved in insurgent organizations on the basis of (often uncorroborated) testimony of a single informer (supergrass)—was used disproportionately against Loyalists. In ten trials from 1981 to 1983, 217 persons were prosecuted, 44 percent of whom were Loyalists—high, given their much lower involvement in "terrorist" offenses than Republicans.[18]

It should not be surprising, then, that the UDA and UVF now consider the RUC at best an unreliable ally in the fight against Republican terrorism and at worst an enemy, views subscribed to by some other Loyalists not involved in insurgent activities, as shown later in the chapter. We shall also see that, although some Catholics are impressed by robust police actions against Loyalist offenders, many others flatly deny that this occurs or believe that it pales in comparison to the police–state atmosphere in Republican communities.

POPULAR ATTITUDES

A fundamental determinant of the quality of police-community relations in Northern Ireland is the public's evaluation of the RUC's counterinsurgency actions. The data in this chapter show that counterinsurgency policing is evaluated more critically than the RUC's ordinary law enforcement, though sections of both Protestant and Catholic populations are unhappy with the ways

TABLE 5.1
Terrorist Incidents and Charges

	Republican						Loyalist					
	Murder		Attempted Murder		Explosions		Murder		Attempted Murder		Explosions	
	Incidents[a]	Charges[b]	Incidents	Charges	Incidents	Charges	Incidents	Charges	Incidents	Charges	Incidents	Charges
1988	62	10	166	38	208	28	22	13	21	8	7	1
1987	69	8	176	10	164	21	11	20[c]	23	11	0	1
1986	41	5	87	24	117	29	14	7	31	4	1	2
1985	42	17	140	36	162	36	5	7	11	16	1	1
1984	40	36	185	41	189	14	7	5	22	27	3	7
1983	54	23	286	37	178	36	7	52	13	23	6	12

	Republican						Loyalist					
	Murder		Attempted Murder		Explosions		Murder		Murder		Attempted Explosions	
	Incidents[a]	Charges[b]	Incidents	Charges	Incidents	Charges	Incidents	Charges	Incidents	Charges	Incidents	Charges
1982	71	32	401	88	212	31	13	18	12	8	7	10
1981	69	27	461	39	159	36	12	21	26	33	3	3
TOTAL	448	158	1,902	313	1,389	231	92	143	159	130	28	37
RATIOS[d]	.35:1		.17:1		.17:1		1.55:1		.82:1		1.32:1	

[a]Incidents = "known terrorist activity" in the source.
[b]Charges = "persons charged with terrorist offense" in the source.
[c]A higher number of charges than incidents for a year is a reflection of more than one person being charged in some incidents and/or that the charge was made for an offense occuring in a previous year.
[d]Ratio of persons charged per incident for 1981–1988.
SOURCE: Chief Constable, *Annual Report for 1988*, Belfast: Police Authority, 1989.

in which conventional policing is affected by security priorities. Survey data (Table 5.2) show that the RUC's handling of ordinary (nonsectarian) crime is rated fairly high by both Catholics and Protestants, but people draw a distinction between the policing of ordinary and sectarian crime. (Sectarian crimes are those committed by members of one ethnic group against another, motivated not by personal gain but to harm or retaliate against the other group. Part of the larger conflict between Protestants and Catholics, sectarian crime occurs somewhat independently of each side's struggles with agents of the state.) Only a slight majority of Catholics approved of the RUC's record in controlling sectarian crime; 40 percent said they were doing a bad job. And whereas Protestants overwhelmingly applauded the RUC's performance in both areas, they were more critical of the policing of sectarian crime.

A more specific issue is whether the police are impartial when dealing with sectarian attacks on members of opposing communal groups. Chapter 4 presented attitudinal data on this question. Most Protestants think the police try hard to stop Protestant attacks, but a minority of Catholics agree. Protestants and Catholics are in closer agreement regarding police action against Catholic attacks, with large percentages believing the police try hard.

Many Catholics appreciate that the dangers facing the RUC interfere with ordinary police duties, and they accept the need for the police to take certain exceptional measures to protect themselves and fight insurgents. However, less than two-fifths say RUC officers should always carry guns, and four-fifths say the police should need a warrant to search a suspect's house. And large proportions of Catholics believe the security forces too frequently

TABLE 5.2
Attitudes Related to Security Policing by Religion
(% in agreement)

	Protestants	Catholics
Police do a good job in controlling nonsectarian crime (1990)	92	77
Police do a bad job in controlling nonsectarian crime (1990)	6	19

TABLE 5.2 (continued)

	Protestants	Catholics
Police do a good job in controlling sectarian crime (1990)	84	53
Police do a bad job in controlling sectarian crime (1990)	12	40
Vehicle checkpoints are used too much (1990)	8	40
Vehicle checkpoints are used too little (1990)	34	9
Random searches of pedestrians are used too much (1990)	3	41
Random searches of pedestrians are used too little (1990)	32	6
House searches are used too much (1990)	3	35
House searches are used too little (1990)	26	3
Police should always carry guns (1990)	86	37
Police should need a warrant to search a suspect's house (1990)	53	79
Approve use of plastic bullets during riots (1985a)	86	9
Approve increasing undercover intelligence operations (1985b)	90	25
Approve shoot-to-kill action against terrorist suspects (1985b)	61	7
Stories about the RUC beating people in custody are just propaganda (1978)	60	20
Persons who kill police officers should get death penalty (1990)	76	19

SOURCES: 1978 poll: Northern Ireland Attitude Survey, Edward Moxon-Browne, *Nation, Class, and Creed in Northern Ireland* Aldershot: Gower, 1983. (N = 1,277)

1985a poll: Northern Ireland Consumer Panel poll, *Belfast Telegraph*, February 6, 1985. (N = 955)

1985b poll: Ulster Marketing Survey, *BBC Spotlight Report*, British Broadcasting Corporation, May 1985. (N = 1, 008)

1990 poll: *Northern Ireland Social Attitudes Survey.* (N = 324 Catholics, 436 Protestants)

engage in vehicle checkpoints, searches of houses, and random searches of pedestrians. Protestants are at least four times more likely than Catholics to say that these measures are used too little. Large majorities of Catholics also reject the use of plastic bullets during riots, the death penalty for killing a police officer, any increase in undercover intelligence operations, and the so-called "shoot-to-kill" practice where suspected insurgents are shot on sight. Protestants, by contrast, strongly endorse these measures. Attitudes are also polarized with respect to the interrogation of detainees. A majority of Protestants (but only a fifth of Catholics) in 1978 dismissed as "propaganda" reports that suspects were being mistreated in police custody.

Since questions on sensitive issues in Northern Ireland appear to yield results that overstate moderate opinion, it is possible, as Whyte argues, that the extent of polarization between Catholics and Protestants on the issues described above is even greater than the survey findings suggest.[19]

There are also some significant differences *within* each ethnic group. Drawing on the survey data in Table 5.3, my interview data, and some secondary sources, this chapter examines popular opinions and reported experiences of counterinsurgency policing and conventional policing, and the consequences for police relations with our four types of communities.

Moderate Catholics and Staunch Republicans

Sizeable numbers of moderate Catholics express satisfaction with the RUC's performance of its ordinary duties. Eighty percent of SDLP supporters say the RUC does a good job handling ordinary crime (Table 5.3). SDLP leaders echo this assessment: "With regard to mundane crime, the police will try to fulfill their role in as professional a manner as possible. The vast majority try to behave as professional policemen, but all it takes is one bad apple to really spoil a situation."[20] It is counterinsurgency policing that is the source of problems. The SDLP's chief whip insists that "to be acceptable the police must be divorced from a security role."[21] And the party's supporters are more critical of security-related policing than conventional law enforcement. The fact that only one-third of moderate Catholics think the police should always carry guns is surprisingly low given the omnipresent threats and frequent casualties among RUC officers, even when armed. This

TABLE 5.3
Attitudes Related to Security Policing by Political Party Affiliation
(% in agreement)

	SDLP	Sinn Fein	UUP	DUP
Police do a good job in controlling nonsectarian crime	80	43	95	88
Police do a bad job in controlling nonsectarian crime	17	47	1	6
Police do a good job in controlling sectarian crime	57	16	92	72
Police do a bad job in controlling sectarian crime	40	78	5	24
Vehicle checkpoints are used too much	38	80	6	15
Vehicle checkpoints are used too little	9	2	35	41
Random searches of pedestrians are used too much	38	88	2	3
Random searches of pedestrians are used too little	7	0	31	44
House searches are used too much	36	69	2	1
House searches are used too little	4	0	24	37
Police should need a warrant to search a suspect's house	78	95	51	49
Police should always carry guns	33	30	89	94
Persons who kill police officers should get death penalty	15	5	82	79

Note: Figures for Sinn Fein should be treated with caution given the low N.

SOURCE: Northern Ireland Social Attitudes Survey 1990. (N = 143 SDLP, 25 Sinn Fein, 271 UUP, 83 DUP; the last three questions in the table had slightly lower Ns)

low level of support may be a function of a perception that police too often misuse their guns, as evident in attitudes (Table 5.2) on the firing of plastic bullets and shoot-to-kill actions against suspected insurgents.

Still, SDLP supporters are less critical of counterinsurgency policing than Sinn Fein supporters. This is partly a function of class and residential differences: moderates tend to live in middle-class areas that largely escape the RUC's iron fist and are likely to experience more benign policing. According to self-reports, SDLP supporters are much less likely than Sinn Fein supporters to have been stopped by police in the past two years (again, partly a function of residence) and about as likely to be stopped as Protestants. Among those who have been stopped, few report that the police were impolite.[22]

The lower the degree of counterinsurgency policing in a neighborhood, particularly in its most intrusive and disturbing forms, the more positive residents' evaluations of the police should be, holding all else constant. In neighborhoods where security policing is rarely seen, much depends on perceptions of the way in which police handle their ordinary duties. The survey data and some other research on moderate Catholic areas indicate that residents of these communities hold favorable views of the RUC's performance in their neighborhoods, which is confirmed in my interviews.[23] As one informant put it, "People will call police, they come to calls, are very attentive when they come, and give a very unbiased service to people" (NN). Police response to calls is not delayed, unlike in many other parts of Belfast. Because police typify the areas as "soft," "friendly," and relatively "safe," they feel a low sense of threat and treat residents accordingly. Hence, police harassment is rare, as a priest reports: "This place is far removed from those environments where the police are part and parcel of everyday harassment. I travel through Andersonstown [a Republican area] and every road has a roadblock with police interrogating people. You don't have that here and I've never heard a complaint about harassment in my three years here" (KK). In this community,

> Policing is not one of the topics that comes up much in conversation.
>
> *Why isn't it a topic of conversation?*
>
> Because people don't experience policing negatively. The area is totally trouble-free, so it is not at the top of their heads. Over in West Belfast there is perpetual tension and people experience the police negatively all the time. Police are on the doorsteps constantly. Police are involved in ordinary policing here, not counterterrorism. . . . People here can filter out things much more easily if they don't affect them directly. If you are living in West Belfast it's the daily diet, part and parcel of life. It's par-

adise here compared to West Belfast. On the other hand, the excesses have stained the RUC. People living here have a range of opinions—from those who hold the extreme, blanket view that we need the police and should support them to others whose views are tinted by [the RUC's] political coloring, that political decisions affect policing. (KK)

In addition to the policing of ordinary crime in the local area, assessments of the RUC may be based on larger conflicts over counterinsurgency policing, as argued in Chapter 1. The SDLP is almost always involved in these national-level controversies, which helps shape constituents' views. It is true that some people living in peaceful areas have become fairly desensitized to the troubles raging elsewhere in the country. For them, "there is a vague appreciation of what goes on there. . . . The troubles don't impinge on their daily life, so they are fairly removed from issues of policing" (NN). But many others who live in peaceful areas are concerned over reports of incidents elsewhere:

> People are annoyed by excesses. There is a general feeling that we need policing, but the excesses do strike people very deeply. . . . When people read news about incidents in other areas they are affected by that, although some are more affected than others. . . . Middle-class Catholics moved here from other places, many from West Belfast, and they'd be influenced by their memories of those areas. People's attitudes are rooted in their previous experiences; they haven't been insulated from the troubles. (KK)

This is corroborated in a study of a mixed town where "to some extent at least the whole Catholic community [which includes middle-class moderates] was aware and resentful of the difficulties experienced by a section of their community from the security forces."[24] One of my informants states: "There is also cynicism that nothing is really done where policing is really bad. No public apology was made for the events investigated by Stalker and Stevens [see Chapter 6]. People believe that inquiries of such kind will never lead to proper, public justice" (O).

Moderates also worry that overzealous behavior and oppressive practices may have the unintended effect of strengthening support for the IRA. One study found "considerable concern amongst moderate Catholics that the security forces might be solidifying, and even broadening, support for the Republican paramilitaries. . . . "[25] A Catholic priest told me that moderate

Catholics were sensitive to "the bad effects of that sort of thing [aggressive security policing] in the past, when the RUC went into Catholic areas with a vengeance. People know that this is counterproductive; it recruits people for the IRA" (KK).

Not all moderate Catholics live in peaceful middle-class neighborhoods. The closer their proximity to troubled Republican communities or to Loyalist areas, the greater the chances that problems will spill over into the neighborhood and lead to more problems with police. In an enclave surrounded by Protestant neighborhoods, largely moderate but with a few Republicans, policing is not so benign and positive attitudes toward the police are somewhat tempered:

> Police do quite a lot of foot patrols here, unsupported by the military, with only one of their own jeeps [as backup]. Quite often you would see a foot patrol and people will speak to them and quite a number of people would know some officers by name and they wouldn't hurl abuse at them. . . . There are complaints about the opening [and searching] of the back of cars. Street harassment occurs fairly often, and people will complain about it. But we do have a small number of young people involved in paramilitary activity.

People also complain about the occasional house searches:

> If people are innocent it is an unsavory business and it leads to complaints and criticisms. . . . There would be the acceptance that if you are involved in trouble, you are *entitled* to be harassed. If police are searching lads against a wall, and people know the lads are sympathizers or active in the paramilitaries, then up to a point they are entitled to be harassed. But they make a distinction with ordinary people.

> *You mean innocent people don't get harassed here?*

> Harassment may involve the people who are open to [i.e., deserve] harassment, and it is unlikely that innocent people will be harassed. The police are selective here and there is no doubt about it that the police here would know who would be involved [in insurgent activities], actively or passively. (V)

This picture differs significantly from what we find in staunch Republican communities, where people frequently experience and witness abuses resulting from counterinsurgency policing. In Republican areas, counterinsurgency policing is not only evaluated on its own terms but also colors assessments of all other aspects of policing. It helps explain why only 30 percent of Sinn Fein supporters believe the police should always carry guns (Table 5.3) in a context where police are prime targets of insurgents. It amplifies "normal friction" in mundane encounters with the police. And it contaminates perceptions of ordinary law enforcement.

In a society like Northern Ireland, it is not possible for the security forces to act, in areas that harbor insurgents, without inconveniencing the local population. But the police and army also engage in gratuitous abuse of residents in these areas. Republican areas are the locus of fairly frequent, intrusive practices, such as house searches and stopping and searching pedestrians and cars at vehicle checkpoints. The data reported in Table 5.3 show that large majorities of Sinn Fein supporters think the police engage too frequently in these operations; and they are substantially more likely than SDLP supporters to take this view (chi-squares on searches of pedestrians is 21.5, on searches of cars 15.6, both significant at p < .001, and on house searches 10.2, significant at p =.02). The survey data on Sinn Fein supporters are consistent with the findings of two qualitative studies of Republican neighborhoods in West Belfast, where residents were indignant over what they considered rampant street harassment, unwarranted arrests, destructive house searches, and indiscriminate use of force during public order incidents; they also believed the police make deals with common criminals in order to gather intelligence and that they purposely refrain from responding to calls from citizens as a way of punishing the community for its tolerance of Republican insurgents.[26] My informants also lamented the collective punishment meted out to neighborhoods the police typify as "hard-line" or "terrorist-friendly." A clergyman: "The police come in with an aggressive this-is-the-enemy attitude" (A). A city councillor: "When you are stopped here by the cops, you are perceived as the enemy. You can tell by the way they treat you, by how difficult they find it to be relaxed. They perceive you as someone they should *fear*" (U). A priest: "If there is trouble [here], the first thing the police do is to draw a gun. It's their own fear driving them to relate to people in the way they do" (S). In neighborhoods typified as enemy territory, "everyone is a Fenian bastard as far as the police are concerned. You don't have to be a Republican or nationalist to be harassed by police and called a Fenian bastard" (UU). And the mistreatment of individuals appears to have larger neighborhood effects: that is, harassment of some residents is defined as repression of the whole community.[27]

Staunch Republican areas are policed both by regular RUC officers and by Divisional Mobile Support Units (DMSUs). Specializing in riot control but also involved in routine patrolling in troubled neighborhoods, the DMSUs have a reputation for being more combative than other police officers. Informants were very critical of these units, and some surmised that deployment of only regular cops might be less provocative albeit no more acceptable to the community.

Militarized police patrols are a fixture in staunch Republican communities, and almost all of the patrols are connected in some way to the security enterprise. (Because of their preoccupation with security, these patrols play little role in ordinary law enforcement.) My interviewees were critical of this omnipresent "occupation force." Several described their areas as "saturated" with patrols day and night. "The army and police never leave the place," said one informant, and since "they provide no benefit at all to the community," their presence is deemed oppressive (TT).

When asked what people in staunch Republican communities complain most about, my informants unanimously pointed to police harassment. Harassment involves threats against persons or their families, house searches, pressuring individuals to become informers, and, most frequently, the continual stopping and questioning of persons on the street, some of whom are arrested and further interrogated in a police station. In the Northern Ireland Social Attitudes Survey, Sinn Fein supporters were the group most likely to report that they had been stopped by police in the past two years—three times more likely than supporters of the other three parties—and they were most likely to say the police had been impolite or very impolite during these encounters. Several of my informants described degrading public encounters they had witnessed or personally experienced, including searching people in public without apparent cause; interrogating for a lengthy period of time; use of offensive language; forcing people to remove their jackets, shoes, and socks (in a country where it is often raining); aiming a rifle at a person's head while he or she is being questioned; death threats; and physical abuse.

Both adults and youths experience these kinds of harassment. Helsinki Watch interviewed people who reported being frequently hassled by the security forces, and who thought harassment is a deliberate attempt to humiliate and instill fear in people living in Republican communities.[28] A routine experience for politically active people, community workers, and persons suspected of having connections to Sinn Fein, the IRA, or another insurgent organization, street harassment also happens to ordinary residents of neighborhoods typified as "enemy" strongholds:

> If you are a political activist or a community worker, you get special attention. Its just general harassment and it does wear you down. . . . The DMSUs are used here; they give us the most harassment. . . . Ordinary people are also being stopped, but not as often as politically active people. . . . Ordinary people know it's going on, they see it, but they distance themselves from it, until it happens to them. (TT)

> It's actually done to degrade people, a master-servant relationship. Very rarely is it a serious search, with the cops believing you are actually concealing something. . . . They target certain people, community workers and anybody they suspect who has any leanings toward Republicanism. Or if you are a bit cheeky toward officers at one time, they will harass you in the future. . . . Individuals with an activist background seem to get a lot of harassment, but I've also seen ordinary housewives getting the exact same thing. I've seen people getting harassed who aren't Republicans. You can't put it down to anything but pure sectarianism. . . . They are now making people take off their shoes and socks on the street. What can you hide in shoes? (UU)

Individuals who are not politically active, but who have had one encounter with the police, may become candidates for future harassment. A mother reports: "I'm very worried now that my son has come to the attention of the police. It's a pattern I've seen over the years—the police know you and then they keep after you. It happens again and again."[29]

The security forces ask a range of standard questions (name, birthdate, where one is coming from, destination, and knowledge of "terrorist" activities),[30] but interrogations may also include questions having no bearing on law and order:

> They ask about your husband and children, personal questions if they know anything about you. They asked my daughter, "Why did you have a baby out of wedlock?" and "Why weren't you on the pill?" Absolutely improper questions! It's a way of punishing people. (TT)

They stop young girls on their way to school and tell them to open their coats . . . and call them sluts.[31]

Abusive conduct also occurs during house searches:

When they search homes, women are more vulnerable to being degraded. They search drawers and ask questions about their birth control pills, underwear. We hear about this a lot. Police also shout sexual insults at women on the street. . . . (UU)

Harrasment is also discerned in the frequency with which road-blocks are set up in Republican areas—snarling traffic and incon-veniencing travelers—and the specific location of some road-blocks: "If there is a bombing outside [the neighborhood], they will put up roadblocks here; it's useless because the culprits have gotten away. It's a way of harassing the natives" (W). And the obverse: "We can't understand why they put up roadblocks *here* when someone here has been killed [here]" and the killer has evi-dently fled the area (TT). Another form of harassment is to shine police landrovers' spotlights on people and houses at night, leav-ing them on for lengthy periods of time (MM).

Encounters with police on the street and at roadblocks some-times involve physical violence: "For a lot of patrols it's all too easy to knock people around because people can't fight back. It's a power trip" (A). Moreover, harassment sometimes appears to be a deliberate attempt to provoke people to fight back:

It's monotonous to patrol the streets every day. They provoke people to relieve the boredom. . . . They will shout at a girl or a mother, using obscenities to get her man's back up; and then he's easy prey for them. If some nationalist has been killed or shot recently, they will make fun of him to provoke people. The army carries bricks around and they leave them on the road to give people ammunition to throw at landrovers! I've seen this hap-pen. [Respondent gives example]. The cops also do this [act provocatively] but not as often, and they do it more shrewdly. They say, "We'll get you yet" or call us names. (LL)

Some people have grown accustomed to minor forms of harassment as a fact of life in Republican areas, but many recipi-ents leave the encounter embittered and some become more dis-posed to passively accepting insurgent attacks on the security forces or even to joining the IRA. A community worker stressed these effects: "Unless you are stopped and searched on a regular basis, you have no idea how demeaning it is and how bitter people feel about it. This harassment conditions people to condone attacks on the police, people who otherwise might not approve of it" (B). However, even those who have not been stopped and searched may feel the neighborhood effects of harassment, insofar as others' experiences reverberate through the community. Harrassment—whether experienced personally or vicariously—thus becomes decidedly counterproductive.

It is not only the police who act abusively. Some members of the community, particularly young people, act disrespectfully or threateningly toward cops, either in reaction to officers' specific actions or out of general bitterness toward the RUC. More menacing than Skolnick's "symbolic assailants"—persons whose appearance or demeanor is construed by police as a cue to their *potential* dangerousness[32]—are the substantial numbers of real assailants in Republican areas, persons who are overtly confrontational, verbally or physically, to the police. Violent atttacks on police and soldiers are not uncommon, and residents of Republican neighborhoods do not lose much sleep over the IRA's killings of members of the security forces. In Sluka's study of Divis Flats, for example, residents considered attacks on police and soldiers to be "the most acceptable form of offensive action by the guerillas. This is because there is little ambiguity concerning the security forces as the obvious and traditional enemy. . . . Divis residents clearly consider policemen . . . to be acceptable military targets." (Soft IRA supporters, however, were less likely to endorse these attacks than hard supporters, and the latter vary in whether only serving or also retired RUC officers are legitimate targets.)[33] Also significant is the fact that only 5 percent of Sinn Fein supporters favor the death penalty for a person who kills a constable (Table 5.3). Support for attacks on members of the security forces distinguishes Republicans from our other three types; it would not be condoned by moderate Catholics, moderate Protestants, or most staunch Loyalists. From 1969 to 1989, Republicans killed 847 members of the security forces; Loyalists killed only 10.[34]

In addition to lethal assaults on the police, one can observe individuals and small groups in Republican areas acting in a provocative or indignant manner toward police officers. They make a sport out of name-calling, taunting, and spitting at officers and throw stones at foot patrols or police landrovers.[35] Even very young children throw stones and habitually greet the police with jeers like "fuck the peelers." Sluka found that people,

> particularly youths and young adults, often give soldiers and policemen who stop them as hard a time as they can as a form of resistance or protest. They frequently try to not answer the questions put to them. . . . They also sometimes vocally and angrily express their resentment at being stopped. For example, on many occasions I heard people ask, "What gives you the right to stop me on my own street going about my own business?" Once the soldiers or policemen become angry or abusive, or threaten them with arrest or being detained, they generally back off and answer the questions.[36]

Such behavior by citizens helps to explain why RUC officers sometimes act overzealously on the street. Research in the United States has shown that individuals who act in an obdurate or fractious manner toward police officers are more likely to be sanctioned or have their wishes ignored than those who show deference and respect.[37] Officers are inclined to vigorously assert their authority when challenged by civilians.

An inspector in the RUC described to me another way in which officers are "harassed." At roadblocks, people sometimes address the officer by name and ask, "How is your daughter, Mary, doing?" or "Are you still living at [specific address]?" Revealing such intimate knowledge about the officer or his family may be intended as low-level intimidation or to demonstrate that the officer's family has been under surveillance by insurgents.[38]

Some studies of minority neighborhoods in America have found that some residents, in evaluating police performance, take into account the level of community cooperation with the police, which may be limited.[39] They blame some of their neighbors for refusing to assist the police when they are on patrol or conducting criminal investigations. Northern Ireland's Republican communities place the blame squarely on the RUC. Informants laughed at the notion that the police suffer harassment from citizens:

> Ha! They are certainly well protected! We are not sympathetic to that notion that they are harassed. They give us a lot of verbal abuse as well. If they abuse us verbally, it's our right to abuse them. We get stopped seven days a week, three to four times a day, and I've never been arrested for any crime, yet I'm constantly tortured on the street! (TT)

To call that [stone throwing] harassment, against large armored vehicles, that's comical. It's different with adults who are capable of harassing them with petrol bombs. But who has the greater strength? Older people won't normally do such things, because it would be madness; you'd get arrested or shot at. We try to tell younger people not to provoke the police. . . . It's also true that to break the monotony, police will taunt people to provoke an attack. (LL)

People would say it [stone throwing] is justified because of the amount of harassment police give to the locals. This is the only way people can get back at them and anyway it is a *minor* attack on heavily fortified landrovers. It's a way of demonstrating that we don't want them here. Also, stone throwing occurs intermittently, not constantly.

Police also say they get harassed at roadblocks when people ask them personal questions about their families.

This does occur but it would be minimal because most people would know they were asking for trouble; they'd detain you for five hours. You'd be the only one who suffers. Even people who hate the police will be civil toward them at roadblocks. (MM)

Chapter 4 discussed perceptions of police bias in general terms. Staunch Republicans see discrimination as intrinsic to the counterinsurgency enterprise. Sectarian battles at flashpoints are allegedly handled poorly: "The police show bias in dealing with Catholic youths and Protestant youths at flashpoints" (O). Sinn Fein supporters are also twice as likely as SDLP supporters to say that controls on Catholic demonstrations are used too much (Table 4.3), which is understandable since Sinn Fein supporters are more likely to participate in such demonstrations. Permission for marching rights and the RUC's handling of marches are matters Catholics have long felt the police deal with unfairly, proof positive of the RUC's political leanings:

The police would generally favor Unionist, Orange parades over nationalist parades. Definitely, people would see this. The police are very much at fault because they have not been facilitating nationalist marches in the city center [of Belfast]. . . . Police will facilitate Orange marches at any time under any circumstances. Unionists have free reign of this city. (U)

The police have rarely allowed nationalist marches in Belfast's city center and in some other towns, for reasons that have not been disclosed.

Republicans believe that police harassment is either nonexistent or negligible in Protestant areas. The police are simply "much harder on Catholics than Protestants in stopping and searching" people (A). The residents of one neighborhood

> think Protestants are not harassed and raided as much, that they get away with things. Protestants on the Shankill are as harassed as we are here, but people here don't believe it. Nobody would ever believe that the police would saturate an area in the Shankill if a body was found or a shooting occurred. Here they would saturate the place and search every house. They might do the same in a Protestant working-class area, but people would never believe it, because they won't believe anything the police say.
>
> *What if you told them that Protestants were harassed in the same way?*
>
> They simply wouldn't accept it. (W)

Some Republicans acknowledge that Protestants are occasionally mistreated by police, but they are adamant that Catholics suffer the lion's share of abuse:

> People here were very surprised when I told them that kids were harassed by the cops in [a staunch Loyalist area]. I think they believed me but they still thought, and will insist, that harassment here is on a much greater scale. (MM)

> I know that in some Protestant areas some people have just as much hassle on the ground from the police. But in Protestant areas the harassment is aimed at the criminal element; in Catholic areas harassment is aimed at everyone—it is widespread, everyone is suspect, everyone! It certainly doesn't seem to be as widespread in Protestant areas. (LL)

> You can drive down the Shankill Road and you can be sure you won't hit a roadblock. There have been numerous occasions when a Catholic has been murdered and the police come in here and put up roadblocks and don't do anything on the Shankill [the presumed origins of the killers].
>
> *But I've been told by people in the Shankill area that there is also harassment in Loyalist areas.*

I don't believe it! I'd *love* to see it happen on the Shankill the way it does here. I drive up and down the Shankill Road and I've never seen people being stopped and searched there.

I've also been told that the police do house searches in Loyalist areas.

I'd find it difficult to believe that Loyalist homes are raided. Only on a very rare occasion is that going to happen. It's not possible because the RUC works hand in hand with the UVF. That's a known fact. Collusion. (TT)

In fact, counterinsurgency policing in Republican areas *is* more extensive and aggressive than in Loyalist areas. It is readily apparent to anyone who travels through Loyalist and Republican areas that the magnitude of visible security policing (roadblocks, patrolling landrovers) is much more prevalent in Republican neighborhoods, and we know that house searches and less visible security operations have been more frequent in those areas. But Republicans' beliefs that only their neighborhoods experience the dark side of policing are mistaken; these beliefs are shaped by the fact that most Catholics avoid Protestant areas and thus have little or no direct knowledge of policing in those areas. "Catholics say people on the Protestant side just don't know what Catholics have experienced" from the RUC (A), but the policing of Protestant areas is just as invisible to Catholics. However distorted, these perceptions of policing on "the other side" provide the basis for the folk wisdom that the police deal more favorably with "them" than "us."

Abundant police patrols in a neighborhood might be expected to deter sectarian, interethnic shootings by members of the opposing side and violent clashes between Protestants and Catholics in interface areas of adjoining neighborhoods. But staunch Republicans insist that the patrols do not prevent these incidents, and they are generally not impressed with the RUC's record in dealing with sectarian violence. Very few Sinn Fein supporters believe the police are doing a good job in controlling sectarian crime or that they try hard to stop Protestant attacks on Catholics (Tables 5.3 and 4.3). This is because the police are thought to be inherently prejudiced in favor of Protestants. A priest in North Belfast— which holds the record for the highest number of sectarian killings in Ulster[40]—noted that the frequent patrolling in the area makes people wonder how sectarian killers can get away so easily: "The police could close off an area very fast, but it doesn't seem to happen" (O). People conclude from the poor response that police are in cahoots with Loyalist insurgents:

> After a sectarian killing here, there is the regular cry that it must have been organized in conjunction with the police—because the area is intensively patrolled by police. You'll always hear that when gunmen come into the area and are successful in getting away. . . . [Such incidents generate a] resurfacing of a degree of distrust which is fairly deep, which makes it easy for people to believe that the police cooperate with [Loyalist] killers. (S)

> Catholics think the police would cooperate and give information to Protestant groups, information that the police won't be around [a Catholic area] at a certain time. So a gang knows when they can come in and get away without fear of being intercepted. (W)

Other interviewees complained that the police also collude with Loyalist paramilitaries by giving them classified information on suspected Republican subversives, while local constables claim they are powerless to protect the targeted person:

> When you are stopped and questioned, people have in the back of their head that that information may be given to Loyalists. It's routine for the RUC to come to a house and say to a person that their file has gone missing and is probably in the hands of a Loyalist death squad. People are fearful of being on file and being a potential target. (UU)

> It is quite frequent here that an officer comes and tells people their police file has been stolen and he tells the person that the police can't protect him and advises him to put extra security on his home. Where else in the world does that happen? Maybe in South Africa! (TT)

For years there have been allegations about police and military collusion with Loyalist insurgents. A major scandal broke in 1989 after Loyalists gave news organizations copies of secret dossiers on Republican suspects, which they claimed they had received from members of the security forces. A commission of inquiry investigated the matter (see Chapter 6) but it did nothing to alleviate the fears of residents of Republican communities.

Awareness that the police have occasionally acted vigorously against Protestant troublemakers does not translate into an acknowledgement of police impartiality. Even the RUC's vigorous control of Loyalist disturbances in the wake of the Anglo-Irish Agreement had little lasting effect on Republicans' beliefs. A study of a small, mixed border town found that the Catholic inhabitants were not impressed by the robust policing of Protestant protests in the wake of the agreement. Police actions were interpreted as being driven by government pressure on the RUC rather than evidence of genuine impartiality and professionalism within the force. For Catholics the clashes were meaningful not in terms of police liberalization but as confirmation of Protestant political intransigence in the context of the Anglo-Irish accord.[41] One of my informants in Belfast drew a similar picture of her community's views:

> They didn't see the police as being any more neutral, but only noticed the hysteria caused by local politicians over the actions of the RUC. Here, people have clashed with police frequently, so clashes with Protestants wouldn't mean that much. . . . [During the Anglo-Irish disturbances] they just said, "it's about time," and that it was inevitable that it would happen at some point. It was a political decision, not a police decision. (MM)

Asked whether those incidents convinced people that the police had become more impartial, another informant replied, "No! People are deeply suspicious of any such claim. The cops were still a lot more lenient toward Protestant demonstrators; you wouldn't have seen Catholic protestors being allowed to jump on police landrovers, like some Protestants were" (LL).

Republicans do not necessarily want rough treatment to be equally distributed, although some doubtless feel this way. After the Anglo-Irish accord,

> certainly there was an attitude that there was a kind of justice in the police being forced to turn on their Protestant friends. But I didn't hear the argument that, therefore, police were even-handed. There is no way you can accept that just because the police beat up Protestants, they are evenhanded. They must not beat up *anyone*. . . . There was a gut reaction, "It serves 'em bloody right," but also the view that [the clashes] served the *police* right—to have to stand up to Protestants.
>
> *How can you say the police aren't being evenhanded when they treat both Loyalists and Catholics harshly?*

Yes, you're right. But it is not evenhanded in the sense that people want. People want the police to be evenhanded in not beating up anyone. (Z)

With the exception, again, of those who take pleasure in seeing the police clash with Protestants:

During the Anglo-Irish period, people saw Loyalists in armed street fighting with police, and people here said "it's about time."

Were they pleased with it?

They were amused and somewhat relieved, surprised that Loyalists had turned on their own force. People showed a certain amount of gladness; they said, "You deserve it". . . . At the end of the day it was good to see the RUC and Protestants fighting in the streets. People were glad to see Protestants getting a taste of their own medicine. The only benefit of the Anglo-Irish agreement was to see this and to see the police getting battered by their own people. (LL)

The data presented above clearly show that counterinsurgency policing drives a sharp wedge between Republicans and the RUC. Of secondary importance is the way the force handles conventional crimes. Sinn Fein, in contrast to the SDLP, has nothing positive to say about the RUC's performance of its conventional policing duties, in part because the party believes "ordinary policing" is a misnomer since it is driven by sinister interests. However, the party takes a more radical position on this question than some of its supporters. A significant number of Republicans distinguish between security policing and the policing of what people call "ordinary decent crime," and evaluate them differently. Whereas only 16 percent of Sinn Fein supporters say the police do a good job in controlling sectarian crime (one aspect of counterinsurgency policing), 43 percent say they do a good job in controlling ordinary crime (Table 5.3). Still, a large number (47 percent) remain unsatisfied with the police record in this area, and even for those who report satisfaction, this does not necessarily improve their overall impressions of the force.

The chairman of the Police Authority believes that Catholic discontent with the police is less a result of controversial police actions than of inaction: "Some of the anger expressed to us by the community is not a result of police actions, but rather people want more policing; they want more normal policing in their areas and cite difficulties getting police to respond quickly."[42] This characterizes the views of moderate Catholics more than staunch Republicans, although it does apply to some of the latter.

The Northern Ireland Social Attitudes Survey contains a question that illustrates Republicans' reluctance to grant police powers in an unambiguous conventional crime scenario. Respondents were asked whether the police, if they had "an anonymous tip that a man with a long criminal record is planning to break into a warehouse," should be allowed without a warrant to tap his phone, open his mail, detain him overnight, or keep him under surveillance. Republicans were much less likely than any of the other three groups to condone these acts: 35 percent would not allow surveillance; 55 percent, overnight detention; 80 percent, a phone tap; and 80 percent, opening of mail. A spillover effect appears to be operating; that is, for many people general mistrust of police activities (stemming from the security and political roles of the RUC) prevents them from condoning proactive measures against ordinary criminals.

Attitudes about ordinary law enforcement can also be measured by perceptions of how the police respond to calls from the public and the attention they devote to "ordinary decent crime" generally. As a rule, the police do not respond immediately in Republican neighborhoods to calls regarding ordinary crime or other matters unrelated to security or public order, and sometimes they do not respond at all. First they try to ascertain whether the call is genuine or a setup. The response time varies, but there is a widespread feeling among Republicans that it is grossly disproportionate to the risk facing the police. "It's accepted that they must check before rushing to a call," says a priest, "But I do still hear some complaints about the lack of response" (V). Some people are upset with the response; others have come to "accept it as a fact of life" (W). My informants offered the following insights into this matter:

> [The lack of police response] is a complaint by older people, people over 35. Older people ask, "What are police doing about the joyriders, the burglers, and other offenders?" Local people tend to know who is involved in break-ins and joyriding and they wonder why the police don't know who these people are. (RR)

[People want] normal policing, which means the police should investigate ordinary crime, full stop. (W)

Yes, people would like them to come more quickly. They are usually called in by people here only for domestics or accidents or break-ins, to get the insurance claim. Police are not called in for assaults; local people would deal with it. People would complain about the lack of response, especially regarding domestics. Police don't enforce exclusion orders against the men. . . . It took two and a half hours to come out to the last one; you could be dead by then! And this fellow nearly killed her the last time, yet it took police two and a half hours. (MM)

Many people would prefer not to call the police and to sort it out themselves. They call police as a last resort, unless they have to call the police if an insurance claim is involved. But we still hear complaints about the lack of response. (LL)

Informants also contrasted the ways in which police handle ordinary crime and security problems to show that the RUC does have the capacity to deal with common crimes:

Police don't respond at all to [ordinary] calls. If they do come, it will be three or four *days* later! But if there is a bombing or a shooting, they will come in, but they will saturate the area. (W)

The police have no problem saturating the place when it suits them, but when it comes to ordinary crime they ignore it. (LL)

The police don't deal with any common crimes. For instance, battered women; if you ring the RUC they won't come and they'll say it's for security reasons. But they are not worried about their safety when they are knocking down doors and searching places. So there isn't a legitimate concern with the safety of police; it's an excuse for not coming to calls. They *could* deal with domestic disputes and women would like to see them handle this because the law should protect you.

So people want more policing of common crimes?

People are upset that police don't respond to crime incidents. It's a disgrace. (TT)

These data suggest that there is some variation in Republican communities on the question of whether the RUC should do more ordinary law enforcement. A section of the population wants to see this, however much they despise the RUC as an agent of the state and complain about its security practices. One observer found that some people "have broken with the prevailing political culture to demand" ordinary policing.[43] Others are more ambivalent: "Nationalists [here] are still mostly suspicious of the police and only accepting of them with regard to some issues of strict police work. . . . In the more strictly apolitical activities, the police would be accepted reasonably well. But there are always 'buts'" (O). And a third group flatly rejects the RUC's conventional policing, because the force is seen as thoroughly alien and oppressive in all of its activities. But, whatever one's personal preferences about ordinary law enforcement, there are strong neighborhood pressures against actually calling or reporting crimes to the RUC. This is where the paramilitaries enter the picture.

The crime control vacuum in Republican areas is functional for the IRA and Sinn Fein in that it helps to minimize contacts between residents and constables that might pose a threat to these organizations. They are worried that, if more people seek the RUC's help on ordinary matters, it might bring police into the community more often, soften some people's perceptions of the force, and give people more opportunity to report subversive activities to the police. Another concern is the RUC's ongoing efforts to pressure ordinary citizens to assist the police in its counterinsurgency campaign. A Sinn Fein city councillor told me: "When people have called the RUC, at the end of the investigation the police try to recruit them as informers. We would point out to victims, that [if they do call the police] they may risk being pressurized into becoming an informer."[44]

To reduce these threats, Sinn Fein and the IRA strongly discourage people in Republican neighborhoods from reporting crimes to the police, and they have created a system of "popular justice" to replace the official criminal justice system. It is acknowledged that victims must report burglaries and car thefts in order to get reimbursed by their insurance company, but for all other crimes and anti-social behavior, people are expected to call Sinn Fein/IRA, which then investigates and punishes the culprit. As a de facto police force in Republican areas, the IRA routinely dispenses summary justice to those accused of joyriding, burglary, violent crimes, and political offenses such as informing on IRA operatives. Punishment takes the form of an assault with iron bars or sticks, shooting the accused in the knee or elbow, or expulsion from the country. From 1973 to 1991, Republican insurgents administered "punishment shootings" to at least 1,059 persons, and between 1982 and 1991, at least 288 persons received "punishment assaults."[45]

Sluka's study of one Republican community found significant variation in residents' views of the IRA's "policing" role: some strongly supported it; some accepted it but were critical of mistakes and punishments that did not fit the crimes; and others unequivocally rejected this vigilantism. Most people, however, preferred the IRA's policing to the RUC's.[46] This may be true elsewhere, but there is also a feeling that the punishments are too harsh. In one of my neighborhoods, "local people have expected the IRA to act as a policing force here, but when they do, people criticize them for being too extreme in their punishments, like kneecapping" (RR). And a survey of 152 households in a Republican neighborhood in Portadown found that 98 percent of respondents felt kneecapping was wrong.[47]

Republicans are less likely than our other three groups to contact the police for any reason. Only 12 percent of Sinn Fein supporters say they have contacted the police in the last two years,[48] despite the fact that people in Republican communities arguably have more reason to contact the police (because of higher levels of crime and disorder) than the other groups. It appears that the majority in Republican areas refrain from calling the RUC unless they need documentation for an insurance claim. A minority will contact the police "if it isn't a matter directly affecting themselves and if it is quite clearly perceived as being . . . a matter of ordinary crime, and not politically motivated" (RR). And a few are prepared to report insurgent activity, using the confidential telephone number (M). However, frustration with the lack of police response conditions some people, who do not support the IRA and prefer that the RUC handle the matter, to report crimes to the IRA because they expect it to be more successful than the police:

> People have no confidence in the RUC, because they see joyriders every night and nothing is done about it. People who suffer from crime would like to see *anyone* deal with it, but it takes the RUC three hours to come if they come at all. So people will come to Sinn Fein because they think we can deal with it. Sometimes we can, sometimes we can't. (UU)

> [Since Sinn Fein does not have an office in this neighborhood] people use the police initially [for some crimes] and the next day

they call in Sinn Fein to reinforce what the police have done by threatening the culprits with shooting their knees. Nine times out of ten that is a lot more successful than calling the police. (MM)

My informants offered explanations for the RUC's neglect of ordinary crime in their neighborhoods that downplay the police concern with being set up for an ambush. It is thought that the police, by refusing to deal with common crimes, "are punishing people because of the political leanings of the area" (TT). Others reported the following:

People do understand that there have been setups, but it is debatable if the police are using this as an excuse and simply punishing the local community by not responding. . . . They also use these hoods [petty criminals], when they catch them, to get information. They say they will let the kid off and also pay him money if he keeps his eye on someone. Anti-social people in the neighborhood would be useful to the RUC. (LL)

People believe that petty crime is condoned by the police because it keeps people disunited, prevents a sense of solidarity being built up in local areas, and puts family members against each other. . . . They say it suits police to have . . . joyriders in and out of police stations so the police can interrogate them about what is going on in the community. (RR).

It is not in their [the RUC's] interest to control ordinary crime. Joyriders will not be charged if they turn informer. The RUC uses young hoods; they deliberately don't interfere with joyriders, which creates increasing pressure for the IRA to deal with it. Then the criminal element turns against the IRA. It's classic colonial rule, turning people against each other. (UU)

[Pressure to turn informer] happens even to people who go in to pay parking fines. It happens quite a lot if they live in a Republican area. People are taken to a room and told the police will tear up the ticket. There's a never-ending search for informers.[49]

The belief that the police have a vested interest in allowing joyriding and theft because it provides them with a steady supply of informers appears to be widespread in Republican sections of West Belfast. One study reported that residents "believe they live among hundreds of small-time informers who are absolved of petty crime in return for services to the police." Evidence supporting this belief was found in a review of press coverage of "outings," public declarations by young "hoods" that they were pressured by the police to report on Sinn Fein members in return for bribes and the promise that charges against them would be dropped.[50] This is an example par excellence of how counterinsurgency interests can contaminate ordinary policing.

Complaints that conventional policing is inadequate and demands for more of it by no means amount to popular acceptance of the RUC's authority and legitimacy. Some people hold contradictory views—demanding greater ordinary policing but wanting the RUC to withdraw from the neighborhood—while others are ambivalent about dealing with the police on ordinary matters. Portadown's Faith and Justice Group, for example, notes that some of its members and constituents "would resent talking to the RUC even about a road accident although we would phone them if we needed them. We admit that there is an inconsistency here but the uncomfortableness we feel in dealing with the security forces is difficult to describe. It's an awful distrust."[51] It is also possible that *complaints about* the lack of police response are not necessarily tantamount to a *demand for* actual intervention by the RUC. There are two reasons for this. First, people may believe that if they call for more crime control from the police, the heightened police presence in the community will increase the frequency of police abuses and the capacity for surveillance of residents. Second, popular alienation from the RUC may mean that, however much people want crimes dealt with, the RUC is not the preferred candidate for the job. When I asked respondents whether community acceptance of the police would increase if the RUC began to take common crimes seriously, I was told: "Only when you have a united Ireland and we have a different police force" (TT), and "people would like to see police deal with ordinary crime more, but then again they don't like the RUC. They'd like an effective police force, but not the RUC!" (MM). Rejection of this particular police force is therefore not a rejection of policing. And intensification of conventional policing by the RUC would do little or nothing to build confidence in what is perceived as an illegitimate, repressive force propping up an illegitimate state.

Moderate Protestants and Staunch Loyalists

Moderate Protestants tend to live in areas where conventional policing is the norm and there is little security policing. This positively affects attitudes to the police. In one area:

We have normal policing here; police walk on the streets without military backup, just two cops on their own. You rarely see an armored vehicle; the last time I saw one was a year ago. You only see normal police here, no riot police or DMSU. . . . There are no roadblocks around the area. There are fairly good relations between police and people here and most people have a fairly positive view of the police. They think, "If we are good to the police, they'll be good to us." (SS)

This does not mean that residents are entirely happy with policing. They may think ordinary policing is inadequate in their own neighborhood and security policing is deficient elsewhere. It is probably true that "most Protestants would like to see more ordinary policing in their own areas and more security policing in Catholic areas" (VV). Moderate Protestants are strong supporters of the various aspects of counterinsurgency policing, as reflected in Table 5.3. Regarding ordinary policing, some complain about slow responses to calls, want more foot patrols, and think more should be done about vandalism, public drunkenness, and youth gangs. Others think the RUC should not be expected to perform both its security and ordinary roles fully. Although they desire more ordinary policing, "they understand police are busy dealing with terrorists and they excuse a great deal because they understand that terrorism and security has to be the greatest priority" (QQ). Still others seem to want the priorities reversed, being critical of the lax police response to ordinary crime and the degree to which security duties overshadow conventional duties. The police are accused not only of delayed responses but also of not responding at all. A protestant minister described one incident:

An elderly man from our congregation was robbed by two young boys. A police car came along and he flagged it down. He pointed to the boys, who were running, but the police refused to chase them. They said he should just come to the station and make a statement. I [later] took this up with the superintendent and he said he accepted that this could happen. (K)

Frustration over responses to calls is especially pronounced in some moderate Protestant communities adjacent to or surrounded by Catholic neighborhoods. In one such area, "people feel they are inadequately policed":

There are preterrorist activities, like riotous attacks, and internecine warfare [between youth] that aren't being dealt with. The standard response time is half an hour to five hours, even for serious things like petrol bombs, burglary, assault. They treat this Protestant locality as being just as dangerous to them as Catholic areas. Well-disposed Protestants have thus developed the same attitude to the police as you would expect from paramilitary-connected people or paramilitary supporters. [At a public meeting on vandalism a] sergeant said he had checked his ledger and he said there hadn't been many calls for assistance or reports of crimes. People at the meeting responded, "That's because we don't expect police to respond to calls." So people refuse to accept that the police will respond. . . . People here say the police trivialize problems, which in a normal society people would consider unacceptable. A man working at a supermarket, twenty yards from _____ RUC station, was beaten up. It took police *two hours* to respond. . . . Police didn't respond when Protestant youth were throwing stones at black taxis, which they think are Republican taxis, but they aren't. . . . A sergeant dismissed a stone-throwing incident between Protestant and Catholic youths as childish behavior. . . . If there are clashes at flashpoints, the police don't come. When I spoke to police outside the station about a fight nearby and I said, "Why aren't you responding?" they became belligerent and ordered me into the station. I spoke to the sergeant, who again was belligerent and aggressive. He did not note my report in his log book. . . . At the meeting, local people accused police of not logging reports.

Why don't the police respond to these requests?

The excuse the police would give is that they are "busy elsewhere." (R)

The public meeting on vandalism mentioned by this respondent drew around 250 residents of the community. The minutes of the meeting reveal public discontent with underpolicing:

Police need to support the . . . community effectively, as they did in the 1970s. . . . People have lost faith in police responding to incidents. A Neighborhood Watch could be set up to combat vandalism. . . . More police patrols are needed on the ground of the estate—foot patrols which are specific to needs and effective and which restore community confidence. . . . Security forces, Community Relations, and the Housing Executive should be invited to see [the neighborhood] and hear the people. The decision makers must be made accountable and more funds made available. . . . People can use 999 emergency phone to "log" complaints and response time [of police].[52]

The reasons for police inaction are not limited to their assessments of immediate danger but also a function of a more general retrenchment in response to years of dealing with security problems. "Some police become laid-back and don't respond to requests because they have had colleagues killed, which makes them unresponsive," said a Protestant minister. "There is a feeling in the community that the police aren't interested in ordinary crime and that petty crimes are overlooked, because they are preoccupied with security concerns" (K). In other words, the security situation may desensitize officers to ordinary problems even in relatively peaceful areas. This is amplified in less peaceful areas, such as a Protestant enclave surrounded by Catholic neighborhoods:

> Security police who drive around in landrovers . . . ignore or deal insensitively with normal policing incidents, antagonizing people. . . . The top priority of commanders is that they should protect their men and a lessor priority is to police the area. . . . Police in this area have a consistent response throughout the area. They respond in the same way in Protestant and Catholic areas, which means that because they deal with security their response to normal policing is abysmal. (R)

Unlike in Republican areas, the police in moderate Protestant areas are not accused of exploiting petty criminals as informers, nor are they accused of neglecting crime in order to punish the community (these areas do not harbor insurgents). If in these communities police sometimes respond half-heartedly to ordinary crimes, it is largely because they have lost enthusiasm for this kind of work in a context where the RUC as a whole faces such major security problems, even if their actual involvement in counterinsurgency in these communities is limited.

Staunch Loyalists are more critical or more ambivalent about policing than moderate Protestants. As Chapter 4 showed, this ambivalence is manifested in some combination of conditional support for the RUC, suspicion of some of its practices, and worries about the direction the force seems to be headed. Problems in policing are blamed on government interference and on the RUC itself. Loyalists are more critical of the RUC's handling of sectarian crime than moderate Protestants (chi-square is 30.9, significant at p < .001), and they are more dissatisfied with security policing in their own neighborhoods and what they see as the "velvet glove" approach in Republican areas. Generally speaking, the greater the degree of counterinsurgency policing in a Loyalist locality, the greater the discontent of residents, who see it as misdirected against them when the police should be cracking down on Republicans. My interviews indicate that Loyalists' complaints about counterinsurgency measures in their own communities bear some remarkable similarities to Republicans' grievances. One local political leader stated:

> I hate to say this, but at the moment their attitude is hardening toward the RUC because of all the major problems over the years. Shoot-to-kill incidents have happened in Protestant areas, not just Catholic. People are arrested on false evidence. The supergrass system exposed the police as people prepared to go to any lengths to make arrests. People are now questioning the RUC's attitude to Loyalists. (PP)

Some Loyalists are also outraged over harassment.[53] A city councillor hears frequent complaints:

> Yes, believe you me there is harassment. I have had two meetings with officers this week about police harassment [in the neighborhood].

> *But many people don't think harassment is a problem in Protestant areas.*

> It *does* take place in Protestant areas. It's misleading to think this is only happening in Catholic areas.

> *But is it less frequent here than, say, on the Falls Road?*

> Yes. Here it happens and then it stops, usually because community leaders bring it to the attention of senior officers. I'm continually having to meet with the police about this; I meet them at fairly close intervals. This seems to have a positive effect in the short term. (PP)

Why would the police harass people living in staunch Loyalist areas? An informant explained:

> Because people here are suspects, suspected of being linked to paramilitary groups. And if the police don't harass the UDA, they won't please the nationalists. The police are trying to make themselves impartial to both sides. . . . The police have *always*

hammered the Loyalist community. For the past seventeen years, they've been arresting people in the night to get information and then releasing them.

Do Protestants resent this?

A certain part of the community would resent it because they know it goes on. Others, who don't know about it, see the police as legitimate—until they find out about incidents of harassment. (E)

A community worker suggested that many ordinary people do not automatically condemn what some brand harassment; they reserve judgment until they learn the identity of the person on the receiving end: "People would find out who he was and whether he deserved it before passing judgment. On the Falls Road, people would be more likely to denounce it immediately" (Y). "The police know who the paramilitaries are," said another informant. "When something happens, the police lift the same people every time. Some people would be aggrieved at this, but most people would think that if the person has done something, they deserve it" (X).

It is not just insurgents who experience abuse from police. Ordinary people also suffer because derogatory police typifications of these neighborhoods are conducive to indiscriminate treatment of residents:

Police judge people by the place they live; they have a picture in their mind of the type of person living in an area. People living in [this neighborhood] are not to be trusted. They think we have paramilitary sympathies or that members of our families are in the paramilitaries. . . . They categorize everybody [here] as being not worthy of the services they offer, and we don't get value-for-money here. (OO)

Residents of staunch Loyalist areas may also be harassed when they travel outside their communities and encounter roadblocks, because the police treat people from disreputable neighborhoods with suspicion:

A lot of people here have had bad encounters [elsewhere] in Belfast—arrests, being stopped—and now they see the police as absolutely bad. One bad incident can cloud their attitude for the rest of their lives, and this has happened to a lot of people. If you are stopped and you say you are from [here], you may be taken in for questioning.

Why?

[This neighborhood] has a very bad image, very negative. It has always been known as a massive Loyalist estate where everyone is bad. (X)

The level of danger facing police officers is higher in Loyalist than in moderate Protestant areas. In many Loyalist areas, the RUC's standard response to calls from the public is delayed, sometimes for a long time, to minimize the risk of being set up for an ambush, much as it is in Republican areas. People appear somewhat tolerant of this:

Police will not respond quickly to calls and people can understand it, because it can be a trap. You will not get a quick response in this area. . . .

So people aren't upset by this?

Upset would be the wrong word. They used to get upset, but now people's heads are down and they just accept it. (T)

People now take delayed reponses "for granted" and have become "used to it" (II). Acceptance of *delayed* police responses, however, does not mean that people accept *no response*, which informants claim happens occasionally.

A high percentage of DUP supporters are satisfied with the general performance of the RUC in handling ordinary crimes (Table 5.3). But other data suggest that a segment of the Loyalist population believes the RUC's preoccupation with security matters detracts from ordinary policing. A report of a conference of Protestant community workers is unequivocal: "The police are not fulfilling their role in crime prevention and are more interested in anti-terrorist work."[54] My informants were equally blunt:

There are a lot of complaints that the police have become an anti-insurgency force and are not involved in normal law and order. Break-ins and other crimes are not dealt with. (Y)

Yes, absolutely, people would like more ordinary policing. The police are all seen to be doing anti-terrorist activity, not dealing with crime. It's time the RUC got back and did their duty for ordinary shopkeepers and other ordinary people.

But do people complain to you about this or is this just your sense?

Oh yes! Daily I get comments about this. When problems arise people say, "Where's the police, where's the police?" (PP)

They should concentrate on policing, not intelligence gathering and other security work. But police don't want to concentrate on house break-ins and other ordinary crimes. The majority of people say the police are concentrating too much on security. . . . The police should have to provide figures on the hours they spend on ordinary work and security work. We've never seen those figures. . . . Victims of crimes are neglected very, very much. If anyone phoned and said, "There is a gunman in the area," the place would be swamped with cops. But if you call and say, "A person has been mugged," you'd be lucky to see them in an hour. . . . Drinking, drugs, vandalism, joyriding—all of that is swept under the carpet by the police. If people are breaking the law the police should act. It is a big, big problem. (OO)

The tactics of the police are completely connected to the anti-terrorist war. . . . They should demilitarize the RUC and have a greater community-based effort. The emphasis is put on the fight against terrorism and not on the civilian dimension. . . . If there is an escalation of Loyalist anger against the police—like after the Anglo-Irish Agreement—then the police are more justified in taking a security response, but usually we have normal times here, so that response is unjustified. (F)

The overreach of counterinsurgency policing in these locales means that it not only detracts from, but also debases, ordinary law enforcement. For one thing, it adversely affects the demeanor and conduct of the police when they do respond to calls. Although it is appreciated that police cannot become complacent about security risks, the militarized style of patrolling and the formidable appearance and sometimes belligerent behavior of the police are deemed inappropriate in Loyalist areas because people think constables are not in serious danger there:

They treat [the neighborhood] as if it is a nationalist area. . . . Police have been heavy-handed in dealing with normal crimes. They won't use minimum force. The police are not being trained properly, not being disciplined. (F)

Look at the way they carry their weapons and their stance, and the way they approach a situation—you can tell they are not trained to be friendly to the public. . . . No one approves of hooligans throwing rocks and vandalism, but when the police come in to deal with this, they tend to overreact. It's hard for a policeman to come into the [neighborhood] and treat people decently. . . . If you visit [the three local] police stations you will find that the police have developed a blanket aggression toward people in this area.

What do you mean by aggression?

They show no courtesy. Basically they just ask you, "What do you want?" You find it difficult to have a pleasantry spoken to you. Whereas when I go to a police station [in a mixed, middle-class area], you get a very different kind of reception. The police there and in Bangor and other places on the outskirts of Belfast are more helpful and laid-back. You can go in with exactly the same problem, like a lost kid, and get two different responses [in police stations in the different areas]. The security situation has taken a toll on police. . . . Detectives give the impression they don't care. There was a case here of a lady who'd been mugged, whom I helped go to the police, and they asked her, "Why were you carrying money anyway?" and "Where did you get that kind of money?" (OO)

Despite the RUC's preoccupation with insurgency, its record in combatting sectarian crimes between Protestants and Catholics has been rather poor. This is because the counterinsurgency campaign is targeted primarily at anti-state activity and only secondarily at interethnic violence. In communities that are especially vulnerable to sectarian attacks, such as those bordering opposing communities, the lack of police intervention causes great resentment. During the frequent sectarian clashes in one area, the police are "not seen to be there when you actually need them" (C). In another area, where Protestants and Catholics live on opposite sides of the street,

Protestants feel that the police do not defend them in the way they should and, when they cry out for help, police don't always respond as quickly as they should. . . . People [here] say that when they call the police, they don't come, even when there is a riot. . . . These people assume they have a *right* to police protection and investigation of crimes and they are frustrated with the lack of response. (P)

Frustration over inadequate policing causes some people to opt for a form of popular justice, by calling on Loyalist insurgents to deal with anti-social and criminal activity. Emulating their

Republican counterparts, Loyalist insurgents have meted out punitive shootings and assaults, albeit on a lesser scale than in Republican areas.[55] In some neighborhoods, "a lot of people will call the paramilitaries to handle common crimes, or call both the paramilitaries and the police" (Y). And the police have been known to *refer* people to the UDA and UVF to handle problems the police wish to ignore. Examples of this were cited by some of my informants and in a Helsinki Watch report.[56] It was also a matter of concern raised at a conference of Protestant community workers, whose report bluntly states:

> The police appear to have abdicated responsibility for tackling petty crime in some Protestant areas, and have even been known to encourage communities to turn to the paramilitaries to solve such crimes. A very serious consequence follows: the RUC . . . are inadvertently supporting the paramilitaries by allocating the territory of petty crime to paramilitaries, while they, paradoxically, concentrate on anti-terrorist offenses. The police should address the problem of petty crime in Protestant areas.[57]

A community worker pointed to the same paradoxical approach to Loyalist paramilitaries: "They do refer a lot of people to the paramilitaries, and at the same time crack down on paramilitaries. They know that if they don't take action, the paramilitaries will. People are very concerned about this" (OO).

This raises the question of how Loyalists view the RUC's treatment of Loyalist paramilitaries. A much greater proportion of Loyalists than Republicans have been charged with political offenses, as we saw in Table 5.1, and staunch Loyalists interpret this, as well as arrests for purposes of interrogation, as grossly unfair. Naturally these sentiments are strongest among insurgents and their sympathizers. "Loyalists hate the police because they arrest our men," a UDA member laments, "but we're just shooting the guys who are shooting the peelers."[58] And the UDA's magazine, *Ulster*, claims that "there are senior officers in the force who—faced with failure over gaining convictions against the IRA—are now turning on the Loyalist community to bolster their success-rate in convictions."[59] The article criticized the RUC's "double standards," its alleged iron fist approach to Loyalist insurgents and velvet glove treatment of Republicans. Another article in this issue of *Ulster* condemned the "general 'boot-on-the-loyalist-neck' tactics" of the RUC.

The interview data indicate that other Protestants (not just insurgents and their supporters) share the concern that Loyalist insurgents receive unwarranted attention from the police, either harsher treatment than they deserve or harsher treatment than their Republican counterparts:

> In ODC [ordinary decent crime] matters, the police are not very effective, but impartial. In political crime matters, people expect the police to be pro-Unionist or -Loyalist and anti-Republican. They think that there are more Loyalists being picked up [than Republicans] and therefore that the police aren't impartial. People believe that the IRA can get away with anything. (Y)

Another informant stated:

> Police have a higher success rate, conviction rate, against terrorists in Loyalist areas. They come in and investigate more easily in the Shankill. The vast majority of crimes are committed by the Republican movement yet most [sic] arrests are of Loyalists. This poses serious questions about policing. (PP)

The attention police accord Loyalist insurgents can spill over into their encounters with civilians. It is felt that ordinary Protestants are "victimized" or "picked on" by the RUC, when the police should instead be targeting Republican insurgents (C), and that "the Protestants get as bad treatment [as Catholics] from the police at roadblocks, but it is never publicized" (E). One informant reflected on the resentment caused by "misplaced" police zealotry:

> When they observe police overdoing it in handling minor crimes, they have a sense that serious problems are not getting enough attention. When someone says, "Why don't you go catch some real terrorists instead of hassling me?" this reflects a sense that one's innocence is being violated: "I've never done anything wrong and you're bothering me." There is a feeling that the police should be concentrating their efforts on more serious things, what people perceive to be the real problems. (JJ)

There appears to be fairly widespread indignation over unfair police treatment of Loyalist communities, although the resentment felt by ordinary people is naturally of a different order than insurgents'. As one informant explained,

> There is generic resentment among all the Protestant population, who feel . . . that Protestants are not protected and are left to defend ourselves. The general feeling is that the police, UDR,

and [Loyalist] paramilitaries are all involved in fighting the same enemy. Protestants feel they are participating in the same enterprise with the police and wonder, "Why are you picking on us and our paramilitaries?" . . . Loyalist resentment at the police is greatest among people who are involved in political activities—in the UVF, UFF, UDA—or who support them. Here we are fighting on the same side as the police and the police are putting us behind bars! (Y)

The notion that Loyalists living in troubled areas are frequently mistreated by the police is diametrically opposed to Catholics' beliefs that Protestants are largely free of police and army control. "Catholics believe that Loyalist paramilitaries never get raided," a community worker stated. "I told someone [a Catholic] that the police go into Loyalist homes on raids in the early hours of the morning and he was shocked" (Y). As I noted earlier, these asymmetrical perceptions are shaped in part by ignorance—staunch Loyalist and Republican neighborhoods are generally avoided by people of the opposite group—and in part by a refusal to believe that the other side might receive the same medicine from the police as one's own side.

That Loyalists hold rather strong grievances about specific aspects of policing is one of the major findings of this study, something that has been ignored or underplayed in other writings on Northern Ireland. Loyalists' main complaints are that the police have deprioritized ordinary crime; act abusively toward civilians, in part because they have been hardened by their security role; pay too much attention to Loyalist paramilitary groups; and are not satisfactorily fighting insurgency in Catholic areas, where the problem is most serious. The solution offered by Loyalists—reducing counterinsurgency efforts in their communities to free police to intensify their efforts against ordinary criminals there and insurgents in Republican communities—is rejected by RUC chiefs as one-sided sectarianism.

CONCLUSION

Appreciating the dangers facing RUC officers, many people in Northern Ireland do not expect policing to be "normalized" along the lines of the rest of the United Kingdom. They accept that constables must be cautious in responding to calls, that foot patrols often require military support, that police stations must be heavily fortified, and that patrol officers need to use armored land-rovers rather than ordinary police cars. But the findings reported in this chapter also point to important grievances about matters at the very core of policing in Northern Ireland, problems arising out of the RUC's dual roles. Criticism of both of these roles—counterinsurgency and ordinary law enforcement—puts the force in something of a dilemma, which one station commander called a "vicious circle": "If you try to deflect the manpower away from terrorism and toward common crime, you leave yourself open to terrorist incidents. If you concentrate on terrorism, you sacrifice ordinary policing."[60] But popular grievances are not limited to complaints about more or less ordinary or security policing; they also center, more importantly, on the *quality* of each kind of polic-ing. On both sides of the ethnic divide, discontent exists over the following:

- Perceived overzealous and biased counterinsurgency polic-ing in certain neighborhoods, including various forms of street harassment, unwarranted arrests and interrogations, discriminatory handling of marches, destructive house searches, use of informers, and other undercover police operations.
- The contamination, not just dilution, of conventional polic-ing by security priorities.

The intensity and kinds of complaints differ for our four types of communities. Moderate Protestants who voice criticisms of the police—many do not—stress the RUC's unsatisfactory perfor-mance of its ordinary crime control function; their satisfaction with its security role is high, though they want to see it expanded. This reverses the concerns of moderate Catholics, who worry most about security practices that they deem repressive. Staunch Republicans are somewhat ambivalent about the policing of ordi-nary crime. They complain that it is scarce in their neighborhoods and eclipsed by security policing, but their desire for more con-ventional policing is leavened by their suspicion of the RUC. Staunch Loyalists appear to want greater ordinary policing, though some fear that this might give police more opportunities to gather intelligence on Loyalist insurgents.

Both Loyalists and Republicans want counterinsurgency policing intensified in communities on the opposite side and relaxed or scrapped in their own communities. Both are incensed over insensitive and repressive practices in their neighborhoods, although the grievances over, as well as the objective reality of, this kind of policing are much more pronounced in Republican areas. A relaxation of certain offensive practices in both Republican and Loyalist communities, discussed in more depth later in the book, would not be sufficient to generate popular acceptance of the RUC if other factors contributing to estrangement remain constant, but it might help to attenuate one of the sources of poor relations between police and residents of these communities.

CHAPTER 6

Police Accountability

Police accountability can be said to exist when police officers are answerable for their conduct. Institutional mechanisms—in the police force, state agencies, or civil society—can enhance accountability, but what seems necessary is a receptive organizational culture, one that is infused with a spirit of accountability. Unfortunately, many police forces around the world lack this kind of spirit as well as adequate internal and external controls.

In Northern Ireland the problem of accountability came to the fore in the late 1960s during a period of escalating crisis. Since then, several oversight agencies have been created. In assessing the current situation, some scholars highlight the areas in which the RUC appears most unaccountable, dismiss existing controls as cosmetic, and conclude that the police are a "law unto themselves."[1] Others claim that the RUC is more accountable than police forces in other ethnically divided societies.[2] My position is that some genuine and important reforms have been made, helping to check police misconduct, but further changes are required in a context where the police enjoy especially broad powers.

Structures of police accountability are important not only in their own right—in controlling the police—but also in terms of their symbolic value and effects on police-community relations. Under normal conditions, we might expect that the greater the perceived accountability, the greater the level of public confidence in the police. But this is not necessarily the case in divided societies, as this chapter shows. Over the years the evolving system of accountability has generated heated conflicts. New controls have met with resistance from social forces who feared that they would hinder police efforts to fight insurgent groups and contain popular unrest, and they have sparked criticisms from other forces who deemed the changes insufficient. We shall also see that most of the problems of accountability can be traced to counterinsurgency policing, the source of the most serious grievances and formal complaints. Moreover, the most disturbing actions arising out of the security enterprise—assault, use of deadly force—are least likely to be punished.

The chapter begins with a brief discussion of controls that are only occasionally activated from London—from parliament or the executive branch. Analysis of these remote controls is followed by a discussion of three local agencies: the Police Authority, the civilian complaints board, and the office of public prosecutions, which prosecutes officers accused of criminal offenses. Later in the chapter I examine changes in the structure of accountability as a function of popular discontent with the status quo and the implications for police-community relations.

REMOTE CONTROLS

The police in the United Kingdom often insist that they are "accountable to the law" and, as such, directly accountable to parliament. Since the demise of Stormont in 1972, Westminister has been responsible for legislation affecting Northern Ireland, and 17 Ulster MPs (most of whom are Unionists) hold seats there (out of 635). Such a small number obviously means that Ulster's MPs have no leverage over legislation, but parliamentary debates do allow for questioning and criticism of statutory provisions, executive policies, and controversial policing incidents. The practical effect of such debate has been limited to sensitizing ministers to MPs' concerns, which at the end of the day may be ignored. Some MPs have called, without success, for the creation of a standing Parliamentary committee that would be empowered to examine and report on any policing matter, thus expanding legislative oversight over policing.

Westminster has shown little interest in reviewing and tightening legal controls over the RUC, and it has done so only after long periods of popular pressure. Instead, it has leaned toward *empowering* the force, granting it broad powers over the past two decades. There is no question that it is a weak mechanism of accountability.

Prior to the Hunt Committee's inquiry in 1969, the RUC was not regularly evaluated, as are other constabularies in the United Kingdom, by Her Majesty's Inspectorate of Constabulary, attached to the Home Office in London. Now it is. This might be considered a small improvement in the RUC's accountability, were it not for the fact that the inspectors are former chief constables whose investigations have been rather superficial and ineffectual, rarely resulting in serious criticisms.[3] The value of the inspectorate might be enhanced if their reports were published and if civilians were included in the teams conducting site visits and drafting evaluations.

A novel and fairly new check on the RUC is the Anglo-Irish Conference—the regular meetings between representatives of the British and Irish governments created under the 1985 Anglo-Irish Agreement. Policing issues have figured prominently at their meetings, with the Irish side arguing for changes that would reduce abuses and improve police relations with Catholics. The British government claims that the meetings have been partly responsible for: creation of the Independent Commission for Police Complaints; the plan for each UDR patrol to be accompanied by a police officer; a code of conduct for the RUC; police-community liaison committees; and new efforts to recruit Catholics.[4] However, when Unionists have charged that such changes reflect government capitulation to Irish pressures, ministers have insisted that the reforms were on the agenda prior to or independent of consultations with Dublin and would have materialized even without Dublin's encouragement. The government is wary of giving the impression that the RUC is becoming even faintly influenced by, let alone accountable to, a foreign regime. But it is clear that the Anglo-Irish Conference has helped to broaden the system of accountability in a unique way.

Highly controversial incidents or larger problems in security policing have sometimes been investigated by commissions of inquiry. Several commissions were formed during the crisis of 1969–1972, some of which recommended significant changes (Chapter 3). Since then, a number of inquiries have been set up, usually as a result of public clamor. Some have identified significant problems and have helped catalyze reforms. Others have essentially endorsed the status quo, recommending only minor adjustments where serious changes seem necessary. Both of these outcomes are illustrated in the following examination of the most important commissions formed since the late 1970s, each of which dealt with problems caused by counterinsurgency policing.

The treatment of persons in police custody has been a recurrent matter of controversy. In 1971, the Compton Commission reported that "physical ill-treatment" had occurred during police questioning.[5] Subjection of detainees to hooding, noise, threats of violence, and prolonged standing were among the third-degree methods used to extract information or confessions. Some of these practices were abandoned as a result of the commission's report, but complaints about abuses continued. From 1976 to 1979, mistreatment of suspects in police custody was apparently tolerated by police chiefs and top government officials. They had received evidence of brutality from physicians and others,[6] but insisted that detainees' wounds were "self-inflicted" and that allegations of brutality were part of the IRA's propaganda war. Independent investigations found otherwise. In 1978 the European Court of Human Rights ruled that the use of rough interrogation techniques in Ulster constituted "inhuman and degrading punishment,"[7] and Amnesty International concluded that "maltreatment of suspected terrorists by the RUC has taken place with sufficient frequency to warrant the establishment of a public inquiry to investigate it."[8] The government responded by forming the Bennett Commission, which confirmed that injuries had been sustained in police custody that were not self-inflicted.[9] After the implementation of most of the commission's recommendations, including television monitoring of interrogation sessions, allegations of mistreatment in custody diminished considerably, although they have risen in recent years.

For years it has been alleged that the security forces have a "shoot-to-kill" policy with regard to "known terrorists," which means tracking and liquidating them on sight. During the peak of the shoot-to-kill incidents, from 1982 to 1985, 23 persons were shot and killed in covert operations. After each killing, questions were raised as to whether the victim could have been arrested, whether the use of lethal force was necessary in the circumstances, and whether the killings were planned in advance, with the blessing of senior officers.

John Stalker, the deputy chief constable of Manchester, headed an official inquiry into the killings of six unarmed suspects by Special Branch units in 1982. Stalker's lengthy investigation met with stiff resistance from senior Special Branch officers, repeated obstruction from the chief constable of the RUC, and ultimately his own dismissal from the investigation and replacement by another British police officer. Prior to his removal, Stalker had uncovered evidence of a host of serious problems: a

Special Branch "inclination" (if not a policy) to shoot suspects without attempting to make arrests; official coverups of the circumstances surrounding such shootings; insulation of the Special Branch from the rest of the RUC, which made it virtually an unchecked force within a force; questionable use of informants and agents provocateurs; police perjury; dubious surveillance operations across the border in the Irish Republic; mishandling of critical pieces of evidence in cases of police shootings; and poor supervision of the RUC by the Inspectorate of Constabulary.[10]

Stalker was removed before he could complete his final report, but his interim report recommended improvements in each of these areas. The government flatly rejected the conclusion that there had been any shoot-to-kill "inclination" and was cool to his other findings. But it did commission a follow-up investigation of the Special Branch, by Charles McLachlan, a member of the Inspectorate of Constabulary. His report noted that changes already had been made to increase the monitoring of branch officers by local RUC chiefs and to reduce its insulation from other sections of the RUC.[11] It remains unclear if any of Stalker's other recommendations have been acted on, with the exception of his recommendation that eleven officers be criminally prosecuted. In February 1988 the British attorney general stated that national security considerations prevented prosecution of these officers. Instead, twenty constables and sergeants underwent disciplinary proceedings and received light sanctions: eighteen were reprimanded, one cautioned, and one case dismissed. This action, coupled with the controversial firing of Stalker, caused a furor in Northern Ireland at the time and continues to be seen by Catholics as a major coverup.

Another commission, the Stevens inquiry, examined allegations that the RUC and Ulster Defense Regiment (UDR) had colluded with Loyalist insurgents, giving them information on suspected Republican political activists and insurgents. Before discussing the inquiry, some background is necessary. One-page documents on suspicious persons are routinely distributed to the security forces on patrol, at roadblocks, and at border-crossing outposts. They contain photos, names, addresses, car information, telephone numbers, notes on a person's movements, and intelligence assessments like "heavily traced as IRA suspect" or "believed to be high-ranking member of a terrorist organization." Without tight safeguards, intelligence material can fall into the wrong hands, and constables and soldiers who are frustrated with a legal system that requires stronger evidence than they often have to convict "known terrorists" may be tempted to supply classified information to vigilantes with the understanding that it will be used to execute summary justice.

Claims that the security forces have over the years passed sensitive information and classified files to Loyalists are not new; such allegations have been made since the early 1970s,[12] and the RUC has long known about the problem.[13] Though rarely publicized, intelligence documents and information stored in computers have been recovered in searches of the homes of Loyalist paramilitaries, sometimes after the persons identified in the documents had been attacked. Events in 1989 gave further weight to allegations of collusion. Loyalist groups, apparently motivated by a concern to demonstrate that their victims were not innocent civilians, gave the press a stream of documents on Republican suspects. In addition, one RUC officer claimed he was one of three dozen members of a secret police "inner circle" committed to "removing" Republican suspects; he showed 233 documents to a Belfast journalist.[14] A 1992 documentary on British television, "The Committee," interviewed another RUC officer who made identical claims. Loyalist insurgents claim that the majority of their victims appeared on police documents,[15] and were thus legitimate targets, but an independent monitoring group concluded that 90 percent (632) of those killed by Loyalists from 1969 through 1989 were civilians. Of the insurgents killed, only one third (21) were Republicans; two-thirds (40) were fellow Loyalists, killed because of internecine conflicts or because they were thought to be informers.[16]

A scandal broke after the press gave sensational coverage to the leaked documents in 1989. The government responded with the appointment of a commission headed by John Stevens, deputy chief constable of Cambridgeshire. Interviewing almost 2,000 persons (including 213 RUC officers) and analyzing over 2,600 intelligence documents recovered from Loyalists, the commission attempted to trace the origin of each of the seized documents.[17] It concluded that the passing of information from the security forces to Loyalist insurgents "is restricted to a small number of individuals and is neither widespread nor institutionalized."[18] However, since the commission admitted that it was unable to trace "many" documents to the persons who supplied them to Loyalists,[19] the leaks may be more widespread than the commission asserts, though this does not mean that collusion is condoned by the commanding heights of the security forces.[20]

The investigation led to the arrests of 94 persons, 59 of whom were charged and 44 convicted of offenses. Although Loyalists claimed that members of both the RUC and UDR had supplied intelligence dossiers, the Stevens Commission uncovered evidence only against UDR members. It found that screening procedures for UDR recruits were grossly lax; recruiters admitted candidates with partisan prejudices, even if they had already been adversely vetted by the RUC. Unlike police officers, UDR members often live in staunch Loyalist areas, where there are constant opportunities to socialize with insurgents in pubs and elsewhere and pressures to reveal sensitive information about Republicans. The Stevens Commission felt that this should not disqualify recruits from joining the UDR, but "more account should be taken of such pressures" by screening teams and more weight should be given to adverse assessments from the RUC.[21] The commission also recommended tighter control over intelligence documents; today, they no longer leave the station and officers must examine them before going on patrol. The commission felt that such changes might reduce collusion, but that it could not be eradicated. In the years since the Stevens inquiry new allegations have surfaced about police collusion with Loyalist killers of Catholics.

Predictably, the rather tame report (but not the subsequent arrests) was greeted with applause from Protestants, while Catholics complained that it barely scratched the surface.

The fact that commissions of inquiry are rare events does not mean that their contribution to police accountability is necessarily episodic or inconsequential. Their findings and recommendations can have lasting, positive consequences. This was certainly the case for the Hunt and Gardiner commissions—discussed in Chapter 3—but since the late 1970s, commissions have had modest effects on policing (e.g., the Bennett Commission) or no appreciable impact. As for police-community relations, their effects have almost always been the opposite of what the government hoped for in appointing the commissions: far from improving opinions of the police, they have *heightened criticisms* and left the impression that police will not be held accountable for serious crimes, including those resulting in fatalities.

THE POLICE AUTHORITY

Under Unionist rule a highly politicized Ministry of Home Affairs was responsible for the RUC. In 1970 the Police Authority was created to administer the RUC in a more neutral fashion than the Home Affairs Ministry. Members of the Authority are not elected, as two-thirds are in Britain, because elected members might politicize the agency or be in a position to place sectarian demands on the RUC. The secretary of state for Northern Ireland appoints members in accordance with the 1970 Police Act, which stipulates that the membership should be representative of Northern Ireland. That the secretary of state appoints these members may result in a body that is maximally impartial with regard to communal interests, but the members may also be rather conservative and deferential toward the RUC.

The Authority has taken a fairly low profile since its inception, neither publicizing its work nor criticizing the police in public, to avoid bringing the RUC into even more controversy. Nor does it disclose the names of its members, given the dangers of doing so. The IRA considers the Authority "an integral part of the British apparatus of repression, and as such its members can expect no leniency. Anyone who works for the RUC, in whatever capacity, will, once positively identified, be executed."[22] When this threat was issued in June 1986, it specifically mentioned one member of the Police Authority. He resigned a few days later. Two members had been murdered in the 1970s.

The Authority is responsible for administering the RUC's finances, personnel, buildings, and supplies, and it has standing committees that address matters of general policing policies, public order problems, the handling of complaints, and police-community relations.[23] This suggests that the Authority could play an important policy-making role with respect to the handling of demonstrations, marches, and riots; police-community relations problems and programs; use of undercover units; use of weapons; and public complaints. But, until recently, it has devoted most of its time to technical and administrative matters.[24] Controversial incidents have received little attention, and the root causes of recurrent policing problems have not been a major concern.

There are two basic reasons why the Authority's performance as the premier agency of police accountability has been unsatisfactory and why it has thus had difficulty convincing the public that the RUC is truly under control.[25] These are the strong pro-police orientations of members and its limited power, either on paper or in practice, over RUC chiefs. Composed of police-friendly persons from both populations (in 1989 it had eight Catholic and ten Protestant members), the Authority maintains that "Northern Ireland has one of the best police forces in the world."[26] This praise is not merely intended for public consumption but reflects the views of most members. According to a former member,

> The predilection was to not upset the status quo. The Police Authority's orientation was as a sympathetic vote of confidence in the RUC. . . . There was always the view that we had to balance our criticisms of the police with praise. . . . Most members of the Authority would say that we . . . have to trust the police. And they wouldn't believe the police were acting in a partial manner. Members had a great disinclination to believe that the police were acting in a manner that kept the tensions going with the community.[27]

Over the years the Authority has had a few members who were less enamored with the RUC, but they had virtually no influence inside the agency. In the late 1970s, for example, there were several protracted conflicts among members over the handling of allegations of police brutality against detainees, but the conservative majority prevailed.[28] This was reflected in public statements praising the RUC and insisting that instances of police mistreatment of suspects were "relatively few indeed,"[29] a conclusion based largely on assurances from RUC chiefs.

In theory the Police Authority has important powers over the RUC, but in practice these powers seem illusory. On those few occasions when the Authority has pressed for a wider remit or asserted itself against the decisions of the chief constable, it usually has encountered stiff resistance. In 1976 it was denied a request to attend security meetings at the NIO and it was also refused access to files on complaints against officers. In a submission to a task force on complaints, the Authority claimed a right of access to such files under the Police Act and complained that its role in monitoring how complaints were being handled was being thwarted by the RUC.[30] A former member summarized the problems of the 1970s:

> We couldn't get access to files, or a file would be provided but . . . Special Branch officers' names were removed. . . . The

> Authority was circumvented when files went from the RUC to
> the DPP [Director of Public Prosecutions] and back to the
> RUC. . . . We couldn't find out what was in the police code
> regarding the handling of prisoners. . . . We were being muffled
> all the time, running around in circles. . . . We were battling at
> all stages with a legal system that favors the police. . . . The
> Police Authority wasn't able to counter the triumvirate at the
> top—the chief constable, GOC [army commander], and secre-
> tary of state—and they determined policy. The Authority's role
> was reduced to more mundane matters.[31]

Recently, the Authority has clashed with the RUC over another
controversial matter, whether lay visitors (teams conducting spot-
checks of centers where suspects are held for interrogation, to
determine if they are being mistreated) should be allowed access
to persons detained for insurgent offenses. Currently they visit
only persons suspected of ordinary crimes. The Authority wants
both types of detainees visited, but it has been rebuffed by the
RUC.[32]

In recent years, the Police Authority seems to have moved
toward a more visible, vanguard role in policing issues.[33] The current chairman claims that members are increasingly active during
regular meetings with NIO ministers and the secretary of state:
the agency "has become much more forceful over the three years
I've been here. A more challenging debate goes on now." The
same is true for its monthly meetings with the chief constable:

> We use persuasive consultation. We tell him what we believe is
> counterproductive and antagonistic. We have authority to ask
> for explanations for any controversial matters and we exercise
> that authority every month. The chief constable is quite open
> about this. There have been a number of occasions when polic-
> ing policy has changed as a result of our suggesting changes in
> policy. This is not a result of Police Authority action by itself,
> but usually in conjunction with the pressures of others. . . . It's
> not an afternoon cup of tea where people do not speak with full
> force. . . . What we don't do is to make this public.[34]

According to the chairman, the Authority helped to change how
the police handle the funeral processions of slain insurgents; contributed to the drafting of the RUC's 1987 Code of Conduct; and
was the driving force behind the creation of Police-Community
Liaison Committees, which are intended to increase consultation
between police and local populations (see Chapter 7).

These recent accomplishments notwithstanding, the Police Authority retains its strong pro-police orientation, which reduces the chances for trenchant examination of problems and corrective action; and it has rarely been able to prevail over the RUC hierarchy when they resist the Authority's requests. An oversight body actively involved in shaping policies and identifying and addressing ongoing problems can make a real contribution to policing, and this is especially important in divided societies where the police wield extensive powers and are frequently in conflict with members of the public. But in Northern Ireland this would require much more robust action than what we see from the current Police Authority.[35]

THE COMPLAINTS SYSTEM

The way in which citizen complaints are handled is one important measure of the quality of police accountability in a society, bearing in mind that the annual number of complaints lodged against members of a police force is but a fraction of the number of bona fide grievances that might result in formal complaints. Among the standard reasons that aggrieved persons do not file complaints are ignorance of the procedures, belief that complaining will be useless or too time-consuming, and fear of police retribution. Even serious acts of police deviance may not generate formal complaints. The "dark figure" of unreported complaints means that the standard analyses based on reported complaints tell only part of the story.

In Northern Ireland, complainants' religion is not recorded in their files, but the majority of complaints come from Catholics.[36] Approximately one-third of the population, Catholics are therefore disproportionately represented as complainants. Areas with heavy concentrations of staunch Republicans account for a sizeable proportion of all complaints. The RUC records complaints by police division. In 1989, B Division (which includes West Belfast) and N Division (which includes Londonderry) generated one-fifth of all complaints; in 1990 they accounted for almost one-fourth of all complaints.[37] Both areas have high Catholic and Republican populations.

It is likely that the number of complaints coming from Republican areas would be even higher were it not for some countervailing factors. In these areas there is widespread feeling that the complaints system is a farce and that, by complaining, a person risks some kind of police retaliation, such as harassment or a countercharge.[38] Alienation from the RUC and a person's prior unsatisfactory experiences with the police or the complaints system itself also militate against filing complaints.

Persons living in Republican areas often report complaints to Sinn Fein, even if they are not ardent Sinn Fein supporters, and people who complain to community organizations in Republican areas are usually referred to Sinn Fein. The party is experienced in filing compensation claims with the help of sympathetic solicitors and individuals are sometimes urged to bring civil proceedings rather than file complaints with the police, because of the greater chance of winning awards. Both former detainees and ordinary people have been paid handsome sums in court or in out-of-court settlements.

Northern Ireland's unique security and public order problems are reflected in complaints arising out of encounters that consume little police time elsewhere in the United Kingdom. Many complaints result from officers' alleged misconduct during paramilitary street patrols, house searches, vehicle stops, interrogation sessions, demonstrations, marches, and riots. It is counterinsurgency policing, in other words, that causes a high proportion of aggravating encounters with civilians that may culminate in formal complaints. And popular discontent with the complaints system is driven largely by the perception that constables are not accountable for actions related to their counterinsurgency role.

The Complaints Machinery

From 1970 through 1974 the number of complaints in Northern Ireland was much lower (an average of 697 per year) than afterwards (an average of 1,944 for 1975–1979; 2,779 for 1980–1984; 3,532 for 1985–1989). The lower figure for the early period may seem surprising since it registered the highest level of political violence of the past two decades. There are two explanations. First, the absence until 1977 of any body outside the RUC specifically responsible for receiving and handling complaints limited the number of complaints to those lodged at RUC stations. Second, the policy of military primacy from 1970 to 1976 (under which the RUC was essentially replaced by the British army in security and public order duties) greatly reduced the number of police-citizen interactions in troubled communities and hence the number of encounters that could go awry and generate complaints. Once the Police Complaints Board was formed (1977) and the RUC regained responsibility for internal security (1976), the number of complaints rose sharply.

Traditionally, the RUC alone received and adjudicated complaints. Departmental procedures were rather elastic and vested wide discretion in senior officers. This changed somewhat in 1970 when a Complaints and Discipline Branch was formed at RUC Headquarters, which was required under the Police Act to record all complaints and monitor investigations. After 1974 the branch itself began to investigate complaints.[39] The creation of the Police Authority in 1970 introduced a modicum of external review since one of its duties is to monitor trends in complaints.[40] However, the handling of specific complaints remained the sole responsibility of the RUC during the first half of the 1970s.

In other societies, the ethnic group with the most troubled relations with the police typically has taken the lead in demanding civilian review boards.[41] Similarly in Northern Ireland, it was Catholic leaders who pressed for an independent complaints body. Partly in response to this pressure and partly to bring Ulster into conformity with earlier changes in England and Wales, a Police Complaints Board (PCB) was created in June 1977. The board reviewed allegations of disciplinary breaches by officers but had no role in the investigation of complaints and it relied on evidence supplied by the police. All complaints were referred to an investigating officer in the RUC's Complaints and Discipline Branch, who interviewed the complainant, the accused officer, and any witnesses and submitted a report to the deputy chief constable (DCC). The latter decided whether to charge the officer with a disciplinary offense, and then forwarded the file to the PCB for review. The board's involvement did not begin until after the police investigation was completed, and then its main role was to decide—when the DCC declined to charge an accused officer— whether a charge was warranted. If the board disagreed with the DCC's decision not to prefer disciplinary charges, it could recommend or direct that specific charges be made.

Although the board occasionally voiced dissatisfaction with some of the regulations governing its operations, it consistently expressed confidence in the thoroughness of police investigations and rarely saw fit to use its statutory power to insist on charges against accused officers.[42] In well under 1 percent of the cases it reviewed between 1977 and 1987 did it disagree with the DCC and recommend or direct disciplinary charges. This record did little to generate the public confidence in the complaints system that the board itself considered of "prime importance."[43]

Concerned about what the board called "the prevailing critical attitude by the public towards police complaints"[44] and following the creation of a new Police Complaints Authority in England and Wales, the government replaced the board in February 1988 with the Independent Commission for Police Complaints (ICPC). The new body was a symbolic gesture on the part of the government, an attempt to defuse conflict over the existing system rather than truly enhance control over deviant cops, since the authorities had always expressed full confidence in the PCB. Still, the ICPC has powers its predecessor lacked. It (1) must supervise police investigations of all complaints regarding death or serious injury (involving a fracture, deep cut or laceration, damage to internal organ, or impairment of bodily function); (2) may supervise other investigations if the commission deems it in the "public interest" (e.g., questionable use of firearms, pressure on a person to turn informer); (3) examines certain exceptional, controversial matters where no complaint has been made; and (4) reviews the reports of all investigated complaints, on the basis of which it may override the chief constable's decision not to charge an accused officer. If the commission overrides the chief constable and directs that disciplinary charges be brought, the case must then be heard by a tribunal consisting of two commission members and the chief constable.

Like the PCB, the ICPC is constrained by a "double jeopardy" arrangement restricting its jurisdiction over certain kinds of complaints. In cases where a criminal offense may have been committed, the DCC must submit the investigative report to the Director of Public Prosecutions (DPP). Officers whom the latter prosecutes—whether convicted or acquitted—are not subject to being charged by the RUC or ICPC with a disciplinary offense for the same act. If the DPP declines to prosecute, disciplinary charges may be made.

Technically confined to supervising police investigations (on the specific kinds of complaints mentioned above) rather than conducting its own investigations, the commission maintains that its actual role is greater than passive supervision. The chairman claims that commission members "can direct and control" investigations,[45] and the secretary reports that police investigators are in effect "working for" civilian overseers:

> We go to great lengths in supervising the investigations. For example, we sit in on interviews of complainants and some police officers and often tell the IO [investigating officer] what further action to take. It's a workable marriage between civilian supervision and police investigation. We're taking supervision to its utmost parameters.

The commission can also insist that specific questions be asked and that additional witnesses be interviewed: "In one incident recently, where a number of officers were saying something didn't happen, we suspected it had happened and asked the investigator to go back and question them again."[46] The secretary claims that cooperation between commission members and investigating officers is generally high, although there are occasional disagreements over how to weigh evidence and whether more information is needed.

The commission's power to supervise investigations is more extensive than the powers entrusted to most civilian oversight bodies elsewhere in the world, but it has not satisfied a citizenry overwhelmingly favoring independent investigation of complaints (documented later in the chapter). The ICPC does not accept that such a mechanism would serve as a further check on the police or build public confidence in the system.[47] The commission also declines to appoint investigating officers from other United Kingdom police forces to examine serious complaints, although this is frequently done elsewhere in Britain. The reasoning: "Outside investigators would still be policemen. We have confidence in the RUC's Complaints and Discipline Branch. Outside investigators could undermine the morale of RUC officers. . . . As independent civilians, we are deeply involved in the investigation of all serious complaints."[48] In other words, the commission's involvement obviates the need for outside police investigators, who might adversely affect morale and signal a vote of no confidence in the RUC's complaints branch.

The new complaints system differs from its counterpart in England and Wales in two respects. First, it allows for the scrutiny of policing incidents of exceptional gravity for which no formal complaint is made. Incidents in which the police use firearms or engage in other serious actions may generate public controversy and media attention, but not always a specific formal complaint. The ICPC may examine such noncomplaint matters provided they are referred to it by the chief constable, the Police Authority, or the secretary of state. Only four such cases were referred to the commission in its first four years, although several highly controversial incidents occurred without formal complaints. None of the "shoot-to-kill" incidents nor the leaks of intelligence documents from the RUC, which led to the Stalker and Stevens inquiries, were referred to the ICPC. In light of the reluctance of the three authorities to refer noncomplaint matters, the commission has requested discretionary power to supervise investigations of such matters without a referral.[49]

A second difference between Northern Ireland and England/Wales is that the former now allows for examination of complaints by a third party without the written consent of the injured party. After a third party has made the complaint, the injured party is interviewed by an RUC investigator to determine if he or she wants to pursue the complaint. If not, the complaint ordinarily will be dropped. But the ICPC may pursue the case if it is serious and evidence is obtained, although this can be difficult if the injured party refuses to cooperate. In one case, three people complained after witnessing an assault on another person. Although the injured party refused to make a statement to the commission, medical evidence and the testimony of the three witnesses provided the basis for recommending disciplinary charges against two officers.[50]

Outcomes

The RUC publishes statistics on the number of complaints that are registered, investigated, and substantiated annually. Whereas many complaints systems use the "preponderance of evidence" test to substantiate a complaint,[51] Northern Ireland uses a more rigorous standard: the accused officer's guilt must be established beyond a reasonable doubt.[52] An unsubstantiated decision means that police investigators judged the allegations incapable of proving beyond a reasonable doubt—not that they were demonstrably false. Complainants are not informed of the specific reasons their complaint succeeded or failed, since the law prevents the authorities from discussing the details of a case.[53]

Table 6.1 shows that the annual substantiation rates in both Northern Ireland and England/Wales have not been high. For some observers, low substantiation rates spell police coverup, on the assumption that many other complaints *should* have been sustained. This reasoning is perhaps understandable in light of the invisibility of police investigations, but there are important procedural and evidential factors intrinsic to the adjudication process that *commonly* limit substantiation rates. Complaints systems necessarily filter out a proportion of complaints at various stages of the process. Some are dismissed as ineligible at an early stage, and others are withdrawn by complainants. Shaping the outcomes of the remaining, investigated complaints are the following: (1) witnesses and material evidence are often lacking, (2) accused officers typically refuse to admit guilt or otherwise incriminate themselves, and (3) their fellow officers are not forthcoming about what they know. Cases often boil down to the conflicting testimony of a complainant and an accused officer. In these cases, and in those where the evidence is ambiguous, the requirement that the allegations be established beyond a reasonable doubt makes "unsubstantiated" verdicts inevitable.

Notwithstanding the factors that universally militate against substantiation of complaints, significant variations in substantiation rates may be found across jurisdictions,[54] raising questions about the reasons for these different outcomes. Annual substantiation rates in Northern Ireland are consistently and significantly lower than in England and Wales, whether the number of registered complaints or only those investigated (after withdrawals and disqualifications) is used as the base (see Table 6.1). Using the latter, more conservative figure, *the mean substantiation rate in Northern Ireland during the 1980s was about one-third that of England/Wales* (3.2 percent and 8.9 percent, respectively). Perhaps the differential substantiation rates can be explained by something peculiar to Ulster's complainants, the kinds of complaints they make, and/or the official investigation process. Later in the chapter I suggest that Northern Ireland's special circumstances do indeed have a bearing on the kinds of complaints filed and on decisions about complainants' credibility, both of which may lower substantiation rates in comparison to England/Wales.

In Northern Ireland a large proportion of registered complaints are withdrawn every year—approximately 40 percent in

TABLE 6.1
Complaints Against the Police

Northern Ireland[c]

	Withdrawn/Not Proceeded With	Unsubstantiated	Substantiated	Informally Resolved[a]	Substantiation Rate[b]	Total
1981	1,133 (39.4%)	1,636 (56.7%)	108 (3.8%)		6.2%	2,877
1982	1,249 (39.4%)	1,832 (57.8%)	87 (2.7%)		4.5%	3,168
1983	1,183 (43.3%)	1,508 (55.2%)	38 (1.4%)		2.5%	2,729
1984	1,249 (41.0%)	1,753 (57.6%)	43 (1.4%)		2.4%	3,045
1985	1,349 (41.7%)	1,837 (56.8%)	51 (1.6%)		2.7%	3,237
1986	1,474 (43.2%)	1,901 (55.7%)	40 (1.2%)		2.1%	3,415
1987	1,381 (33.8%)	2,676 (65.5%)	26 (0.6%)		1.0%	4,083
1988	1,631 (55.6%)	1,208 (41.2%)	39 (1.3%)	56 (1.9%)	3.1%	2,934
1989	2,404 (60.3%)	1,326 (33.2%)	58 (1.5%)	201 (5.0%)	4.2%	3,989
1990	2,291 (55.5%)	1,590 (38.5%)	61 (1.5%)	190 (4.5%)	3.7%	4,132
Mean	45.3%	51.8%	1.7%	3.8%	3.2%	

	Withdrawn/Not Proceeded With	Unsubstantiated	Substantiated	Informally Resolved[a]	Substantiation Rate[b]	Total
			England and Wales[d]			
1981	15,638 (48.2%)	15,263 (47.0%)	1,542 (4.8%)		9.2%	32,443
1982	14,904 (46.5%)	15,395 (48.0%)	1,787 (5.6%)		10.4%	32,086
1983	14,880 (48.5%)	14,353 (46.8%)	1,448 (4.7%)		9.2%	30,681
1984	13,661 (43.8%)	15,992 (51.2%)	1,561 (5.0%)		8.9%	31,214
1985	13,266 (47.0%)	11,670 (41.3%)	1,155 (4.1%)	2,162 (7.6%)	9.0%	28,253
1986	11,277 (38.7%)	12,734 (43.6%)	1,129 (3.9%)	4,038 (13.8%)	8.1%	29,178
1987	11,410 (40.9%)	10,513 (37.6%)	924 (3.3%)	5,085 (18.2%)	8.1%	27,932
1988[e]	8,823 (40.4%)	7,541 (34.6%)	669 (3.1%)	4,792 (21.9%)	8.2%	21,825
1989	9,301 (41.5%)	6,558 (29.2%)	662 (3.0%)	5,918 (26.4%)	9.2%	22,439
Mean	43.9%	42.1%	4.2%	17.6%	8.9%	

aInformal resolution became an option in Northern Ireland in 1988 and in England and Wales in 1985.
bSubstantiated complaints as a percentage of total complaints investigated (substantiated and unsubstantiated, excluding informally resolved).
cSource: Chief Constable, *Annual Reports*, 1981–1990, Belfast: Police Authority.
dSources: *Report of the Commissioner of Police of the Metropolis*, 1981–1987, and *Report of Her Majesty's Chief Inspector of Constabulary*, 1981–1989, London: Her Majesty's Stationary Office.
eFigures for 1988 and 1989 exclude the London metropolitan police since the commissioner did not include them in the 1988 and 1989 *Reports*.

1981–1987, rising to 57 percent in 1988–1990. Reasons why complainants decide to withdraw complaints include the following: a reluctance to pursue the matter until resolved; intention to express a grievance or to receive an explanation or apology, rather than seek punishment of the offending officer; complainants' intoxication or emotional condition at the time the complaint is lodged; discovery that accused officers are entitled to sue complainants for defamation; and police pressure to withdraw allegations (such as threats to charge the complainant with a criminal offense).[55]

Complaints related to counterinsurgency policing (most of the allegations of assault, harassment, unlawful arrest, improper house search) account for a substantial proportion (over half) of all complaints investigated in Northern Ireland, and it is the failure to substantiate all but a few of these complaints that generates the greatest public concern over the complaints system. Assault is the single largest category of complaint, accounting for around a third of all investigated complaints for 1980–1990. A substantial number of complaints in the 1970s stemmed from allegations of assault and mistreatment during police interrogations. This problem was studied by several commissions of inquiry (mentioned at the beginning of the chapter), which resulted in some improvements in interrogation procedures. The proportion of total assault complaints that come from detainees remains high, however. In 1978, 24 percent of assault complaints were made by persons arrested under the security laws who alleged that an assault occurred during interrogation; from 1986 to 1989 that figure varied from 21 percent to 42 percent.[56] (An additional, smaller number of complaints of assault-during-interrogation come from persons arrested under the ordinary criminal law.) Allegations of assault in settings outside detention centers (on the street, in police landrovers) are also relatively high.

Complaints regarding the most serious offenses, like assault, are less likely to be investigated and, if investigated, substantiated by the RUC than allegations of more minor offenses such as incivility, neglect of duty, and procedural irregularity.[57] A huge proportion of assault complaints are withdrawn and never investigated, roughly twice the number of assault complaints that are investigated and about a third of all complaints filed.[58] Of those assault complaints that are investigated, the mean substantiation rate was 1.9 percent for 1981–1989, half the rate for all other complaints, 3.9 percent.[59] The lower substantiation rate for assault, which is by no means unique to Northern Ireland,[60] may be a function of the higher "cost"—to the officers implicated and to the image of the force—of substantiating the more serious complaints, and the relatively low cost of verifying minor complaints.[61] In a study of two British police forces, Russell found that citizens who made serious complaints were more likely to be discredited by the police and therefore less likely to have their complaints substantiated.[62] The Police Complaints Board in Britain suggested that investigating officers were more inclined to accept the accused officer's account in cases of assault than in cases of corruption or fraud,[63] perhaps because corruption and fraud are more difficult to excuse than assault, which may border on the legitimate use of force.

Also noteworthy is the lack of action on the complaints of individuals arrested under the security laws, many of whom claim they were assaulted during interrogation at holding centers like Castlereagh. From 1988 through 1991 the complaints commission handled 1,329 such cases, of which 1,000 (75 percent) were dismissed because the complainant "failed to cooperate" with the investigating officer; 33 others withdrew their complaints. *All* of the 296 remaining cases "were regarded as unsubstantiated because of insufficient evidence."[64] The commission's annual reports offer no explanation for the large number of complainants who refuse to cooperate nor for the paucity of evidence in these cases, but the secretary told me that most of the complaints involve slaps on the head or punches to the stomach, leaving no visible signs of injury.[65] He also argued that some complainants, when faced with criminal charges, complain as a "countertactical measure," and others file both an assault complaint and a civil suit for damages and then refuse to be interviewed until the outcome of their suit. RUC chiefs make the same claims about countertactical motives and add that detainees' complaints are a propaganda exercise, designed to denigrate the holding centers.

Allegations of police harassment are widespread in black inner-city neighborhoods in the United States and Britain.[66] In Northern Ireland's staunch Republican and Loyalist areas, harassment complaints are also common, although many of them are never formally filed because harassment is seen as a fact of life and because people doubt that such complaints will be sustained. Harassment ranges from petty to more serious actions, usually

TABLE 6.2
Most Frequent Complaints[a]

	Assault			Harassment/Oppressive Conduct[b]			Incivility		
	Substantiated	Not Substantiated	Substantiation Rate (%)	Substantiated	Not Substantiated	Substantiation Rate (%)	Substantiated	Not Substantiated	Substantiation Rate (%)
1978	5	1,026	0.5	NA	NA	NA	1	280	0.4
1979	2	1,016	0.2	0	195	0.0	2	305	0.7
1980	1	994	0.1	0	183	0.0	1	325	0.3
1981	18	519	3.3	3	132	2.2	19	269	6.6
1982	16	662	2.3	2	141	1.4	16	312	4.9
1983	5	480	1.0	2	191	1.0	10	264	3.7
1984	8	577	1.4	1	292	0.3	5	312	1.6
1985	15	655	2.2	1	370	0.3	9	283	3.1
1986	11	639	1.7	7	517	1.3	3	280	1.1
1987	4	1,099	0.4	1	410	0.3	7	428	1.6

	Assault			Harassment/Oppressive Conduct[b]			Incivility		
	Substantiated	Not Substantiated	Substantiation Rate (%)	Substantiated	Not Substantiated	Substantiation Rate (%)	Substantiated	Not Substantiated	Substantiation Rate (%)
1988[c]	9	484	1.8	1	219	0.5	6	197	3.0
1989	16	569	2.7	5	158	3.1	11	280	3.8
1990	18	659	2.7	5	150	3.2	8	297	2.6
Total	128	9,379	1.6	28	2,958	1.1	98	3,832	2.6
Mean	9.9	721.5	1.6	2.2	227.5	1.1	7.5	294.8	2.6

[a]Complaints investigated during each year. Harassment is defined in the text; incivility includes mild verbal abuse and insults.

[b]Figures for 1979–1982 include "threats," which were reported separately for these years, but collapsed into harassment/oppressive conduct for subsequent years.

[c]Informal resolution became an option in 1988 and a number have been resolved in this manner, not included in these figures but included in Table 6.1.

NA = Not available.

SOURCE: Chief Constable, *Annual Reports*, 1978–1990.

repeated over a period of time, and includes unnecessary stops and searches of pedestrians and cars, unwarranted house searches, intimidation and threats, and pressure to become an informer. Proving harassment is extremely difficult. For example, the police may frequently stop and question a person whom they genuinely believe to be involved in or knowledgeable about subversive activities; claims that this constitutes police misconduct are unlikely to succeed. Even when officers have subjected a citizen to unnecessary, oppressive treatment, verification by the RUC's Complaints and Discipline Branch or the ICPC is extremely rare. In fact, complaints alleging harassment and oppressive conduct[67] are the least likely of any to be sustained; only 1 percent were substantiated from 1979 to 1990 (Table 6.2).[68]

The ICPC is responsible for reviewing police investigation reports, after which it may reverse the chief constable's decision on whether an accused officer should be charged with a disciplinary offense. From 1988 through 1991 it examined 8,511 cases, two-thirds of which were withdrawn or dispensed with (because they were anonymous, repetitious, or impossible to investigate). The commission also supervises investigations of complaints involving serious injury or death and those it considers of substantial public interest. Supervised investigations constituted about 8 percent of the total cases received by the commission from 1988 to 1991. The commission notes in its annual reports that it would supervise more cases ("public interest" cases) were it not for its limited resources.

The ICPC's new powers have not increased the number of disciplinary charges or substantiated verdicts. During its first four years (1988–1991) of reviewing case reports and supervising police investigations, the ICPC initiated 56 charges, resulting in 7 substantiations. This is not significantly different from the PCB's record. The substantiation rate for RUC-initiated charges is much higher than the ICPC's: from 1986 through 1991 the RUC initiated 27 charges resulting in 20 convictions. The RUC's higher rate may be a result of treating its own charges more seriously than the commission's and/or because it is more selective, preferring charges against officers only when reasonably satisfied that a violation occurred.[69]

Although there is some debate in the literature on the effectiveness of civilian review boards, their substantiation rates are not as a rule much higher than those of police department boards and may be lower, as we have just seen. A study of 35 American cities found that the mean substantiation rate for external, civilian boards (30 percent) was not very different from the rate for internal, police boards (21 percent).[70] Nevertheless, some civilian boards have trumpeted their "success" in fostering accountability, both by ensuring that deviant cops are punished and by contributing to a climate that discourages future wrongdoing—the notion that police misconduct would be more frequent if no complaints board existed. The ICPC believes it has had success in both areas.

The ICPC also sometimes informs divisional commanders or the chief constable of patterns of complaints.[71] Examples of corrective action taken by the chief constable as a result of these efforts include revised arrest procedures in one RUC Division and circulation to the force of advice on the sensitivity of searching citizens in public places.[72] For the most part, however, the ICPC focuses on the individual complaint, as is true for most other civilian review boards,[73] rather than the larger problems (policies, supervision, training, etc.) giving rise to complaints. The Police Authority, which is mandated to monitor patterns in complaints, also has brought its findings to the attention of senior officers,[74] but this has not been systematic enough to make much difference in police practices. The net effect is that the *root causes* of misconduct receive insufficient attention. In his report on the 1981 riots in Brixton, England, Lord Scarman called for creation of a complaints agency that would address citizens' grievances over general policing problems, and a Home Office study concurred on the need for an agency "capable of exerting some remedial influence on police misconduct beyond the individual case," exposing "systematic defects" in policing.[75] A stronger monitoring and feedback role for the ICPC and Police Authority in Northern Ireland would highlight and perhaps help remedy some of the structural causes of police misconduct. And the capacity of civilian review mechanisms to expose and remedy systemic problems will be enhanced if all complaints (not just substantiated ones) are used as a basis for identifying institutional defects and problem officers who accumulate numerous charges and require closer supervision.

Police Perspectives

The police have abiding interests in keeping complaints low. A high number of complaints may consume police resources (assuming the complaints are investigated), adversely affect officer morale, increase public alienation, and ultimately lead to reforms that "handcuff" officers. Few police forces see complaints in a positive light—useful not only for disciplining or purging deviant cops but also as valuable public feedback that may highlight faulty policies, training, and/or operational styles and, if remedied, help to enhance police professionalism and public acceptability.[76] Instead, police managers are prone to see complaints in an entirely negative light, as an embarrassment to the force. It seems vitally important that police managers recognize that complaints may provide opportunities for self-correction and that an unwillingness to take them seriously may sour police-community relations.

Resisting Outside Intervention.   A standard police argument is that the control and punishment of wayward officers is the proper jurisdiction of senior officers and the courts, not civilian review boards. Police unions and management in many countries have opposed civilian review as encroachment on their professional autonomy; unqualified civilians have no legitimate role to play in this area. Like other police forces, the RUC and its British counterparts have over the years tried to block reforms in this area. In Britain the Police Federation fought the creation of the Police Complaints Board and then urged its members not to cooperate with it.[77] Northern Ireland's Police Federation was no more impressed with the proposal for a similar board in the mid-1970s: "We categorically refute and resent the implied suggestion of partiality where police are involved in investigating complaints of this nature. . . . In the present abnormal situation we consider any change undesirable and indeed unnecessary."[78] Because of their experience and "expertise," police investigators were viewed as "superior to any civilian type investigation."[79] The literature shows, however, that outside investigation can work if the investigators are well trained and command the necessary resources and police cooperation to conduct their inquiries.

The federation argued against the legislation creating the Police Complaints Board on the grounds that it was redundant (the RUC's handling of complaints was already sufficiently reviewed by the Police Authority) and that the existence of a civilian review board "almost encourages malcontents to get police officers suspended from duty by making frivolous and unfounded complaints against them."[80] It was assumed that the board would favor complainants over officers.[81] In fact, the PCB (and the ICPC today), like civilian review boards in Britain and the United States, have ruled overwhelmingly on the side of the police. Once it became clear that the PCB was not the adversary feared, police suspicion subsided,[82] only to be rekindled when a new body was proposed. The federation subsequently tried to block the ICPC's power to examine noncomplaint matters and third-party complaints, on the grounds that these powers were not shared by the complaints board in England and Wales. At Westminster the federation's parliamentary representative branded the proposed commission a "kick in the teeth" of every RUC officer and called the provision for third-party complaints "the ultimate in mischievous busy-bodying."[83] A third party could make a complaint in order "to make a name for himself in the press, to show his community that he is vigorous on their behalf, to pick up any tittle-tattle, or [to exploit] a malicious or frivolous complaint that might have been made in the heat of the moment."[84] (The ICPC later reported that third-party complaints have not been frequent.)[85] The power to investigate noncomplaint matters was offensive, according to the federation, because it might somehow infringe on "the private business of police officers in their own homes" and intrude on their civil liberties.[86] No indication was given of how this power might be abused in this way.

In order to function effectively civilian review boards need to establish credibility with the police, but they are also interested in winning popular confidence. The PCB sought to achieve "that delicate and necessary balance between public confidence and acceptance by the police," and the ICPC positions itself "in the middle, looking after the different interests of the public and the RUC."[87] But it is extremely difficult to gain and retain the confidence of both, as many boards have learned. The history of civilian review shows that a board that leans too far in trying to build credibility with one of these audiences will damage its standing with the other. The question of public confidence in the system is explored later in the chapter. On the police side, the federation initially worried that commission members would interfere with the work of investigating officers and it disliked the idea of members being present during interviews with accused officers.[88] The ICPC has tried to allay these concerns. Similarly, when the federation claimed that many officers were suspended because of pending complaints, the commission showed that this perception was mistaken, that only a handful of suspensions had occurred.[89]

The federation has not suspended its own suspicions of the ICPC, which it views as "not much different" from the previous board:

> We didn't oppose [the commission's] creation but we opposed the increase in its powers. . . . The perception of the new board is that it encourages complaints.

> *Do you think any kind of outside complaints body is needed?*

> I suppose there should be something outside the force to maintain the public confidence. But the commission wants to increase its scope, which we don't like.[90]

At the federation's 1993 convention, the chairman launched a scorching attack on the commission:

> So zealous has the commission been in pursuing its duties that my Federation believes that they are in danger of jeopardizing their credibility with my members beyond recovery. . . . The commission does not understand its own remit. Independent implies impartial, an objective weighing up of evidence. The ICPC must be aloof from political expediency. Collecting the scalps of police officers will not win public confidence because that kind of aggrieved public has an insatiable appetite for police humiliation.

He also complained that the ICPC was trying to hold tribunals against accused officers when investigating officers already had found insufficient grounds to pursue the charge and that the federation was being burdened by legal fees (£20,000 in 1992) in defending accused officers.[91]

After years of fighting any increase in the power of the complaints agency, the federation has recently done a volte face, by supporting the idea of transferring the *investigative* function from the RUC to the ICPC. Why? "The current system is tying up an awful lot of police officers, and involves a lot of hassles with officers investigating officers. Everyone is sick to death of hearing about 'police investigating themselves.'"[92] Support for outside investigations is not, therefore, based on an acknowledgement of deficiencies in departmental investigations or in the ICPC's supervision of those investigations. Instead, it is now being favored for practical and symbolic reasons: because it might free police resources now devoted to investigating complaints, increase public confidence in the system, and silence critics once and for all. And, while independent in certain respects, such bodies remain dependent on the cooperation of the police, in providing complete files and otherwise facilitating investigations. On the other hand, it is fair to assume that the federation realizes that external investigation can be risky: it might increase the "scalping" of officers whom the federation considers innocent.

Whether complaints are investigated by police officers or by an outside agency, accused cops and their colleagues typically comply with investigations in a minimalist fashion. A major British study concluded that "police officers will normally tell lies to prevent another officer from being disciplined or prosecuted, and this is the belief of senior officers who handle complaints and discipline cases."[93] The literature on policing suggests that this is the norm in police forces around the world. Northern Ireland is no exception. In one of its reports, the PCB wondered "whether any attempt is ever made to break" the "remarkable solidarity" among accused RUC officers and their colleagues, a solidarity that militates against convictions.[94] An official inquiry concurred: "The evidence from police officers seems often to consist of short statements to the effect that the allegations are wholly denied (from detective officers who interrogate prisoners) or that nothing untoward was seen or heard (from uniformed officers)."[95] Today, both the secretary and chairman of the ICPC admit that the RUC's nearly seamless blue curtain continues to shield accused officers.[96]

The universal police tendency to close ranks in the face of outside scrutiny is amplified among RUC officers, who feel under constant fire, politically and physically. The complaints system is yet another vehicle through which civilians can "attack" the police and its routine operations may erode officer morale. Morale may suffer even if the number of cases sustained is small, because of the resources devoted to processing registered complaints and the feeling that there are many false accusations. One way to bolster police morale and perhaps win some public sympathy is to cast aspersions on complainants.

Discrediting Complainants. Police investigators routinely include in their reports comments about the credibility of complainants and witnesses. An examination of the complaints files of two British police forces found that police investigators often reported information that seemed designed to denigrate complainants and thereby reduce the chances that complaints would be upheld: the complainant's alleged mental illness, prior record of arrest, prosecution, and conviction, and intoxication at the time of the complaint. None of the complainants with two or more of these stigmata had their complaints sustained, but 40 percent of those with no discredits were successful. And the more serious the complaint, the greater the likelihood of discrediting information being discovered.[97]

The same stigmata may affect outcomes in Northern Ireland, but some unique factors also seem to be present. First is a complainant's real or alleged associations with Loyalist or Republican insurgents. The Bennett Commission found that some reports of investigating officers "go beyond the immediate facts of the case" and "incorporate an assumption that a complaint by a suspect terrorist is unlikely to be genuine."[98] There is also a presumption that persons arrested under the security laws complain as a matter of course, without cause.[99] This helps to explain why their complaints are almost never substantiated.

Persons who are not tied to insurgent groups may nevertheless hold anti-police attitudes, which brings us to the second discredit. Investigators look for any indication that a person has malicious motives and is complaining to malign the RUC or tie up police resources. Not only can this shape case outcomes, but it is also invoked in the public domain to impugn the motives and character of complainants and thereby neutralize criticism. Senior RUC officers have frequently complained about the malicious motives of some, if not most, complainants. Chief Constable Kenneth Newman even drew a connection between complaints and police casualties:

> Allegations of torture and brutality are the spurious "justification" put forward by terrorists for murder of police officers. People who recklessly engage in purveying serious and unproven allegations against the RUC are playing a dangerous game with policemen's lives. It has already proven fatal for some officers.[100]

In fact, there is no evidence that police work in Ulster would be any safer were unfounded complaints to cease. Newman put an even more twisted spin on the problem of complaints when he declared,

"The volume and nature of the allegations should be interpreted not as a worrying indication of police misconduct but as a barometer of growing police success"—that is, success in apprehending political criminals had motivated IRA supporters to manufacture spurious complaints to discredit the RUC.[101] Insofar as these views are shared by other RUC chiefs, who have also criticized complainants' motives, questions may be raised about the extent to which the leadership of the RUC takes complaints seriously.

Rank-and-file officers in other countries typically see complainants as enemies, and this is no less the case in Northern Ireland, judging by the discourse of the Police Federation. Accepting that "genuine complaints" must be investigated, the federation, like its English counterpart, considers most complaints trifling, groundless, or malicious.[102] The federation's chairman put the blame on the government: "It would appear that the Government would prefer to waste police officers' time investigating complaints rather than try to put a stop to frivolous and unfounded complaints."[103] The federation even believes many officers have been unfairly subjected to disciplinary charges where the evidence was thin. It claims that officers charged with assault "suffer the humiliation and indignity of investigation, suspension, and trial on alleged assaults for propaganda purposes. . . . "[104]

The chairman of the Police Authority agrees that malicious motives may account for rises in the number of complaints. Witness his explanation for the increase from 1988 to 1989 in complaints alleging assault:

> It is possible that someone saw an opportunity to attack the police and tie up resources by getting a number of people to make complaints. If they see that someone won a case alleging assault, and got compensation, it might be encouraged. . . . The IRA is organized and could take a decision to make mass complaints.[105]

The 1979 Bennett Commission accepted that some persons deliberately make false accusations in order to tarnish the RUC and tie up police resources, but it concluded that such motives "can scarcely account for the volume of complaints."[106] The secretary of the ICPC is more skeptical of the notion of the malevolent complainant: "I've never seen a malicious complaint. . . . If someone is taking the trouble to make a complaint, they are probably serious." The exception may be prisoners: "A lot of complaints by people in holding centers are dispensed with because the complainant won't cooperate. These complaints are the most likely to be made for tactical reasons."[107] As a way of reducing illegitimate allegations, the commission's two leaflets on the complaints system warn that, since "some people deliberately make false complaints," accused officers are entitled to sue for defamation. A Northern Ireland Office leaflet, *Police and Public*, contains the same warning.[108] In England and Wales the Police Federation fought for this right as a means of defense and as leverage to persuade people to withdraw complaints.[109] RUC members doubtless see it in the same light.

The literature on police accountability recognizes that some complaints are indeed spurious, that people sometimes complain for tactical reasons (if charged with a crime) or out of revenge. (At the same time, many would-be complainants decline to file complaints.) However, the notion that a sizeable number of complainants in Northern Ireland have malicious motives is an *assertion*; neither the RUC, the Police Federation, nor the Police Authority has offered any evidence to support this claim.

This analysis suggests that the RUC has abiding interests in minimizing the number and gravity of complaints that are filed and upheld—to limit damage to the image of the force and to officer morale, the draining of resources in investigations, and the possibility of new reforms that would tighten controls on police conduct. The RUC now reluctantly accepts as inevitable some measure of outside intervention, but it insists that all bona fide complaints are fully investigated and that wayward cops are duly punished. Low substantiation rates (relative to filed complaints) are largely a function of the false claims of disreputable complainants, not a symptom of faulty procedures or police coverup. Further reforms are unwarranted, except to appease public demands for greater external intervention, which may increase popular confidence in the system. The experience of other countries shows that the success or failure of civilian review boards depends largely on their acceptability to police officers at all levels of a force.[110] In Northern Ireland police resentment toward the complaints system has been constant, and the evidence presented above suggests that it is seen in an entirely negative light by the Police Federation and RUC chiefs.

CRIMINAL PROSECUTIONS

Under Unionist rule, decisions regarding the criminal prosecution of police officers rested with the RUC and the attorney general. The RUC's prominent role in decisions of whether to prosecute its own members had obvious shortcomings and resulted in few court cases against officers. The attorney general's role was also problematic. His decisions on whether to prefer charges depended entirely on his assessment of reports of prior investigations carried out by the RUC, and as a member of cabinets that were always Unionist, his decisions may have been influenced by political considerations.

A new office of Director of Public Prosecutions (DPP) was established in 1972, following recommendations of the Hunt Committee and a Working Party on Public Prosecutions. The government hoped that a public prosecutor would "not be open to the same allegations of bias" that were leveled at the previous system of police prosecution.[111] The DPP is responsible for the prosecution of all serious crime including crimes by police officers.

In terms of his primary responsibility of prosecuting civilians, the DPP has helped to ensure that most Protestant and Catholic defendants are treated impartially.[112] The DPP's contribution to police accountability is another question, and there are several reasons why it is less than optimal. First, he relies on police investigators in deciding whether to prefer charges against accused officers, which favors the accused. Second, the DPP is highly dependent on the cooperation of the RUC in the performance of his primary prosecutorial duties; they are essentially on the same side in the adjudication of crimes by civilians. Such close ties may compromise, at least on some occasions, the DPP's willingness to prosecute accused officers.[113] Third, the same evidentiary problems facing RUC investigators and the ICPC affect the DPP's decisions. Witnesses and material evidence are often absent, and the police code of silence for the most part prempts any damaging testimony by colleagues. Fourth, the DPP takes into account the fact that courts rarely convict police officers. He prosecutes only those cases he believes hold a "reasonable prospect" of securing a conviction, prospects that are lower for police than civilians.[114] It is appreciated that police officers enjoy a strong presumption of innocence in court, which means that more evidence is effectively required for prosecutions of police than what is required for civilians.[115]

The "accountability" of the DPP himself is also problematic.[116] He is required under law to "discharge his functions under the direction of the attorney general," who appoints him, and the attorney general can direct that a prosecution not proceed if he concludes that it may threaten "the public interest." The attorney general examines cases of killings by the police before a decision is taken on the propriety of criminal charges. Although he is no longer tied to a Unionist regime (he is a British cabinet member), his views can still be influenced by concerns about possible political fallout from prosecutions of RUC officers, including embarrassment of the government and revelation of unseemly or covert police practices.[117] A case in point involved a controversial decision in the wake of the Stalker inquiry. Stalker had implicated senior officers in obstruction of his inquiry and perversion of justice, and the DPP concurred that there was evidence of such actions. Yet the attorney general prevailed on the DPP not to prosecute on the grounds of the "public interest" and "national security," which prompted allegations of a coverup.[118]

Authorizing few criminal prosecutions of police officers over the years, the DPP has consistently refused to disclose the reasons behind his decisions. When he has declined to prosecute constables, especially for killings, he has been accused of concealing police criminality. One commission of inquiry recommended that he be required to supply more information about his decisions to complainants, the complaints board, and the Police Authority.[119]

When serious cases against police officers have come to court, how has the accused fared? The answer depends on the type of offense. Table 6.2 above reports figures on the annual number of complaints of assault investigated by the RUC. Almost all of these are forwarded to the DPP for a decision on whether prosecution is warranted. Comparing the figures in Tables 6.2 and 6.3, we find that only a tiny fraction of investigated complaints resulted in prosecution in the last half of the 1970s and the last half of the 1980s (data for other years are unavailable). On the other hand, a significant proportion of the cases where officers were charged resulted in guilty pleas or verdicts (Table 6.3). This suggests either that the DPP is correct in prosecuting only those cases of assault with a high likelihood of conviction *or* that if a greater number of cases went to court they might also result in conviction.

A different pattern of prosecution and conviction is evident in figures on the disposition of cases of injury or death resulting

TABLE 6.3
RUC Officers Prosecuted for Assault

	Total charged	Guilty	Acquitted	Pending trial
1974	6	4	2	—
1975	9	5	4	—
1976	7	3	1	3
1977	6	3	—	3
1978	18	6	3	9
1979	17	6	2	9

	Total charged	Guilty plea	Convicted in court	Acquitted	Pending trial
1986	16	1	2	13	—
1987	16	5	4	7	—
1988	12	2	5	5	—
1989	21	10	5	3	3
1990	12	4	3	2	3

SOURCES: Chief Constable, Annual Reports, for 1974–1979 figures; Department of the Director of Public Prosecutions, for 1986–1990 figures, supplied to the author.

from the firing of plastic bullets during public gatherings and disturbances. Of the 182 such cases evaluated by the DPP from 1981 through 1989 (11 of which involved deaths), a prosecution was directed in only 4 cases.[120] None resulted in conviction.

This pattern of low prosecution and conviction rates holds for the total number of killings by police and soldiers (including those resulting from plastic bullets and live ammunition). From 1969 through 1989, 327 people were killed by members of the security forces—about 85 percent by the military. Forty percent of the victims were identified as insurgents (mostly Republicans), and the remainder included civilians and common criminals. Only 21 members of the security forces were prosecuted for these killings, 6 of whom were RUC officers. Nineteen were acquitted; 1 (a policeman) was convicted of manslaughter and given a suspended sentence; and 1 (a soldier) was convicted of murder and given a mandatory life sentence (he was inexplicably released after three years and reinstated in the army). In most of these cases, the court accepted the accused's claim that he thought the victim was armed and ready to shoot, although in several cases no guns were found at the scene.

The low prosecution and conviction rates in cases of injury or death from plastic bullets and killings in general may be explained by one or more of the following factors: the *prima facie* legality of some of the actions, particularly where insurgents were armed; a strong presumption of innocence in cases involving members of the security forces; collusion between the accused and colleagues present at the scene, who corroborate the accused's version of events; and insufficient evidence. Two other factors serve to keep convictions low in cases of fatalities. First, the law permits use of force if "reasonable in the circumstances."[121] The reasonableness standard, as applied in cases of lethal force, has led courts to find most killings by the police and army justifiable. It is likely that a higher standard, that of *absolute necessity* to protect life, would result in higher conviction rates and might help to reduce the number of incidents resulting in fatalities.[122] Second, the law allows members of the security forces who have killed in the line of duty to be charged only with murder, not manslaughter or excessive use of lethal force. Certainly there are incidents in which intent to murder is not present, but the shooters acted with reckless disregard for life or made a serious error of judgment. Prosecution and conviction rates in cases of fatal shootings would arguably increase if the DPP was able to charge officers with these lesser offenses.[123]

What is most important for our purposes is the cumulative effect of these low prosecution and conviction rates on popular confidence in the system of accountability. The virtual impossibility of a conviction is cited as proof positive, particularly by Catholics, that the police are free to injure and kill civilians with impunity.

DISCONTENT WITH THE SYSTEM

The problem of police accountability in Northern Ireland is important not just in terms of the adequacy of control over the police but also in terms of its effect on police-community relations. Under normal conditions, the greater the perceived accountability, the greater the public's acceptance of the police.[124]

But in divided societies, communal divisions may mean that reforms in the direction of enhanced accountability are not universally appreciated, and may instead have a differential effect on each communal group. Dominant groups may believe the police are already sufficiently controlled or that the constraints are too tight. New controls may be defined as sheer appeasement of the subordinate group, not justified in their own right. And the subordinate group may not endorse the reforms introduced, even those they previously demanded. Insofar as other important aspects of policing remain contentious, expansion of the system of accountability may be insufficient to bolster confidence in the police. Moreover, new controls can intensify struggles over accountability, rather than defuse them.

The problem of police accountability has generated bitter conflicts in Northern Ireland since the troubles began in the late 1960s, and oversight agencies continue to grapple with the problem of public skepticism and criticism. Recognizing that their own satisfaction with the handling of complaints is not shared by the public, officials invoke the old adage that "justice must not only be done, but must also be seen to be done." The PCB lamented "the prevailing critical attitude by the public toward police complaints,"[125] and the ICPC, whose powers are greater than the PCB, was created expressly to alleviate public concerns that police investigators were covering up for accused cops. Yet its symbolic value in this regard is undermined if few people know the body exists. The commission's secretary surmised that "the man on the street probably doesn't know we exist."[126] Even some community workers I interviewed expressed surprise when told about the commission.

When asked what the commission is doing to educate the public, the secretary referred to two leaflets informing citizens about the complaints system and the procedures for filing a complaint, and he noted that the agency meets with community groups. But he also underscored the dangers of high visibility:

> We publicize ourselves without being seen as attracting complaints. We don't want to alienate the police or destroy police cooperation; it's a tightrope situation. . . . If we put adverts in papers [publicizing our role] it would damage the relationship, because we'd be seen to be touting for business by attracting complaints.[127]

The Police Complaints Board expressed the same concern in the early 1980s about "appearing to invite complaints" if it publicized itself.[128]

The literature suggests that, with regard to popular attitudes toward complaints procedures, there is an "inherent lack of credibility of internal review."[129] And in his report on the riots in Brixton, England in 1981, Lord Scarman concluded that "if public confidence in the complaints procedure is to be achieved any solution falling short of a system of independent investigation . . . is unlikely to be successful."[130] Yet external investigatory systems are also unlikely to generate much public approval if most defendants are exonerated. Popular perceptions about the integrity of a system are colored by the final verdicts, rather than by the fairness of the less visible investigatory process.[131] In a divided society like Northern Ireland external investigation would do little to assuage the public not only if substantiation rates remain low but also if they were *high*. High rates would only confirm for many people that the RUC is a repressive, undisciplined force, one whose officers are perhaps "accountable" after the fact, but insufficiently controlled proactively.

Neither of the nationalist political parties is impressed with the existing mechanisms of accountability. A survey of four Sinn Fein and nine SDLP politicians found unanimous agreement on the need for additional controls on police officers.[132] A Sinn Fein leader told me that bodies like the Police Authority and complaints board have not been

> in any way effective in holding the RUC in check. The Police Authority said [after the Stalker inquiry] that shoot-to-kill wasn't happening when most people now accept that it exists. . . . Regardless of the system of complaints, no action is taken. People get a standardized reply from the commission saying "no evidence exists and no action will be taken." . . . The Police Authority, complaints commission, and Diplock courts are all part of [the] counterinsurgency strategy.[133]

The SDLP would be skeptical of the claim that the Police Authority and complaints board are part of the counterinsurgency enterprise, but it is just as critical of their record in curbing police misconduct. A 1985 policy paper states, "The Police Authority is nothing more than an official smokescreen, aimed at suggesting that the RUC are controlled and are accountable. . . .

In the Police Authority, like other institutions, we witness abuse, injustice, apology for serious crimes, and silence on widespread wrongs." Also of dubious value is the complaints board and the independence of the DPP.[134] Instead of working within the Police Authority and the ICPC to make them more effective, the SDLP refuses to accept positions on them. There are several reasons. First, it is claimed that these bodies are powerless and that participation on them would be a meaningless exercise. Second, the SDLP is concerned that it might lose some votes among its more radical constituents if it was seen to be associated with the RUC, even indirectly through membership on oversight agencies. Third is the danger that if SDLP members sat on these bodies, they would be targeted for assassination by the IRA.[135]

Although the SDLP boycotts all bodies connected to the RUC, members do meet privately with police officers. They consider this more effective, less politically embarrassing, and less physically dangerous than formalized connections, which are harder to keep secret. A Belfast city councillor, who has dealt with the police on many occasions over the years, states: "I know I will get a positive, sympathetic response when I go to the police. I don't go to them unless I have specific information. . . . I will simply ring them up and request a meeting . . . and they will have several senior police and military officers there" (U). Sinn Fein, by contrast, will have nothing to do with the RUC, apart from rare negotiations over the policing of Republican marches and funerals.

Ordinary Catholics historically have been leery of agencies involved in policing matters, including those that handle police misconduct, and suspicion of these bodies has not lessened over time. Nearly three-quarters of SDLP supporters and 9 out of 10 Sinn Fein supporters agreed with the statement, "When the police or army commit an offense in Northern Ireland, they usually get away with it."[136] Republicans are strongly convinced of this (66 percent strongly agree, 23 percent agree), whereas moderate Catholics are somewhat less critical (34 percent strongly agree, 38 percent agree). These opinions may reflect general impressions or more specific perceptions of the complaints commission (and its low substantiation rates as reported in the press), the courts (and acquittals in controversial cases), and/or internal RUC disciplinary mechanisms.

My interview data help us understand why Catholics have such a low opinion of the complaints system. A priest told me that the moderate Catholics in his parish believe the police get away with crime: "If an investigation is carried out by police officers, people wouldn't have faith that it was impartial. People would laugh at it and be cynical about it" (KK). Similarly, another priest reported that in his Republican community "people think the complaints process is a farce and they have no perception of internal [RUC] disciplinary procedures" (D). He hears frequent complaints, but has grown weary of helping people make formal complaints: "It's hard to get energized about harassment. You need the time, date, number of the policeman. Even if you do get this information and ring up the police, nothing will be done about it. But it is something superior officers *could* handle" (D). A prominent priest claims to have personally lodged 2,000 formal complaints since 1971 on behalf of other people, "without a single success." Claiming that the authorities dealing with complaints are involved in a "conspiracy" to obstruct justice, he now pursues other avenues:

> I've stopped making official complaints. I've had more success with unofficial complaints. If I contact senior officers, they may shift the [accused] officer around, to Derry, as punishment. When you do this, you don't have to go through formal channels and you don't have to prove anything. Quite a number of senior officers are open to this; they are interested in community relations. (Q)

Other informants stressed the unwillingness of people to lodge a complaint:

> Catholics would be hesitant to file complaints with the police. I've heard comments that if they filed a complaint, they would be hassled at checkpoints. There's a real foundation to that. In the RUC, word about complaints can leak to the boys on the ground [ordinary constables] and they may take action. I'm convinced it does happen. The police have incredible intelligence on people. (G)

> Very few people would go through [the complaints] process. We wouldn't advise them to complain at an RUC station. At the station all these different officers come in and stare at you and you feel you will be targeted for further harassment. So people would avoid making a complaint. When people here do make a complaint they don't feel they will be listened to or that anything will be done about it. (UU)

Most ordinary people . . . would be reluctant to make a formal complaint. It would have to be a serious issue and they wouldn't do it on their own but would go to a political party. . . . People also think if they make a complaint they will be arrested by the police. People who do make a formal complaint do so as a last resort, not a port of first call. (RR)

Some people, however, believe that making a complaint can have a temporary deterrent effect on the accused officer, but the initial contact person is a local politician or a solicitor, not the RUC or ICPC:

We try to get people to file a complaint through their solicitor. . . . No one has ever had a satisfactory outcome from [filing a complaint at a police station].

Why would anyone make a complaint at all if they know nothing will be done about it?

Because a complaint goes down in the officer's record. And I've found that when I make a complaint they ease off a while. Now they harass my husband instead! The officer actually told me the harassment won't stop. But it has eased off a little. (TT)

Instead of going to a police station, a person might go to a solicitor, but only if it was a case of physical abuse or something serious. People who get a lot of verbal abuse at roadblocks might log a complaint with a solicitor to protect themselves in the future. Or if they were under threat from the police, they might do this to highlight the case, in the hope that it might afford some protection. . . . It might get the police to back off a bit, give him a break. . . . The officers at roadblocks in the area would be informed to back off. Harassment would not end, but it might cease for a while. (LL)

Many people are unaware of the existence of the ICPC, but those who know of it dismiss it as cosmetic:

They would have no faith in the commission; they would think it would be of the same mind as the RUC. The commissioners would be seen as the police out of uniform, just like the police in uniform. They wouldn't see it as neutral or independent. (LL)

It's a joke. It's police policing themselves. People don't see the board as independent; they see it as part of the RUC. People would see making a complaint as a waste of time. . . . People think they have to complain at a RUC station, but even if they knew they could complain at the commission, it wouldn't matter. (MM)

These findings are supported by Sluka's study of Divis Flats in West Belfast:

> Divis residents have no confidence at all in the complaints procedures against members of the security forces. . . . Many Divis residents have withdrawn complaints because they say that they were threatened that if they went ahead with them they would be arrested, countercharged, or harassed. . . . [They say that] the army and police often try to intimidate people into withdrawing their complaints by threatening them. . . . They believe that members of the security forces invariably cover up for each other. . . . [137]

Fear of police retaliation as a reason for not filing a complaint was also found by a Helsinki Watch investigation, which quotes a community worker: "If they file a complaint with the RUC, the RUC then files a criminal complaint against the kid. . . . So it's a pointless exercise to complain. And the kids know that you just get more hassle if you complain." A youth worker cited an example of a youth who had taken a car for a joyride: "[He] was stopped by the RUC and dragged out through the windscreen—he was badly hurt. He charged the policeman with assault. Then the RUC counter-charged him, and the RUC said, 'If you drop your charges, we'll drop ours.' And he did."[138]

In short, staunch Republicans see the complaints system as a farce, see the members of oversight bodies not as independent but as "the police out of uniform," and fear police retribution if they make a complaint. Most moderate Catholics concur that the system is terribly deficient or mere window dressing. Both groups overwhelmingly endorse the idea, asked in a poll, that serious complaints against the police "should be investigated by an independent body, not by the police themselves" (86 percent of Sinn Fein, 94 percent of SDLP).[139]

Protestants generally perceive the system of accountability differently, believing that controls on police are either adequate or too severe, not too lax. The Unionist parties insist that RUC officers are already under excessive control. The Democratic Unionist Party's security spokesman argues that the police

> are always looking over their shoulder at the implications of any action they might take against the IRA. Of course, there

have to be restrictions on the security forces; you can't let them do whatever they want. But you also must realize that it's a guerilla war and quick decisions must be made on the ground. They realize that if they make the wrong decision they will not be reprimanded but will be *gutted* . . . and that their careers will be finished. . . . So the police and military are not having the freedom that they ought to have in defending the community.[140]

The Ulster Unionist Party's security spokesman described other demands and constraints on constables:

The police are working through a court system that was not designed to deal with terrorism; it was designed to deal with ordinary crime. There is a lot on the side of the terrorist. . . . There is enormous pressure on police to get convictions when they don't have the evidence required by the courts. We know who the terrorists are. But witnesses often will not give evidence to the police. . . . The police by and large act within the law. They know they are constantly under scrutiny from Republicans and others. Its not so much bad apples as bruised apples. They are pressurized so much that they at times succumb and occasionally act in a way that perverts the course of justice.[141]

The problem lies not with the police but with the evidentiary requirements of the courts, which are so demanding that officers sometimes act improperly. The solution: "The government is wrong not to give the police the means by which they can disrupt the terrorists, and that means internment."[142]

Unionist leaders are also dissatisfied with the overreach of oversight agencies. The UUP and DUP have fought virtually every measure to promote police accountability, including creation of the Police Authority, the PCB, and the ICPC, and they have opposed attempts to make these agencies more powerful. During the 1970s and 1980s, for example, they denigrated demands from Catholics and human rights groups for a stronger civilian complaints body.[143] A 1985 proposal for changes in the complaints system was branded a "smear on the police" which would "only lend assistance and a cloak of respectability to those who wish to abuse the procedure for . . . their own subversive objectives." A stronger complaints body was unnecessary since complaints are made "for no other purpose than to frustrate the police in the performance of their duty."[144]

Today, the Unionist parties are reluctant to advocate the complete dismantling of the oversight agencies, but neither do they endorse them. The DUP's security spokesman half-heartedly concedes the need for these agencies but cites a litany of problems with them:

> Yes, you need a Police Authority; it is valuable. But those who are picked to sit on it are not broadly representative. They [government ministers] try their best to get people who will do what the government wants them to do. They should not be lackeys of the government. . . . On all of these bodies . . . the people come from one political party: the Alliance Party [a small, centrist, nonsectarian party]. They are overrepresented on all appointed bodies. Why? Because they are yes-men and yes-women. There is certainly not enough DUP representation on appointed bodies. . . . But I'm not casting any reflection on the current Police Authority; I don't know who's on it. You do need a Police Authority and a complaints body. But if they spent as many man-hours in fighting terrorism as they do in dealing with the foolish complaints against the police. A lot of complaints are made with political motivation and they take a tremendous amount of time. [The RUC is] spending so much time in investigating complaints that they are being deviated from their main purpose. We are not in a normal situation where genuine complaints will be dealt with. If an officer has wronged the community, he deserves to suffer. But today officers are looking over their shoulder and are not allowed to do their duty.[145]

His counterpart in the UUP was less critical, but he also wondered about the persons sitting on such bodies:

> We don't feel they hinder proper policing, although at some times they have. We recognize the need that we do not become a police state.
>
> *Then the party supports these bodies?*
>
> Like any government-appointed body, in the difficult circumstances we have here, one must look at the pressures which can be put on that body. Having a Police Authority or complaints commission doesn't mean you have an end to problems, because those bodies may become infiltrated or pressurized. We've had members of the Police Authority pressurized to resign. And the vice-chairman called [chief constable] Hermon a black bastard [i.e., biased against Catholics]. One has got to be careful that these bodies are not infiltrated.[146]

What irritates Unionists is that these agencies have taken pains to distance themselves from Unionist influence and that they sometimes appear to act in ways that violate Protestants' traditional visions of law and order.

Unionists' disdain for mechanisms of accountability is also evident in their stance toward the various commissions of inquiry that have investigated special policing problems. Each of these commissions has been castigated as efforts to placate Catholic critics and accused of interfering with proper policing. A UUP officer and head of the Orange Order doubted that any investigation would satisfy the critics: "Those who criticize and pre-judge the RUC would not be satisfied even if the angel Gabriel came down from heaven to carry out the investigation."[147] Responding to calls for an inquiry into the killing of a Catholic demonstrator by a plastic bullet, another UUP leader remarked that "our police force needs investigation and inquiry like they need a hole in the head."[148] And an independent Unionist complained that "nobody is . . . setting up committees of inquiry to inquire into the activities of the IRA and the way it murders and mutilates innocent people."[149]

Unionists' blanket opposition to tighter controls on the RUC may be tempered during those rare periods when serious conflicts flare up between Protestants and the police. Their standard claim that any greater accountability would only undermine the RUC was suspended after the 1985 Anglo-Irish accord, which led to periodic clashes between police and Protestants in the street. Suddenly, a stronger complaints board looked more attractive. The DUP's security spokesman labeled the complaints system a "farce" requiring "drastic overhaul," and the party passed a motion in 1986 calling for a review of the system.[150] It came as news to some that many Protestants, according to the security spokesman, had misgivings about the handling of complaints and that the police often apply pressure on Protestant complainants to withdraw complaints, including threats of police retribution and loss of the complainant's job.[151] Unionists' criticisms of the complaints system abated, however, once struggles over the Anglo-Irish agreement subsided, and now they appear to have reverted back to their traditional opposition to reforms.

Agreeing with the Unionist parties, many Protestants believe that the oversight agencies were established to placate Catholics and have detracted from effective policing. Some people hold double standards, believing that there should be more leniency toward police officers operating in Catholic areas but greater accountability if an incident happens in a Protestant area. People might be disturbed if police deviance went unpunished in their neighborhood, but they "would be happy if the police shot someone in West Belfast and then they would not want the shooter held accountable for those actions! There's a lot of double standards here" (JJ). Moderate Protestants do not subscribe to the idea that police usually get away with offenses (only 10 percent think so), which may reflect a belief that guilty officers are indeed punished or a belief that officers rarely *engage* in misconduct in the first place, which would follow from moderates' diffuse confidence in the RUC. But their confidence in the complaints mechanisms apparently is not high. Two-thirds of UUP supporters say they favor an agency with power to investigate complaints against officers. An informant described the prevailing opinion:

> People don't have much faith in the police complaints system. I know because people tell me this. And persons who make a complaint are not satisfied with the outcome. . . . Most people aren't aware the commission exists. Ordinary Protestants who know about it would like to see a board that is completely independent with greater powers and doing totally independent investigations.
>
> *Do they tell you that?*
>
> On, aye! I do hear those kinds of comments from Protestants. (VV)

Few staunch Loyalists (17 percent) believe the police usually get away with offenses, but like the other three groups they are not confident in how complaints are presently handled. Seventy percent want a body that independently investigates accused officers. For Loyalists as well as moderates, this may reflect ignorance that a commission already exists, frustration with the commission, or a distrust of police investigations of RUC officers:

> Most people would think [lodging a complaint] would be a waste of time. Police are investigating each other. There is a vision that they are all in it together, so what's the point of complaining? (X)
>
> I've never known anyone to use [the commission]. But, then again, what's the sense in going to it, because complaints never get anywhere. The board doesn't work. And if you complain the police not only cover it up but charge you with an offense. (II)

The normal person would not be aware of the complaints board, but we tell them about it. It is not generally known that the board exists. They would be worried because they think it would cost money because you are dealing with the law. When we tell them they won't incur costs, then they would be concerned about harassment by police and this would deter them from complaining. . . . People are surprised to learn a board exists. They want to know if the accused officer will be involved, sitting in on the hearing. They are very skeptical. (OO)

Even those who are aware of the commission may refrain from using it: "By and large the impression is that it is stacked in favor of the police, and this may prevent people from using it" (T). Instead, some people complain to community workers, clergy, or paramilitaries: "Partly they feel there is no use in making a formal complaint and partly it's an alien world to them. They would feel nervous, especially those who are illiterate, about going through the procedures and filling out forms. It's much easier to go to local paramilitaries to complain" (Y).

In sum, Protestants and their Unionist political leaders hold two negative and seemingly contradictory views of Ulster's system of accountability. On the one hand, controls on the police are called too severe under Northern Ireland's exceptional circumstances, handcuffing police and oversensitizing them to the legality of their actions. On the other hand, although people believe that officers involved in serious crimes are punished, they do not want complaints investigated by the police. The apparent contradiction between these opinions is partly dissolved when we factor in the target group. The principal concern is that restrictions on police behavior in Catholic neighborhoods not be too tight, and the complaints system is seen as a hindrance. When Protestants are involved, there is more concern about unchecked overzealous police actions and criticisms that officers accused of misconduct are falling through the cracks. In other words, patently sectarian sensitivities and interests help shape popular perceptions of the complaints machinery and the larger system of accountability.

CONCLUSION

This chapter has identified some progressive changes in Northern Ireland's system of accountability as well as problems that continue to generate public discontent. This raises the question of the kinds of structures appropriate to such a divided and strife-torn society.

The adequacy of the complaints machinery has been a matter of controversy throughout the period under examination. It commands little public confidence, and there is overwhelming support for civilian investigation of complaints, rather than police investigation. I have argued that this kind of change probably would not markedly increase substantiation rates, but even if it did it would not substantially inflate popular confidence in the complaints system or the police force. If low substantiation rates continued, people would conclude that civilian investigators are either unwilling or unable to deal with police wrongdoing. Substantially higher rates would be taken as proof positive that the RUC is a rotten police force; *police accountability after the fact might increase without any increase in the RUC's overall credibility or deterrence of officer misconduct before the fact.* Greater accountability in a divided society like Northern Ireland would therefore do little to enhance police-community relations, contra the conventional wisdom. It might impress some moderate Catholics, but would probably be lost on the other groups.

Complaints bodies, even where they operate fairly well, typically put almost all of their resources into the detection of individual-level deviance *ex post facto*. In addition to punishing those guilty of specific offenses, controls are required to discourage deviance before the fact. Police-community relations might improve if more attention is given to *patterns* in complaints over time and place. This may be facilitated by an agency that monitors complaints and marshalls its findings to remedy at least some of the causes of problem behavior (such as training, department policies and priorities, and supervision). If certain police stations or branches are disproportionately implicated in abuses or specific kinds of abuses, this can be brought to the attention of local commanders and corrective action taken. The complaints commission and the Police Authority claim to do this, but not systematically or frequently. When it comes to policing problems, these agencies are primarily reactive, not proactive.

Another limitation of the system of accountability is that misconduct is addressed within a narrow legal framework. Many of the police practices that are experienced as oppressive are legal under the criminal and security laws: the powers to stop and search pedestrians and vehicles, to arrest and detain persons for questioning, to raid and tear up houses in search of weapons and ammunition, to ban, restrict, and intervene in demonstrations and marches, and to use firearms if "reasonable under the circumstances" (instead of when absolutely necessary to protect life). In a context where legal powers are so extensive and, when used, so potentially disruptive of people's lives, it is incumbent on RUC commanders and the Police Authority to make greater efforts to ensure that the laws are enforced in the most sensitive manner possible. The corollary is that there should be greater sanctioning not only of conduct that is illegal but also of behavior that is technically legal but gratuitously harsh and aggravating.

State-centered controls on the police (from courts, legislatures) may be insufficient. It is frequently argued that the police should also be accountable, in a meaningful way, to civil society. But how is this possible where civil society is divided along communal fault lines? Is "democratic" or "popular" accountability (involving all major sections of the population in oversight structures) at all possible where civil society is intensely polarized, where a shared political culture (based on trust, compromise, and accommodation) is lacking, and where there is a high danger of partisan interference in affairs properly relegated to the police? Highly inclusive oversight bodies theoretically would be open to fiercely ethnocentric persons intent on using the police for sectarian purposes; to persons who have anti-police agendas, bound to create havoc inside the organization; and to sympathizers of insurgent groups, who may present security risks. This could put "the police at the mercy of the rawest emotions, the most demagogic spokesmen, and the most provincial concerns"[152] or lead to unproductive, bitter struggles between opposing interests, each making extravagant demands on the police. Even less extreme members might be tempted to use the police as a political football, or find it difficult to reach agreement with persons holding radically different visions of proper policing. All of this illustrates how ethnic conflict in a divided society can complicate or subvert the otherwise lofty goal of "democratizing" controls over the police. For precisely this reason, the leading human rights body in the country flatly insists that "fully democratic accountability is not a realistic option in Northern Ireland."[153]

Clearly, some degree of police insulation from communal pressures is healthy if it reduces politicization or manipulation by narrow interest groups.[154] Police should be sensitive to community concerns without being governed by them; citizens' preferences should be weighed in relation to the larger imperatives of law enforcement and order maintenance. At the same time, there is a danger in excessive police autonomy from civil society, which makes them dismissive of citizen grievances and resistant to cooperation with oversight bodies. The RUC already leans in this direction, ignoring citizens' criticisms and demands, many of which appear to be genuine and legitimate, and this costs the RUC popular support. The dangers described in the preceding paragraph do not mean we should abandon altogether the idea of civic accountability in divided societies. Even in the most sharply polarized societies, it is possible to locate candidates for oversight bodies who do not have a sectarian axe to grind. Drawn from both the majority and minority populations, they must be maximally apolitical, committed to working with (but not co-opted by) the police, able to articulate the grievances of the communities most disturbed by policing, but also conscious of the larger public interest and dedicated to defending liberal policing ideals. The Police Authority and the Independent Commission on Police Complaints would argue that their members have these attributes. However, their social distance from the most troubled neighborhoods and their pro-police leanings interfere, at least to some extent, with their mandate of increasing police accountability.

The public is certainly not convinced that these agencies are playing their proper role in overseeing the police, although definitions of "proper" oversight vary across our four types of communities. Clearly, compared to the primitive system of accountability that existed prior to 1970, the present, more elaborate system has not helped to improve police relations with any of our four communities. It remains an open question as to what effect more robust agencies would have. From the data presented here, it is predicted that if any group would be impressed by greater oversight, it would be moderate Catholics. Stronger proactive controls and reactive sanctions are unlikely to be appreciated by staunch Republicans, whereas many staunch Loyalists and moderate Protestants would see them as fetters on the police, wholly inappropriate given Northern Ireland's security situation. New reforms would thus continue to spark new conflicts, just as they did in the past.

PART 3

Improving Police-Community Relations

CHAPTER 7

Community Policing in the Shadows

The criticisms and demands of Protestants and Catholics highlighted in the preceding chapters are frequently discounted by the RUC—dismissed as unreasonable, politically motivated, or mutually incompatible. These views often appear in editorials in the Police Federation's magazine, *Police Beat*, and were expressed in interviews with RUC members:

> In acting impartially, on one day you will offend one community and the next day the other.[1]

> It's certainly not possible for the police to take decisions that get [cross-community] support. The conflicting views about policing are simply not reconcilable.[2]

> Policing in Northern Ireland is like intervening in a marital dispute. Both sides are thumping you, and you can never really win.[3]

The comments stand in stark contrast to the official line that most Protestants and Catholics support the police, and they suggest an underlying skepticism about the prospects for building popular consent for impartial, nonsectarian policing. Many RUC officers have now concluded that, no matter *how* the police perform, they cannot satisfy both sides simultaneously in light of their opposed, and apparently irreconcilable, views and demands on matters of law and order. Consequently, the authorities in Northern Ireland, preoccupied as they are with security problems, have given relatively little attention to the problem of popular discontent or alienation from the police.

Nevertheless, the Police Authority and the RUC are formally committed to devising programs to enhance police-community relations; each has specialized bodies working in this area. The Police Authority has a Community Relations Committee that meets with community leaders, monitors patterns in complaints against the police, and promotes police-community liaison arrangements. The RUC has its own community policing units. Before I examine these structures, a few general points are in order about community policing.

Community policing is designed to bring police and communities closer together, a sort of "partnership" with the goal of reducing crime and confronting other local problems. In practice, it can take the form of neighborhood foot patrols, meetings with community groups, youth programs, police lectures in schools, neighborhood watch programs, and so forth. By opening channels of communication and cooperation between local citizens and the police, community policing aims at making police more responsive to community needs, increasing crime prevention, and improving police-community relations.

These efforts have not produced major improvements in relations where police are unpopular or scorned.[4] In America's inner-city neighborhoods, for instance, few community policing initiatives have addressed the problems most disturbing to people, generated greater understanding between police and citizens, or reduced chronic tensions. The motives underlying community policing programs are central; often they are driven by police interests in image enhancement or in mobilizing citizens to assist with crime problems, rather than being sincere efforts to engage residents in constructive problem solving or to seriously entertain their preferences when decisions are made.[5] Keeping citizen intervention to a minimum reduces police exposure to criticism, but it also limits possibilities for the growth of mutual understanding and popular confidence in the police.

Most community policing initiatives have little effect on the kinds of police-citizen interactions that drive poor relations. Meetings, youth work, recreational activities, and other programs are peripheral and virtually irrelevant to the core activities of the police. A 1967 presidential commission in the United States concluded that community policing would do little good if confined to isolated programs or the exclusive business of specialized police units having little influence over regular officers, which is precisely how community policing has usually manifested itself.[6] James Q. Wilson observes that "police-community relations [in America's black ghettos] cannot be substantially improved by programs designed to deal with the citizen in settings other than encounters with patrolmen. . . . "[7] What does seem to positively affect relations is located precisely at the level of street interactions, namely, foot patrols. Foot patrols have the potential to personalize contacts and humanize the police, and research in a number of cities suggests that they seem to improve citizens' perceptions of the quality of police service and reduce fear of crime.[8]

This chapter examines three community policing mechanisms in Northern Ireland: the Police-Community Liaison Committees sponsored by the Police Authority, the RUC's Neighborhood Branch which conducts foot patrols, and its Community Relations Branch. These structures, and their reception in our four types of communities, warrant close scrutiny because the RUC and the Police Authority present them as critical to building better relations between civilians and the police. We will see that each mechanism has both internal deficiencies and external limitations not unlike what we find in community policing structures in other societies, but also with some unique twists.

POLICE-COMMUNITY LIAISON COMMITTEES

Lord Scarman's report on the 1981 riot in Brixton, England, documented several problems in police relations with the black population and advocated changes to elicit greater community involvement in the development of policing policy and operations. In 1982, the Home Office responded with a circular containing guidelines for consultative arrangements between police and local communities.[9] The 1984 Police and Criminal Evidence Act (s. 106.1) required police authorities to establish mechanisms for obtaining the views and cooperation of local people about matters concerning the police. Today, most British police authorities have established some liaison machinery, usually in the form of a consultative committee.

Northern Ireland gradually followed suit. Liaison committees already existed in some areas, but they were restricted to members of the security forces and district and city councillors. They operated with "too much secrecy and little meaningful discussion," according to a former member of the Police Authority, and they "were not much use in community terms."[10] In 1984 the Police Authority produced a report advocating that committee membership should be broadened to include lay members, "so that the roots of the consultative process can anchor more firmly throughout the community."[11] The report fell on deaf ears. In 1988 the Police Authority renewed its efforts to convince councils to adopt liaison committees with lay representation. The proposals were discussed at a meeting of the Association of Local Authorities, where they met with opposition. Most councils with liaison committees were reluctant to broaden them to include lay members. A few Unionist members objected to the very idea of liaison bodies, on grounds that it amounted to appeasement of Catholics.[12] Declining to take a position on the matter, the association left the decision up to each council. By 1990, 23 of the 26 councils had some kind of liaison arrangement, but almost all restricted membership to police and elected councillors, excluding lay members of the community.

According to the Police Authority's model, a Police-Community Liaison Committee (PCLC) should strive to do the following:

1. Cultivate good relations between the police and the community.

2. Obtain the views of local people regarding policing matters.

3. Promote understanding of the constraints on police responses to local problems.

4. Foster solutions to local problems.[13]

The committees were expected to discuss issues of local crime and security, neighborhood watch programs, traffic problems, and the role of local Community Relations constables.[14] Matters excluded from committee purview include cases under police investigation and complaints against individual officers.[15]

This section reports data drawn from interviews with representatives of 17 (out of 23) PCLCs, conducted in the autumn of 1990.[16] The 17 committees represent all the major areas of Northern Ireland: rural and urban; Protestant, Catholic, and mixed areas; and low-, moderate-, and high-violence areas. One member of each PCLC was interviewed, in most cases, the committee chairman or town mayor.[17] Interview transcripts were analyzed separately by the author and an independent researcher in order to enhance the reliability of the data analysis. A 1991 report of a conference attended by members of all the liaison committees provided further support for my interview findings.[18]

Given Northern Ireland's unique security problems, where anyone having connections to the RUC can be targeted for attack by the IRA, I have kept anonymous the identities of my respondents and their respective district locations.

Research on other societies points to problems that often plague police-citizen consultative bodies. In the United States, neighborhood advisory bodies are usually made up of middle- or upper-class business and civic leaders who are pro-police and detached from the concerns of populations most aggrieved about police actions on the street. Consequently, there is little discussion of controversial matters or criticism of policies.[19] Similarly in England and Wales, police consultative committees are run by people who are disproportionately male, middle class, middle aged, and "respectable."[20] Most are strong champions of the police, rarely questioning priorities, policies, and use of resources; nor (surprisingly) are questions raised about serious crime problems. Instead, the committees are preoccupied with nuisances, traffic problems, disorderly youths, and environmental conditions (litter, graffiti, street lighting, etc.). Although the committees appear moderately successful as a means of ventilating local concerns, "the majority are rather cosy ritualistic affairs that achieve little practically and have no discernible impact on what the police do. . . . "[21] Only a few see themselves as making a genuine contribution to police accountability, and it is questionable whether they have had any appreciable positive impact on police-community relations, the official *raison d'être* of these bodies.

My findings show that almost all of Northern Ireland's PCLCs deviate even more dramatically from the models advocated by the Home Office and the Police Authority. I will argue that Northern Ireland's security situation explains some, but not all, of the structure and practices of the PCLCs. Other factors are also important, some of which are peculiar to Ulster whereas others are also evident elsewhere in the United Kingdom.

The data analysis included an examination of whether the organization and activities of PCLCs are associated with the geographical location of a committee, the ethnic composition of a district (heavily Protestant, heavily Catholic, mixed), or the level of political violence in a district (high, moderate, or low numbers of bombings and fatalities).[22] I found no significant variation in committee organization and practices by geography, ethnicity, or insurgency. PCLCs in low-strife areas expectedly paid little attention to security issues, but this was also (surprisingly) the case in districts with high levels of political violence. Only one PCLC did so frequently. The following sections address four major findings and suggest explanations for the basic uniformity of committees irrespective of differences in their respective district's location, ethnic profile, and level of violence.

Weak Links to Communities

A 1985 Home Office circular stated that a consultative "group can only command the confidence of the local community if its meetings are in general open to press and public. ... "[23] In Northern Ireland meetings are not open to the public, ostensibly because closed meetings "encourage freer discussion," particularly with respect to sensitive issues, and open meetings might endanger committee members, both police and councillors.[24] "There is an element of protecting members who raise particular issues," one committee member remarked. "Should they be identified with championing a particular issue or arguing against a certain security measure, it could present difficulties." In fact, few PCLCs actually deal with sensitive matters. A more important concern is the sheer exposure committee members would get from open meetings; the public is now generally unaware of who sits on these committees, and open meetings might endanger members' safety, given the standing threat to anyone who regularly deals with the RUC. It has been suggested that committees might at least sponsor occasional public forums to allow ordinary people to express their views, but for safety reasons committee members have shunned even that degree of visibility.[25]

The Police Authority encourages PCLCs to inform local people of the committee's existence and how it may be contacted, and urges them to publicize the issues currently under discussion.[26] Yet most committees have operated rather secretly, with no publicity or press coverage. In 11 out of 17 PCLCs, meetings have never been publicized. Seven of my informants claimed that the public is aware of the existence of the local PCLC, but no independent evidence exists to verify the claim; 7 others doubted that the local population knew of the committee. Some cited the recency of the committee's formation to explain the public's lack of awareness. Others blamed the public, claiming that ordinary people take little interest in *any* council matters. Still others took the elitist position that "a councillor has a feel for what needs to be done," thus obviating the need for involvement of the public. A minority of informants wanted their PCLC to do more to publicize itself and generate popular input.

PCLCs are typically made up of elites who may not be well "anchored" in any particular community, as the Police Authority had hoped. Of the 23 existing PCLCs, most (18) are restricted to police and district councillors; only 5 include lay members of the community. The Police Authority continues to argue for inclusion of lay members, but it cannot dictate to the district and city councils and thus defers to their wishes: "We want a liaison committee that suits the needs of each community," says the chairman of the Authority. "The councillors are the legitimate elected representatives, so they legitimately can claim that they are representative of the community . . . [and] have a fair view of the needs of their community."[27] Most of my PCLC interviewees agreed, arguing that the main reason for excluding laypeople from committee membership was that elected councillors are themselves community representatives. Though not an unreasonable claim, the political and class composition of the PCLCs suggests that the interests of some important populations are being ignored while the influence of established interests may be heightened, a point taken up below.

Other reasons were given for excluding laypersons. Doubt was expressed about whether they would truly represent any constituency. One interviewee predicted that they "would only end up representing themselves." Lay members might also present a security risk because they might divulge sensitive or restricted information or because they may have covert ties to insurgent groups. Councillors might accept "the right type" of lay member, I was told, but not "people who want to disrupt things or get information on policing" for sinister purposes. This is an understandable concern, given Northern Ireland's security situation, but it can also be used as a pretense for excluding all laypersons.

Councillors may also want to monopolize liaison arrangements out of fear of being confronted or outvoted by lay members. Lay members might create tensions on a PCLC if they frequently challenged councillors or criticized the police. One interviewee noted that "there is always an element of friction between elected officials and community representatives." "Councillors feel these people would be usurping their position," another said. "They don't like nonelected people coming in and taking their rightful position. It's a matter of pride. . . . We feel that community leaders would dictate to us if there were six of them and six of us"—the numbers recommended by the Police Authority. Lay members might even present a future electoral threat to councillors, as one PCLC member pointed out:

> Councillors would see it as being a threat to their own position. They are jealous of their position. They are afraid that the community representatives would stand against them in the next election. . . . That's the underlying motivation. . . . But this [inclusion of laypersons] is what the committee needs—fresh ideas. It would be a way of developing links with the community, which must help solve sectarian problems.

I studied four of the five committees with lay members. Two of them have existed for many years (since 1970 and 1977) in border areas with Catholic majorities and a record of high political violence. Each sees itself as a model for other committees. Two others operate in low-violence areas, one in a mixed area and one in a heavily Protestant area.[28] These committees have taken pains to select "responsible" persons. In one, lay members are drawn from the chamber of commerce, farmers' union, secondary schools, and hotel owners' association. Another committee includes a Protestant clergyman, a youth worker, an educator, and members of trade and farmers' associations.

As expected, their opinions of community members differ radically from the councillor-monopolized committees. On two of the committees with lay members, the chairmen (who were themselves councillors) argued that lay members were "on the ground" and "closer to ordinary people and their problems" than the members who were councillors. When asked whether lay members might pose any kind of threat to elected members, the chairman of another PCLC (who is also the town major) responded:

> I don't see any threat whatsoever from community members. In fact, it's a real value to have their views. They are not there trying to overtake the elected representatives. And no councillor has ever expressed that view to me. . . . If elected members perceive it as a threat, you'll never have a successful committee. If you can't trust each other you shouldn't be in the business.

Relations between the elected and lay members were said to be cordial.

Interpersonal relations on these PCLCs may be friendly or collegial, but this leaves open the question of whether lay members make any real contribution by articulating the views of populations that might otherwise fall through the cracks. Much depends on the layperson's social base: members of a chamber of commerce, a business association, or a farmers' union represent rather different constituencies than clergy, community workers, or teachers, who are closer to residential populations that might have problems with the police. The presence of persons close to the grass roots increases the potential that a PCLC will address problematic relations between the police and communities. With a few exceptions, however, both the lay members and elected councillors on Ulster's PCLCs are middle-class, "respectable" individuals, rather far removed from the issues of greatest concern to working-class inhabitants of troubled areas (unlike the community-based informants discussed in earlier chapters).[29] The most striking exception is a lay member who is deeply involved in community work in two such neighborhoods.

I discovered two unofficial liaison groups in North and East Belfast. Both were recently formed on the initiative of local RUC commanders seeking greater community input than that afforded by the liaison committee attached to Belfast City Council. They operate out of the spotlight to protect members and ensure the integrity of the decision-making process. "Members would be concerned if their views on the committee were made public." For instance, "If Loyalist members said that rerouting a parade is OK, they wouldn't want that publicized" because they might be attacked by other Loyalists for acquiescing (L). Members include local clergy, community workers, businessmen, politicians, and officers of tenants and residents associations. Like the official PCLCs with lay members, the two unofficial groups reportedly operate in a noncontentious manner and value the presence of lay members (J, L, V). Unlike Belfast City Council's PCLC, the unofficial groups pride themselves on their success in getting things accomplished. I was told that the North Belfast committee is taken more seriously by the police than Belfast's official PCLC: "The police view the Belfast City Council as being discriminatory and not representative of the community [given its control by Unionists], so it can be dismissed. The police will listen to it, but they often discount it" (L).

The North Belfast group seems particularly valuable in light of the high level of interethnic violence there. Although a large proportion of the committee's time is devoted to ordinary crime, it has also addressed problems of sectarian killings, altercations during the marching season, ways to deal with recurrent clashes at flashpoints, and occasionally security policies (L). The East Belfast committee is concerned with improving the image of the neighborhood, dealing with graffiti, reducing crime, and promoting reconciliation between Protestant and Catholic schoolchildren (J, V). It appears that the presence of lay members (at least some of whom are close to the grass roots) on these unofficial bodies increases the probability that serious issues will be raised and that problems of police-community relations might be addressed. But, again, this model contrasts with most of the official liaison committees, where lay representation is lacking altogether.

Unionist Domination

Not only are most of the PCLCs devoid of lay representation, but almost all are chaired and dominated by members of one religion and one political persuasion: they are *Protestants and Unionists*. Only three committees are chaired by non-Unionists (two Alliance and one independent nationalist). On at least six committees there is no Catholic member and on eight there are only one or two Catholics. There are two reasons for this. First, some districts have totally Protestant councils because of small Catholic populations. Second, where Catholics are represented on a council, their political party affiliations determine whether they will participate on a PCLC. Catholics in the Alliance Party participate, but Sinn Fein and the SDLP boycott the PCLCs, and where these parties form the majority on a council, they have usually blocked the creation of a liaison committee altogether.

Sinn Fein councillors refuse all contact with the RUC, but the SDLP appears more ambivalent. SDLP councillors boycott PCLCs but meet privately with local police as the need arises and claim they are entirely satisfied with this arrangement. However, SDLP members have participated in formal contacts with police where they take place under the auspices of another council committee (not a PCLC) or where police meet with the entire council. This kind of participation affords some "cover" for SDLP members, who worry that visible "liaison" with the RUC might be interpreted as "collaboration," which would be politically risky (alienating radical SDLP supporters) or physically dangerous. An independent nationalist member of a Special Committee expressed the concerns of fellow nationalists:

All of us nationalists would find it difficult to join a police liaison committee. It's not that we wish the police ill; on the contrary, we wish the police well and cooperate with them. But a police liaison committee would formalize the contacts between the nationalists and the police and then there is the question of attitudes toward the security incidents. . . . There is an ongoing risk to nationalists who have formal links to the police. . . . The Special Committee wasn't set up to deal specifically with policing. It's only because it's a broader thing that you are confortable discussing security [and policing].

The only SDLP councillor who sits on a PCLC is conscious of the political and physical risks:

I shouldn't be on the committee, since I'm SDLP. But being able to speak to the police is important. . . . The SDLP says there's no useful purpose, since we can approach the police individually. . . . I don't think that is enough. . . . But I'm taking a low profile. I'm not advertising it, because of the threat to anyone who has connections to the police.

The party's boycott of the liaison committees is motivated not only by the political and physical risks but also by the expectation that participation would only lead to unproductive battles with Unionist members. The party's general secretary:

The reality would be that SDLP members would be sitting with . . . DUP extremists. There would be problems discussing issues like UDR targeting of nationalists, the location of Orange bonfires, the routing of Orange parades. . . . The committees are not an arena for working together on policing issues. . . . To bring policing [issues] to a local district council would only ensure that it would become more divisive, a slanging match, polarized.[30]

Another party officer pointed to the futility of participation: "We feel the liaison committees are a sop to the Unionists. They don't serve any useful purpose. . . . Unionists would be in the majority and they narrow things down to their own little patch. They dominate" (U).

Although none of my Unionist and Alliance informants wanted Sinn Fein councillors to participate on a PCLC—for some understandable reasons—there was broad agreement that the SDLP should participate, and these members had repeatedly tried to recruit SDLP councillors onto their liaison committees. In most cases, this appears to reflect a genuine interest in broadening a PCLC's base, but two respondents confided that such prodding was done to embarrass and needle SDLP councillors.

That almost all of the PCLCs are Unionist-dominated predisposes them to be fairly uncritical and deferential toward the police. One Unionist member reported that his committee "would want to hear what the police would feel is best. . . . The police are the professionals, not the committee members." Few committee members have any expertise or experience in policing, and most are strongly pro-police—both of which contribute to a generally passive approach. I was informed that "the police are completely unbiased here" and that Northern Ireland has the "best police force in the world." Those members who are less enamored with the RUC and more assertive at meetings nevertheless take pains to avoid an adversarial style, which would place them in the company of Sinn Fein.

The pro-police orientation is illustrated by responses to a question about a proposal under which teams of laypersons would visit police stations to observe and report on the conditions under which detainees are held to ensure compliance with the rules.[31] The program is widely supported by my Unionist informants, some of whom see it not as a check on police practices but rather as a stamp of approval for the police. Their responses reveal a strong presumption in favor of the police. One member believes lay-visiting is an opportunity to dispel the "propaganda" about police maltreatment of detainees, a mechanism for "proving what the police have been saying all along, that they are not misbehaving and that prisoners are being well looked after." "Not that [lay visitors] are policing the police," says another committee member, "but if an outside person is visiting, it provides backup for the police. He's not going in to find faults but to give praise." By contrast, Alliance and some SDLP politicians view lay-visiting as an important means of oversight on police conduct.

Not only are most PCLCs controlled by Unionists, but most are dominated by one party: the Ulster Unionist Party. This party has traditionally been less critical of policing policies and practices than the right-wing Democratic Unionist Party. *UUP domination of most PCLCs thus reduces the potential for spirited debate and for serious criticism of the police.* Were the SDLP or Sinn Fein involved, discussions would be more animated and issues of biased law enforcement, policing of marches, harassment, and brutality would figure prominently. On the other side, DUP members are not as likely as their UUP counterparts to act as cheerleaders for the RUC; they are more inclined to criticize the police for inaction and urge them to act more forcefully against Catholic troublemakers and the IRA. In one of the two committees chaired by a DUP councillor, the chairman made the following complaints:

> There are not enough RUC on the ground doing road checks and being seen to be there. It is essential that road checks be done more frequently. They say there's a shortage of men. . . . I don't believe there is a shortage of manpower. But it's not being put to use. The higher powers in the background [senior officers] are not putting them to use. I think it's a political matter.

> *Do the police respond to the committee's requests?*

> I don't see any tangible results. If you ask for road stops, they may put up a few more for a while and then you don't see them. . . . They should put more officers on the beat, community policing, and they'd have more information on the community and better relations with the community. Instead they use cars and landrovers. I advocate beat patrols at every meeting and it falls on deaf ears.

Mundane Issues

Two-thirds of the PCLCs are preoccupied with mundane issues such as traffic problems, teenage drinking, vandalism, street lighting, and so on. Larger problems never make it onto their agendas—because the mundane matters are deemed manageable and resolvable, because the police are considered unreceptive to broader concerns, and/or because of a denial that certain problems even exist. PCLCs might be expected to examine ways of improving police relations with local communities, patterns and trends in local complaints against the police, and major police policies. All of these were cited in the 1985 Home Office circular as important topics for discussion in England; these matters arguably require even more attention in Northern Ireland.

Northern Ireland's committees have also been urged to consider policing policies and to plan for the future.[32] "We challenged them to suggest changes in policing in their areas that they'd like to see in five years' time, to get them to take a broader view," the chairman of the Police Authority told me.[33] When informed that most committees are not doing this and are instead reacting to fairly minor matters, he responded:

> I don't want to detract from what they are talking about. The issues may seem trivial to an outsider, but they are important to that community. . . . Where normality is the rule, one should expect more mundane discussions. I would expect that in areas where terrorism and racketeering are common, the committees should be looking at them.[34]

Even in tranquil districts, however, discussion of issues such as police policies and relations with communities, in addition to more mundane matters, can be valuable. In troubled districts PCLCs might be expected to give priority to discussing sectarian attacks, provocative marches through opponents' neighborhoods, controversial police actions, the location of roadblocks, ways of improving police-community relations, and so forth. Remarkably, only one PCLC in a highly disturbed district gives serious attention to these problems. In three other troubled areas, security issues are only occasionally discussed. In one of these, "the major issues are speeding, drinking and driving, and underage drinking. . . . This area has suffered terribly under terrorism. . . . That's an area we try not to address ourselves to because it can be difficult to get the officers to respond. It's nearly taboo." No liaison committee exists in two other high-violence areas (Armagh, Newry).

Members of six committees thought that serious issues should be dealt with in private meetings with the police, not in the PCLC, but others wanted their committee to deal with the most important matters. One interviewee contrasted his experience on two committees:

> In [one PCLC] so much of the liaison business dealt with routine problems, not the major ones. Some members saw this as misguided and tried to divert the routine questions. They said, "That's not what we're really here to talk about." It was a continual battle. . . . Our committee [another PCLC] is aware of the danger of the routine matters, and it wants to deal with the larger issues.

What is striking is that the first PCLC operates in an area plagued by serious disorders and policing problems. The informant's characterization of that committee is confirmed by a current member who predicted that he would get nowhere if he raised major issues:

> Before I became a member, I thought that because it was so secretive, it would be interesting. But I was disappointed. . . . Sometimes there can be absolutely nothing of importance raised. . . . Harassment and public alienation from the police are things that have never been discussed, and should be. . . . The whole makeup of the committee is so loaded that discussing larger issues would do no good. If I raised an issue, five or six Unionists would contradict it. . . . The committee would be a fairly hostile environment in which to raise major or delicate issues. It would end up in a slanging match.

Some police representatives on the PCLCs also want to discuss more than the minor problems. One committee member remarked, "Divisional commanders don't want to talk about broken street lights. They want to talk about the more major problems." Another revealed that "it was the police themselves who, at the first meeting, said 'Can we get away from those trivial issues like road safety?'" "We would be anxious that the committee should not restrict itself to mundane matters," says an RUC superintendent sitting on this PCLC. "It was agreed on the committee that we would not deal with mundane issues. We want any issue discussed. We're quite happy to face critical views as well."[35] In many other districts, however, I was told that the police are reluctant to discuss controversial police actions and policies and sensitive matters related to counterinsurgency. They prefer to discuss ordinary matters because they are "safe" and to focus on specific issues because that keeps larger policy questions off the agenda.

Impact

For the reasons identified above, the PCLCs have had rather limited impact on police-community relations and police accountability. As in Britain, members of most of Northern Ireland's liaison committees were hard pressed to identify significant outcomes of their efforts.[36] In only a few cases were specific accomplishments cited, such as the reopening of a police station that had been closed against the wishes of local people. Interviewees appeared skeptical that the PCLCs had helped to improve policing or increase police accountability. Instead, they claimed that the *process* itself was important; they cherished the opportunity for regular, structured dialogue between senior police officers and other committee members, and expressed satisfaction that the police "take note" of their concerns. My research indicates that this is precisely the primary role of the liaison committees: they provide *a formal channel of communication between police and the other committee members*.

Unfortunately, the quality of that communication falls short of what seems necessary in a divided society where policing is so controversial. And the tangible effects of this discourse—in terms of police policies, priorities, and practices—are rather limited. One member called his committee a "talking shop," a notion that troubled the chairman of the Police Authority: "If they are a talking shop where nothing much happens, then one has to ask why they exist."[37] Institutionalized dialogue between police and citizens might have some positive symbolic effect on police-community relations, but this would require radical changes in the way the PCLCs operate. The fact that most of the committees are secret affairs, dominated by middle-class Unionists, and preoccupied with minor matters suggests that their impact on community relations, particularly in Northern Ireland's most troubled neighborhoods, is slight at best. Conversely, the five committees with lay members have a greater potential to affect police-community relations, although this would depend on the social bases of lay members (which are limited in Northern Ireland) as well as a community's receptivity to efforts to improve relations. Later in this chapter I show that the residents of some neighborhoods have little or no interest in better relations with the RUC. They would not be amenable to any overture from a PCLC.

If the committees have any value on the community relations front, it is limited to the Protestant population, given Unionist control of most of them. The value of one liaison committee to a Protestant community (and to the RUC) is revealed by the town major:

> People saw that, if an incident happens, they could phone a councillor or liaison committee member and express their views. . . .
> One example: people called up and said Sinn Fein was putting leaflets around for a march. This information could be transmitted to the RUC and you could have this vital role of nipping

things in the bud, by setting up roadblocks. Another example: people phoned up saying, "Gerry Adams [Sinn Fein's president] is scheduled to address a meeting here; did you know that?"

Some informants in other PCLCs were conscious of the danger of listening to the views and demands of only one ethnic group and even doubted whether PCLCs should take those preferences seriously: "I'm not so sure you can be overly sensitive to what one community or the other is demanding." This concern may seem warranted with respect to Northern Ireland's staunch Republican and Loyalist districts, but it can also be used as an excuse for ignoring the grievances of these communities.

Morgan's conclusion that Britain's consultative committees are "cosy ritualistic affairs" that have little if any impact on policing strongly characterizes most of Northern Ireland's PCLCs. My sources described the police and councillor members as being "part of a team" and "good friends." As I have shown, some of this cosiness is a function of Northern Ireland's ongoing security problems, which make insularity attractive and open or more inclusive meetings problematic and pose some physical threat to committee members by virtue of their contacts with the RUC. But the structure and practices of most of the PCLCs is also determined by the interest of councillors in excluding lay members, the interest of nationalist parties in refusing to accept membership, and a propensity to confine agendas to "safe," mundane matters. The net effect is that established interests are represented on the PCLCs, while the interests of people living in troubled areas are neglected. The PCLCs give local Unionist leaders regular, formal access to the RUC. Over time, it is possible that this access will translate into some measure of influence over the local police station. Because most of the PCLCs are boycotted by nationalists and do not include laypersons, it is primarily the Unionists who stand to gain from this relationship with the police.

On a more positive note, the existing liaison arrangements provide a foundation for building a more robust liaison system: one that incorporates broader representation of various shades of opinion, encourages discussion of more serious issues, and places a premium on enhancing police-community relations. At present, however, Northern Ireland's polarized political culture, ethnic strife, and chronic security problems present important obstacles to the progressive development of these bodies.

THE RUC'S COMMUNITY POLICING

Police-Community Liaison Committees are the responsibility of local councils and the Police Authority, not the RUC per se. This section focuses on the RUC's own efforts to improve police-community relations.

Foot patrol is a staple of many community policing projects, and evidence from England and the United States suggests that foot patrols are favored by the public.[38] Patrols are designed to increase the visibility of police on the street, operate in a personalized manner, cultivate positive relations with the public, attend to various problems, and prevent crime.

There are two kinds of foot patrols in Northern Ireland. Regular constables sometimes walk the streets, often accompanied by soldiers. In addition, the RUC's Neighborhood Branch specializes in foot patrols to develop contacts with local people, routinely visiting shops and community centers in certain neighborhoods. Some see these patrols as vital to the improvement of police-community relations. According to the chairman of the Police Federation, "Getting men on the street again is really the only thing that will improve community relations—talking to people on the street."[39] And a police superintendent remarked, "We'd like to see more foot patrols. It improves the quality of policing, if not the number of crimes we can control. Without foot patrols, police-public interaction suffers."[40]

The police walk the beat unaided by military cover in fairly peaceful areas (although joint police-army patrols also occur there). In high-violence areas like West Belfast, West Londonderry, Newry, and Strabane, foot patrols by Neighborhood Branch officers are either absent altogether or are major displays of force, under the guard of heavily armed soldiers and two or more landrovers. Without this backup, the officers on foot patrol would be walking targets in these communities. But bearing no resemblance to conventional foot patrols, the militarized patrols are hardly capable of constructive engagement with civilians, the very purpose of foot patrols. Patrolling officers rarely speak to people on the street—and when they do they try to disguise it—because it might increase their vulnerability to sniper attack and because they do not wish to compromise citizens in the eyes of onlookers. The RUC knows that "even talking to a policeman" in Republican areas may be "seen as an act of treachery."[41] Officers also avoid food shops in these areas (even those willing to serve them) so as not to endanger the proprieters by giving the appearance of being on good terms. In turn, residents rarely approach these patrols to ask for help, report incidents, or otherwise converse with the officers. As I show later in the chapter, these communities draw little distinction between the Neighborhood foot patrols and other kinds of policing, and many people doubt that the patrols are motivated by good intentions.

That these formidable armed convoys are such a perversion of the foot patrol ideal raises the question of why the RUC even bothers with them. The patrols play little role in the control of ordinary crime or insurgent activities. Low-level intelligence gathering and monitoring of suspicious activities can be done more effectively from landrovers or hidden outposts or via informants. Brewer and Magee claim that foot patrol reflects the RUC's "commitment" to improving community relations and that it is "the style of policing which comes nearest to breaching the divide between the police and the community."[42] They are wrong on both counts: the RUC has little institutional commitment to community relations (as I show below) and the armed convoy incarnation of its foot patrols hardly bridges the gulf between the police and the public. Rather, the goal appears to be more symbolic: the RUC can claim it does community policing in every neighborhood and the patrols are another way of demonstrating, with officers on foot as well as in landrovers, that the authorities remain "in control" of the area or at least have not been driven out by insurgents. It is yet another display of the police presence in an area, preventing the establishment of "no-go" areas, like those that appeared during the disturbances of the early 1970s when Catholics erected barricades blocking entry to their neighborhoods.[43]

Precisely because Neighborhood foot patrols cannot interact freely with the public in troubled areas, the onus of building better relations has fallen on a separate branch. Created in 1970, the Community Relations Branch sponsors a host of programs, works to develop ongoing relationships with neighborhood leaders, and seeks to reconcile members of each community to the RUC.[44] Community Relations (CR) officers spend most of their time dealing with youth, because they are seen as more malleable than adults and because it is young people who typically have the most negative attitudes to the police—a pattern evident in other societies.[45] CR officers organize sports activities, "rambles" or nature outings, "blue lamp" discos, quiz competitions, holiday camps, and lectures in schools.

Community Relations training is not particularly sophisticated. Training might be expected to stress skills for effective communication, dealing with youth, and sensitivity to local concerns. The four-week course covers teaching and mediation skills, but

> there is a heavy emphasis on the Outward Bound dimension—training in canoeing, hiking, etc. Community Relations officers are just good policemen who can communicate with people and have common sense. . . . It is not a branch where a high degree of specialized skills is required. You need to be able to listen to people.[46]

A study of five neighborhood policing schemes in Britain also found specialized training to be lacking, again eclipsed by the wisdom of "common sense."[47]

The branch is run by a chief superintendent at RUC Headquarters in Belfast; branch units exist in every RUC subdivision, but not every station. CR officers enjoy considerable job autonomy: they have their own offices and staff and set their own priorities and daily tasks. This autonomy is highest in Republican areas because the unique obstacles to community policing there demand more creative approaches.

Notwithstanding the freedom CR constables have in their daily activities, there are major shortcomings in the RUC's approach to community policing. In Northern Ireland (as in mainland Britain)[48] community policing is *marginal to the paramount organizational imperatives of the police force.*

One measure of its status is the number of officers employed in this kind of work. As of September 1993, the Neighborhood Branch had 342 officers, 4 percent of the regular force; 151 officers were attached to the Community Relations Branch, 1.8 percent of the regular force.[49] In the West Belfast area where policing is the most dangerous, 10 officers out of a total of 400 are attached to Community Relations units (1 inspector, 3 sergeants, 6 constables).

CR officers are rarely promoted within the branch, since the RUC, like British police forces, believes that specialization makes officers ill suited to engage in other kinds of police work. This means that most of these officers, even the best ones, do not remain long in the branch (around four years). Such turnover may adversely affect the goal of improving police-community relations insofar as continuity of personnel is valuable.[50] Although the high turnover exposes more officers to community policing than would be the case if it was confined to a select group of officers, the relatively small number involved has a limited effect on the force as a whole.

Not only is community policing limited in terms of the number of officers involved, but it is marginalized within the organization. The contribution of community police officers is maximized if they have a role in catalyzing departmentwide sensitivity to community relations and if they are involved in evaluating policies and practices that affect community relations.[51] This is not the case in Northern Ireland, where community constables are isolated from the rest of the RUC and where community policing is confined to a set of programs, not a philosophy shaping the actions of all officers. As in other societies, many RUC officers view community policing skeptically, not as "real" police work but as social work—as leaning too much toward the demands of the community and undermining the goals police consider most important. Brewer and Magee cite officers who hold these attitudes in East Belfast, and Graef quotes a constable involved in a Neighborhood unit near the border: "Nobody wants our end of the work. They think we are silly. A lot of people have got it into their heads that community relations in Northern Ireland is a lost cause and the only way you can police Northern Ireland is by riot squads."[52] A CR constable told me:

> It's easier if you mix with uniformed men, involve them with the work we do. But other cops are led to believe what we do is office work, although a lot would be interested in the job. Many officers are quite ignorant of what Community Relations does.
>
> *So other cops doubt that Community Relations work is real policing?*
>
> Maybe, but is standing at a roadblock all day questioning motorists real policing?[53]

Of course, not all RUC officers are skeptical of community policing. When asked whether other officers doubt that CR work is genuine policing, a sergeant replied:

That view exists, but surprisingly enough I found it more in the previous station I worked where they thought it was a joke. I used to work in the Neighborhood Branch in an orange [Protestant] area where they thought there was little need for it. Here, they realize the necessity for [community policing]. They see that I am going out and putting my life on the line too. They probably see that it is the way forward, because they are aware of the alienation of the community. But [skepticism] always exists.[54]

An inspector in West Belfast estimates that at least 50 percent of ordinary officers "see us as wasting our time, because of their lack of knowledge," but others "will say Community Relations is doing a good job. We take some uniformed officers with us on community programs. They get to see that Community Relations can help in their work. . . . Once they get the message they start to appreciate it and see that we're not having an easy time."[55] Divisions within the RUC over the merit of community policing also exist among commanding officers. Some are quite supportive, convinced that it is the way to build popular consent for the RUC. Others are cynical, believing police-community relations in troubled neighborhoods are so frozen that no amount of constructive engagement with residents will make a difference.

Whatever the attitudes of RUC officers toward community policing, it remains programmatic and largely segregated from the rest of the force; ordinary officers are not routinely sensitized to the importance of community relations, and community constables have little role in shaping the policies that have the greatest impact on relations with the public. Consequently, community policing has little if any impact on most officers' *behavior*, particularly in neighborhoods where counterinsurgency is the norm.

The RUC refused me formal permission to interview or observe CR units at work. Nevertheless, with the help of third parties, I arranged informal contacts with officers in a Republican part of West Belfast and a much less troubled, mixed, middle-class part of Southwest Belfast. The findings indicate that community policing contrasts sharply between the two areas. The findings on Southwest Belfast were similar to those of a study of Protestant East Belfast.[56]

In the mixed, middle-class area, I accompanied two CR officers, a sergeant and a constable, on visits to a Catholic school and a Protestant school. (To my knowledge, no other researcher has

observed CR work inside Northern Ireland's schools.) In this part
of Belfast popular suspicion of the police does not appear to be
strong. Police access to Protestant schools in the area is a piece of
cake. With regard to Catholic schools, the constable said,

> It is not as bad here as in West Belfast. Some Catholic parents
> would already be pro-police even before we approach them.
> Parents get a letter asking if they object to our lectures in school.
> Rarely do they say no. We've had no difficulty getting into
> Catholic schools here; the Board of Governors of the school
> gives permission.

Classroom visits may involve lectures on various mundane topics,
taking kids' fingerprints, demonstrating how police dogs are handled, showing police equipment, and so forth. A lecture I
attended, in a class of 35 ten-year-old primary school children,
involved the following exercises: tests on bicycle safety and road
signs, a crossword puzzle on road safety, and a game where students were asked to guess the month and day the constable was
born. The officers had no difficulty establishing immediate rapport, and the entire class was remarkably attentive and enthusiastic, but at the end some kids said they enjoyed it because "we got
out of work" for the hour. Aside from introducing themselves as
police officers, there was nothing in the lecture about police work.
The sergeant's reasoning is revealing:

> You have to be careful; kids might tell their parents we talked
> about what police do and get annoyed. It's better to let kids see
> there is another side to the police—to develop rapport with top-
> ics unrelated to policing. Then, in later visits, we could ask them
> questions like "Why do you have police?" and "What do police
> do?" Then you have already got them on your side and got their
> confidence.
>
> *Wouldn't parents object to lectures on policing during your
> return visits?*
>
> The school will always ask parents for permission. We couldn't
> do it without permission. If a parent objects, then the kid would
> be taken out of class or the lecture wouldn't occur at all. This
> happens rarely here.

These CR officers encounter very little neighborhood resistance to their work with schools and community organizations

and are not preoccupied with their personal safety. The constable said,

> Security precautions are not so important here. I feel fairly safe, but I still can't be complacent about my security. I'd be an easy target [traveling alone and unarmed]. I don't like traveling in uniform and that's why I wear a jacket over it. As long as you don't have a breakdown [of the car] on the road!

Most community relations programs in Britain and America have failed to involve those sections of the public most alienated from or hostile to the police—precisely those populations most in need of constructive contacts with the police. In Northern Ireland community policing is also unevenly distributed. Programs thrive in untroubled Protestant, Catholic, and mixed areas like the one just described, which arguably least need these programs. They are not well received in some Loyalist areas and in Republican areas where, as a CR sergeant told me, the people "who are most alienated wouldn't come anywhere near us." The community policing vacuum in these neighborhoods exists not because the police do not try to make contacts and launch programs (they try hard); it is a function of popular rejection of the whole policing enterprise. CR officers try to entice youth to participate in football matches, quizzes, interethnic retreats, and discos, but these programs are unpopular in staunch Republican areas, and even the mention of such a program is likely to meet with stiff resistance from parents, teachers, and Republican political activists. This reception is discussed in the next section.

It is noteworthy that CR officers persist in their efforts to include in their functions youth from Republican areas, despite the possibility that their family members may be involved in Sinn Fein politics or IRA activity, which can increase the danger to the officers involved. This persistence is a function of the RUC's interests in maintaining a foothold in troubled areas (not to be seen as driven out by the IRA) and in trying to win at least some young hearts and minds, despite the enormous obstacles.

West Belfast contains both Catholic and Protestant neighborhoods. Working with Protestants there is much easier and quite functional for CR officers, in several respects. One sergeant said:

> We use the Protestant side of the community to give us something to do, to keep the monthly returns right and to show that we are doing things. We try to do cross-community projects to

involve both sides. There is a danger that you could forget the Protestant community. But we must remember that they have their paramilitaries too. You have too keep your finger on their pulse.

Do you sometimes forget the Protestants?

No. Most of our work is done with the 20 percent [Protestants in West Belfast], but most of the effort is done with the 80 percent [Catholics]. The Protestants are not forgotten because it's nice for us to hit the doorsteps and talk to people in relative safety.

What's the difference between "work" and "effort"?

Work is the practical going out into the community. We are frequently involved with community groups on the Protestant side. Setting up discos, football matches, school visits are Protestant things. You couldn't do a disco or anything in the evening in the Catholic area. Effort is the time you spend trying to think up some project that will be acceptable to Catholics and to get some involvement from them. We spend more time trying to get it right and acceptable in that community. We have to adjust what we do in the Catholic community. In the orange area, we can give them something off the shelf. In the Catholic area, schools projects, for instance, are always quiet, behind the scenes. It would be counterproductive to be too visible.[57]

In Britain and the United States, lack of close contact between police and communities is largely a function of the impersonal, remote, rapid-reaction style that characterizes modern policing. This obtains in Northern Ireland as well, but there are also some unique conditions that divide the police and civilian population. Policing in general is more detached from civil society, and community policing is infinitely more difficult there than elsewhere in the United Kingdom because of the extreme alienation or suspicion of the RUC in certain neighborhoods and because of intimidation of residents who want to participate in CR programs. And any success officers have in building ties to residents of Republican areas (which inevitably becomes known in these small communities) typically leads to IRA/Sinn Fein efforts to undo it, via pressure on the residents involved (discussed later in the chapter).

It is not only the intimidation of civilians that restricts and distorts CR work in Republican areas but also the omnipresent threat of attacks on the police; a concern for personal safety forces community constables to sacrifice much of their work in these neighborhoods. Given the chronic danger to police officers in Republican areas, it is understandable that safety considerations would have a decisive effect on CR work, as a sergeant stressed:

> The number one cap we wear is the security cap. . . . Security is the first and last consideration and everything you do is based on that and you can't even look at the normal problems. Security prevents me from doing anything. All the problems are security-based. I don't have normal problems that you'd have in an ordinary area. Our problem is security, security, security. If you are asked to set up a meeting, you go into an area, are spotted, and set up [for ambush].

The greater the security precautions required, the more they impinge on and limit community policing activities. The paradox of trying to cultivate community relations in dangerous areas is underscored by a CR sergeant: "To go wherever we want, we need security cover and you can't do this work with security cover because you are bringing danger to the people you visit." "I can't visit people on the Falls without taking troops with me," an inspector complained. "I don't want to take three landrovers with me to go into the community."

There is also a concern that CR work is perceived in Republican areas as a charade for intelligence gathering, a notion that bothers CR officers, as one told me:

> Community Relations officers would be branded by Sinn Fein as part of the Special Branch, trying to gather intelligence. That's not true at all. We try to avoid any impression that we are doing any intelligence gathering. For us to get involved in intelligence gathering would ruin our work. The most important war is for the hearts and minds.

At the same time, CR officers working in Republican areas are sometimes mobilized for large-scale police operations such as riot control and crowd management at marches and funerals. Although this is rare, my police informants considered it problematic:

> Community Relations men put on uniforms to police public order incidents, but here they tend to keep us on the outskirts of those situations if they can, so the public don't recognize us. (an inspector)

We'd be used in a public order situation, but we wouldn't be put in at the sharp end. You'd find us on the perimeter.

Why?

It seems a trifle dishonest [to be prominently involved in such operations]. I would see it as detrimental to the work we're trying to do. We need to take a detached, middle view between the community and other cops. (a sergeant)

The commitment of the Community Relations Branch to winning hearts and minds also makes CR officers sensitive to any action of other police officers that might undermine their achievements. Whether or not citizens draw distinctions between street cops and CR officers, the latter's credibility (in Republican areas, among people who are not already opposed to them) is rather easily shaken by controversial incidents involving regular constables and Divisional Mobile Support Units: "If someone is shot by the RUC, Community Relations work comes to a halt for a week," an inspector observed. "Things get canceled and you have to go back to the start of the board again." Even in communities that are not so inhospitable to the police, this dynamic is present. A superintendent in one such area noted: "Sometimes when we do get something [a CR project] organized and going along nicely for a while, an incident happens and puff, it's up in smoke." Community policing in Republican areas therefore cannot progress in a linear fashion but is, as a CR inspector put it, "very much two steps forward, one step back."

One might expect that these officers would find their work frustrating in the extreme, but my informants disagreed:

The reward you get for one little step forward is so much more rewarding than the buckets of response you get in a normal area. Here you have to battle to get anything done and I really enjoy it. It's a challenge and one you enjoy. . . . Success would be one more school taking part in one more function for the year or having a school coming in that hasn't had contact with us before. (a sergeant)

It is not frustrating work at all. We have to struggle for everything we get and this makes it more satisfying than Community Relations work in Bangor [a peaceful, Protestant town], where they turn people away. In Bangor, Community Relations officers don't have to work hard to cultivate relations with the community. Here, job satisfaction is *higher*; it's more challenging here. If you get an extra 20 kids going to a camp, you've made improvements. If you make contacts with the SDLP, that's progress. (an inspector)

This rather meager progress may indeed be less frustrating than one would expect; what is more frustrating, as an officer quoted earlier noted, are the contaminating effects of other kinds of policing on the work of the CR Branch. And this is a one-way street, since the efforts of CR officers have little effect on other officers. Community policing is detached from the rest of the force, and other officers receive little feedback from the CR Branch as to how their actions may run contrary to the goals of community constables.

NEIGHBORHOOD RECEPTIVITY TO COMMUNITY POLICING

My analysis of Police-Community Liaison Committees noted that the public is, for the most part, unaware of their existence and activities. The committees might have some effect on police-community relations, behind the scenes, if they addressed citizen's major grievances. But the issues typically dealt with by most of the PCLCs are such that their contribution to police-community relations is slight at best. This section focuses on neighborhood orientations toward the more visible community policing mechanisms sponsored by the RUC, the Neighborhood Branch foot patrols and Community Relations programs.

For some analysts, it is police behavior exclusively that sours relations with communities, and it is the police alone who bear the onus for improving relations.[58] But relations are never a one-way street, and the variable of community receptivity should not be left entirely out of the picture. Some neighborhoods are thoroughly alienated from the police and stridently reject all overtures that might help to improve relations. The present study supports the argument that improvements are a "matter of accommodation on both sides" in the sense that both the police and communities must be receptive to forging new relationships.[59] Although police bear the primary responsibility, it is also important, as an American commission argued, that community members criticize police responsibly (based on the facts), refrain from blaming police for problems that are not of their making, and demonstrate support for the police in carrying out their normal functions.[60] This is extremely difficult, however, in communities where the police and the state lack any semblance of moral capital.

The success of community policing is therefore affected not only by the activities and resources of community police officers but also by the status of the police force in the neighborhood culture. In Northern Ireland, some neighborhoods enthusiastically welcome Neighborhood foot patrols and Community Relations initiatives, some are indifferent or ambivalent about them, and others reject them unequivocally. The level of receptivity is shaped by a community's political identity, the neighborhood culture's definition of policing, and patterns in residents' experiences with the police.

Foot patrols in Britain and the United States have for the most part been welcomed by the public, including minority groups.[61] Although they have had little if any impact on crime, they have reduced citizens' fear of crime and increased their regard for the police. Skolnick and Bayley write, "Properly carried out, foot patrol generates goodwill in the neighborhood" and "humanizes" the police.[62] Even in Northern Ireland it might be expected that community policing would be defined more favorably—in each of our four types of community—than the RUC's conventional or security policing because community constables personify the RUC's benevolent, friendly side. Moderate Protestants and Catholics are, for the most part, favorably disposed toward community policing. But this is far from the case in staunch Republican and some Loyalist areas, which are the focus of the remainder of the chapter. In Republican neighborhoods, community policing is rejected out of hand as a transparent glove covering the RUC's iron fist. Even for persons who accept that the intentions of Neighborhood and CR officers are benign, these officers are not insulated from the larger context of policing, which tarnishes everything they do. Staunch Loyalists are more ambivalent and divided over community policing, but there is a strain of suspicion running through the culture of their neighborhoods.

Neighborhood receptivity to community policing can be measured by prevailing definitions of it in the neighborhood culture and by the ways in which community constables are treated by residents. The data presented below are drawn primarily from interviews with community informants and from some CR officers who work in these neighborhoods.

Loyalist Communities

Peaceful, middle-class Protestant areas tend to welcome foot patrols, and residents freely interact with officers walking the beat.[63] I was told that in one such area "people are 100 percent for foot patrols" and they "constantly" tell their city councillor they would like to see more patrols to deal with vandalism, drunkenness, and other crime (VV). In areas where crime and other problems are rarer, I found less demand but still high regard for foot patrols. CR officers are also esteemed, and their programs thrive in moderate Protestant areas. "Community Relations officers are excellent people," says a community worker. "They are of a different quality to security police who drive around in landrovers . . . antagonizing people" (R). Whether contacts between CR and Neighborhood constables and the residents of a particular community are frequent or infrequent, moderate Protestant areas are distinguished by their generally favorable relations with them.

Community policing is more problematic in staunch Loyalist areas. Some people support foot patrols and complain that they are too scarce. A city councillor:

> Certainly the people I represent are calling out for more foot patrols. We believe the RUC should get back to being the bobby on the beat. Instead, the police are driving around in armored landrovers. This creates an "us-versus-them" situation. They don't get to know the people. We see the bobby on the beat as a way of cutting down on vandalism and other crime. (PP)

And a community worker: "The police used to be on the beat and they knew the area quite well. Today there are *some* foot patrols, but never at the right time. We have never seen police here when incidents are happening" (OO). People living in Loyalist areas may favor more patrols but also personally avoid them: "People are very cautious of having relations with police even if they support the police because the people with power [paramilitaries], even if they're a minority, can make a lot of trouble for you. It's fear" (JJ). Neither police nor residents are prone to exchange pleasantries: "Here, they wouldn't stop for a casual conversation. If they talk, it's an interrogation. The police are fearful of sniper attack. And the public doesn't want to talk to them and doesn't want to be seen talking to them for fear of who might be watching" (C). Foot patrols in these areas became more risky after the Anglo-Irish Agreement: "Foot patrols ceased with the agreement and they haven't been accepted back. . . . Some Loyalists would shoot at foot patrols. . . . Ordinary people would like more foot patrols" (T).

Perceptions of Community Relations programs are also mixed in Loyalist areas, ranging from very positive to very negative. On the positive side, there are neighborhoods where such programs are in high demand, a demand apparently not being met in some areas. One community worker says that more money should be spent on community relations work, that CR officers should have more responsibility, and that they "should be visiting community groups more often, running seminars for community workers" (E). Some neighborhoods seem to get little or no attention from Community Relations:

> For a while community policing was the in thing, but community policemen are taken away [transferred] and others are put in. There's no continuity. We don't have contact with the Community Relations cops now. I wouldn't even know the Community Relations officers in the area now. I haven't heard of any working here. . . . People think some Community Relations cops are different from ordinary cops. We had two very good lads working here; then they took those lads out of the area, probably because they got to know the area and told their superiors that not all the people here were bad! (OO)

There is also a sense that resources are diverted from Protestants to Catholics:

> Community Relations officers are seen to be doing more for the nationalist side than the Protestant side. (E)

> Community Relations officers from Grosvenor Road [a police station in a Republican area] have meetings with nationalist community groups,[64] but officers from [the] station [here] don't have meetings with Loyalist community groups. . . . We need more community policing, more resources. (F)

> We used to use Community Relations' minibuses, but they would often say they were being used by people in [a specific Catholic area]. People would complain that only Catholics get buses and resources from Community Relations. There's a sense that if a Catholic area asked for a bus, all stops would be pulled out [to satisfy them], but in a Protestant area getting positive

responses from Community Relations cops is difficult unless the natives are restless. Whenever there is a backlash from the Protestant community, then Community Relations would bend over backwards to help us. I actually pointed that out to one officer and he said "that's the way the cookie crumbles." (JJ)

Not only are Catholic areas thought to be disproportionately blessed with CR programs because the police bend over backwards to placate them, but residents also complain that community constables "take for granted Loyalist support for the police" (F) and "are dubious about coming in because they don't want to be too closely associated with Loyalist groups" (E). The notion of favoritism toward Catholics is consistent with a more general Protestant belief that Catholics are today benefiting from "reverse discrimination" in other spheres of life, such as jobs and public housing. It is difficult to verify whether CR resources are disproportionately devoted to Catholic neighborhoods; the Community Relations Branch is clearly anxious to maintain whatever contacts it has with Catholics, although it is appreciated that Loyalists' support for the police can no longer be assumed and must be actively reproduced.

If favoritism is one grievance, the effectiveness of CR programs is another:

> They usually take only one side to events and when they sponsor cross-community activities they are not very successful. Community Relations officers would have good working relations with community workers here, but at the end of the day there is not much that results from their efforts. Community relations programs in general in Northern Ireland are the flavor-of-the-month approach—new projects, but little thought as to where they are going. (SS)

In some Protestant areas people have been anxious to attend public meetings with the police to air local problems. Chapter 4 described one such meeting in a moderate Protestant neighborhood. But it appears that meetings between the RUC and members of the public are almost as rare in Loyalist areas as they are in Republican areas, perhaps because the police wish to avoid facing the intense public criticism they anticipate receiving. One Protestant minister noted that when the police have held a public meeting at his church, they have been "on the receiving end of criticisms from people who say 'the police are unfair to us' or that the police are bending over backwards to accommodate the other side" (P). In another locale the police have rarely held meetings with community leaders or the public, though residents apparently would welcome such meetings:

The police have to take the initiative. It would be a very well attended meeting and there would be many things to discuss. There is a bad sore opening up here about joyriding, which should be discussed. . . . They should be brave enough to listen to all views and take criticism from people who are very unhappy. They should ask people what they expect from the RUC. . . . Police would have to stand up and take the stick, what's coming to them. But you'd have to have a community leader chairing the meeting and controlling people, and you'd have to have a prefixed agenda. Many paramilitary people and their wives would turn up at the meeting and they'd try to turn it into something else; they might try to turn it around to the security situation [police actions against Loyalist insurgents]. You have to make sure that paramilitary sympathizers—who should be there—are not there for a personal vendetta or to attack every word the police said, but there because of conditions in the area. The meeting would have to deal with *ordinary policing.* (OO)

Not all Loyalist neighborhoods are anxious to see Community Relations officers become more involved in their affairs. In one community residents seem apathetic or suspicious of the CR Branch: "The police have never been instrumental in starting something like that. Its very hard to get people to go to any kind of meeting. People stay in their own houses and mind their own business. They are battle-weary and think nothing is changing, so 'what's the point?'" (X). In other Loyalist areas, Community Relations and Neighborhood patrol officers seem as disreputable as they are in Republican areas (discussed below). A worker at a community center notes that people

think the police are spying on them—earie-wiggin', as they say.

What is earie-wiggin'?

You know, like earwigs, getting in your ears, listening for things. People won't speak to them when they come into the center; people immediately stop talking—you could cut it with a knife. (WW)

One of her colleagues elaborated:

> Meetings [between police and] community groups happen rarely. People get suspicious if there is too much of that kind of contact. I don't think people would like more contact with Community Relations officers, but they will use them occasionally. They are suspicious of what the police are trying to do. They also fear being seen as touts [informers]. . . . If someone is talking to police in this area, they would be called an informer. . . . If policemen were hanging around [the community center], people would think they were waiting for the UDA men to come in or doing surveillance and people would get suspicious. If they are here for a short time, on business, its OK. . . . When buses are driven for our events, it is by the two Neighborhood police. But even the Neighborhood cops are not fully accepted. I don't like them coming into the center at times, because the center itself might get a bad reputation. We have twenty-two user groups [connected to the center] who would be suspicious if the police came in a lot. When they do come in, it's usually for only half an hour. (II)

A former director of this community center expanded on these observations and concerns:

> People have no illusions about what Neighborhood police are there for. You don't tell them anything. The workers at the center knew the Neighborhood cops were coming in to access information, to get an ear on the ground. People would talk to them and be civil toward them, but they wouldn't tell them anything important. The Neighborhood cops are still seen as police. As soon as a Neighborhood cop came into the center, people would adjust their conversation. They would tell us community workers things they would never tell a cop, and they were afraid [if they spoke to a constable] of being accused later of saying something they shouldn't have said. . . . Our caretaker got beaten up by paramilitaries because he talked to the Neighborhood officers. . . . The cops occasionally came in looking for certain people and we'd [community workers] say, "No, we haven't seen them," for survival reasons. We were concerned with the center's survival. You don't cultivate a police presence in a center because there's always a chance that someone will let something slip. We'd be very careful not to be seen meeting the police privately much. When I knew police were planning a visit I made a point of telling people, making a general announcement, saying that the police are coming in to talk about a spe-

cific thing. This would relieve people and protect the center. But sometimes the police would have an open agenda; I then had to be very careful in terms of what I'd discuss. At the same time, the center needed the police for certain things, like threats against the center from paramilitaries. There were times when it was in the best interests of the center to give cops information on paramilitaries, selectively. But police create pressure when they want to. They give you a sense that if you don't cooperate with them, then you are against them. (JJ)

Allegations of community constables' involvement in intelligence gathering cannot easily be verified. One CR officer quoted earlier in the chapter seemed to be referring to this when he said that Loyalists "have their paramilitaries too. You have to keep your finger on their pulse." But the other officers quoted above deny any involvement in covert security work. In the course of their routine work, however, these officers are bound to observe and hear things that may be useful to the RUC. They may actively refrain from seeking out security-related information, but discoveries about suspicious persons or events are no doubt passed on to other police officers, just as community cops do in other countries.

If some people evaluate police officers solely on the basis of their membership in the RUC (i.e., the institution determines attitudes), others' assessments are influenced by the demeanor or reputation of individual officers. A community worker describes how the behavior and standing of even one officer can make a difference:

I had terrible trouble with Neighborhood cops. They stop kids (even in Protestant areas) and accuse them of stealing things to provoke the kids. They ask, "Where did you get that radio?" or "that watch?" "Did your mother buy you that?" They would come in to the community center and sit around for as long as possible and the staff didn't want to make them coffee, and this was in a *Protestant* area! . . . They were asking kids what their brothers and fathers were up to. No way would Protestant families let kids talk to these Neighborhood cops. The Community Relations cops were accepted there, but the two Neighborhood cops were not accepted at all because they asked too many questions and made derogatory statements about kids and their families. When one of the cops was later posted to Crossmaglen, the people had a field day. Before these two officers came into the area, people loved the Neighborhood police, but when they took over relations changed drastically. It's amazing how one or two officers in an area can influence community perceptions about the RUC as a whole. The Community Relations officer up there . . . had a brilliant attitude, great rapport with kids. . . . He took a great interest in the kids and asked questions that showed his interest, like a question about a kid's parent being ill.

Didn't people see the questions as intelligence gathering?

No, because of the sensitive manner in which he spoke to people. He was genuinely concerned. He always said to me, "If there's anything I can do to help with anything, let me know." He volunteered to give references for kids if they were in court charged with a petty crime; he personally would act as a character reference for those kids! (MM)

Republican Communities

Moderate Catholics who live in middle-class, quiet neighborhoods generally see foot patrols and CR programs similarly to moderate, middle-class Protestants. These neighborhoods send children to CR functions and welcome school visits by police. Community policing is simply not very problematic for moderate Catholics; it is counterinsurgency policing that troubles them. But even while supporting community policing, they realize that the RUC as a whole does not operate as if improving community relations is a priority.

Some academics believe community policing spells an insidious form of control, a means of manipulating the public and bolstering the image of the police without incorporating citizen demands into decision making.[65] It is a promotional affair, not one of bilateral engagement. Community policing in the United States has been called a "velvet glove" designed for pacification of the public, and in Britain it has been described as nothing short of police "colonization" of civil society, the purpose of which is to manufacture consent for the police.[66] These claims are exaggerated with respect to liberal democracies, but closer to the mark in ethnically divided societies, where some neighborhoods define community policing in precisely these terms. They are a staple of the neighborhood culture in Northern Ireland's Republican areas, where there is no appreciable demand for community policing, where few people distinguish Neighborhood and Community Relations constables from anyone else in the RUC, and where "community relations" is seen not only as a euphemism for public relations but also a ruse for more sinister aims, namely, intelligence gathering to further the repression of the Catholic population.

James Baldwin once described the status of the police in America's black ghettos in the following terms: "Their very presence is an insult, and it would be, even if they spent their entire day feeding gumdrops to children."[67] Baldwin overstated the extent of black hostility to the police in the early 1960s, but his assessment applies with full force to Northern Ireland's staunch Republican neighborhoods. Community cops are no less "legitimate targets" than their counterparts in other branches of the RUC. One example is a Community Relations officer who, I was told, was shot and killed while giving candy to a young girl. Rejection of these officers is also expressed in less violent ways in Republican areas, chiefly by residents' studious avoidance of all contact with them.

My data indicate that foot patrols, either by regular constables or by the Neighborhood Branch, are totally unwelcome in Republican neighborhoods: "The public at large don't see that foot patrols present anything other than a threat. They serve no useful purpose. The message is to show that they [the security forces] are present in an area. You know that sooner or later officers are going to relieve their boredom by harassing people" (U). Seeing foot patrols as nearly as unapproachable as armored landrovers, people religiously shun them:

> People are very reluctant to talk to police on the street. They might say hello and walk on but wouldn't want a long conversation. (RR)

> You wouldn't see anyone stopping and talking to a policeman. . . . Civilians won't initiate conversations with officers on foot patrol; the police initiate if anything is said. . . . If a policeman says "hello," most people would respond and walk on. . . . Or maybe you don't speak to them, but nod pleasantly as you pass by. (U)

If officers try to initiate conversations, some people will say nothing at all and others keep their responses brief, dubious of the officers' motives:

Police will speak to people during foot patrols today; they will ask, "How are you today?" or "I saw you downtown." Small talk. . . . The police mostly initiate the conversation. They even engage in some banter with hoods. . . . Adults are less likely to speak to the police. It's more the younger people and the known hoods in the area who would talk to them. . . . Striking up a conversation, especially with women with prams [containing babies], is a way of giving the police cover [from possible attack]. Women won't talk to them except to say, "You are just using me." They would give police abuse; they'd tell them to get away from them, that they were using them for cover. (W)

Foot patrols are therefore hardly a means of improving relations in these neighborhoods. One informant thought there might be conditions under which such patrols would become slightly more acceptable: "You want to be sure that the officers on the beat are trained, have met the local people and know them by name (not as strangers), and would not play with the kids, because mothers would be suspicious that it would be a con job" (D). But this informant was skeptical that this could be done. Others were unequivocal when asked if people wanted to see more foot patrols:

No, are you joking? The army and police never leave the place. We'd like them out completely. (TT)

People . . . wouldn't want to see more foot patrols, because they don't like them, the police are outsiders, and people are afraid it would lead to rioting by the kids. (D)

People don't want either the army or the RUC doing foot patrols. They don't trust the police, they basically don't trust them! (MM)

We want the patrols done away with altogether. . . . (U)

The idea of a bobby on the beat is ridiculous. Even if only one officer walked around, his presence would still be unacceptable. It wouldn't make what he stands for any more acceptable. (LL)

The RUC would be shot at more often if they did do [more] foot patrols. (B)

My interview findings indicate that it would be quite difficult for people to suspend assumptions that foot patrols are involved in a "con job," or some covert security work:

We had a cop who learned people's names and would say "Hi Jim" or "Hi Mary" and it wasn't appreciated at all! He was seen as a greater threat than the cop who just went about his job. Community relations efforts like that would normally be interpreted as having a hook.

A hook?

They wouldn't be seen as goodwill efforts. In the present context, they are perceived as part of the overall security exercise, intelligence gathering. This notion of a community relations officer of goodwill doesn't exist in this area. People would say he really doesn't exist! (S)

There is a general impression that intelligence gathering is one motive, even among older people. . . . Even those who support a police presence would not do so without having doubts in their mind. (RR)

Young kids might talk to cops out of curiousity. . . . But when kids have asked about the cops' guns, police have said, "Does your daddy have a gun?" They are always doing intelligence gathering, always. (LL)

Police go out of their way to strike up a conversation—for intelligence gathering.

Do people realize that intelligence gathering is going on?

Adults would see it as intelligence gathering and avoid speaking to them. (W)

In sum, residents of Republican neighborhoods avoid foot patrols for pragmatic reasons (the encounters might turn nasty or they wish to conform to the neighborhood street code, which forbids contact) and out of principle (because patrol officers are members of a discredited organization or involved in covert security work). That the patrols are defined as part of the security apparatus turns on its head the conventional wisdom about their promise. Rather than improving police-community relations, foot patrols have a backfiring effect, *worsening* those relations by intensifying residents' fear and loathing of the forces "occupying" their neighborhood.

Are Community Relations officers viewed any differently? A CR sergeant working in a Republican area believes that residents think "we are doing ordinary, simple police work and are not involved in sensitive matters."[68] But my community-based informants disagreed. One reported:

> They are viewed exactly the same as other peelers; they work for the same organization and they all carry guns.[69] Police coming into schools or setting up discos would be viewed as part of the same organization.
>
> *So people don't draw distinctions between Community Relations cops and other cops?*
>
> No. That Community Relations officer can be shifted to any branch or into any police operation, so he is not really separate from other cops. People believe those community cops didn't go into the RUC for community relations work. (LL)

Indeed, in Republican areas CR constables are occasionally mobilized for other duties, including crowd control during marches, funerals, and riots. Though rare in Republican areas, this public order deployment compromises CR officers' expressed interest in avoiding direct involvement in counterinsurgency.

Intelligence gathering, however infrequent and low level, is another way they may become involved in security work:

> At the end of the day, every RUC man is gathering at least low-level intelligence. His primary thing is his security role. What a Community Relations cop would hear kids talking about, he feels duty bound to pass it on to other cops, which could lead to a serious incident. Some kids will jokingly say [to other kids], "You're dad's in the IRA" or "You have guns in your house." These things are bound to occur in the presence of Community Relations cops. Also, officers *must* be asking kids for information related to Republican activities, subtle intelligence gathering. . . . Another goal is turning kids against Republicanism. (UU)

CR officers are also involved in trying to normalize the RUC's image. A CR sergeant told me that during his (rare) visits to schools in a Republican area

> we'd present ourselves as ordinary policemen. In talks to primary school children we present a general idea of what a policeman's job is. The police here come across as a very military-type force, and we try to emphasize other things. We say we are here to protect life and property, to detect crime, and to protect you. Rather than jumping out of landrovers.

Would the children question this image, saying that they don't see police doing the normal things?

Primary school children wouldn't have such a response, but secondary school children would.

Informants labeled such normalization efforts "propaganda" and complained that CR officers were "trying to make it look like the RUC is a normal force" (UU).

My interview data show that the dominant theme in the neighborhood culture of Republican areas is that community policing is designed for "public relations or for intelligence gathering" (D). But there are also some countervailing views which are sociologically significant albeit subordinate to the prevailing definitions. Community leaders and ordinary people living in troubled Catholic areas are not uniformly antagonistic to CR programs. One informant indicated how the minority in his neighborhood, who might like to participate in a CR venture, are overshadowed by dominant local forces:

Hard-core Republicans wouldn't want to and other people, around 40 percent, would like to be involved, would be happy to take part, but they know it's just not politically feasible. They'd be leaving themselves open to intimidation or harassment or problems for their family living in the community. One priest tried to organize a ramble, which involved use of a police van, and when it hit the headlines it didn't help his reputation at all. (RR)

It is also the case that some Republican communities show slightly more civility than others toward Neighborhood or Community Relations officers. A community worker contrasted two areas where she had worked:

Here people would cut them to shreds [verbally] if they tried to start a conversation. In [another community] there may be some more banter [between officers and some residents] than here. I offered the police tea at [that] community center and a worker at the center even went and bought coffee for one of the officers who didn't drink tea. That would be a no-no here. I once offered a cup of tea to a cop I had called in to the center because my purse had been stolen, and people were outraged! (MM)

A few of my sources in Republican areas spoke positively about the caliber and intentions of officers attached to the Community Relations Branch (C, Q), but they also pointed out that

these officers seemed to be powerless to do anything about problems or influence officers outside the branch. For instance, a clergyman who sometimes deals with CR officers finds them polite
and helpful, but he questions "whether they actually do anything
about problems" and notes that it is difficult to see their concern
for improving relations "filtered down to the rank and file" (A).

Notwithstanding the positive feelings about community constables held by some people in Republican neighborhoods, the
dominant orientation is one of disdain. And there are personal risks
to anyone having contacts with the police; such persons are widely
regarded with suspicion, and the more frequent the contact, the
more dangerous the liaison. This applies to ordinary individuals
and community leaders alike, although Catholic clergy are somewhat exempt. Working *with* the police, in virtually any capacity, is
tantamount to working *for* them. And working for the police
means that one is working against the IRA. (Persons who are
employed in any supportive capacity to the RUC and army are considered "legitimate targets" by the IRA; from 1985 to 1993 it killed
30 people for doing contract work for the security forces, such as
repairing bombed police stations or supplying food to police.)

Both CR officers and my community informants agreed that
police access to young people in Republican areas is often hindered by parents, teachers, and political activists.[70] In those areas
Catholic school officials are reluctant to allow police visits
because of their own anti-RUC attitudes, anticipated resistance
from parents, or threats from Sinn Fein/IRA. CR officers are not
allowed into some schools in West Belfast, for example, and in
others the lecture topics are narrowly restricted. For example,
officers may be allowed to lecture on topics like avoiding
strangers or crime prevention but not on policing as a career or
the "role of the police."[71] A sergeant describes the situation in
Catholic schools in the area:

> No principal has said, "No, we don't *want* you in." But they say
> they can't have us in because of concern for the police officers'
> security and the security of the schools. The Provos [IRA]
> would take active steps to prevent that. . . . Most of the break-
> throughs come when you get a new headmaster who doesn't
> realize the dangers. But the times we've been into Catholic
> schools are very, very few, and then there has not been a reac-
> tion from the Provos. But we do little because we expect they
> would put a stop to it. We'll go and have liaison with the head-

master, but we won't go into the classroom. If he and I have a productive meeting, that's how I would measure success. In other areas, officers are in the schools every day. . . . The few times we've been in grade schools, we wouldn't be in uniform, . . . we'd be very sensitive in what we do, and we'd present ourselves as ordinary policemen.

Primary school children may not challenge the officers, but on the rare occasion when police have managed to visit a secondary school in one Republican area, "some students would say, 'What the fuck are you doing here?' during a lecture. They'd challenge us, but we'd take it in stride. Usually teachers would back officers up. Community Relations officers expect to be haggled in these schools. They faced a lion's den."[72]

My community informants confirmed that community constables were unwelcome in the schools:

People would be very suspicious of anything the police would ask of them. The police would know that they shouldn't try anything here. None of our kids would go on a ramble or to a disco sponsored by the RUC. Parents wouldn't allow their kids to attend. (W)

Most people here wouldn't let their children get involved in [school visits by police]. Community Relations officers are creating an illusion. . . . The whole point would be to turn people against the Republicans, to try to depoliticize the situation and to try to make Sinn Fein and the IRA out to be hoods to be turned against and informed on. This would be their ultimate goal; they probably would not say these things in the lecture, but this is what they'd be working towards. (UU)

The majority of parents would object if they knew Community Relations officers were coming into schools here. There would be an uproar about it. The majority would resent those visits and if they knew about it beforehand they wouldn't send their kids to school for that day. People might even protest and picket the school. That has happened before in other parts of the city. And they would have sharp words for the school's Board of Governors for letting the police in.

But a minority of parents would approve?

Few. There is a small minority who would say—after they found out about the visit from their kids—that the lecture focused on road safety or something else innocuous and they would be prepared to accept it on those grounds. But even these people might be skeptical of allowing the visit, if they knew beforehand, for security reasons. The police would have to have the military swamp the place to protect the Community Relations cops for one lecture! This might endanger the kids. The majority of parents, if they learned a visit had occurred, would be up there voicing their indignation. Group pressure would also prevent the minority view from being heard in most cases. . . . I've never heard of school visits by Community Relations cops here, and we would have heard if it had happened. (LL)

Also telling is the response from a SDLP politician when it was announced in 1991 that the chief constable planned to begin police recruitment efforts in Catholic schools. He publicly branded it as impractical and so unacceptable that parents would resist the initiative.[73]

The IRA and Sinn Fein also try to prevent police visits to schools, although they are not always successful. A Sinn Fein city councillor told me:

I had an argument with a headteacher regarding the ramble scheme. The school wanted to use Community Relations for a ramble and I said that is wrong. I tried to convince him not to have contact with the RUC. I reminded him that one of his pupils was shot dead by a plastic bullet [fired by the police]. But I wasn't successful in convincing him to refrain from dealing with the Community Relations cops. I told him that a Community Relations cop this year might be firing plastic bullets at demonstrators next year. It's a moral dilemma for him. The last thing I asked was whether he did not see the possible security threat in allowing children to accompany the police on a ramble. . . . He responded that there were a number of Catholic schools doing it and that if the parents let them go, they should be allowed to go. (UU)

The difficulties community constables face in working with youth in Republican areas is mirrored in their efforts to build relationships with adults, either on an individual or group basis. It might seem natural for CR officers to develop links to community organizations, but this is impossible in Republican areas. A CR sergeant confided that community groups in Republican parts of Belfast "would be the *last* people to get involved with us":

Community groups in the green [Republican] area, it would be very difficult for them to meet with us. We are striving to get more contacts with them. If they meet us they will be told they can't do it and there will be boys [IRA operatives] at their door. We have hardly any contact with community leaders, and when we do we must meet in a secure area away from the station.

Lacking contacts with community leaders, CR officers are obviously in no position to intervene or mediate when serious problems arise, such as Orange marches through the community or problems with other police and army units.

The neighborhood taboo on civilian contacts with community constables is not watertight, however. Catholic clergy are in a rather unique position in these neighborhoods in that they are not pressured to eschew contacts with the RUC. Insurgent groups have been careful not to be seen interfering with the Catholic Church, which traditionally has been outside their sphere of influence. Although the majority of Catholic clergy seem to agree with the Church hierarchy that political violence is sinful,[74] they are divided in their views of the courts, army, and police.[75] Some priests have repeatedly and publicly condemned police misconduct; others are less critical and have expressed qualified or unqualified support for the RUC. Some clergy religiously keep the RUC at bay, refusing all overtures from community constables. Others have no hesitation in dealing with the police. They help to facilitate CR programs by trying to recruit young members of their church to participate, regularly approach the police on behalf of parishioners, or attend functions or meetings with the police. Others are selective in their contacts. A priest said: "I'll see them privately at any time, but I'm not going to dinners with them. I'm not into the wining and dining. Meetings between clergy and the police don't go well. The Protestant ministers say 'how are ya Sammy?' [to an officer], which shows that the officers get on with the Protestants. It looks bad" (Q). Another priest believes that lunches for local clergy are "a PR effort" and "fairly artificial," but he attends anyway (O). A Protestant minister described the atmosphere at these meetings:

> The cynic in me wonders how far the meetings are a PR job, trying to soften me up. But I still tend to think that the officers are genuinely concerned. . . . Only occasionally do criticisms arise in those meetings. Those of us who would attend would be the clergy who would already have an interest in improving community relations. So we would not be likely to enter into

heated debates. If clergy on the fringes attended, it might be different. (P)

Insurgents grant community groups much less latitude than clergy in liaising with the RUC. One exception is a civic group in Londonderry that has fairly frequent contacts with CR officers as well as Republican insurgents. The police have asked the organization to transmit messages, to mediate incidents, and to help the police in dealing with people in a notoriously dangerous area or during some street disturbances. In turn, the group has had some success with its efforts on behalf of citizens, helping families get visits to their detained children and arranging for the release of some detainees. Some of these people are associated with Sinn Fein, which leads it to tolerate the organization's contacts with the RUC, as a member confides: "Sinn Fein aren't mad about us, but they see us doing them a favor by going to the police for their constituents" (M). This group clearly has a unique relationship with the RUC that other community groups in Republican areas lack—apparently because both senior police officers and Republican insurgents in Londonderry know that the group is capable of helping them.

As a general rule, however, civic organizations in Republican areas have either negligible contact with the RUC or none at all. Community workers in several Republican areas pointed to the constraints insurgent groups place on their organizations:

> We walk a tightrope in what people see as our business. We would be putting the organization at risk if we were seen to be liaising with the police. The Republican paramilitaries see a role for our organization, which is nonpolitical and noninvolved in policing. To liaise with the police would be stepping over the mark. Nationalists don't mind us making representations [to the police] if people are lifted or harassed. But they don't want us involved in positive policing because it's against their interests. They *want* police kicking down doors!

> *How do you know what the limits are?*

> We have an instinct that certain work is OK. One-to-one dealing with people's rights is OK, but if I get involved with police in terms of how to police a certain area, it would be unacceptable. (C)

> We'd have to be careful not to be seen working on behalf of the police. You could be regarded as being a police apologist. We

have to be more indirect. Rather than going to the police directly, we work through other agencies. We try to keep the center here as neutral as we can—neither part of the controlling function of the state nor the struggle against the state. (RR)

In [one neighborhood] we tried to use Community Relations but we had a lot of opposition from the local Sinn Fein councillors. They said, "Don't use police vehicles because they are legitimate targets." We said, "Even with children in them?" He said, "It doesn't matter, they are still legitimate targets and they are targets even if my children are in them, which they won't be." He was very blasé about it. We said that we wanted to continue to use them. (SS)

Some community workers in Republican areas avoid liaisons with the police for reasons other than pressure from insurgents. For some, personal distrust of the police is reason enough. An organization's constituents may be another deterrent. At one community center, CR officers "have rung and asked us to come to a meeting about joyriders. But if the people around here found out, that would be the end of the center!" No one in the neighborhood, it was claimed, would attend a meeting to discuss crime problems (W). Another community center avoids police for similar reasons: "Our committee is elected by other community groups. These groups would not want us to liaise with the RUC. Their views are too jaundiced now. . . . If it was known that we had contact with the RUC, people would pull out of our group" (B). Another said:

Community Relations cops, we can't deal with them at all. People here would say any contact with police is a no-no. People see it [CR programs] as a way of pumping their kids for information. I've been warned off about even bringing them into the [community center].

By whom?

By ordinary people, not the paramilitaries. I dropped hints about the possibility of doing some cross-community work with police help—I'd done it before in other communities—and people here said "absolutely not." Here they don't make distinctions between Community Relations cops and other cops. People don't even want to find out if the Community Relations cops are well intentioned. I've said to them, "You don't even know any of these cops, so how can you make a judgment?" And people said they didn't want to meet them or know anything about them. They simply wouldn't entertain the idea. They're seen as just police. Later I asked for clarification as to why they were so hostile to these cops and they said the Community Relations Branch was an information-gathering branch of the RUC. (MM)

Organizations that work to promote interethnic reconciliation also consider close contacts with the RUC problematic. One such organization sponsors conferences for community activists and functions for Protestant and Catholic youths, some of which RUC members have attended. The director reflects:

> We ran into some problems with these meetings. We were a little afraid of being *used* as an organization to promote the police point of view. We wanted to be seen as honest brokers to give people the opportunity to express views freely. . . . We were invited by the RUC to do more at one time and I regret that we didn't. We were a bit afraid the police were using us. We don't want our organization to lose its own integrity and credibility. You need to retain some distance for credibility. (I)

These interview data show just how stigmatized the police have become in Republican areas and how easily that stigma can rub off on groups associating with the police. This extreme disrepute-by-association with the RUC is not a significant factor in police relations with minorities elsewhere in the United Kingdom or in the United States.

In sum, there are three main reasons why people living in staunch Republican areas take pains to avoid community constables: the norms of the neighborhood culture proscribe contacts with all police officers; community constables are contaminated by the RUC's general lack of authority and by recurring problems of police brutality, harassment, unaccountability, and so on; and community police are thought to be involved in covert security work. Not only is there profound opposition to community policing in Republican neighborhoods—perhaps the strongest for any ethnic group in the Western world—but community policing also has a backfiring effect. Not only does it fail to improve relations with these communities, it worsens those relations. It follows that more foot patrols and more robust Community Relations activities in these neighborhoods would only compound the problem.

CONCLUSION

This chapter has identified several obstacles in the path of official efforts to improve police-community relations in Northern Ireland: (1) the context of political violence and counterinsurgency, (2) shortcomings in existing community policing approaches, and (3) the lack of receptivity in staunch Republican and Loyalist neighborhoods to state-sponsored efforts to improve police-community relations.

Certainly the protracted political violence in Northern Ireland, which includes lethal and nonlethal attacks on police, hampers community policing. CR constables are softer targets than other RUC officers because their greater interaction with the public puts them in greater danger and because they are normally unarmed. (Neighborhood patrolmen are less vulnerable since they carry guns.) In troubled areas, the omnipresent danger makes their work a pale imitation of what normally passes for community policing.

Also critical is the fact that community policing operates in the shadows of counterinsurgency policing, which determines perceptions of all police activities in the most troubled neighborhoods. Specific counterinsurgency operations also affect, in a more direct way, the work of CR constables. When an operation goes awry and sparks controversy, this causes a ripple effect in the neighborhoods most exercized by the event, derailing community constables' efforts or at least interrupting their progress in the neighborhood. A single police shooting of a civilian or even an insurgent, for instance, may unravel whatever minor achievements community police might have made with some people prior to the incident.

There are also limitations in the nature and scope of the state's response to community relations problems. As for the Police Authority, its definition of the problem and its solutions seem rather limited. When asked what the Authority is doing to build public confidence in the police, the chairman emphasized attempts to improve communication:

> Much of it boils down to a communication gap between officers and the community. Apart from that, there is no magic formula. [We are] trying to dismantle the *perception* of policing inherited from the 1960s and 1970s, and showing that policing today is

different. . . . Community leaders are invited in for discussions with the police. The police are constantly probing the attitudes of the community and trying to reflect the wishes of the community. So it *does* happen, frequently but informally. Divisional commanders do take great care to open dialogue with people. They contact those community leaders who are fair and unbiased. And the Police Authority tries to sound out people from various communities—political and religious leaders and community workers—and we take their views on board.[76]

We have seen that the problem goes far beyond a communication breakdown: it is driven by real conflicts between police and civilians over police practices, reforms, and the very legitimacy of the RUC.

The Police-Community Liaison Committees have similarly minimalistic views of the problem and its solution, and they have failed—by design or default—to address the interests of the most discontented sections of society.

As for the RUC, the compartmentalization of community policing dilutes its potential. Community policing has the greatest promise not when it is a narrowly defined set of *programs* monopolized by special units detached from other police officers, but when it is a *philosophy* of policing shaping the policies and practices of the entire police force, especially with regard to street-level encounters between police and civilians.[77] In the RUC as in most other police forces,[78] community policing is segregated from other police work and foreign to most officers. What is needed is a thorough reconstitution of the RUC's occupational culture in line with the principles of community policing—sensitivity and respect toward civilians, a service orientation, and communication rather than confrontation—to reduce the most unsettling conduct. Such subcultural change requires, at the minimum, steadfast efforts by commanding officers to ensure that community constables are not isolated from the rest of the force and that the lessons they learn are routinely disseminated throughout the organization. This does not mean that the entire police force should do what community police do now; instead, it involves ongoing feedback to foster a broader sensitivity to community concerns.

Unfortunately, the growth of these values and behavioral inclinations is almost impossible in a context where security policing is so prominent, where some communities see the RUC as altogether sinister, and where constables are routinely stoned, shot at, and petrol bombed. For community-friendly policing to thrive, a climate of goodwill and mutual acceptance is required, but this is almost entirely absent in neighborhoods where the police and residents see each other as enemies and where residents are belligerent and uncooperative with officers. Moreover, it is difficult to see how a meaningful kind of community policing can be grafted onto a system so dominated by security priorities. On the other hand, there are many interactional settings—checkpoints, house searches, demonstrations, and marches—where police officers could treat citizens much more sensitively and thereby help to lessen the RUC's ill repute.

Predictably more enlightened than other officers about the importance of cultivating police-community relations and the possible dividends accruing from such efforts, Community Relations and Neighborhood constables are rather atypical of the force. Moreover, their efforts are repeatedly undermined by the actions of other officers, particularly those stationed in troubled areas and those heavily involved in security-related duties. In inhospitable neighborhoods, community policing will continue to fail to ameliorate police-citizen relations as long as other kinds of policing remain constant. This does not go unnoticed by community constables. "Community Relations policing is bolting the stable door after the fact," a CR sergeant observed. "It should be there to prevent problems from arising and to help realize what the problems are."[79] Counterinsurgency policing, with all of its aggravating and alienating effects on those who suffer from it, thus lies at the very heart of the community relations problem in Northern Ireland, yet it has remained largely impervious to the reforms instituted in other areas of policing.

None of my informants, even those who praise the efforts of Community Relations and Neighborhood officers, believe that their efforts are having much positive impact on police-community relations. However well intentioned, community policing programs have yielded little or nothing positive in neighborhoods where relations with the police are abysmal. In fact, in these neighborhoods, community policing has had the opposite effect of what is intended. Rather than improving police-community relations, it *negatively affects* those relations. People associate community constables with other "forces of oppression" and take pains to avoid all contact with them. The presence of CR and

Neighborhood officers in a community is only another means of "occupying" or surreptitiously controlling it. It is extremely difficult to envision how community policing might be destigmatized, absent a transformation of Northern Ireland's political system. And more robust community policing programs, more foot patrols, and more inclusive police-community liaison committees would only meet with more resistance in Republican and some Loyalist neighborhoods.

None of this is to suggest that police-community relations are frozen in Northern Ireland. Relations *can* be improved within certain limits. But we have seen that such improvement is not going to occur through formal community policing programs and liaison arrangements. Relations will not improve unless counterinsurgency policing improves and, more fundamentally, until a political settlement is reached.

CHAPTER 8

Conclusion

In this concluding chapter I review the book's major findings and draw some conclusions about the conditions under which police-community relations may improve or deteriorate in Northern Ireland. I then make some broader points that should have implications for our understanding of police-community relations in other societies.

Under Unionist rule the Royal Ulster Constabulary came very close to the divided society model of policing outlined in Chapter 1. In some respects, the RUC today bears a striking resemblance to its former incarnation under the Unionist state. It remains armed and militarized, involved in both ordinary law enforcement and counterinsurgency, and overwhelmingly Protestant despite efforts to recruit Catholics. The RUC's role in internal security and public order has increased dramatically under British rule, largely because the level of political violence has remained high and the British army has assumed a reduced role, with the RUC filling the vacuum. Yet there are also important ways in which the RUC has progressed since the demise of Unionist rule. It enforces the law in a more universalistic manner; its mission is no longer that of upholding Protestant supremacy; it is more autonomous of external, sectarian forces; training has improved; and outside mechanisms of accountability now exist.

In short, under British rule policing reflects both traditional commitments and new demands. It departs from certain dimensions of the divided society model, but not others. Despite the reforms, police relations with Catholics have not markedly improved, and precisely because of the reforms, police relations with a section of Protestants have deteriorated.

Central to my analysis is a more refined picture of divided societies than we find in conventional perspectives that paint divisions in black and white. The central dynamic in divided societies, of course, is the conflict between the major communal populations,[1] but intracommunal divisions may also be important and deserving of investigation in their own right. The differences in how the police are experienced and regarded by subgroups within a particular communal population may mean that a subgroup has more in common *on some issues* with a section of the opposing communal group than with other sections of the communal population of which it is a part. In Northern Ireland, we have seen that moderate Protestants and Catholics are not worlds apart in all of their opinions of the police; they have some similar views. Similarly, staunch Loyalists hold some grievances that bear striking resemblance to those of staunch Republicans. These cross-cutting cleavages are most likely to develop after a new regime takes power if the regime prompts changes that alter traditional relations between police and dominant and/or subordinate groups. The changes may, for example, irritate a section of the dominant population, leading to some convergence with the complaints of the subordinate population. Explanations for the similarities and differences between the groups can be traced, I have argued, to our four variables: counterinsurgency policing, legitimacy of the state, national-level conflicts over policing, and ordinary law enforcement. This explanatory framework is not specific to Northern Ireland; it should prove useful, I believe, in understanding other deeply divided societies.

Staunch Republicans have the worst relations with the RUC. They live in neighborhoods whose culture is militantly opposed to the British state and the security forces, neither of which commands moral authority. These neighborhoods bear the brunt of counterinsurgency policing but receive little in the way of conventional policing. Residents criticize the RUC's "abdication" of its responsibility for ordinary crime, but their profound suspiciousness of the police creates ambivalence about whether the RUC should play a greater role in this area. Anti-police feelings are pervasive in these communities. Even persons who have had good experiences with individual officers tend to hold negative views of the RUC as an organization because of the neighborhood reputation of the force, which is shaped by historical antipathy to the RUC (part of the socialization of each new generation) and contemporary events both inside and outside the community. National-level conflicts over policing only bolster Republicans' alienation from the RUC and willingness to tolerate, applaud, or participate in violent attacks on constables.

Moderate Catholics are in something of a dilemma. They express more satisfaction with the police than Republicans and their interactions with officers are less strained, largely because they tend to live in neighborhoods where security policing is relatively light. They want ordinary crime dealt with more vigorously. Even if the counterinsurgency enterprise has little direct impact on their lives, however, they are critical of it. Serial conflicts at the national level over this kind of policing have an ongoing effect on the perceptions of moderate Catholics, which casts a shadow over improvements in policing and gives a hollow ring to the authorities' praise for the RUC's accomplishments. Added to this is the low status of British rule, which limits the degree to which confidence can grow in institutions of law and order. Until a political settlement is reached, the legitimacy of the RUC will remain precarious, though moderates are less likely than Republicans to insist that it has absolutely no credibility.

Protestants are more favorably disposed toward the police than Catholics. The predominant Protestant orientation (strongest among moderates) entails a presumption in favor of the police, which is solid enough to cast suspicion on allegations of police misbehavior, at least when the charges come from Catholics. (This "halo effect" is not so bright, however, that it necessarily blinds people to serious or repeated departures from expected policing practices.) Protestant support for the RUC is consistent with the pattern for dominant ethnic groups in other divided societies, but Northern Ireland now differs from the model divided society because of the dominant group's loss of state power in 1972. This loss of control over the levers of executive and parliamentary power can set in motion a process in which the dominant group's relations with authorities like the police become strained, and Protestant support for the RUC has indeed grown less categorical and more qualified since 1972. A residue of the historical affinity between the RUC and the Protestant population remains, but it has diminished significantly over the past two decades, leaving a degree of ambivalence among Protestants unknown during the era of Unionist rule.

Nowhere is this more evident than among staunch Loyalists. Historically the fiercest champions of the RUC, they have grown increasingly frustrated and resentful during the two decades of British rule. This will come as no surprise to those who study divided societies undergoing transformations, but it does not figure prominently in the literature on Northern Ireland. Loyalists revere iron-fist policing when it is targeted at Catholics, but are incensed that the use of "kid gloves" is the norm. What's more, the police are now accused of treating Loyalist communities with the same bitter medicine they should be using against Catholic rebels. As in Republican areas, harsh policing affects not only insurgents and criminals but also the law-abiding population, who are not immune from police behavior that is uncivil and provocative. Loyalists frequently complain that the police are acting against the wrong people, people who are "loyal" to Ulster. The cumulative effect of years of such "misdirected," oppressive policing is a palpable erosion of confidence in the RUC. For this, Loyalists blame both the police and the British government. The police are faulted for their willingness to carry out British policies, the British government for debasing the entire law-and-order enterprise. State intervention usually results in "unwarranted" restraints on the policing of Catholics and sometimes harsh sanctions against Protestants, and a basic distrust of this state also diminishes Loyalists' confidence in the RUC. As for national-level conflicts over policing, they affect Loyalists' attitudes in a positive manner only when the grievances or demands come from Catholics and when they are rejected by the authorities. When the controversy arises out of Protestants' complaints, it is likely to reinforce Loyalists' doubts about the RUC or bitterness over the government's role in policing.

Moderate Protestants have the best relations with the police of any of our four groups. They consider the British state somewhat more legitimate than the other groups, are generally satisfied with the RUC's performance of its ordinary policing duties, and have little direct experience with security policing. However, the latter indirectly affects, via national-level struggles, their perceptions of policing. When the disputes are initiated by Catholics, moderate Protestant leaders typically jump to the defense of the police, belittling criticisms and symbolically demonstrating their confidence in the police. The cumulative effect of these struggles is a reinforcement of their support for the RUC. Like staunch Loyalists, moderates believe the RUC is unduly restricted in its fight against Republican insurgency, and they favor "untying" officers' hands. Demands for tighter restrictions on the use of force and greater accountability to oversight bodies may be acceptable in a "normal" society, but in strife-torn Northern Ireland they are seen as handcuffing the police. This automatic defense of the security forces may disappear, however, when criticisms come from other Protestants.

It bears repeating that although moderate Catholics and Protestants live in areas where counterinsurgency operations are subdued on the ground, their views are indirectly and differentially affected by counterinsurgency policing because it is fiercely contested at the national level. These conflicts have had a net negative effect on moderate Catholic perceptions, a net positive effect on moderate Protestants.

We have also seen that in a divided society like Northern Ireland, police-community relations are not only a function of the way the police treat "us" but also the way they purportedly treat "them." Communities, particularly the troubled ones, hold strong beliefs about policing in neighborhoods on the opposite side. Both staunch Republicans and Loyalists believe the RUC is unresponsive to their needs and too lenient on the other side. They also seem to resent police attempts to improve relations with the other side, which can be construed as placating people who deserve stiff medicine. (This dynamic is perhaps unique to deeply divided societies.) What is remarkable is that such strident opinions about the opposite community are formulated largely without the benefit of firsthand observations or other reliable information. And media reports or other accounts that challenge taken-for-granted assumptions about policing on the other side are either defined as exceptions to the rule or rejected outright.

Conflict theorists have exaggerated the degree to which conflict theory explains policing and police-community relations in relatively integrated, democratic societies lacking civil strife. I have argued that conflict theory has much more explanatory power in authoritarian and communally divided societies. In divided societies, conflict occurs both between ethnic groups and the police and between different ethnic groups over policing issues. In Northern Ireland we have found a high degree of discord between Protestants and Catholics over the state and state intervention in policing; we have found that, on specific aspects of policing, there is considerable disagreement between Catholics and Protestants and our four subgroups; we have found that some neighborhoods are entirely inhospitable to the police; we have found deep discontent over counterinsurgency policing and dissatisfaction with ordinary law enforcement and community policing. This does not mean that conflict rages over every aspect of policing or that it is equally intense in all areas, but contested policing is clearly endemic in Northern Ireland, unlike the more episodic disputes elsewhere in the United Kingdom. Conflict over policing is rooted in Northern Ireland's sociopolitical order, with its real and perceived ethnic inequalities, enduring ethnic prejudice and hostilities, the legacy of Protestant political domination, and the existing system of British rule which lacks moral authority for Catholics and Protestants alike. In this context, are there any changes that might help to improve, even slightly, police-community relations?

IMPROVING POLICE-COMMUNITY RELATIONS

Since the model of police-community relations in divided societies presented in Chapter 1 is more complex than what we find in more integrated societies—that is, there are more interrelated determinants—we should expect that relations would be harder to change in divided societies. Judging from this study's findings, it appears that much of the conventional wisdom on improving police-community relations, which we find in the literature on Britain and the United States, does not apply very well to divided societies:

1. Recruiting more cops from a subordinate ethnic group is hardly a sufficient condition, and may not even be a necessary condition, for building confidence in the police. It will have little positive effect on police relations with the subordinate group in the absence of larger changes. Even moderate Catholics in Northern Ireland, who seem to want more Catholic constables, would see this as a minor change. Moderate Protestants would have the same reaction, but many staunch Loyalists would be alarmed by a significantly greater number of Catholics in the RUC.

2. Organizational changes that improve police training, redefine the mission of a police force, increase the commitment to more impartial law enforcement, and induce autonomy from political forces are valuable in their own right. But it is unlikely that such reforms, in the absence of other changes, will have much positive effect on a subordinate group's relations with the police. This is partly because these reforms are at least one step removed from policing on the ground, where repressive incidents continue

to occur. For Northern Ireland's Catholics, as long as policing remains so obtrusive at the neighborhood level and so controversial at the national level, it colors or neutralizes the progressive changes in other areas of policing. Reforms are overshadowed by continuing problems, both real and perceived, of harassment, verbal abuse, use of excessive force, oppressive "occupation" of neighborhoods, collusion between police and Loyalist insurgents, and biased law enforcement (over half of Catholics believe the police continue to favor Protestants).

Dominant groups, by contrast, are likely to interpret reforms that depart from traditional policing as a threat to the maintenance of law and order and to their superordinate position in society. Ulster's Protestants have fought virtually every progressive change for precisely these reasons. Many endorse universalistic, apolitical, and accountable policing in principle, but this support wanes when these ideals are too heavily reflected in practices that violate what Protestants traditionally expected from the RUC. Hence, many Protestants complain about "excessive" restrictions on the use of force, due process norms governing the treatment of suspects in police custody, actions of the complaints commission, and overly evenhanded law enforcement. Reforms too often translate into unwarranted intervention in Protestant areas when police should instead be intensifying their control of subversive Catholic neighborhoods.

3. Civilian oversight bodies, such as policy-making agencies or complaints boards, may serve the dual role of increasing police accountability and building public confidence in the police. The creation of such a body is, of course, no guarantee that the public will be satisfied that the police are under meaningful control and that misconduct is being punished. Northern Ireland is a case in point. Catholics roundly dismiss the oversight bodies as window dressing. The Police Authority's power over the RUC seems hollow, and the complaints commission seems ineffective because of low substantiation rates, because its actions against wayward cops are largely invisible, or because of a failure to act decisively in the most notorious cases of police misconduct. Nearly three-fourths of SDLP supporters and nine out of ten Sinn Fein supporters believe that members of the RUC who commit offenses usually do so with impunity; and 90 percent of Catholics want a complaints commission with investigatory powers, rather than one that relies on police investigations. Even this kind of change

probably would do little to increase the number of substantiated complaints, which means that distrust of the system will persist. As a general rule, it can be argued that mechanisms of accountability have very limited potential to improve police relations with populations that are already highly critical of the police.

Protestants have a rather different opinion of the existing mechanisms of accountability. Unionist leaders opposed the creation of the Police Authority, the Police Complaints Board, and the Independent Commission for Police Complaints, and they continue to blame them for straightjacketing the police. Whereas Catholics criticize these bodies for being weak, Protestants are more likely to say that they prevent police officers from acting vigorously against troublemakers, fearful that they might be dragged before the complaints commission. At the same time, a majority of Protestants do not trust the police to investigate themselves and want an independent body to do this. But very few (13 percent) think the police usually get away with serious crimes.

4. "Community policing," in different forms, has been embraced in a number of countries as a means of improving relations. It is promoted as a way of building a "partnership" between police and citizens in dealing with crime and other local problems, making officers more responsive to the community, and helping to "humanize the police" in the eyes of neighborhood residents.[2] These claims would seem surrealistic to subordinate ethnic groups in divided societies. In Northern Ireland's staunch Republican, and even some Loyalist, neighborhoods, we have seen that residents avoid foot patrols, refuse to participate in Community Relations programs, stigmatize civic groups that have anything to do with the RUC, brand liaison committees as window dressing, and may even condone violent attacks on community constables. Republicans are most hostile to community policing ventures, but many Loyalists also greet them with skepticism or suspicion.

Community policing promises little—particularly in neighborhoods where relations are already strained—if it is based on any of the following premises, each of which obtains in Northern Ireland: (i) The assumption that relations can be improved via specific programs, liaison committees, or special police units. However laudable, such efforts typically are marginal to the core activities of the police force and have little, if any, impact on the practices of regular officers. (ii) The assumption that police-community problems are essentially due to poor communication and that community policing will help to promote mutual understanding. Poor communication usually is only a minor part of the problem where police-community relations are poor. (iii) The assumption that the velvet glove of community policing can succeed in a context where iron-fist measures are common, or that the former can even compensate for the latter. The obverse dynamic is more likely. Where harsh, counterinsurgency policing is institutionalized and routine, it overshadows, makes irrelevant, and may even contaminate all community policing experiments. We have seen that, in Ulster's most troubled neighborhoods, community policing has a *backfiring effect*; far from improving relations, it reinforces poor relations. People lump community constables together with other "forces of oppression" and community policing is seen as a hollow PR effort and a thinly disguised mode of repression, in the form of intelligence gathering. It is difficult to imagine how community policing, even if expanded significantly, could improve police relations with Republican and some Loyalist neighborhoods. These neighborhoods simply lack the requisite receptivity to community policing overtures.

If these four conventional solutions are deficient, how, then, might relations between police and communities be improved? To answer this question, we need to reexamine the two most important factors shaping relations in Northern Ireland.

First, the state. The police may be evaluated not only for what they do but also for what they symbolize, such as a particular social or political order. Where the legitimacy of the state is not problematic, this should redound to the benefit of the police, bolstering their status in public opinion. Unfortunately, this point is apparently so taken for granted in the literature on liberal democracies that it is not even incorporated into models of police-community relations.[3] For the bulk of the population in these societies, the state's basic legitimacy either enhances the status of the police or at least does not diminish that status. Even for people who are alienated from the political system, this appears to have only a slight effect on their attitudes toward the police.[4] The state is a background factor shaping police-community relations in these societies, playing a relatively invisible but positive role (given its overall legitimacy for most people), but it is very much in the foreground in deeply divided societies, where the state's moral authority, at least for certain ethnic groups, is precarious or negligible. The image of the police suffers by virtue of their association with the state, and genuine attempts to depoliticize them may be met with derision by groups who insist on defining the police force as nothing but an instrument of the regime. In Northern Ireland, Republicans never lose sight of the state-police connection and are emphatic that the legitimacy of the RUC depends on a new, acceptable state; Loyalists are also sensitive to the state-police relationship. Moreover, attacks on the police, whether physical or verbal, are often driven by anti-state or other political motives. This dynamic is virtually absent in contemporary Britain and the United States.

In divided societies, replacement of a regime rooted in the old order is a necessary condition for marked improvement in relations. Much depends, of course, on the nature of the new regime; it must signal a break with the past sufficient to alter the symbolic status of the police. In South Africa the reformist government of President Frederik de Klerk did nothing to engender black's confidence in the police force; most observers believe popular acceptance of the police is contingent on the installation of a regime based on majority rule, although this is hardly a sufficient condition for legitimation. In Zimbabwe and Namibia, where majoritarian governments replaced white minority regimes in 1980 and 1990, respectively, police relations with blacks seem to have improved, although some mistrust lingers.[5] In Northern Ireland, British rule commands no more moral authority among Catholics than did Unionist rule because both power structures are associated with the partition of Ireland and political marginalization of the Catholic minority. And the RUC is considered no more autonomous of the British state than its Unionist predecessor; it is still seen as an instrument of state repression. In other words, the transition from Unionist rule to British rule has been wholly insufficient to elevate the RUC's symbolic status in the eyes of most Catholics. Confidence in the RUC will remain low as long as it is defined as an arm of an illegitimate state, as my informants stressed:

> Most people would believe a political solution is required for real change in policing. (LL)

> Catholics have to feel they can identify with the state before they can identify with the police. (U)

There will never be proper, civilian policing here until Britain withdraws.[6]

[The police will be acceptable] only when you have a united Ireland and we have a different police force. (TT)

If a more radical political change than British rule is required for Catholic legitimation of the police, there is no consensus on the preferred type of arrangement. Approximately one-quarter of Catholics identify a united Ireland as the best political system; about one-third favor a power-sharing arrangement in Northern Ireland; and the other options have less appeal.[7]

Protestant support for the police is also ultimately contingent on the larger national question: Ulster must remain either part of the United Kingdom or become independent; Ireland must never be reunited. Protestants see the current system of British rule as preferable to a united Ireland,[8] but only slightly preferable. A lingering distrust of the British administration in Ulster colors their views of the RUC. Ever since the beginning of British rule in 1972, Protestants have worried about whose interests the police would protect. The fact that reforms in the RUC were gradual helped to mute Protestants' fears, but in the past decade they have increasingly questioned the leanings of the force, sometimes labeling it an agent of the British state or even anti-Protestant. When asked what the police could do to improve relations, some respondents in Loyalist areas point to the symbolic status of the police: "People are confused; they don't have a sense of who the police are. The police need to change so people can feel some empathy with them" (JJ). "People no longer see it as their police force. Since the Anglo-Irish accord, people [believe] they've been sold down the river" (II). Even for persons who continue to define the RUC as "our police force," there is no doubt that British rule and the accompanying changes in policing have heightened concerns. A similar dynamic is apparent in South Africa today, where confidence in the police among a section of the white population has reached an all-time low. Embryonic reforms in the police force and dissolution of the apartheid system have brought right-wing whites into conflict, sometimes bloody, with police, who stand accused of being traitors to the white population.

Without a political settlement in Northern Ireland that would transform the state in a direction endorsed by Protestants as well as Catholics, and holding all else constant, basic perceptions of the police are likely to remain fairly stable. The problem is that a political system acceptable to both sides remains elusive. Not only does the current system of British rule command very little support among Protestants and Catholics, but, on the major alternatives, attitudes are polarized. Only 1 percent of Protestants see a united Ireland as the best form of government, and very few Catholics endorse the options favored by Protestants, such as complete integration of Ulster into the United Kingdom. There is some interethnic support for power sharing, but half as many Protestants (18 percent) as Catholics (35 percent) consider it the best form of government for the country.[9] In a nutshell, the political requirements for the growth of police legitimacy across the ethnic divide are absent, and the endemic conflict over the state will remain a significant impediment to improvement in police-community relations.

The second critical factor impeding improvement in police-community relations is counterinsurgency policing, which is important at both the national level and the street level. At the national level, it sparks frequent, well-publicized controversies over policing, which have a cumulative impact on popular attitudes. In Northern Ireland, like contemporary South Africa, accusations about police misconduct, if not full-fledged scandals, have become daily fare.

Counterinsurgency actions at the street level are equally important. The sociology of policing has established that face-to-face interactions between police and citizens play a critical role in shaping relations. This literature focuses on societies where ordinary law enforcement is the norm, but street-level conduct is no less important in societies where counterinsurgency practices figure prominently, as in Northern Ireland. By their very nature, counterinsurgency actions on the street are more conducive to problems than conventional law enforcement practices. In societies where at least part of the population experiences counterinsurgency policing as the norm on the ground, it does far greater cumulative damage to relations with the police than in societies where counterinsurgency actions are rare or absent altogether. In the latter, there is little hesitation on the part of community members to call for more policing and greater protection in their neighborhoods, and this is also true for minority-group members who are critical of other aspects of policing. In deeply divided societies, subordinate ethnic groups may complain about the lack of conventional policing, but their experience with counterinsurgency policing contributes to a reluctance to demand more law enforcement in their neighborhoods. Instead, the police may be totally unwelcome in the community and prime targets for attack, as in Ulster's Republican areas and many of South Africa's black townships.[10]

Counterinsurgency policing is a fact of life in the context of Northern Ireland's civil strife and political violence. Police primacy in the security area is firmly institutionalized (military primacy was abandoned in 1976 for reasons that still obtain today), and as long as counterinsurgency policing continues, even in a more relaxed form, it will generate some popular discontent. However, some progressive changes are possible in this area, and those that might help to reduce discontent are suggested in the interview and survey data. My informants in Catholic areas repeatedly criticized police harassment, brutality, abuse of power during public order situations, and every other practice related to the security situation. The survey data show that Catholics overwhelmingly disapprove of covert intelligence operations, shoot-to-kill operations against suspected or "known terrorists," and the use of plastic bullets to control unruly crowds. Large numbers think the police too often impose restrictions on Catholic demonstrations, set up vehicle checkpoints, stop and search pedestrians, and conduct house searches. In a context where police are responsible for fighting insurgency, it is not feasible to discontinue these measures (with the exception of the shoot-to-kill practice).[11] But they should be used more selectively and in accordance with norms of minimum force and the presumption of innocence. Too many of the RUC's counterinsurgency efforts involve gratuitous harassment and violence against civilians.

This raises the question of how to reduce police abuses. Some changes are easier to implement than others. More selective and less destructive house searches and tighter controls on the use of weapons might be implemented fairly swiftly. Unfortunately, despite the liberal rhetoric of RUC chiefs, there appears to be little institutional commitment to curbing repressive practices. Some of the top management and station commanders continue to tolerate or actively encourage actions that result in serious abuses (misuse of plastic bullets during riots, abuse of persons in police custody, and shoot-to-kill incidents). These individuals should be replaced with leaders who will not hesitate to punish serious misconduct and who will anticipate and take steps to prevent it in the first place.[12]

Such changes may reduce serious abuses, but what about the more frequent misconduct on the street—during routine patrols, at roadblocks, or during stops of pedestrians? The policing litera-ture is duly skeptical about the extent to which street behavior can be modified, given the autonomy of officers on the ground and the "low visibility" of most of their actions (which makes them effectively unreviewable),[13] but it does suggest two ways in which street conduct may be improved: The first is reconstitution of the police subculture.[14] In Northern Ireland, this would mean an emphasis (during training and at the police station) on norms of civility and minimum force in police contacts with the public, and a redefinition of neighborhoods that are now labeled "enemy territory" so that residents are no longer stereotyped and indis-criminately treated as foes. What needs to be appreciated, how-ever, is the tremendous difficulty of changing any subculture, par-ticularly where values and beliefs are daily refueled by working conditions and events, and where the police are themselves treated as enemies. The second is stricter supervision over consta-bles by their superior officers on the ground, which requires meaningful rewards for good behavior and punishments for unambiguous misconduct. This is complicated by the fact that superior officers do not always accompany regular constables, but when they do, they are in a unique position to control their subor-dinates' actions. Since this change occurs at the street level itself, rather than the more amorphous subcultural level, it has greater capacity to produce immediate and meaningful results.

The idea of liberalizing counterinsurgency policing is not a contradiction in terms. The changes I have advocated would not jeopardize internal security or hamper the RUC's ability to con-trol troublesome populations. At the same time, Northern Ire-land's serious security problems place limits on the degree to which counterinsurgency measures can be relaxed and, hence, on the extent to which relations with the public can improve. Polic-ing in Northern Ireland is extremely demanding and frustrating to constables who are under fire from a host of enemies. First, there are political opponents who constantly clamor for tighter control over officers; for changes in patrolling, interrogation practices, and crowd control methods; and for commissions of inquiry into serious incidents of police misconduct. Then there are the omnipresent physical risks. Officers are perhaps understandably tempted to behave overzealously toward civilians in neighborhoods where they command no respect from people, some of whom act belligerently in their presence or greet them with stones and petrol bombs, and where their colleagues have been injured or killed. Dangerous and trying working conditions create strains that make officers unreceptive to reforms imposed from above and incline them to act in indiscriminate, obnoxious, or violent ways. But this only increases popular discontent and generates new recruits for insurgent organizations—powerful arguments in favor of curbing repressive policing at the street level.

We should not be overly optimistic about the dividends that reforms in counterinsurgency policing, as outlined above, might pay, in a context where a discredited state remains in place. But the investment seems entirely sound. For those moderate Catholics whose support for the RUC is diffuse and for those who are ambivalent about the force, the relaxation of certain security practices probably would have some positive effect, since it is precisely those practices that concern moderates most. What about staunch Republicans? A decrease in the number of incidents in which altercations and police abuses occur may not substantially alter Republicans' overall relations with the police, but would *reduce one source of problems* and perhaps the intensity of their bitterness toward the RUC. Consider a comment of a community worker in a Republican neighborhood:

> The RUC could stop using plastic bullets tomorrow. It could seriously sort out the RUC-[Loyalist] paramilitary links. Officers could be better trained in their dealings with the public. They don't have to be cheeky or provoke events. They should stop blanket raids [on houses], and conduct searches only on firm evidence. [These changes] might not make the RUC *accepted* in the community, but it would improve relations between the police and the community. (B)

It would be surprising if the changes required to improve police relations with one side of a divided society would be the same as those necessary to improve relations with the opposite side. The data show that Protestants overwhelmingly support the very measures Catholics oppose. They do not believe searches of houses or pedestrians are conducted too often, and few think vehicle checkpoints and controls on Catholic demonstrations are excessive. Most Protestants say these measures are used too infrequently or in the right amount. Similarly, they almost unanimously support the use of plastic bullets (though Unionist leaders express outrage when a Protestant is on the receiving end) and undercover intelligence operations, and a majority approve of shoot-to-kill operations. Protestants are united in their demand for more intensive policing in Republican areas, but some moderates also want Loyalist troublemakers treated with the same strong medicine. Loyalists on the whole want the medicine reserved for Republicans alone. When asked what the police could do to improve relations with Loyalist communities, informants wanted security policing in their neighborhoods scaled back—they called for fewer armored landrovers patrolling their streets, an end to the various kinds of harassment, and the exercise of "much more restraint, treating people as human and not as enemies, until they are proven to be enemies" (A).

If intensification of counterinsurgency actions in Republican areas would help to improve Protestants' opinions of the RUC, its relaxation in those areas would have the opposite effect. Unionist politicians panic at the slightest hint that a particular security measure is being tempered or might be discontinued, and they would greet my proposals with alarm. However, these changes could be implemented without fanfare, making their visibility low for persons not directly affected, and perhaps avoiding contentious debate. Even if Unionists become aware of certain changes, and offer the usual opposition, this is arguably a small price to pay. And if the changes were implemented in both Republican and Loyalist areas, this might dilute the power of arguments that they were meant to appease Catholics.

Liberalizing counterinsurgency practices may have secondary positive effects in addition to any direct improvement in police-citizen interactions. It might help to reduce the number of incidents that fuel the fires of national controversies over policing. Insofar as the frequency of these spectacles is reduced, their net effect on police-community relations will be lessened and policing may become less politicized. More selectivity in house searches and stops, searches, and arrests of citizens on the street might free some police resources for use in conventional law enforcement, more of which would be greeted with approval in many neighborhoods.

In sum, police-community relations in Northern Ireland are not frozen. They can be thawed, at least to some extent, by the measures described above, although substantially warmer relations will have to await fundamental changes in the security situation and in the state.

ENDNOTES

CHAPTER 1. POLICING ETHNICALLY DIVIDED SOCIETIES

1. Many of the classics deal with the organization and occupational culture of police forces in the United States and Britain. There is, however, a body of research on police relations with minority groups that is relevant to the present study. Most of this literature is based on survey research which shows that blacks in Britain and the United States consistently hold more negative views than whites on a range of policing questions. Most blacks do not categorically reject the police, as some commentators claim, but they are clearly more inclined than whites to believe that the police engage in harassment, abuse people physically and verbally, discriminate against minorities, show disrespect for citizens, and are not held accountable for misconduct. At the same time, inner-city blacks believe their communities do not receive adequate law enforcement and want more police protection and services. Though critical of certain aspects of policing, they do not want the police to withdraw from their communities. Whites, by contrast, generally find policing much less problematic and they are less likely than blacks to experience unpleasant contacts. See President's Commission on Law Enforcement and Administration of Justice, *Task Force Report: The Police*, Washington, DC: U.S. Government Printing Office, 1967; David Bayley and Harold Mendelsohn, *Minorities and the Police: Confrontation in America*, New York: Free Press, 1969; Herbert Jacob, "Black and White Perceptions of Justice in the City," *Law and Society Review* 6, 1 (August 1971): 69–90; Angus Campbell and Howard Schuman, "Racial Attitudes in Fifteen American Cities," in *Supplemental Studies for the National Advisory Commission on Civil Disorders*, Washington, DC: U.S. Government Printing Office, 1968, pp. 42–43; Joseph Lohman and Gordon Misner, *The Police and the Community*, Vol. 1, Report for the President's Commission on Law Enforcement and Administration of Justice, Washington, DC: U.S. Government Printing Office, 1966; Harlan Hahn and Joe Feagin, "Riot-Precipitating Police Practices: Attitudes in Urban Ghettos," *Phylon* 31 (1970): 183–193; *Los Angeles Times*, March 28, 1988 and March 10, 1991; *New York Times*, April 5, 1991; *Washington Post*, May 3, 1992; David Smith, *Police and People in London*, Vol. 1: *A Survey of Londoners*, London: Policy Studies Institute,

1983; Mary Tuck and Peter Southgate, *Ethnic Minorities, Crime, and Policing*, Home Office Research Study 70, London: Her Majesty's Stationary Office, hereafter HMSO, 1981; Wesley G. Skogan, *The Police and the Public in England and Wales: A British Crime Survey Report*, Home Office Research Study 117, London: HMSO, 1990.

2. Samuel Walker, *A Critical History of Police Reform*, Lexington, MA: Lexington Press, 1977; Robert M. Fogelson, *Big-City Police*, Cambridge: Harvard University Press, 1977; Stanley H. Palmer, *Police and Protest in England and Ireland: 1780–1850*, Cambridge: Cambridge University Press, 1988; Jerome Skolnick and David Bayley, *The New Blue Line: Police Innovation in Six American Cities*, New York: Free Press, 1986. Few studies examine the more rapid reform efforts that sometimes follow in the wake of major riots or scandals (Lawrence Sherman, *Scandal and Reform: Controlling Police Corruption*, Berkeley: University of California Press, 1978).

3. On the neglect of politics and the state in the policing literature, see Otwin Marenin, "Police Performance and State Rule," *Comparative Politics* 18, 1 (October 1985): 101–122.

4. Citing a number of surveys, Whyte concludes that there is even greater disagreement between Protestants and Catholics on law-and-order issues than on constitutional questions (John Whyte, *Interpreting Northern Ireland*, Oxford: Clarendon, 1990, p. 88).

5. Since religious preference in Northern Ireland is nearly synonymous with ethnic background (Irish Catholics and Scottish or English Protestants), I will refer to Protestants and Catholics as ethnic groups. Specifically religious differences between Catholics and Protestants are secondary to ethnic struggles over state power, socioeconomic advantages, and nationality (British, Irish, or Ulster).

6. Egon Bittner, *The Functions of the Police in Modern Society*, New York: Aronson, 1975; David Bayley, "Police Function, Structure, and Control in Western Europe and North America," in N. Morris and M. Tonry (eds.), *Crime and Justice*, Vol. 1, Chicago: University of Chicago Press, 1979.

7. Conflict theorists who write on policing focus almost exclusively on class, not race, ethnicity, or gender. In the crudest formulations, policing is reduced to class control and the police to instruments of the capitalist class, repressing the working class (see Sidney Harring, *Policing a Class Society*, New Brunswick, NJ: Rutgers University Press, 1983; and Richard Quinney, *Class, State, and Crime*, New York: Longman, 1977). For others, the police have a broader role, enforcing class, race, and gender oppression (Center for Research on Criminal Justice, *The Iron Fist and the Velvet Glove: An Analysis of the U.S. Police*, Berkeley: CRCJ, 1973).

8. Marenin, "Police Performance and State Rule," pp. 103–104.

9. Otwin Marenin, "Parking Tickets and Class Repression: The Concept of Policing in Critical Theories of Criminal Justice," *Contemporary Crises* 6 (1982): 241–266.

10. Nancy Travis Wolfe, *Policing a Socialist Society: The German Democratic Republic*, New York: Greenwood, 1992; Maria Helena Moreira Alves, *State and Opposition in Military Brazil*, Austin: University of Texas Press, 1985; Americas Watch, *Police Abuse in Brazil*, New York: Americas Watch, 1987; Americas Watch, *Police Violence in Argentina*, New York: Americas Watch, 1991.

11. Alvin Rabushka and Kenneth Shepsle, *Politics in Plural Societies*, Columbia: Merrill, 1972, pp. 67–68; Hermann Gilomee and Jannie Gagiano (eds.), *The Elusive Search for Peace: South Africa, Israel, Northern Ireland*, Oxford: Oxford University Press, 1990; Leo Kuper and M. G. Smith (eds.), *Pluralism in Africa*, Berkeley: University of California Press, 1969.

12. Cynthia Enloe, *Ethnic Soldiers: State Security in Divided Societies*, Athens, GA: University of Georgia Press, 1980; Philip Frankel, "South Africa: The Politics of Police Control," *Comparative Politics* 12 (1980): 481–499; *Acta Juridica*, 1989, special issue on policing in South Africa; John D. Brewer with Kathleen Magee, *Inside the RUC: Routine Policing in a Divided Society*, Oxford: Clarendon, 1991; Ronald Weitzer, "Policing a Divided Society: Obstacles to Normalization in Northern Ireland," *Social Problems* 33, 1 (October 1985): 41–55; Weitzer, "Accountability and Complaints Against the Police in Northern Ireland," *Police Studies* 9, 2 (Summer 1986): 99–109; Weitzer, "Elite Conflicts over Policing in South Africa: 1980–1990," *Policing and Society* 1 (1991): 257–268; Weitzer, "Transforming the South African Police," *Police Studies* 16, 1 (Spring 1993): 1–10.

13. The model was originally proposed in my unpublished paper, "Police Liberalization in Northern Ireland" (1989). John Brewer ("Policing" in Gilomee and Gagiano, *The Elusive Search for Peace*) subsequently added some elements that are neither common in nor unique to divided societies, such as a chronic manpower shortage; recruitment restricted to one community (the police in South Africa and Rhodesia are or were 60 percent black, and Namibia's counterinsurgency police unit, Koevoet, was 90 percent black); a "lack of autonomy" from the political system (an exaggeration); and close links between the police and the military (not found in Northern Ireland under Protestant rule or in Rhodesia until the outbreak of a guerilla war in the early 1970s).

14. At the same time, policing may have unintended, dysfunctional consequences, catalyzing resistance from below and ultimately undermining relations of domination, as in South Africa since the mid-1980s.

15. Together these elements also distinguish policing in a divided society from authoritarian states lacking sharp ethnic cleavages. How-

ever, some of the elements (political bias, weak accountability, excessive police powers, responsibility for internal security) are very prominent in authoritarian police forces. See, for example, Wolfe, *Policing a Socialist Society*.

16. The police are hardly apolitical or detached from the dominant political culture in integrated societies; they enforce laws that are political products and they are indirectly involved in the maintenance of prevailing political and social structures. What varies across societies is whether that order commands moral authority and the degree to which police are responsive to the expectations of ruling elites. The sociopolitical order in divided societies is highly contested, and the police are more readily mobilized by the regime for political purposes than is true in integrated societies. This undermines the authority of the police among members of the subordinate group, to a degree that is unparalleled for any group in integrated societies.

17. John Brewer et al., *The Police, Public Order, and the State*, New York: St. Martin's, 1988, p. 149.

18. Quinney, *Class, State, and Crime*.

19. Weitzer, "Transforming the South African Police."

20. This claim is made by Brewer and Magee, *Inside the RUC*.

21. The literature on the United States and Britain contains ample evidence that the most important determinant of police-community relations in these societies is police performance, at the local level, of their ordinary law enforcement duties and their conduct toward neighborhood residents in the course of this work. Evidence on the role of other factors (experiential, subcultural, demographic) is scattered, and the conclusions of this literature have not been synthesized into a coherent explanatory framework for understanding police-community relations. See the citations in note 1 above and Scott Decker, "Citizen Attitudes Toward the Police," *Journal of Police Science and Administration* 9 (1981): 80–87; Douglas Smith, Nanette Graham, and Bonney Adams, "Minorities and the Police," in M. Lynch and E. Patterson (eds.), *Race and Criminal Justice*, New York: Harrow and Heston, 1991; Darlene Walker et al., "Contact and Support: An Empirical Assessment of Public Attitudes toward the Police and the Courts," *North Carolina Law Review* 51 (1971): 43–79; Nancy Apple and David O'Brien, "Neighborhood Racial Composition and Residents' Evaluation of Police Performance," *Journal of Police Science and Administration* 11, 1 (1983): 76–83; Komanduri Murty, Julian Roebuck, and Joann Smith, "The Image of the Police in Black Atlanta Communities," *Journal of Police Science and Administration* 17 (1990): 250–257.

22. The literature has paid scant attention to extra-neighborhood influences on citizens' attitudes toward the police, such as the possible spillover effect of controversial police behavior in other locales.

23. Jean-Paul Brodeur, "High Policing and Low Policing," *Social Problems* 30, 5 (June 1985): 507–520; Rodney Stark, *Police Riots*, Belmont, CA: Wadsworth, 1972; and P.A.J. Waddington, *The Strong Arm of the Law: Armed and Public Order Policing*, Oxford: Clarendon, 1991. Similarly understudied are the authoritarian societies where counterinsurgency policing, particularly in the form of proactive targeting of suspected subversives, is extreme, as in military dictatorships and state socialist countries (see Wolfe, *Policing a Socialist Society*).

24. One study found only a slight relationship between American minorities' feelings of political alienation or powerlessness and negative attitudes to the police (Stan Albrecht and Miles Green, "Attitudes Toward the Police and the Larger Attitude Complex," *Criminology* 15, 1 [May 1977]: 67–86). It is likely that some black ghetto residents in the United States see police as agents or symbols of white domination, but those who make this argument provide no data on the proportion of the population holding these views (Bayley and Mendelsohn, *Minorities and the Police*, pp. 141–142; Robert Fogelson, "From Resentment to Confrontation: The Police, the Negroes, and the Outbreak of the Nineteen-Sixties Riots," *Political Science Quarterly* 83, 2 [June 1968], p. 221).

25. The much-publicized, videotaped beating of Rodney King in Los Angeles in 1991 is a case in point. Opinions of the Los Angeles Police Department plummeted after the beating. In polls of Los Angeles residents, the approval rating of the LAPD by blacks dropped from 64 percent in 1988 to 29 percent in 1991, just after the beating (*Los Angeles Times*, March 10, 1991).

26. Gerald Suttles, *The Social Construction of Communities*, Chicago: University of Chicago Press, 1972.

27. Whyte, *Interpreting Northern Ireland*, pp. 34–35.

28. *Independent*, March 22, 1993. This was the case in 35 of Belfast's 51 wards.

29. David J. Smith and Gerald Chambers, *Inequality in Northern Ireland*, Oxford: Clarendon, 1991, p. 100.

30. Georg Simmel, *Conflict and the Web of Group-Affiliations*, New York: Free Press, 1955.

31. Studies using intensive interviews include Irving Wallach and Collette Jackson, "Perception of the Police in a Black Community," in J. Snibbe and H. Snibbe (eds.), *The Urban Policeman in Transition*, Springfield, IL: Thomas, 1973; Penny Green, *The Enemy Without: Policing and Class Consciousness in the Miners' Strike*, Milton Keynes, England: Open University Press, 1990; Mike McConville and Dan Shepherd, *Watching Police, Watching Communities*, London: Routledge, 1992.

32. Community relations with the police and army are discussed in observational studies of two Republican neighborhoods in Belfast (Jef-

frey A. Sluka, *Hearts and Minds, Water and Fish: Support for the IRA and INLA in a Northern Irish Ghetto*, Greenwich, CT: JAI Press, 1989, Chap. 5; Frank Burton, *The Politics of Legitimacy: Struggles in a Belfast Community*, London: Routledge and Kegan Paul, 1978, Chap. 3).

33. John Van Maanen, "On Watching the Watchers," in P. Manning and J. Van Maanen (eds.), *Policing: A View from the Street*, Santa Monica: Goodyear, 1978, p. 63.

34. The IRA is the premier insurgent organization on the Republican side, far more prominent than the small Irish National Liberation Army. Insurgent groups on the Loyalist side include the Ulster Defense Association, the Ulster Freedom Fighters, and the Ulster Volunteer Force. These groups are often called "terrorists" or "paramilitaries" in Northern Ireland. Here, I avoid use of the pejorative term *terrorist* and use either *paramilitary* or the more generic term *insurgent*.

35. It is possible that Brewer and Magee's study (*Inside the RUC*), which had been completed, but not yet published, just as I was entering the field, made the RUC's gatekeepers wary of any further research.

36. Names of voluntary civic organizations were provided by the Community Relations Council and the Northern Ireland Council for Voluntary Action. Permission to interview workers at community centers was given by Belfast City Council's Community Services Department, with the help of someone connected to the department.

37. After a decade of recording interview responses by hand, I am reasonably confident that I recorded most statements verbatim or nearly verbatim, with the help of abundant abbreviations. Although awkward, I sometimes asked respondents to repeat statements that seemed especially precious. Gaps in the recorded material were filled in immediately after each interview.

38. John Lofland and Lyn Lofland, *Analyzing Social Settings*, Belmont, CA: Wadsworth, 1984, p. 40.

39. For a perspective emphasizing macro-micro links in ethnographic studies, see Michael Burawoy, "The Extended Case Method," in Burawoy et al., *Ethnography Unbound*, Berkeley: University of California Press, 1991.

CHAPTER 2.   PROTESTANT POLICING: 1922–1968

1. Kevin Boyle, Tom Hadden, and Paddy Hillyard, *Law and State: The Case of Northern Ireland*, Amherst: University of Massachusetts Press, 1975, p. 173.

2. Stanley H. Palmer, *Police and Protest in England and Ireland, 1780–1850*. Cambridge: Cambridge University Press, 1988, pp. 342, 274, 260.

3. Palmer, *Police and Protest*, pp. 345–346, 538.

4. [1864 Commission] *Report of the Commissioners of Inquiry, 1864, Respecting the Magisterial and Police Jurisdiction Arrangements and Establishment of the Borough of Belfast*, Presented to Parliament, c. 3466, Dublin: HMSO, 1865, p. 6.

5. Andrew Boyd, *Holy War in Belfast*, New York: Grove, 1969, pp. 53, 55.

6. *Report to the Lord Lieutenant of Ireland of Messrs. Fitzmaurice and Goold into the Conduct of the Constabulary During the Disturbances at Belfast in July and September 1857*, House of Commons papers, c. 333, 1858, pp. 2–3.

7. 1864 Commission, p. 6.

8. 1864 Commission, p. 20.

9. [1886 Commission] *Report of the Belfast Riots Commissioners, 1886*, Presented to Parliament, c. 4925, Dublin: HMSO, 1887, p. 6.

10. Charles Townshend, *Political Violence in Ireland: Government and Resistance since 1848*, Oxford: Clarendon, 1983, p. 87.

11. 1886 Commission, pp. 17, 16.

12. 1886 Commission, p. 16.

13. 1886 Commission, p. 21.

14. 1886 Commission, p. 19.

15. Charles Townshend, "Policing Insurgency in Ireland, 1914–1923," in D. Anderson and D. Killingray (eds.), *Policing and Decolonization*, Manchester: Manchester University Press, 1992.

16. Farrell examines only part of the 1920s (Michael Farrell, *Arming the Protestants: The Formation of the Ulster Special Constabulary and the Royal Ulster Constabulary, 1920–1927*, London: Pluto, 1983); Ryder devotes a chapter to the period of Unionist rule, but fails to document any of his sources (Chris Ryder, *The RUC*, London: Methuen, 1989).

17. All volumes of debates from 1921 to 1940 and 1965 to 1968 were reviewed because these periods marked the formative years of the Unionist state and the prelude to its dissolution; for 1940–1965 alternate volumes were examined. Generally, there was a high degree of intraparty consistency and redundancy in MPs' comments over the years. The material examined included debates on appropriations for the force, specific disturbances and other law and order matters, and debates specifically on the RUC.

18. Mr. Devlin, Commons, *Debates*, May 26, 1925, col. 816.

19. Mr. Healy, Commons, *Debates*, May 3, 1932, cols. 1138–1140.

20. Mr. McAteer, Commons, *Debates*, March 18, 1952, col. 363.

21. Farrell, *Arming the Protestants*, p. 218.

22. For a discussion of these attacks, see Tim Pat Coogan, *The IRA*, London: Fontana, 1980, Chap. 7.

23. In local government elections, however, Unionists gerrymandered electoral boundaries in some areas, such as Londonderry, where Catholics were the majority but could not win control of the city council. In addition, property and other qualifications in local elections reduced the number of eligible voters in the disproportionately disadvantaged Catholic population.

24. The number of MPs representing nationalist, independent Unionist, labour, and liberal parties ranged from 12 to 19 (Sydney Elliott, *Northern Ireland Parliamentary Election Results: 1921–1972*, Chichester: Political Reference Publications, 1973, pp. 114–117).

25. Paul Bew, Peter Gibbon, and Henry Patterson, *The State in Northern Ireland: 1921–1972*, Manchester: Manchester University Press, 1979, pp. 131ff.

26. Edmund A. Aunger, *In Search of Political Stability: A Comparative Study of New Brunswick and Northern Ireland*, Montreal: McGill-Queens University Press, 1981, p. 123.

27. Minister of Home Affairs Topping, Commons, *Debates*, May 2, 1957, col. 910.

28. Minister of Home Affairs Warnock, Commons, *Debates*, January 29, 1948, col. 3595.

29. Minister of Home Affairs Maginess, Commons, *Debates*, November 21, 1951, col. 2250.

30. Mr. West, Commons, *Debates*, November 12, 1969, cols. 1216–1217.

31. Mr. Porter, Commons, *Debates*, November 29, 1955, col. 2925.

32. Robert Megaw, Parliamentary Secretary to the minister of Home Affairs, Commons, *Debates*, May 24, 1922, col. 652.

33. *Interim Report of the Departmental Committee of Inquiry on Police Reorganization in Northern Ireland*, Belfast: HMSO, March 1922.

34. Megaw, Commons, *Debates*, May 24, 1922, col. 654.

35. Minister of Home Affairs, Commons, *Debates*, June 5, 1923, cols. 1304, 1307.

36. Wickham, quoted in Farrell, *Arming the Protestants*, p. 189.

37. Commons, *Debates*, June 9, 1966, col. 201.

38. *Interim Report*, Reservations to Committee Recommendations.

39. Farrell, *Arming the Protestants*, p. 267; Commons, *Debates*, June 9, 1966, col. 160.

40. Ryder, *The RUC*, p. 60.

41. [Hunt Committee] *Report of the Advisory Committee on Police in Northern Ireland*, Cmnd. 535, Belfast: HMSO, October 1969, Lord Hunt, Chairman, p. 30.

42. Farrell, *Arming the Protestants*, p. 267.

43. Commons, *Debates*, November 28, 1944, cols. 2459–2460.

44. Mr. Gormley, Commons, *Debates*, April 14, 1965, col. 1103.

45. Mr. Diamond, Commons, *Debates*, November 21, 1951, col. 2332.

46. Ryder, *The RUC*, p.41.

47. Bates, quoted in Farrell, *Arming the Protestants*, p. 194.

48. Wickham, quoted in Farrell, *Arming the Protestants*, p. 194.

49. Commons, *Debates*, April 26, 1927, col. 860.

50. Commons, *Debates*, November 21, 1951, cols. 2251, 2253.

51. Less than a year after recruiting began, there were 3,515 A Specials, 15,903 part-time B Specials, and 1,310 C Specials (Farrell, *Arming the Protestants*, pp. 53–54).

52. Farrell, *Arming the Protestants*, pp. v, 155.

53. Commons, *Debates*, May 26, 1925, col. 824.

54. Clause 3 of the Craig-Collins pact, 1922, cited in Farrell, *Arming the Protestants*, pp. 104–105.

55. Quoted in Farrell, *Arming the Protestants*, pp. 156, 157.

56. Interview, August 2, 1984.

57. Mr. Diamond, Commons, *Debates*, May 25, 1955, col. 1550.

58. Ronald Weitzer, *Transforming Settler States: Communal Conflict and Internal Security in Northern Ireland and Zimbabwe*, Berkeley: University of California Press, 1990, pp. 57–58.

59. Patrick Buckland, *The Factory of Grievances: Devolved Government in Northern Ireland, 1921–1938*, New York: Barnes and Noble, 1979, pp. 200–206.

60. John McGuffin, *Internment*, Tralee: Anvil, 1973, p.84.

61. Michael Farrell, *Northern Ireland: The Orange State*, London: Pluto, 1976, p. 24.

62. Mr. McMullen, Commons, *Debates*, October 29, 1925, col. 1655.

63. Mr. Campbell, Commons, *Debates*, March 24, 1936, col. 640.

64. Mr. Campbell, Commons, *Debates*, March 24, 1936, col. 640.

65. Mr. Connellan, Commons, *Debates*, November 30, 1955, cols. 2948–2949.

66. Boyle, Hadden, and Hillyard, *Law and State*, p. 38.

67. Mr. Campbell, Commons, *Debates*, April 29, 1936, col. 1166.

68. National Council for Civil Liberties [NCCL], *Report of a Commission of Inquiry Appointed to Examine the Purpose and Effect of the Civil Authorities (Special Powers) Acts, 1922 and 1933*, London: NCCL, 1936, p. 26.

69. Mr. Diamond, Commons, *Debates*, February 16, 1955, cols. 233–234; May 25, 1955, col. 1551.

70. Mr. Healy, Commons, *Debates*, May 9, 1951, cols. 887–888.

71. NCCL, *Report*, p. 26.

72. NCCL, *Report*, p. 27.

73. Mr. Maginess, Commons, *Debates*, August 21, 1951, col. 2099.

74. Farrell, *Arming the Protestants*, pp. 191–192.

75. Quoted in Ryder, *The RUC*, p. 92.

76. Quoted in Commons, *Debates*, May 15, 1924, col. 967.

77. The speeches of Inspector Nixon, an extreme Orangeman, challenged the British government during a period when relations between the British and the Unionist state were sensitive. Nixon was subsequently elected to the Stormont parliament as an independent Unionist.

78. Mr. Healy, Commons, *Debates*, May 3, 1932, col. 1140.

79. Mr. McAteer, Commons, *Debates*, March 22, 1951, col. 630.

80. Mr. Healy, Commons, *Debates*, May 9, 1951, cols. 887–888.

81. See Rodney Stark, *Police Riots*, Belmont, CA: Wadsworth, 1972.

82. Farrell, *Northern Ireland*, p. 138.

83. Mr. Campbell, Commons, *Debates*, July 10, 1935, cols. 2419–2420.

84. Mr. Beattie, Commons, *Debates*, July 10, 1935, col. 2421.

85. Commons, *Debates*, July 10, 1935, col. 2429.

86. Attorney General Babington, Commons, *Debates*, July 10, 1935, col. 2431.

87. Attorney General Babington, Commons, *Debates*, July 10, 1935, col. 2435.

88. Mr. O'Reilly, Commons, *Debates*, December 4, 1968, col. 2169.

89. Mr. Minford, Commons, *Debates*, May 3, 1955, col. 1162.

90. Mr. Healy, Commons, *Debates*, November 21, 1951, col. 2227.

91. Minister of Home Affairs Maginess, Commons, *Debates*, August 21, 1951, col. 2093.

92. Minister of Home Affairs Maginess, Commons, *Debates*, March 22, 1951, col. 638.

93. Mr. Nelson, Commons, *Debates*, August 21, 1951, col. 2071.

94. Mr. McSparran, Commons, *Debates*, August 21, 1951, cols. 2088–2089.

95. Cf. Ryder, *The RUC*, p. 82.

96. Mr. Hanna, quoted in Farrell, *Northern Ireland*, p. 208.

97. Mr. O'Reilly, Commons, *Debates*, May 7, 1968, col. 931.

98. Mr. Healy, Commons, *Debates*, November 21, 1951, col. 2225.

99. Mr. Diamond, Commons, *Debates*, May 6, 1952, col. 673.

100. Mr. O'Connor, Commons, *Debates*, March 12, 1969, col. 309.

101. Ryder, *The RUC*, p. 84.

102. Patrick Buckland, *A History of Northern Ireland*, Dublin: Gill and Macmillan, 1981, p. 64.

103. Mr. Healy, Commons, *Debates*, October 20, 1936, col. 2097.

104. Mr. Conlon, Commons, *Debates*, February 21, 1946, col. 2303.

105. Mr. McAteer, Commons, *Debates*, March 18, 1952, col. 366.

106. Mr. Diamond, Commons, *Debates*, November 13, 1968, col. 1696.

107. Mr. McAteer, Commons, *Debates*, March 18, 1952, col. 365.

108. The minister of Home Affairs reported figures on police clearance rates in Northern Ireland from 1939 to 1965 that ranged from 57 to 63 percent, while in the rest of the United Kingdom from 1955 to 1964 the rates ranged from 40 to 45 percent (Commons, *Debates*, June 11, 1940, col. 1376; May 6, 1952, col. 687; May 2, 1957, col. 910; May 13, 1964, cols. 876–877; April 14, 1965, col. 1069; May 4, 1966, col. 684).

109. Commons, *Debates*, March 29, 1962, col. 488.

110. Hunt Committee, p. 19.

111. Hunt Committee, p. 32.

112. Prime Minister, Commons, *Debates*, May 15, 1924, col. 968. No other information was provided.

113. Minister of Home Affairs Bates, Commons, *Debates*, April 10, 1930, col. 762; March 16, 1932, col. 371.

114. In criminal cases involving civilians accused of ordinary crimes, senior police officers personally conducted the prosecutions in court. Lacking an external check, this system of police prosecution, which also existed in England and Wales, was open to ethnic discrimination against defendants. It also may have left the impression that the magistrates' courts were "police courts in which contests between the police and the citizens take place" (*Report of Working Party on Public Prosecutions*, Cmnd. 554, Belfast: HMSO, 1971, p. 9).

115. Minister of Home Affairs Craig, Commons, *Debates*, December 12, 1963, cols. 1667–1668; December 18, 1963, col. 1823.

116. Hunt Committee, p. 19.

117. Dermot Walsh, "The Royal Ulster Constabulary: A Law unto Themselves?" in M. Tomlinson et al. (eds.), *Whose Law and Order?* Belfast: Sociological Association of Ireland, 1988, pp. 96–97.

118. Mr. Fitt, Commons, *Debates*, March 10, 1965, col. 1760.

119. An exception is an inquiry ordered by the minister of Home Affairs in 1965 into allegations of police harassment and misconduct made by a nationalist MP. Two years later, a new minister reported that the police had been "vindicated" and that he trusted that "this public exoneration . . . will have a salutary effect on any hon. Member who may be tempted, on the flimsiest of evidence, to impugn the character

and integrity of members of the RUC" (Commons, *Debates*, February 25, 1965, cols. 1227–1239; March 22, 1967, cols. 311, 338–339).

120. Mr. Diamond, Commons, *Debates*, March 10, 1965, col. 1757.

121. Mr. Beattie, Commons, *Debates*, April 29, 1936, cols. 1152, 1154.

122. Ms. Murnaghan, Commons, *Debates*, December 15, 1965, col. 63.

123. Mr. Fitt, Commons, *Debates*, March 27, 1968, col. 246.

124. Mr. Fitt, Commons, *Debates*, November 26, 1968, col. 1989.

125. Mr. Grant, Commons, *Debates*, May 29, 1924, col. 1185.

126. Mr. Boal, Commons, *Debates*, December 12, 1963, col. 1668.

127. Mr. Hanna, Commons, *Debates*, May 9, 1951, col. 924.

128. Minister of Home Affairs Maginess, Commons, *Debates*, June 27, 1951, col. 1670.

129. Gresham Sykes and David Matza, "Techniques of Neutralization: A Theory of Delinquency," *American Sociological Review* 22 (1957): 666–670; see also William Waegel, "How Police Justify the Use of Deadly Force," *Social Problems* 32 (1984): 144–155.

130. Minister of Home Affairs Topping, Commons, *Debates*, November 12, 1957, col. 2436.

131. Commons, *Debates*, October 29, 1940, cols. 2508, 2509–2510. Opposition MPs had complained that the police were engaging in unnecessary identity checks, interrogations, and oppressive searches.

132. Minister of Home Affairs MacDermott, Commons, *Debates*, October 8, 1940, cols. 2323–2324.

133. Minister of Home Affairs Topping, Commons, *Debates*, December 19, 1957, col. 2880.

134. Minister of Home Affairs Craig, Commons, *Debates*, October 29, 1968, col. 1842.

135. The first minister of Home Affairs refused to make a copy of the RUC Code available to members of parliament because the code "has always been regarded as a confidential document" (Commons, *Debates*, April 9, 1936, cols. 1100–1101). Three decades later a copy of the code was finally placed in the Parliamentary Library, but the minister deleted all official instructions to the force because they might include confidential information, the dissemination of which would be "against the public interest" (Commons, *Debates*, November 20, 1968, col. 1814).

136. Mr. Hanna, Commons, *Debates*, May 20, 1936, col. 1704.

137. Michael MacDonald, *Children of Wrath: Political Violence in Northern Ireland*, New York: Blackwell, 1986, pp. 22, 24.

138. Commons, *Debates*, December 15, 1965, cols. 63–64.

CHAPTER 3. REFORMING THE RUC

1. Richard Rose, *Northern Ireland: A Time of Choice*, London: Macmillan, 1976, p. 21.

2. One of the best is by the Sunday Times Insight Team, *Northern Ireland: A Report on the Conflict*, New York: Vintage, 1972. See also the reports of the Cameron and Scarman commissions, cited below.

3. Minister of Home Affairs Craig, Commons, *Debates*, October 16, 1968, col. 1017.

4. [Cameron Commission] *Disturbances in Northern Ireland*, Cmnd. 532, Belfast: HMSO, September 1969, Lord Cameron, Chairman.

5. Minister of Home Affairs Craig, Commons, *Debates*, November 12, 1968, col. 1635; Minister of Home Affairs Porter, Commons, *Debates*, January 28, 1970, cols. 2403–2405.

6. [Scarman Tribunal] *Violence and Civil Disturbances in Northern Ireland in 1969*, Cmnd. 566, Belfast: HMSO, April 1972, Justice Scarman, Chairman, p. 16.

7. Scarman Tribunal, p. 15.

8. Mr. Diamond, Commons, *Debates*, October 22, 1968, col. 1112.

9. Mr. Fitt, Commons, *Debates*, November 20, 1968, col. 1826.

10. Mr. O'Hanlon, Commons, *Debates*, March 19, 1969, col. 578.

11. Mr. Hume, Commons, *Debates*, May 28, 1969, col. 944.

12. Mr. O'Reilly, Commons, *Debates*, April 30, 1969, col. 1865.

13. These findings are reported in a book by former British Prime Minister James Callaghan, *A House Divided: The Dilemma of Northern Ireland*, London: Collins, 1973, pp. 54ff.

14. [Hunt Committee] *Report of the Advisory Committee on Police in Northern Ireland*, Cmnd. 535, Belfast: HMSO, October 1969, Lord Hunt, Chairman.

15. Hunt Committee, pp. 41, 21.

16. The Inspectorate of Constabulary was formed in 1856 as a mechanism through which the Home Office in London could evaluate provincial police forces. Inspectors are former police chiefs who are inclined to offer constructive support, rather than serious criticism, to the forces they review.

17. Police Authority for Northern Ireland, *The First Three Years*, Belfast: Police Authority, 1973.

18. Interview, August 2, 1984.

19. Arthur Hezlet, *The "B" Specials: A History of the Ulster Special Constabulary*, London: Tom Stacey, 1972, p. 223.

20. "Ulster's Police Force Speaks Out," *The Newsletter*, September 6, 1969.

21. Poll conducted by the Representative Body of the RUC, cited in Richard Rose, *Governing Without Consensus: An Irish Perspective*, Boston: Beacon, 1971, p. 147.

22. Chief Constable, *Annual Report for 1970*, Belfast: Police Authority, p.1.

23. Ronald Weitzer, *Transforming Settler States: Communal Conflict and Internal Security in Northern Ireland and Zimbabwe*, Berkeley: University of California Press, 1990, Chap. 5.

24. Paddy Hillyard, "The Normalization of Special Powers: From Northern Ireland to Britain," in P. Scraton (ed.), *Law, Order, and the Authoritarian State*, Philadelphia: Open University Press, 1987; State Research, "The RUC: A Sectarian Police Force," *State Research Bulletin*, no. 26 (1981): 17–23; Dermot Walsh, "The Royal Ulster Constabulary: A Law Unto Themselves?" in M. Tomlinson et al. (eds.), *Whose Law and Order?* Belfast: Sociological Association of Ireland, 1988.

25. Chris Ryder, *The RUC*, London: Methuen, 1989; William Hart, "Waging Peace in Northern Ireland," *Police Magazine* 3 (May 1980): 23–30; John Reed, "Northern Ireland: Progress in Policing Within a Divided Society," *Police Journal 55*, 1 (January 1982): 20–27.

26. See Ronald Weitzer, "Policing a Divided Society: Obstacles to Normalization in Northern Ireland," *Social Problems*, 33 1 (October 1985). Brewer and Magee accept this perspective but sometimes exaggerate the degree to which the RUC has reformed (John D. Brewer with Kathleen Magee, *Inside the RUC: Routine Policing in a Divided Society*, Oxford: Clarendon, 1991).

27. Weitzer, "Policing a Divided Society."

28. Robert Reiner, *The Politics of the Police*, New York: St. Martin's, 1985, Chap. 3.

29. Brewer and Magee, *Inside the RUC*.

30. Robert M. Fogelson, *Big-City Police*, Cambridge: Harvard University Press, 1977, Chap. 4; Simon Holdaway, *Inside the British Police*, Oxford: Basil Blackwell, 1983, Chap. 11.

31. Report by Her Majesty's Chief Inspectorate of Constabulary, cited in Chris Ryder, "RUC Will Toe the Line on Ulster, Report Says," *Sunday Times*, April 6, 1986.

32. Figures provided by RUC Headquarters, Belfast.

33. From 1986 to 1989, 7 to 10 percent of new recruits were Catholic (House of Commons, *Written Answers*, November 4, 1988, col. 823 and July 20, 1990, col. 735).

34. *Police Review*, June 2, 1989, p. 1108.

35. Letter to author from Senior Assistant Chief Constable W. J. McAllister, October 29, 1991.

36. Nicholas Scott, NIO minister responsible for law and order, House of Commons, *Oral Answers*, July 3, 1986, col. 1158.

37. *Independent*, January 28, 1993.

38. Interview with Maginnis, October 8, 1990.

39. Speech by chairman of the Police Federation, "Annual Conference 1986," *Police Beat*, June 1986, p. 22.

40. Personal communication, July 19, 1990.

41. The average RUC constable earned £30,370 in 1991, which is within the top tenth income bracket in Ulster. Sergeants, inspectors, and senior officers naturally earn more. These incomes allow cops to live in nice neighborhoods, thereby putting distance between them and working-class communities ("High Wages Seen to Sever Police from Their Roots," *Independent*, December 20, 1991).

42. Fogelson, *Big-City Police*, pp. 282–283.

43. "Known terrorists" are persons alleged by the police to have committed offenses, but the evidence is not sufficient to stand up in court or securing a conviction would mean blowing the cover of an informant who fingered the terrorist. The authorities may also allow a known terrorist to remain at large because, under surveillance, he might act in ways that aid in intelligence gathering or lead them to other terrorists.

44. Kevin Boyle, Tom Hadden, and Paddy Hillyard, *Law and State: The Case of Northern Ireland*, Amherst: University of Massachusetts Press, 1975, pp. 42–47.

45. [Gardiner Committee] *Report of a Committee to Consider, in the Context of Civil Liberties and Human Rights, Measures to Deal with Terrorism in Northern Ireland*, Cmnd. 5847, London: HMSO, January 1975, Lord Gardiner, Chairman.

46. Frank Burton, *The Politics of Legitimacy: Struggles in a Belfast Community*, London: Routledge and Kegan Paul, 1978.

47. Interpol reports that the RUC suffers the highest casualty rate of any police force in the world (*Belfast Telegraph*, January 20, 1983; *Irish Times*, June 24, 1985).

48. Interview with chairman of federation, September 20, 1990.

49. *Police Beat*, July–August 1990.

50. Basil Stannage, "Address by the Chairman of the Police Federation," *Constabulary Gazette*, October 1974, p. 10.

51. Editorial, *Police Beat*, January 1981, p. 1.

52. Alan Wright, quoted in *Belfast Telegraph*, January 24, 1986.

53. Alan Wright, "Address to the Annual Conferance 1989," *Police Beat*, June 1989, p. 11.

54. Interview, September 20, 1990.

55. "Conference Special," *Police Beat*, September 1991, p. 2.

CHAPTER 4. POLICE LEGITIMACY
AND PROFESSIONALISM

1. Chief Constable, *Annual Report for 1988*, Belfast: Police Authority, p. xviii.

2. Interview, July 30, 1990.

3. Continuous Household Survey, Northern Ireland Office, *A Commentary on Northern Ireland Crime Statistics*, Belfast: NIO, 1989.

4. House of Commons, *Written Answers*, November 4, 1988, col. 823 and July 20, 1990, col. 735.

5. Northern Ireland Social Attitudes Survey, 1990.

6. Northern Ireland Social Attitudes Survey, 1990.

7. Douglas Smith, Nanette Graham, and Bonney Adams, "Minorities and the Police," in M. Lynch and E. Patterson (eds.), *Race and Criminal Justice*, New York: Harrow and Heston, 1991. This difference was not found among blacks in London (David Smith, *Police and People in London*, Vol. 1: *A Survey of Londoners*, London: Policy Studies Institute, 1983, p. 246).

8. David Smith, *Equality and Inequality in Northern Ireland: Perceptions and Views*, London: Policy Studies Institute, 1987.

9. Northern Ireland Social Attitudes Survey, 1990.

10. Scott Decker, "Citizen Attitudes Toward the Police: A Review of Past Findings and Suggestions for Future Policy," *Journal of Police Science and Administration* 9, 1 (1981): 80–87.

11. Northern Ireland Social Attitudes Survey, 1990.

12. See Frank Wright, "Protestant Ideology and Politics in Ulster," *Archives Europeennes de Sociologie* 14, 2 (1973): 213–280; Jennifer Todd, "The Two Traditions in Unionist Political Culture," *Irish Political Studies* 2 (1987): 1–26.

13. On some of the survey questions reported in this book significant proportions answer "don't know," "no opinion," or "neither." This should not be interpreted as neutrality. Some of those who give these responses may be choosing "safe" options in a context where suspicion of the police is high and where the credentials of survey interviewers may be suspect, causing concern about confidentiality of the views expressed. With regard to the political party affiliations of respondents analyzed in Chapters 4–6, it should be noted that I have excluded the small, centrist Alliance Party—whose members strongly support the police—and the smaller fringe parties.

14. Carl Werthman and Irving Piliavin, "Gang Members and the Police," in D. Bordua (ed.), *The Police*, New York: Wiley, 1967, pp. 76–79.

15. The distinction between diffuse and specific support is made by David Easton, *A Systems Analysis of Political Life*, Chicago: University of Chicago Press, 1965, pp. 62–63.

16. Interview with Seamus Mallon, SDLP security spokesman, August 9, 1984.

17. *Belfast Telegraph*, September 25, 1989.

18. John W. Soule, "Issue Conflict in Northern Ireland," *Political Psychology* 10, 4 (1989): 725–744.

19. *Irish News*, April 16, 1986.

20. Interview, October 20, 1990.

21. SDLP, *The Northern Ireland Police Service*, policy document adopted by fifth annual conference, Belfast, 1975.

22. Quoted in Conor Cruise O'Brien, Letter to the Editor, *The Times*, May 20, 1989.

23. Interview with Mallon, August 9, 1984.

24. Interview with Alliance Party district councillor, July 21, 1991.

25. Interview with SDLP district councillor, October 20, 1990.

26. Northern Ireland Social Attitudes Survey, 1990.

27. Jeffrey A. Sluka, *Hearts and Minds, Water and Fish: Support for the IRA and INLA in a Northern Irish Ghetto*, Greenwich, CT: JAI Press, 1989, Chap. 4.

28. Herbert Jacob, "Black and White Perceptions of Justice in the City," *Law and Society Review* 6, 1 (August 1971): 78–79. See also Nancy Apple and David J. O'Brien, "Neighborhood Racial Composition and Residents' Evaluation of Police Performance," *Journal of Police Science and Administration* 11, 1 (1983): 76–83.

29. Peter H. Rossi and Richard A. Berk, "Political Leadership and Popular Discontent in the Ghetto," *Annals of the American Academy of Political and Social Science* 391 (1970), p. 121.

30. Robert McVeigh, *Racism and Sectarianism: A Comparison of Tottenham and West Belfast*, unpublished doctoral dissertation, Queen's University, Belfast, 1990, pp. 194–202.

31. The findings are based on participant-observation and in-depth interviews with a random sample of 76 of the 775 families in Divis Flats in West Belfast. Policing was not the main topic of the study, but the author concludes that negative views of the police are widely shared among his subjects (Sluka, *Hearts and Minds*, Chap. 5).

32. James Baldwin, *Nobody Knows My Name*, New York: Dell, 1962, p. 67.

33. Gerry Adams, quoted in *Belfast Telegraph*, March 7, 1986.

34. Irving Wallach and Collette Jackson, "Perception of the Police in a Black Community," in J. Snibbe and H. Snibbe (eds.), *The Urban Policeman in Transition*, Springfield, IL: Charles Thomas, 1973; Joseph Lohman and Gordon Misner, *The Police and the Community*, Vol. 1, Report for the President's Commission on Law Enforcement and Administration of Justice, Washington, DC: U.S. Government Printing Office, 1966, pp. 78–79.

35. Unpublished *Los Angeles Times* poll, no. 148, March 20, 1988.

36. Smith, *Police and People in London*, p. 208.

37. Interview with Paddy McManus, Sinn Fein legal affairs spokesman and Belfast city councillor, October 24, 1990.

38. Interview with McManus, October 24, 1990.

39. Andrew Hamilton, Clem McCartney, Tony Anderson, and Ann Finn, *Violence and Communities*, Coleraine: Center for the Study of Conflict, University of Ulster, 1990, p. 48.

40. The term "normal friction" is used by James Q. Wilson, "The Police in the Ghetto," in R. Steadman (ed.), *The Police and the Community*, Baltimore: Johns Hopkins University Press, 1972, p. 68.

41. Brewer and Magee field notes, May 15, 1987, p. 22 and October 9, 1987, p. 16.

42. Interview, October 22, 1991.

43. Robert Fogelson, "From Resentment to Confrontation: The Police, the Negroes, and the Outbreak of the Nineteen-Sixties Riots," *Political Science Quarterly* 83, 2 (June 1968); Wilson, "The Police in the Ghetto," p. 63.

44. In the United States there is evidence that cops working in predominantly black areas are more likely than their counterparts in racially mixed areas to hold anti-black attitudes (Donald J. Black and Albert J. Reiss, "Patterns of Behavior in Police and Citizen Transactions," in *Studies in Crime and Law Enforcement in Major Metropolitan Areas*, Vol. 2, Report for the President's Commission on Law Enforcement and the Administration of Justice, Washington, DC: U.S. Goverment Printing Office, 1967, pp. 133–137).

45. Brewer and Magee field notes, October 9, 1987, pp. 37, 38; John D. Brewer and Kathleen Magee, *Inside the RUC: Routine Policing in a Divided Society*, Oxford: Clarendon, 1991, p. 140.

46. In their study of Boston, Chicago, and Washington, Black and Reiss ("Patterns of Behavior") found that prejudiced officers generally did not discriminate against blacks when accompanied by researchers. This is also found in an observational study of London (David Smith and Jeremy Gray, *Police and People in London*, Vol. 4: *The Police in Action*, London: Policy Studies Institute, 1983, Chap. 4). By contrast, a study of 5,688 police-citizen contacts in Rochester, St. Louis, and Tampa found that police were significantly more likely to threaten or use force against members of black or racially mixed neighborhoods than in other neighborhoods (Douglas Smith, "The Neighborhood Context of Police Behavior," in A. Reiss and M. Tonry [eds.] *Communities and Crime*, Vol. 8 of *Crime and Justice*, Chicago: University of Chicago Press, 1986). Another American study found that patrol officers more frequently stopped and interrogated black youths than other youths, often without cause, and that black youths suspected of violating the law were treated more

severely than others (Irving Piliavin and Scott Briar, "Police Encounters with Juveniles," *American Journal of Sociology* 70 [1964]: 206–214).

47. See the discussion of the "working personality" of police officers by Jerome Skolnick, *Justice Without Trial*, New York: Wiley, 1966.

48. One study argues that blacks and Hispanics in the United States are similarly alert for signs of police prejudice and that they may over-dramatize their contacts with police (David Bayley and Harold Mendelsohn, *Minorities and the Police: Confrontation in America*, New York: Free Press, 1969, p. 194).

49. Soule, "Issue Conflict."

50. President's Commission on Law Enforcement and Administration of Justice, *Task Force Report: The Police*, Washington, DC: U.S. Government Printing Office, 1967; [Kerner Commission] *Report of the National Advisory Commission on Civil Disorders*, New York: Bantam, 1968.

51. United States Commission on Civil Rights, *Who Is Guarding the Guardians?* Washington, DC, 1981, p. 5.

52. Northern Ireland Social Attitudes Survey, 1990.

53. Brewer and Magee, *Inside the RUC*, p. 250.

54. Richard Mapstone, "The Attitudes of Police in a Divided Society," *British Journal of Criminology* 32, 2 (Spring 1992): 183–192. The attitudes of Protestant police officers were very close to those of the Protestant population.

55. A study of Detroit suggests that black attitudes to the police improved as the number of black police officers increased, with a more restrictive policy on the use of firearms, and with the installation of a black major and police chief. But the study is flawed by a lack of longitudinal data with which to measure changes in citizens' attitudes (Edward Littlejohn, Geneva Smitherman, and Alida Quick, "Deadly Force and Its Effects on Police-Community Relations," *Howard Law Journal* 27 [1984]: 1131–1184). See also Lawrence W. Sherman, "After the Riots: Police and Minorities in the United States, 1970–1980," in N. Glazer and K. Young (eds.), *Ethnic Pluralism and Public Policy*, Toronto: Lexington, 1983, pp. 220–222.

56. See Stephen Leinen, *Black Police, White Society*, New York: New York University Press, 1984, Chap. 7. In addition, although attitudes do not necessarily translate into behavior, some black cops hold anti-black prejudices. In the three American cities studied by Black and Reiss ("Patterns of Behavior," p. 135), 28 percent of the black officers working in predominantly black neighborhoods expressed prejudice or extreme prejudice against blacks, compared to 79 percent of the white officers.

57. In London, two-thirds of blacks believe more black police would make no difference in the quality of policing, and a third thought

it would improve policing (Smith, *Police and People in London*, p. 216). In the United States, a study of Baltimore found that 28 out of 50 blacks saw no difference in the behavior of white and black officers, and 36 had no preference as long as the officers performed their duties adequately (Wallach and Jackson, "Perception of the Police in a Black Community"). See also Leinen, *Black Police, White Society*, Chap. 6, and Nicholas Alex, *Black in Blue: A Study of the Negro Policeman*, New York: Appleton-Century-Crofts, 1969, Chap. 6.

58. Wallach and Jackson, "Perception of the Police in a Black Community." Bayley and Mendelsohn (*Minorities and the Police*, p. 122) found that only 8 percent of blacks and 5 percent of Hispanics in Denver considered minority cops traitors. Reiss found that 71 percent of the residents of a black lower-class Boston neighborhood and 62 percent of the residents of a black lower-class Chicago neighborhood disagreed with the statement that a black male would be making a mistake if he chose a police career over a job paying as much in construction (Albert Reiss, "Public Perceptions and Recollections About Crime, Law Enforcement, and Criminal Justice," in *Studies in Crime and Law Enforcement in Major Metropolitan Areas*, Vol. 1, Washington, DC: U.S. Government Printing Office, 1967, p. 55).

59. Northern Ireland Social Attitudes Survey, 1990.

60. Northern Ireland Consumer Panel poll, *Belfast Telegraph*, February 6, 1985.

61. Hamilton et al., *Violence and Communities*, p. 48.

62. Herbert Jacob, "Black and White Perceptions of Justice in the City," *Law and Society Review* 6, 1 (August 1971): 69–90.

63. Interview with UUP security spokesman, Ken Maginnis, October 8, 1990.

64. Interview, October 17, 1990.

65. Except in the Shankill, which has a history of supporting independent Unionists.

66. Sarah Nelson, *Ulster's Uncertain Defenders: Loyalists and the Northern Ireland Conflict*, Belfast: Appletree, 1984, Chap. 11.

67. *Times*, September 19, 1988.

68. Hamilton et al., *Violence and Communities*, p. 37.

69. *Community Development in Protestant Areas*, report of a conference of Protestant community workers in Lisnaskea, April 1991, pp. 40, 50.

70. Interview with DUP security spokesman, Rev. William McCrea, October 19, 1990.

71. A "supergrass" is one who informs on several people. In the early 1980s the authorities were successful in convincing a number of paramilitaries to finger colleagues, who were subsequently tried in court, in return for reduced sentences and handsome financial payoffs.

72. Interview with McCrea.

73. Northern Ireland Assembly, *Debates*, May 1, 1985, p. 252.

74. Alan Kane, Northern Ireland Assembly, *Debates*, March 19, 1986, p. 23.

75. Interview with McCrea.

CHAPTER 5. DUAL POLICING: FIGHTING CRIME AND INSURGENCY

1. G. H. Boehringer, "Beyond Hunt: A Police Policy for Northern Ireland of the Future," *Social Studies*, 2 (1973): 403; Patrick Buckland, *A History of Northern Ireland*, Dublin: Gill and Macmillan, 1981, p. 64.

2. *Irish Times*, June 24, 1985.

3. Chief Constable, *Annual Report for 1982*, Belfast: Police Authority, p. xii.

4. John D. Brewer with Kathleen Magee, *Inside the RUC: Routine Policing in a Divided Society*, Oxford: Clarendon, 1991, p. 267.

5. Brewer and Magee (*Inside the RUC*, p. 186) exaggerate somewhat when they claim that in troubled areas "no routine policing exists."

6. Paddy Hillyard, "Political and Social Dimensions of Emergency Law in Northern Ireland," in A. Jennings (ed.), *Justice Under Fire: The Abuse of Civil Liberties in Northern Ireland*, London: Pluto, 1988, p. 196.

7. From 1975 to 1988, half of the persons arrested were detained longer than the initial 48-hour period (Northern Ireland Information Service).

8. Helsinki Watch, *Human Rights in Northern Ireland*, New York: Helsinki Watch, 1991, p. 13.

9. Dermot Walsh, *The Use and Abuse of Emergency Legislation in Northern Ireland*, London: Cobden Trust, 1983, pp. 33, 39, 69.

10. Under the Emergency Provisions Act, residents can claim financial compensation for damages. The NIO paid £1.26 million in compensation to householders in 1988–1989, more than double the figure for the previous year (*Fortnight*, no. 276, September 1989, p. 21).

11. NIO figures cited in Helsinki Watch, *Human Rights in Northern Ireland*, p. 23. The NIO defines a "positive search" as one in which weapons, ammunition, illegal radio equipment, or hiding places are found.

12. House of Commons, *Written answers*, March 7, 1988, cols. 69–70 and April 17, 1989, col. 12.

13. Martin Dillon, *The Dirty War*, London: Arrow, 1991, pp. 404–409.

14. Sir John Hermon, quoted in William Hart, "Waging Peace in Northern Ireland," *Police Magazine* 3 (1980), p. 30.

15. [Kilbrandon Inquiry], *Northern Ireland: Report of an Independent Inquiry*, London: British Irish Association, 1984, Lord Kilbrandon, Chairman, p. 39.

16. Republicans were responsible for 80 percent and Loyalists for 20 percent of the murders by insurgents in the 1980s (Chief Constable, *Annual Report for 1989*, p. 58).

17. Several of these factors are discussed in Steve Bruce, *The Red Hand: Protestant Paramilitaries in Northern Ireland*, Oxford: Oxford University Press, 1992.

18. Steven Greer, "The Supergrass System," in A. Jennings (ed.), *Justice Under Fire: The Abuse of Civil Liberties in Northern Ireland*, London: Pluto, 1988.

19. John Whyte, *Interpreting Northern Ireland*, Oxford: Clarendon, 1990, pp. 87–88.

20. Interview with Patsy McGlone, SDLP general secretary, July 25, 1990.

21. *Belfast Telegraph*, October 8, 1988.

22. Northern Ireland Social Attitudes Survey, 1990.

23. Andrew Hamilton, Clem McCartney, Tony Anderson, and Ann Finn, *Violence and Communities*, Coleraine: Center for the Study of Conflict, University of Ulster, 1990, p. 69.

24. Hamilton et al., *Violence and Communities*, p. 48.

25. Hamilton et al., *Violence and Communities*, p. 51.

26. Jeffrey A. Sluka, *Hearts and Minds, Water and Fish: Support for the IRA and INLA in a Northern Irish Ghetto*, Greenwich, CT: JAI Press, 1989, Chap. 5; Robert McVeigh, *Racism and Sectarianism: A Comparison of Tottenham and West Belfast*, unpublished doctoral dissertation, Queen's University, Belfast, 1990, pp. 194–202.

27. McVeigh, *Racism and Sectarianism*, p. 199.

28. Helsinki Watch, *Children in Northern Ireland: Abused by the Security Forces and Paramilitaries*, New York: Helsinki Watch, 1992; Helsinki Watch, *Human Rights in Northern Ireland*, pp. 17–20.

29. Quoted in Helsinki Watch, *Children in Northern Ireland*, p. 23.

30. Under the EPA, the police or soldiers may stop any person or vehicle in order to ascertain the person's "identity and movements" and what he or she may know about any explosion or incident endangering life.

31. Mother of three, quoted in Helsinki Watch, *Children in Northern Ireland*, p. 19.

32. Jerome Skolnick, *Justice Without Trial*, New York: Wiley, 1966, p. 45.

33. Sluka, *Hearts and Minds*, p. 150.

34. Irish Information Partnership, *Agenda*, London: IIP, 1990.

35. Sluka (*Hearts and Minds*, p. 276) claims that police riding in landrovers sometimes try to provoke attacks from people on the street in order to relieve their boredom while on patrol.

36. Sluka, *Hearts and Minds*, p. 191.

37. Irving Piliavin and Scott Briar, "Police Encounters with Juveniles," *American Journal of Sociology* 70, 2 (September 1964): 206–214; Donald Black, "Production of Crime Rates," *American Sociological Review* 35, 4 (August 1970): 733–748; Donald Black, "The Social Organization of Arrest," *Stanford Law Review* 23 (June 1971): 1087–1111.

38. Interview with inspector, July 25, 1990.

39. Irving Wallach and Collette Jackson, "Perception of the Police in a Black Community," in J. Snibbe and H. Snibbe (eds.), *The Urban Policeman in Transition*, Springfield, IL: Charles Thomas, 1973, p. 387; David Bayley and Harold Mendelsohn, *Minorities and the Police: Confrontation in America*, New York: Free Press, 1969.

40. From 1969 through 1990, 632 persons were killed in the RUC's D Division—which includes North Belfast and northern parts of greater Belfast—compared to 430 in B Division or West Belfast (House of Commons, *Written answers*, June 27, 1990, col. 235).

41. Hamilton et al., *Violence and Communities*, pp. 49–50.

42. Interview, July 30, 1990.

43. Malachi O'Doherty, "Fear and Loathing on the Falls Road," *Fortnight*, no. 304 (March 1992), p. 23.

44. Interview with Paddy McManus, October 24, 1990.

45. Figures provided by RUC Headquarters, Belfast. These figures are conservative since some victims do not seek hospitalization or otherwise come to the attention of the authorities.

46. Sluka, *Hearts and Minds*, Chap. 4.

47. Survey conducted in Portadown in 1990, cited in Helsinki Watch, *Children in Northern Ireland*, p. 48.

48. Northern Ireland Social Attitudes Survey, 1990. The figures for the other parties are 22 percent for SDLP supporters and 27–28 percent for UUP and DUP supporters.

49. Interview with McManus.

50. O'Doherty, "Fear and Loathing," p. 24.

51. Quoted in Helsinki Watch, *Children in Northern Ireland*, p. 37.

52. Minutes of public meeting, March 26, 1991.

53. See also Sandra Barwick, "Penalizing Protestants," *The Spectator*, June 15, 1991, pp. 17–18.

54. *Community Development in Protestant Areas*, report of a conference of Protestant community workers in Lisnaskea, April 1991, p. 25.

55. From 1973 to 1991 Loyalist insurgents administered 598 punishment shootings and from 1982 to 1991 136 punishment assaults (figures provided by RUC Headquarters, Belfast). It appears that the majority of these sanctions were directed at anti-social and criminal elements in Loyalist neighborhoods, with the remainder given to political offenders such as informers or members of opposing Loyalist paramilitary groups. The magazine of the Ulster Defense Association, *Ulster*, sometimes publishes threats to persons it labels criminals or anti-social to cease their behavior or face punishment.

56. Helsinki Watch, *Children in Northern Ireland*, pp. 37–38.

57. *Community Development in Protestant Areas*, p. 50.

58. Quoted in Anton La Guardia, "Living in the North," *The Spectator*, September 17, 1988, p. 15.

59. "Ulster's One-Sided Police Force," *Ulster*, October–November 1989, p. 15.

60. Interview with superintendent, May 28, 1992.

CHAPTER 6. POLICE ACCOUNTABILITY

1. Dermot Walsh, "The Royal Ulster Constabulary: A Law unto Themselves?" in M. Tomlinson et al. (eds.), *Whose Law and Order?* Belfast: Sociological Association of Ireland, 1988.

2. John D. Brewer with Kathleen Magee, *Inside the RUC: Routine Policing in a Divided Society*, Oxford: Clarendon, 1991, p. 271.

3. John Stalker, *The Stalker Affair*, New York: Viking, 1988.

4. "Developments Since the Signing of the Anglo-Irish Agreement," government paper reprinted in House of Commons, *Written answers*, May 24, 1989, col. 541.

5. [Compton Commission] *Report of the Enquiry into Allegations Against the Security Forces of Physical Brutality in Northern Ireland Arising out of Events on the 9th August, 1971*, Cmnd. 4823, London: HMSO, November 1971, Sir Edmund Compton, Chairman.

6. Peter Taylor, *Beating the Terrorists*, Harmondsworth: Penguin, 1980.

7. European Court of Human Rights, *Case of Ireland Against the United Kingdom: Judgment*, Strasbourg, January 1978, p. 82.

8. Amnesty International, *Report of an Amnesty International Mission to Northern Ireland*, London: Amnesty International, June 1978, p. 70.

9. [Bennett Commission] *Report of the Committee of Inquiry into Police Interrogation Procedures in Northern Ireland*, Cmnd. 7497, London: HMSO, March 1979, Judge Bennett, Chairman.

10. Stalker, *Stalker Affair*.

11. House of Commons, *Debates*, February 17, 1988, cols. 978–980.

12. Martin Dillon, *The Dirty War*, London: Arrow, 1991, Chap. 10.

13. *Independent*, September 16, 1989.

14. *Irish News*, October 2, 1989.

15. *Independent*, August 31, 1989.

16. Irish Information Partnership, *Agenda 1987–1989*, London: IIP, 1990.

17. [Stevens Commission] *Summary of the Report of the Deputy Chief Constable of Cambridgeshire, John Stevens, into Allegations of Collusion Between Members of the Security Forces and Loyalist Paramilitaries*, Belfast: RUC Headquarters, May 1990.

18. Stevens Commission, p. 6.

19. Stevens Commission, p. 8.

20. Steve Bruce argues that collusion is not institutionally condoned in the security forces (*The Red Hand: Protestant Paramilitaries in Northern Ireland*, Oxford: Oxford University Press, 1992, pp. 225, 272–273).

21. Stevens Commission, p. 11.

22. IRA statement quoted in *Irish Times*, June 10, 1986.

23. Police Authority, *Working Together to Police Northern Ireland*, Belfast: Police Authority, 1988, pp. 12–13; Police Authority, *Information*, Belfast: Police Authority, n.d.

24. A similar reluctance of English police authorities to exert control over the police is discussed in Mike Brogden, "A Police Authority: The Denial of Conflict," *Sociological Review* 25, 2 (May 1977): 325–349.

25. See Standing Advisory Commission on Human Rights, *Annual Report for 1984–1985*, Belfast: HMSO, p. 29.

26. Police Authority, *Report on the Work of the Police Authority for Northern Ireland: 1970–1981*, Belfast: Police Authority, 1982, p. 6.

27. Interview, May 31, 1991.

28. Interview with former member, May 31, 1991; *Newsletter*, July 3, 1978.

29. *Irish News*, June 23, 1979; *Newsletter*, July 4, 1979.

30. Police Authority, "Proposals by the Police Authority for Northern Ireland," reprinted in Working Party, *The Handling of Complaints Against the Police: Report of the Working Party for Northern Ireland*, Belfast: HMSO, 1976, p. 31, Harold Black, Chairman. The task force rejected the Authority's claim that it had a right to examine the files.

31. Interview, May 31, 1991.

32. *Irish Times*, May 29, 1992.

33. Brice Dickson, "The Police Authority for Northern Ireland," *Northern Ireland Legal Quarterly* 39, 3 (Autumn 1988): 277–283.

34. Interview with chairman of the Police Authority, July 30, 1990.

35. See Committee on the Administration of Justice, *Police Accountability in Northern Ireland,* Belfast: CAJ, 1988.

36. Interview with secretary of Independent Commission for Police Complaints (hereafter ICPC), September 19, 1990. When asked how he determined complainants' religion, the secretary cited their names, residence, and "background."

37. Out of 2,494 total cases of complaints in 1989, B Division generated 242 and N Division 240; out of 2,480 cases in 1990, B Division had 298 and N Division 257 (figures provided by RUC Complaints and Discipline Branch).

38. The literature indicates that police retaliation is feared by complainants in other societies, especially in minority communities.

39. In 1985, 61 RUC officers and 35 civil servants were attached to the branch, at a cost of £2 million for the year (Irish Information Partnership, *Agenda, 1985,* London: IIP, 1986).

40. The Authority ("Proposals," p. 31) claims that its complaints committee regularly examined the register of complaints at RUC headquarters and that "members satisfy themselves that complaints are entered correctly, that they are properly investigated, and that appropriate action is taken."

41. Louis Radelet, *The Police and the Community,* New York: Macmillan, 1980, p. 304.

42. Ronald Weitzer, "Accountability and Complaints Against the Police in Northern Ireland," *Police Studies* 9, 2 (Summer 1986): 99–109.

43. Police Complaints Board (hereafter PCB), *Annual Report,* Belfast: HMSO, 1984, p. 1.

44. PCB, *Triennial Review Report,* Belfast: HMSO, 1980, p. 15.

45. Chairman of ICPC, quoted in *Belfast Telegraph,* January 16, 1989.

46. Interview with secretary of ICPC, September 19, 1990.

47. Committee on the Administration of Justice, *Cause for Complaint,* Belfast: CAJ, 1990.

48. Interview with secretary of ICPC, May 29, 1991.

49. ICPC, *Triennial Review Report, 1988–1991,* Belfast: HMSO, 1991, p. 9.

50. ICPC, *Triennial Review Report, 1988–1991,* p. 6.

51. Douglas Perez, *Police Accountability: A Question of Balance,* unpublished doctoral dissertation, University of California, Berkeley, 1978, p. 401.

52. ICPC, *Annual Report,* Belfast: HMSO, 1989, p. 10.

53. Police (Northern Ireland) Order 1977, sect. 12, replaced by Police (Northern Ireland) Order 1987, sect. 18.

54. Significant variation in substantiation rates is reported in an analysis of internal and external complaints arrangements in 35 American cities (New York Police Department Civilian Complaint Review Board, *Nationwide Survey of Civilian Complaint Systems*, 1986, pp. 66–67).

55. Ken Russell, *Complaints Against the Police: A Sociological View*, Glenfield, England: Milltak, 1976, pp. 59–60; Laurence Lustgarten, *The Governance of Police*, London: Sweet and Maxwell, 1986, p. 150; Jeffrey A. Sluka, *Hearts and Minds, Water and Fish: Support for the IRA and the INLA in a Northern Irish Ghetto*, Greenwich, CT: JAI Press, 1989, pp. 225, 227. The PCB cited two reasons for withdrawal: intoxication and desire for informal resolution (PCB, *Annual Report*, 1982, p. 6). Even some Unionist leaders have claimed that the police sometimes pressure complainants to withdraw allegations (*Belfast Telegraph*, June 6, 1986).

56. PCB, *Annual Reports* for 1986–1988; ICPC, *Annual Reports* for 1988–1989.

57. Chief Constable, *Annual Reports*.

58. Only recent figures are available since the RUC previously did not disaggregate withdrawn complaints by category of complaint: in 1990 1,319 assault complaints were withdrawn, leaving 677 to be investigated; in 1991 the figures are 1,183 and 708, respectively.

59. Calculated from Tables 6.2 and 6.1, respectively.

60. A study of internal boards in 77 police and sheriff's departments in Washington State found that complaints of excessive force and deadly force were least likely to be sustained (John R. Dugan and Daniel R. Breda, "Complaints About Police Officers," *Journal of Criminal Justice* 19 [1991]: 165–171). In London in the 1970s the substantiation rate for assault was 0.5 percent and for other complaints 5.2 percent (Philip Stevens and Carole Willis, *Ethnic Minorities and Complaints Against the Police*, Research and Planning Unit paper 5, London: Home Office, 1981, p. 12).

61. Russell, *Complaints Against the Police*, p. 73.

62. Russell, *Complaints Against the Police*, Chap. 4.

63. Police Complaints Board [England and Wales], *Triennial Review Report*, London: HMSO, 1980.

64. ICPC, *Annual Reports* for 1988–1991.

65. Interview, May 29, 1991.

66. David Bayley and Harold Mendelsohn, *Minorities and the Police: Confrontation in America*, New York: Free Press, 1969, p. 128; [Christopher Commission] *Report of the Independent Commission on the Los Angeles Police Department*, presented to the Mayor of Los Angeles, July 9, 1991, pp. 75–78; David Smith, *Police and People in London*, Vol. 1: *A Survey of Londoners*, London: Policy Studies Insti-

tute, 1983; Wesley G. Skogan, *The Police and the Public in England and Wales: A British Crime Survey Report*, Home Office Research Study 117, London: HMSO, 1990.

67. Harassment and oppressive conduct are considered synonymous by the RUC.

68. Since "informal resolution" became an option in 1988, an increasing number of complaints have been handled in this way: 20 percent of all harassment complaints in 1989 and 28 percent in 1990 (Chief Constable, *Annual Reports* for 1989 and 1990, Belfast: Police Authority).

69. Similar explanations are suggested in a study that found a higher substantiation rate in Philadelphia's internal police board than the civilian board (James R. Hudson, "Organizational Aspects of Internal and External Review of the Police," *Journal of Criminal Law, Criminology, and Police Science* 63, 3 [1972]: 427–433).

70. There was significant variation across cities in substantiation rates within each category (New York Police Department Civilian Complaint Review Board, *Nationwide Survey*, pp. 66–67). A comparable figure (25 percent) for internal boards is reported in a study of 77 police and sheriff's departments in Washington State (Dugan and Breda, "Complaints About Police Officers," p. 167).

71. Interview with secretary of ICPC, September 19, 1990; see also Brian Hilliard, "Complaints and Communication," *Police Review*, June 8, 1990, p. 1147.

72. ICPC, *Annual Report*, 1989, p. 13.

73. Clifford Shearing, *Post-Complaint Management: The Impact of Complaint Procedures on Police Discipline*, Discussion Paper 4, Royal Canadian Mounted Police External Review Committee, Ottawa, 1990.

74. Interview with chairman of the Police Authority, October 18, 1990.

75. Lord Scarman, *The Scarman Report*, Harmondsworth: Penguin, 1982, para. 7.27; David C. Brown, *Civilian Review of Complaints Against the Police: A Survey of the United States Literature*, Home Office paper no. 19, London: Home Office, 1983, p. 27.

76. This issue has received little attention in the literature, but a strong argument for treating complaints positively is made by Andrew Goldsmith, "External Review and Self-Regulation: Police Accountability and the Dialectic of Complaints Procedures," in Goldsmith (ed.), *Complaints Against the Police: The Trend to External Review*, Oxford: Clarendon, 1991.

77. On struggles in England and Wales, see Derek Humphry, "The Complaints System," in P. Hain (ed.), *Policing the Police*, London: John Calder, 1979.

78. Police Federation, "Proposals by the Police Federation for

Northern Ireland," reprinted in Working Party, *Handling of Complaints*, pp. 27–28.

79. Police Federation, "Proposals," p. 27.

80. Alan Wright, "Chairman's Address to Annual Conference," *Police Beat* (July 1979), p. 11.

81. The British Police Federation also objected to the creation of the English complaints board, but muted its criticisms when the Home Office gave officers access to copies of complaints and allowed the federation to use its funds to prosecute complainants.

82. The PCB noted in a 1980 report that, in its first two years of operation, the police personnel dealing with complaints had not been cooperative, but subsequently they adopted a "positive, constructive approach" (PCB, *Triennial Review Report*, 1980, p. 16).

83. Eldon Griffiths, House of Commons, *Debates*, May 6, 1987, col. 820.

84. Griffiths, col. 825.

85. ICPC, *Triennial Review Report, 1988–1991*, p. 6.

86. Griffiths, col. 826.

87. PCB, *Annual Report*, 1984, p. 3; *Belfast Telegraph*, January 16, 1989.

88. *Belfast Telegraph*, January 16, 1989; interview with secretary of ICPC, September 19, 1990.

89. Hilliard, "Complaints and Communication," p. 1147.

90. Interview with chairman of federation, September 20, 1990.

91. Sam Beattie, "Chairman's Speech," *Police Beat* (Conference Special), 1993, p. 3.

92. Interview with chairman of federation, September 20, 1990.

93. David Smith and Jeremy Gray, *Police and People in London*, Vol. 4: *The Police in Action*, London: Policy Studies Institute, 1983, p. 329.

94. PCB, *Triennial Review Report*, 1980, p. 16.

95. Bennett Commission, p. 115.

96. *Belfast Telegraph*, January 16, 1989; interview with secretary of ICPC, September 19, 1990.

97. Russell, *Complaints Against the Police*, Chap. 4.

98. Bennett Commission, p. 119.

99. Interview with secretary of ICPC, May 29, 1991.

100. Kenneth Newman, "Allegations Against the Police: Statement by the Chief Constable," *Constabulary Gazette* (July 1977), p. 5.

101. Newman, "Allegations Against the Police," p. 5.

102. Police Federation, "Proposals," p. 28; Wright, "Chairman's Address," 1979, p. 11.

103. Alan Wright, "Chairman's Address to Annual Conference," *Constabulary Gazette* (October 1977), p. 8.

104. Wright, "Chairman's Address," 1977, p. 7.

105. Interview with chairman of Police Authority, October 18, 1990.

106. Bennett Commission, p. 112.

107. Interview with secretary of ICPC, September 19, 1990.

108. Northern Ireland Office, *Police and Public*, reprinted in PCB, *Annual Report*, 1977.

109. Humphry, "The Complaints System."

110. Brown, *Civilian Review*; Goldsmith, "External Review and Self-Regulation"; James R. Hudson, "Police Review Boards and Police Accountability," *Law and Contemporary Problems* 36, 4 (1971): 515–538; David Bayley, "Accountability and Control of Police: Lessons for Britain," in T. Bennett (ed.), *The Future of Policing*, Cambridge: Cropwood Conference Series, no. 15, 1983.

111. Lord Windlesham, minister of state at NIO, quoted in *Irish Times,* May 2, 1972.

112. Kevin Boyle, Tom Hadden, and Paddy Hillyard, *Ten Years On in Northern Ireland*, London: Cobden Trust, 1980, p. 68; *Fortnight*, September 1983.

113. For the same reason, American prosecutors seem to have a similar reluctance to prosecute police. See Arthur Kobler, "Police Homicide in a Democracy," *Journal of Social Issues* 31, 1 (1975): 163–184.

114. Bennett Commission, p. 123.

115. Boyle, Hadden, and Hillyard, *Ten Years On*, p. 79; Walsh, "The Royal Ulster Constabulary," p. 98.

116. Prosecutors elsewhere typically make low-visibility decisions and lack meaningful accountability for these decisions.

117. Walsh, "The Royal Ulster Constabulary," p. 99.

118. House of Commons, *Debates*, January 25, 1988, col. 22.

119. Bennett Commission, pp. 125–126.

120. Irish Information Partnership, *Agenda 1987–1989*.

121. Criminal Law Act (Northern Ireland) 1967, sect. 3(1).

122. Amnesty International, Helsinki Watch, and Northern Ireland's Standing Advisory Commission on Human Rights have all called for adoption of the necessity standard (see Helsinki Watch, *Human Rights in Northern Ireland*, New York: Helsinki Watch, 1991, pp. 55–60).

123. Introduction of these lesser charges has been recommended by Amnesty International, Helsinki Watch, the Committee on the Administration of Justice, and the Standing Advisory Commission on Human Rights.

124. Scarman, *Scarman Report*.

125. PCB, *Triennial Review Report*, 1980, p. 15.

126. Interview with secretary of ICPC, September 19, 1990.

127. Interview with secretary of ICPC, September 19, 1990.

128. PCB, *Annual Report*, 1982, p. 8.

129. Wayne A. Kerstetter, "Who Disciplines the Police? Who Should?" in William A. Geller (ed.), *Police Leadership in America: Crisis and Opportunity*, New York: Praeger, 1985, p. 173. The only available attitudinal data bearing on this issue appear in a survey of complainants in three American cities with internal police boards. A majority said they were not impressed with the thoroughness, objectivity, and fairness of the board to which they complained (Perez, *Police Accountability*).

130. Scarman, *Scarman Report*, paras. 7.14, 7.21.

131. Kerstetter, "Who Disciplines the Police?" pp. 161–162.

132. John W. Soule, "Issue Conflict in Northern Ireland," *Political Psychology* 10, 4 (1989): 725–744.

133. Interview with Paddy McManus, October 24, 1990.

134. SDLP, "Justice in Northern Ireland," discussion paper adopted at annual conference, 1985, pp. 10, 8.

135. Interview with general secretary of SDLP, July 25, 1990.

136. Northern Ireland Social Attitudes Survey, 1990.

137. Sluka, *Hearts and Minds*, pp. 224–228.

138. Helsinki Watch, *Children in Northern Ireland: Abused by Security Forces and Paramilitaries*, New York: Helsinki Watch, 1992, pp. 31, 32.

139. Northern Ireland Social Attitudes Survey, 1990. This compares to 92 percent of the British public who support the same kind of body (British Social Attitudes Survey, 1990). Attitudinal data on this issue scarce in the United States, but a Los Angeles poll taken a few days after the televised beating of Rodney King found the Los Angeles population overwhelmingly supported creation of a civilian review board to review cases of police misconduct: 75 percent of whites, 78 percent of Hispanics, 88 percent of blacks (unpublished *Los Angeles Times* poll, no. 245, March 7–8, 1991).

140. Interview with Rev. William McCrea, DUP security spokesman, October 19, 1990.

141. Interview with Ken Maginnis, UUP security spokesman, October 8, 1990.

142. "We Long for Normality" (interview with Ken Maginnis by Tony Judge), *Police,* September 1990, p. 27.

143. See, for instance, the comments of Rev. William Beattie, Northern Ireland Assembly, *Debates*, June 26, 1985, pp. 386, 391.

144. Rev. William Beattie, Northern Ireland Assembly, *Debates*, April 16, 1985, p. 7.

145. Interview with McCrea.

146. Interview with Maginnis.

147. Rev. Martin Smyth, quoted in *Belfast Telegraph*, August 31, 1989.

148. Thomas Passmore, quoted in *Irish Times*, August 22, 1984.

149. James Kilfedder, House of Commons, *Debates*, February 17, 1988, col. 987.

150. Alan Kane, Northern Ireland Assembly, *Debates*, March 19, 1986, p. 225.

151. *Belfast Telegraph*, June 6, 1986.

152. James Q. Wilson, *Varieties of Police Behavior*, Cambridge, MA: Harvard University Press, 1968, p. 289.

153. Committee on the Administration of Justice, *Police Accountability in Northern Ireland*, p. 34.

154. The police also need to be insulated from local political structures. In the United States, the tight control of police departments by local political machines in the late nineteenth and early twentieth centuries amounted to "community control run amok" (Samuel Walker, *A Critical History of Police Reform*, p. 15; Herman Goldstein, *Policing a Free Society*, Cambridge, MA: Ballinger, 1977, pp. 143, 149).

CHAPTER 7. COMMUNITY POLICING IN THE SHADOWS

1. Interview with chief inspector, July 26, 1990.

2. Interview with RUC spokesperson, July 18, 1986.

3. Interview with RUC spokesperson, August 3, 1984.

4. President's Commission on Law Enforcement and Administration of Justice, *Task Force Report: The Police*, Washington, DC: U.S. Government Printing Office, 1967; Jack Greene and Stephen Mastrofski (eds.), *Community Policing: Rhetoric or Reality?* New York: Praeger, 1988.

5. Mark Moore, "Problem Solving and Community Policing," in M. Tonry and N. Morris (eds.), *Modern Policing*, Chicago: University of Chicago Press, 1992, p. 135; Jack Greene, "Police and Community Relations," in R. Dunham and G. Alpert (eds.), *Critical Issues in Policing*, Prospect Heights, IL: Waveland, 1989.

6. President's Commission on Law Enforcement and the Administration of Justice, *The Challenge of Crime in a Free Society*, New York: Avon, 1968, p. 258.

7. James Q. Wilson, "The Police in the Ghetto," in R. Steadman (ed.), *The Police and the Community*, Baltimore: Johns Hopkins University Press, 1972, p. 68.

8. Police Foundation, *The Newark Foot Patrol Experiment*, Washington, DC: Police Foundation, 1981; Robert C. Trojanowicz, "An Evaluation of a Neighborhood Foot Patrol Program," *Journal of Police Science and Administration* 11 (1983): 410–419; Stephen Mastrofski, "What Does Community Policing Mean for Daily Police Work?"

National Institute of Justice Journal, no. 225 (August 1992): 23–27.

9. Home Office, *Local Consultation Arrangements Between the Community and the Police*, circular 54/1982.

10. Interview with former member of the Police Authority, October, 23, 1990.

11. Police Authority, *Final Report of the Working Group on Consultative Arrangements Between the Community and the Police*, Belfast: Police Authority, 1984, p. 5.

12. Interview with former chairman of the Association of Local Authorities, October 10, 1990.

13. Police Authority, *Final Report*, p. 6.

14. Police Authority, *Factsheet*, 1989.

15. Police Authority, *Final Report*, p. 9.

16. Of the six PCLCs that were not evaluated, one refused an interview, two had recently been reconstituted, and three did not reply to my inquiries. Five of the six exist in largely Protestant, low-terrorism areas, and the responses to most of the questions probably would have been similar to those gathered from neighboring PCLCs. *Police-Community Liaison Committee* is used here as a generic term that includes committees of that name, functionally equivalent committees with different names, and arrangements whereby the entire district council is permitted to attend police liaison meetings, where no formal liaison committee exists.

17. In three cases the town clerk or chief executive of the district was present to corroborate the responses of the primary interviewee.

18. Police Authority, *Report*, Community-Police Liaison Committee conference, June 19, 1991.

19. President's Commission, *Task Force Report*, pp. 157–158.

20. Rod Morgan, "The Local Determinants of Policing Policy," in P. Willmott (ed.), *Policing and the Community*, London: Policy Studies Institute, 1987; Rod Morgan, "Policing by Consent: Legitimating the Doctrine," in R. Morgan and D. Smith (eds.), *Coming to Terms with Policing*, London: Routledge, 1989; Rod Morgan and Christopher Maggs, *Setting the P.A.C.E.: Police Community Consultation Arrangements in England and Wales*, Bath Social Policy Paper No. 4, University of Bath, 1985.

21. Morgan, "Policing by Consent," p. 232; Morgan, "Local Determinants."

22. Michael Poole, "The Geographical Location of Political Violence in Northern Ireland," in John Darby (ed.), *Political Violence: Ireland in Comparative Perspective*, Belfast: Appletree, 1990. Bombing incidents have been much more frequent than fatalities, but the geographical distribution of bombings is roughly consistent with that of fatalities (Russell Murray, "Political Violence in Northern Ireland,

1969–1977," in F. Boal and J. N. Douglas [eds.], *Integration and Division: Geograhical Perspectives on the Northern Ireland Problem*, London: Academic, 1982). Figures on the geographical distribution of fatal incidents from 1969 to 1990 are provided in House of Commons, *Written answers*, June 27, 1990, col. 235.

23. Home Office, *Arrangements for Local Consultation Between the Community and the Police Outside London*, circular 2/1985.

24. Police Authority, *Final Report*, p. 10; interview with chairman of Police Authority, October 18, 1990.

25. Committee on the Administration of Justice, *Consultation Between the Police and the Public*, Belfast: CAJ, 1985.

26. Police Authority, *Final Report*, p. 11; Police Authority, *Report*, p. 4.

27. Interview with the chairman of the Police Authority, October 18, 1990.

28. The unexamined committee is in a heavily Protestant area with low violence.

29. A point stressed by the Committee on the Administration of Justice, *Consultation*, p. 6.

30. Interview with general secretary of the SDLP, Patsy McGlone, July 25, 1990.

31. In April 1991, 41 lay visitors (whose identities are secret) were selected to visit seventeen police stations where detainees are held. Visits are to occur at least once a month and the visitors are entitled to have access to detention rooms and medical rooms and to speak to detainees. They do not have access to the three holding centers for those accused of security offenses. For earlier proposals, see Committee on the Administration of Justice, *Lay Visitors to Police Stations in Northern Ireland*, Belfast: CAJ, 1989.

32. Police Authority, *Report*, p. 3.

33. Interview, July 30, 1990.

34. Interview, October 18, 1990.

35. I had the opportunity to conduct a group interview with this liaison committee, with two RUC members present.

36. Morgan and Maggs, *Setting the P.A.C.E.*, p. 41.

37. Interview, October 18, 1990.

38. In both countries, fairly large majorities of the public support more foot patrols (David Smith, *Police and People in London*, Vol. 1: *A Survey of Londoners*, London: Policy Studies Institute, 1983, p. 213; Mike McConville and Dan Shepherd, *Watching Police, Watching Communities*, London: Routledge, 1992, pp. 32–36; Robert C. Trojanowicz, "An Evaluation of a Neighborhood Foot Patrol Program," *Journal of Police Science and Administration* 11 [1983]: 410–419; Police Foundation, *The Newark Foot Patrol Experiment*, Washington, DC: Police Foundation, 1981).

39. Interview, September 20, 1990.

40. Comment during author's meeting with a PCLC, October 19, 1990, which police attended.

41. RUC officer, quoted in *Times*, August 30, 1988.

42. John D. Brewer with Kathleen Magee, *Inside the RUC: Routine Policing in a Divided Society*, Oxford: Clarendon, 1991, p. 116.

43. Recalling these events, the chief constable declares that the RUC's philosophy is to "be seen to police on the streets whenever it is necessary to do so. If someone puts up a barricade across the road . . . we would take the ground. . . . We could not give an inch, because if you give an inch, they will take a mile" (interview with Chief Constable Hugh Annesley by John Weeks, *Police*, November 1991, p. 26).

44. Community Relations Branch, *Ramble Scheme*, Belfast: RUC, 1990.

45. Community relations officers in Britain and America also spend a disproportionate amount of their time working with youth, particularly in the schools.

46. Interview with sergeant in Community Relations, October 22, 1990.

47. David Brown and Susan Iles, *Community Constables: A Study of a Policing Initiative*, London: Home Office, 1985, pp. 31–32.

48. Susan Phillips and Raymond Cochrane, *The Role and Function of Police Community Liaison Officers,* London: Home Office, 1988; Lord Scarman, *The Scarman Report,* Harmondsworth: Penguin, 1982, para. 5.48.

49. Figures provided by RUC Headquarters, Belfast.

50. Scarman, *Scarman Report*, para. 5.52.

51. Joseph Lohman and Gordon Misner, *The Police and the Community,* Vol. 2, President's Commission on Law Enforcement and Administration of Justice, Washington, DC: U.S. Government Printing Office, 1966, p. 305.

52. Roger Graef, *Talking Blues: The Police in Their Own Words,* London: Fontana, 1990, p. 98.

53. Interview, June 3, 1992.

54. Interview, October 22, 1990.

55. Interview, July 25, 1990.

56. Brewer and Magee, *Inside the RUC.*

57. Interview, October 22, 1990.

58. Burton Levy, "Cops in the Ghetto: A Problem of the Police System," *American Behavioral Scientist* 11, 4 (March–April 1968): 31–34.

59. David Bayley and Harold Mendelsohn, *Minorities and the Police: Confrontation in America*, New York: Free Press, 1969, p. 170.

60. President's Commission, *Task Force Report*, p. 150.

61. Support for foot patrols is documented earlier in the chapter.

The evidence on attitudes to other community policing programs is more mixed. In San Diego in the 1960s, for example, such programs were seen by blacks as a "con game," a PR effort lacking in merit (Lohman and Misner, *Police and the Community*, Vol. 1, p. 58). The 1967 President's Crime Commission concluded that community relations units had not won the support of minority groups (*Task Force Report*, p. 151).

62. Jerome Skolnick and David Bayley, *The New Blue Line*, New York: Free Press, 1986, p. 216.

63. Brewer and Magee, *Inside the RUC*.

64. This happens rarely, according to my Catholic sources in this area.

65. Carl Klockars, "The Rhetoric of Community Policing," and Peter Manning, "Community Policing as a Drama of Control," in J. Greene and S. Mastrofski (eds.), *Community Policing*, New York: Praeger, 1988. Neither author provides any evidence to support his assertions.

66. Center for Research on Criminal Justice, *The Iron Fist and the Velvet Glove: An Analysis of the U.S. Police*, Berkeley: CRCJ, 1977; Michael Brogden, *The Police: Autonomy and Consent*, London: Academic Press, 1982, Chap. 8.

67. *Nobody Knows My Name*, New York: Dell, 1962, p. 65.

68. Interview with sergeant, October 22, 1990.

69. In fact, CR officers are often unarmed.

70. The data presented below on obstacles to CR work in schools in Republican areas are supported by Brewer and Magee, *Inside the RUC*, pp. 112–113.

71. In tranquil areas officers are able to present wide-ranging lectures as well as more extensive programs of instruction that can last as long as fifteen weeks, for eight to twelve hours per week (Community Relations Branch, *Police Educational Program Policy Document*, Belfast: RUC, 1988).

72. Interview with inspector, May 28, 1992.

73. *Irish News*, March 1, 1991.

74. Jennifer Todd, "The Sin—and the Sinner Perhaps," Religion in Ireland, supplement to *Fortnight*, no. 296, June 1991.

75. A 1986 survey of 232 priests found that they were almost evenly split on the statement "The hierarchy has not done enough to criticize various forms of state violence" (Gerald McElroy, *The Catholic Church and the Northern Ireland Crisis, 1968–1986*, Dublin: Gill and Macmillan, 1991).

76. Interview, October 18, 1990.

77. These points are vigorously made by the President's Commission on Law Enforcement and Administration of Justice (*The Challenge*

of Crime, p. 258 and its *Task Force Report*) and in Lord Scarman's report on the 1981 riot in Brixton (*Scarman Report,* Part 5).

78. Mark Moore, "Problem-Solving and Community Policing," in M. Tonry and N. Morris (eds.), *Modern Policing,* Chicago: University of Chicago Press, 1992.

79. Interview, October 22, 1990.

CHAPTER 8. CONCLUSION

1. Alvin Rabushka and Kenneth Shepsle, *Politics in Plural Societies,* Columbia: Merrill, 1972, pp. 67–68.

2. Jerome Skolnick and David Bayley, *The New Blue Line,* New York: Free Press, 1986, p. 216.

3. The general neglect of the state in the literature on policing is criticized in Otwin Marenin, "Police Performance and State Rule," *Comparative Politics* 18, 1 (October 1985): 101–122.

4. Stan Albrecht and Miles Green, "Attitudes Toward the Police and the Larger Attitude Complex," *Criminology* 15, 1 (May 1977): 67–86.

5. Along with the regime change in Namibia, a broad process of "civilianizing" the police force began after independence. The police no longer carry firearms; only special units are now trained in riot duties, previously part of each officers' training; and the security branch has been abolished (Laurie Nathan, *Marching to a Different Drum: A Description and Assessment of the Formation of the Namibian Police and Defense Force,* Working Paper 4, Center for Southern African Studies, University of the Western Cape, 1991). Along with the regime change in Zimbabwe, the paramilitary role of the police has become less prominent and the security branch was absorbed into the intelligence agency. But a new political police unit, the Police Intelligence and Security Inspectorate, has been created and the regular police still enforce the security laws inherited from the old regime (Ronald Weitzer, *Transforming Settler States: Communal Conflict and Internal Security in Northern Ireland and Zimbabwe,* Berkeley: University of California Press, 1990, pp. 143–145).

6. Interview with Paddy McManus, Sinn Fein legal affairs spokesman and Belfast city councillor, October 24, 1990.

7. See the survey data in Weitzer, *Transforming Settler States,* p. 199.

8. Survey data show that Protestants are considerably more ambivalent about the British state than Catholics, who unequivocally reject it. They are unhappy with the status quo (only around 6 percent support the current system of direct rule), but a near majority supports full integra-

tion of Ulster into the United Kingdom, as an insurance policy against a united Ireland (Weitzer, *Transforming Settler States*, p. 199).

9. Support for power sharing increases, for both Protestants and Catholics, if repondents are asked simply whether they support it, rather than which of several options they consider the best form of government for the country.

10. Ronald Weitzer, "Transforming the South African Police," *Police Studies* 16, 1 (Spring 1993): 1–10.

11. The government claims that there is no policy of summarily executing insurgents, but the Stalker inquiry suggested there was an "inclination" to do so (see Chapter 6). The practice should be abandoned; every effort should be made to arrest suspected insurgents unless they resist arrest by firing at the security forces.

The use of plastic bullets is extremely controversial in Northern Ireland, but I am not convinced that they should be banned. All forceful riot control methods present some risks, and it is arguable that plastic bullets are better suited than some other methods in putting distance between rioters and security forces; in Ulster they have resulted in relatively few casualties. From 1970 to 1989 approximately 110,000 plastic and rubber bullets were fired by the army and police, resulting in eighteen deaths—or one fatality for every 6,100 bullets fired. Waddington argues that this kind of fatality rate is not objectionable in Northern Ireland's circumstances, and he calls plastic bullets the "most appropriate" means of incapacitating rioters (P.A.J. Waddington, *The Strong Arm of the Law: Armed and Public Order Policing*, Oxford: Clarendon, 1991, pp. 195–205). Ulster's record is far better than that of some other countries. Fifty Palestinians in Israel's occupied territories were killed by plastic bullets fired by soldiers in a period of just over one year (Bernard Trainor, "Israel Troops Prove Newcomers to Riot Control," *New York Times*, February 19, 1989). At the same time, the fatality rate in Ulster could be reduced if the bullets were fired strictly in accordance with the regulations; six persons have died from bullets fired at a closer range than what is prescribed.

12. A point stressed by Lawrence Sherman with regard to eliminating police corruption (*Scandal and Reform: Controlling Police Corruption*, Berkeley: University of California Press, 1978, pp. 243–251).

13. Joseph Goldstein, "Police Discretion Not to Invoke the Criminal Process: Low Visibility Decisions in the Administration of Justice," *Yale Law Journal* 69 (March 1960): 543–594.

14. The recent literature on reform of the South African Police places great weight on changes in police culture, excessively so, according to Mike Brogden and Clifford Shearing, *Policing For a New South Africa*, London: Routledge, 1993.

APPENDIX

COMMUNITY INTERVIEWEES

A   director of religious organization, October 9, 1990

B   community worker, October 16, 1990

C   community worker, October 11, 1990

D   Catholic priest, October 8, 1990

E   community worker, October 18, 1990

F   community worker, October 18, 1990

G   community worker, October 23, 1990

H   community worker, September 19, 1990

I   community worker, June 11, 1991

J   community worker, May 22, 1991

K   Protestant minister, May 24, 1991

L   city councillor, Alliance, May 23, 1991

M   community worker, October 5, 1990

N   Catholic priest, May 22, 1991

O   Catholic priest, May 28, 1991

P   Protestant minister, May 28, 1991

Q   Catholic priest, May 30, 1991

R   community worker, May 31, 1991

S   Catholic priest, May 31, 1991

T   community worker, June 3, 1991

U   city councillor, SDLP, June 10, 1991

V   Catholic priest, June 4, 1991

W   community worker, June 6, 1991

X   community worker, June 6, 1991

Y   community worker, June 7, 1991

Z   Catholic priest, June 11, 1991

II   community worker, June 1, 1992

JJ   former community worker, June 2, 1992

KK   Catholic priest, June 2, 1992

LL   community worker, June 3, 1992

MM   community worker, June 5, 1992

NN   Catholic priest, June 5, 1992

OO   community worker, May 20, 1992

PP   city councillor, independent Unionist, May 21, 1992

QQ   community worker, May 22, 1992

RR   community worker, May 22, 1992

SS   community worker, May 26, 1992

TT   community worker, May 27, 1992

UU   city councillor, Sinn Fein, May 27, 1992

VV   city councillor, Alliance, May 29, 1992

WW   community worker, June 1, 1992

INDEX